"Tony Maalouf has presented to the Christ
scholarship on a much neglected topic. The
dants have in sacred Scripture has long be
inform and enlighten both scholars and lay r
day. Although *[Ishmael in the Shadow of Israel]* brings to bear an impressive range of scholarship and deals extensively with original sources, it is highly readable. The Arab background to the book of Job, along with Proverbs 30–31, is convincingly presented. Fresh options for new, legitimate translations of key verses are presented with care and sensitivity. Any Christian trying to sort out the Scriptures and the troubled Middle East of past and present must, by all means, read this book with care."

—Kenneth E. Bailey
Professor Emeritus of Middle Eastern New Testament Studies
The Ecumenical Institute (Tantur), Jerusalem

"Some Christians who believe God's promises to Israel can tend to have a rejectionist's derogatory attitude toward Arabs. Dr. Tony Maalouf, an evangelical Arab Christian scholar, opens our eyes to scriptural teaching about Arabs, much of which is usually overlooked. To bless the Jews does not mean we have to curse the Arabs.

Ishmael in the Shadow of Israel is an excellent study for any believer interested in the Middle East and the Arab world."

—Patrick Cate
President of Christar

"Most Western Christians believe the children of Israel are God's chosen people, but are unsure how to view the sons of Ishmael. They rejoice to hear of Jews acknowledging Jesus as messiah, but know little about Arab believers. [This] highly trained Arab believer's book will help clarify issues, answer questions, and create a concern for all Abraham's children."

—Stuart Briscoe
Minister-at-Large, Elmbrook Church

"Dr. Tony Maalouf tackles the often contentious subject of Arab-Jewish relations with *insight, kindness,* and *clarity*. His *insight* comes from his personal background and years of experience in the Middle East. His *kindness* comes from a heart that loves both God and those created in the image of God—including both Arabs and Jews. And his *clarity* comes from his deep knowledge and skillful handling of God's Word. In tackling a topic that generates more heat than light, Tony seeks to turn down the thermostat and pull back the curtains. Here is a coherent presentation of God's plan for Abraham's 'other son.'"

—Charles H. Dyer
Senior Vice President and Provost
Moody Bible Institute

"I am delighted to recommend with enthusiasm *Ishmael in the Shadow of Israel*, written by my good friend Tony Maalouf. His insistence that the children of Ishmael are loved by God and play a distinctive role in the salvific destiny of those who place their faith in Christ is long overdue. My reading of Tony's fine treatment has expanded my appreciation of Paul's seminal statement that Jew and Gentile are one in Christ (Gal. 3:28). *Ishmael in the Shadow of Israel* is a must-read for every student of current affairs in the Middle East."

—Ronald Youngblood
Professor of Old Testament
International College and Graduate School, Honolulu, Hawaii

"Dr. Maalouf's work is a much needed clarification of pertinent passages and promises concerning the relationship between the Arabs and the Jews. A native Lebanese who received his higher education in both France and America, Dr. Maalouf is uniquely qualified to assess both the ancient and contemporary situation. With his expertise in biblical languages he shows the reader in convincing detail that God's original intent was for the sons of Ishmael to be a blessing for the sons of Abraham, not a threat. They were to live side by side in harmony and protection. And when God took the light to the Gentiles, the sons of Ishmael were the first Gentiles to receive the message. Hopefully, this enlightened understanding of God's original intent will help us here in the West to better understand God's intent for Israel today and in the future."

—David R. Anderson, Ph.D.

"A fascinating study, which gently debunks many of the myths of the Arab peoples. Of particular interest is the defense of the Arab Christian, who stands in the crosshairs of culture, politics, and upbringing. *[Ishmael in the Shadow of Israel]* offers fresh insight into an age-old conflict and will engender much dialogue."

—Ergun Mehmet Caner
Coauthor of *Unveiling Islam*
Associate Professor of Theology and Church History
Liberty University, Lynchburg, Virginia

ISHMAEL
IN THE
SHADOW
ISRAEL

ISHMAEL IN THE SHADOW OF ISRAEL

God's Prophetic Plan for Abraham's Firstborn

TONY MAALOUF

Foreword by Eugene H. Merrill

Ishmael in the Shadow of Israel: God's Prophetic Plan for Abraham's Firstborn

Previously published under the title *Arabs in the Shadow of Israel: The Unfolding of God's Prophetic Plan for Ishmael's Line.*

Published by Kregel Publications, a division of Kregel Inc., 2450 Oak Industrial Dr. NE, Grand Rapids, MI 49505.

978-0-8254-4807-2

Printed in the United States of America

1 2 3 4 5 / 29 28 27 26 25 24 23

To my dear wife and children
for their steadfast encouragement
and support of this book project

CONTENTS

Foreword by Eugene H. Merrill 11
Abbreviations 13
Introduction: Arabs Yesterday and Today 17

Part 1: Biblical Foundations

1. The Unfortunate Beginning (Gen. 16:1–6) 43
2. Hagar's Songs in the Night (Gen. 16:7–16) 61
3. The Pursuit of Destiny (Gen. 17; 21:1–21) 80
4. The Jewish Ishmael (Gal. 4:21–31) 97

Part 2: Arabs in the Light of Israel

5. Sunrise of Abraham's Children 109
6. Job, Son of the Arabian Desert 120
7. Agur and Lemuel, Wise Men from Arabia 136

Part 3: Arabs in the Darkness of Israel

8. What Became of Ishmael? 149
9. Arabs Haunted by World Powers 157
10. The Nabataeans: Ishmael Finally Settled 171

Part 4: Arabs in the Light of Christ

11. Arab Messianic Expectations 183
12. The Magi-Arab Worshipers of Christ (Part 1) 193
13. The Magi-Arab Worshipers of Christ (Part 2) 205

Conclusion: Arabs in the Shadow of Israel 219
Endnotes 225
Bibliography 337
General Index 356

FOREWORD

One of the most intractable cultural and political issues of modern times has been the stormy relationship between the State of Israel and its near and more distant Arab neighbors. Despite repeated wars interspersed with troubled and uneasy times of peace, there appears to be no human solution to the profound distrust and even bitter hatred that characterizes the mutual interaction of these children of Abraham.

In recent years the rise of militant Islamic fundamentalism has added a new dimension to what has been up until now a political problem for the most part. The visit of Ariel Sharon to the Temple Mount, also the site of the Dome of the Rock and the al-Aqsa Mosque, sacred to Muslims, triggered a violent reaction from Palestinian Arabs, one that has resulted in the death of thousands of Israelis and Arabs alike. For every action by one side there has been an opposite reaction from the other, inevitably of a more violent and horrendous nature. There is thus in place a spiraling of animosity, one that threatens to destroy both peoples if left unresolved. And all in the name of religion.

No people are more torn by the ravages of the Middle Eastern conflict than believers in Jesus Christ, especially those whose eschatology teaches that God has an ongoing role for the Jew to play in the unfolding of the kingdom to come. The "messianic" Jew finds himself at odds with his own culture for having abandoned his ancient Jewish traditions and he also stands in jeopardy from Arab terrorism that hardly distinguishes among Israelis of any kind. Even more to be pitied, perhaps, is the Arab Christian, particularly the Palestinian, for he is more likely than not to be linked by his fellow Arabs with Jewish and Christian Zionism and by Israelis as "just another Arab" whose hostilities toward them may be taken for granted. What, if anything, can be done to resolve the impasse, especially as it relates to brothers and sisters in Christ on both sides of the cultural and political fault line?

What has been needed is a well-informed, dispassionate, and articulate response by Arab and Jewish spokespersons who share a common faith in Jesus the Messiah. The present volume makes giant strides toward accomplishing that objective, at least from the Arab Christian perspective. His Lebanese roots and upbringing, his impeccable academic credentials as a biblical scholar, and his years of ministry in the Middle East qualify Dr. Tony Maalouf, with unparalleled insight and sensitivity, to address the complex issues that confront God's people in this vortex of terror and hopelessness.

The great burden of this endeavor is to trace the history of the Arab people back to its biblical roots, back to Abraham and his son Ishmael, recognized by both the Bible and the Qurʾan as the ancestor of the millions of people who call themselves Arab. Reading the biblical text in fresh ways—ways possible, perhaps, only to an Arab—Maalouf displays profound exegetical and theological skills that enable his readers also to view Ishmael and his descendants in a new light. He does not gloss over the sins and shortcomings of his people, nor does he take sides in the struggles between Jew and Arab in the modern world. He does, however, make clear the profoundly important role that the Arab has played in biblical times and since, and he displays his burden, like that of Paul, that his own Arab people might be saved. One can only hope that this effort might be met by one from the pen of a Jewish believer. Between the two could come a message of reconciliation in line with the ministry of our Lord himself who came to make us all one in him.

—EUGENE H. MERRILL

ABBREVIATIONS

AASOR	*Annual of the American School of Oriental Research*
ABD	*Anchor Bible Dictionary.* Edited by David Noel Freedman. 6 vols. New York: Doubleday, 1992.
AJSL	*American Journal of Semitic Languages and Literature*
ANET	*Ancient Near Eastern Texts Relating to the Old Testament.* Edited by James B. Pritchard. Oxford: Oxford University Press, 1955.
AOAT	Alter Orient und Altes Testament
ARAB	*Ancient Records of Assyria and Babylonia*
ARNA	*Ancient Records from North Arabia.* Edited by F. V. Winnett and W. L. Reed. Toronto: University of Toronto Press, 1970.
BA	*Biblical Archaeologist*
BAGD	Walter Bauer, William F. Arndt, and F. Wilbur Gingrich. *A Greek-English Lexicon of the New Testament and Other Early Christian Literature.* Revised and augmented by F. Wilbur Gingrich and Frederick W. Danker. 2d ed. Chicago: University of Chicago Press, 1979.
BAR	*Biblical Archaeology Review*
BASOR	*Bulletin of the American Schools of Oriental Research*

BDB	*The New Brown, Driver, Briggs Hebrew and English Lexicon of the Old Testament.* Edited by Francis Brown, S. R. Driver, and Charles A. Briggs. Peabody, Mass.: Hendrickson, 1979.
BHS	*Biblia Hebraica Stuttgartensia*
Bib Sac	*Bibliotheca Sacra*
BR	*Biblical Research*
BZAW	Beihefte zur Zeitschrift für die alttestamentliche Wissenschaft
CEV	Contemporary English Version
EI	*The Encyclopedia of Islam*. New ed., 11 vols. Edited by E. van Donzel et al. Leiden: E. J. Brill, 1979–2002.
EJ	*Encyclopedia Judaica*. 16 vols. Jerusalem: Encyclopedia Judaica; New York: Macmillan, 1971–72.
EvQ	Evangelical Quarterly
FEI	*E. J. Brill's First Encyclopedia of Islam, 1913–1936.* 9 vols. Edited by M. Th. Houtsma et al. Leiden: E. J. Brill, 1987.
FOTL	Forms of the Old Testament Literature
ICC	International Critical Commentary
ISBE	*International Standard Bible Encyclopedia.* Edited by Geoffrey W. Bromiley. Rev. ed. 4 vols. Grand Rapids: Eerdmans, 1979–88.
JAOS	*Journal of the American Oriental Society*
JB	Jerusalem Bible
JBL	*Journal of Biblical Literature*
JCS	*Journal of Cuneiform Studies*
JETS	*Journal of the Evangelical Theological Society*
JJS	*Journal of Jewish Studies*
JNSL	*Journal of Northwest Semitic Languages*
JPS	Jewish Publication Society
JSOR	*Journal for the Study of Oriental Research*
JSOT	*Journal for the Study of the Old Testament*
JSS	*Journal of Semitic Studies*
KB	Ludwig Koehler and Walter Baumgartner. *The Hebrew*

	and Aramaic Lexicon of the Old Testament. Translated and edited by M.E.J. Richardson. Leiden: E. J. Brill, 1996.
KJV	King James Version
LB	Living Bible
LXX	Septuagint
MT	Masoretic Text
NAB	New American Bible
NASB	New American Standard Bible
NAV	New American Version
NCB	New Century Bible
NEB	New English Bible
NICOT	New International Commentary on the Old Testament
NIDNTT	New International Dictionary of New Testament Theology
NIV	New International Version
NJB	New Jerusalem Bible
NKJV	New King James Version
NRSV	New Revised Standard Version
OBO	Orbis Biblicus et Orientalis
Or	*Orientalia* (NS)
PEQ	Palestine Exploration Quarterly
RB	*Revue Biblique*
REB	Revised English Bible
RSV	Revised Standard Version
TB	*Tyndale Bulletin*
TDOT	*Theological Dictionary of the Old Testament.* 11 vols. Edited by Johannes Botterweck and Helmer Ringgren, translated by David E. Green and others. Grand Rapids: Eerdmans, 1974–2001.
TOTC	The Tyndale Old Testament Commentary
TSF Bulletin	*Theological Student's Fellowship Bulletin*
VT	*Vetus Testamentum*
WBC	Word Biblical Commentary
ZAW	*Zeitschrift für die alttestamentliche Wissenschaft*
ZDMG	*Zeitschrift der deutschen morgenländischen Gesellschaft*

INTRODUCTION

ARABS YESTERDAY AND TODAY

One of the blessings sometimes taken for granted in the United States is the availability of good Christian radio stations, which broadcast challenging messages of life and death, giving people something to think about while pursuing their daily routine. Several years ago I used to turn to one of these stations every morning on my commute to the seminary. I was constantly blessed and challenged with the Word that many times impacted me for the rest of the day. Yet, one morning, a famous preacher from the West Coast preached a message that deeply disturbed me, causing me to turn the radio off and start thinking.

I do not remember the various details of the message, but I still recall that somehow the subject turned to Abraham and Hagar. "If Abraham was not so impatient," said the speaker, "we would have been spared much headache in the Middle East today." Implied was that Abraham's impatience before God—compared to *our* great patience, obviously—led to Ishmael's birth and sustained enmity and struggle between the line of Ishmael and the line of Isaac until today. Though it was not the first time I had heard similar claims about Abraham's role in the birth of Ishmael, it was the first time I stopped to ponder the reasons behind and the consequences of such criticism. What increased my interest in the subject was an earlier discovery of a veiled truth regarding Ishmael.

Over the past few years, I have come to conclude that negative comments like that of the West Coast preacher betray three crucial facts related to the line of the slave woman. First, they show how narrow our view of God's sovereignty is. The same God who planned a redemptive role for the line of Isaac (Gen. 17:19) designed a major historical role for the line of Ishmael as well (16:10; 17:20). God planned to save thousands of those guilty of crucifying Christ through the same death they were culpable for (Acts 2–3). Second, they reveal how much current events in the Middle East influence our interpretation of the biblical text. Finally, they disclose our ignorance of many details in biblical and secular history, for we assume that history supports our theology in the matter of Ishmael's enmity to Isaac, when it does not.

Had Abraham not been so impatient, we might have been spared the headache of the Arab-Israeli conflict in the Middle East today. Yet replacing Arabs with another ethnic group might have only changed the name of the conflict and unfortunately kept the headache. On the other hand, removing Hagar's descendants from the picture would affect many details we tend to ignore in God's design of world history and human redemption. First, it removes large sections of secular history important to the fulfillment of God's purpose. Most important, it removes a multitude of names written in the book of life throughout salvation history. Finally, it removes several inspired portions of the biblical text related to this specific ethnic line.

The West Coast preacher may not have intended his casual comment to cause such damage. It was most likely a passing remark, and not premeditated. It may also have been said as an irony in order to magnify human guilt and vindicate God in his ways. Yet, this passing statement is only one among many signals that betray a negative stereotype concerning the slave woman and her line, common in many Christian circles today. The confusion can only be overcome by an in-depth study of the Word of God and an objective pursuit of the truth. However, the negative image of Ishmael in Christian circles in the West may be related, among other things, to deeply rooted biases against Arabs in general in broader Western societies.

The Status Quo

In a forum held in Oxford on June 7, 1998, "The Arab Image in the West," participants summarized the current feelings toward Arabs common in the West.

> These negative perceptions are seen daily in the Western media, in books, in statements by politicians, in Hollywood films, and in the behaviour and views of members of the public. The results of opinion polls and other surveys, particularly in the U.S.A., confirm these negative images.[1]

The report on the forum goes on to say,

> An analysis of six opinion polls and surveys carried out in the U.S.A. between 1981 and 1996 indicates how perceptions of Arabs and Muslims in the U.S.A. evolved during that period. . . . The analysis shows that security concerns other than historical or cultural factors are the dominant variables influencing the perception and images of Arabs. . . . The Arab image in the U.S.A. can be drastically affected by the latest headlines on violence and terrorism.[2]

After any likelihood of Arab involvement in the Oklahoma City bombing had been disproved, the polls showed a slight improvement in people's disposition toward Arabs.[3] However, since that forum, additional events took place that only caused the picture to go downhill. The worst that could happen to the Arab image came about with the hideous terrorist attacks of September 11, 2001, in New York City and Washington. As a reaction against these events, a global war against terrorism was started under the leadership of the United States. As this book goes to press, we are still watching the different phases of this war unfolding. Amid this disorder, attempts to adjust the picture of the Arabian descendants of Abraham became more needed, though all the more difficult to achieve.

The problem of ethnic partiality has deeper roots than casual preferences. It is caused by several of the sociopolitical factors already mentioned above. But most important for the present study is that it signals a chronic misunderstanding of portions of Scripture that will occupy us in the remainder of this book. However, before this is attempted, it is necessary to sketch the background needed for the upcoming discussion, which will clarify our path and help answer a few subconscious questions.

Arabs Yesterday and Today

Who are the Arabs, and where did they come from? A brief survey of the postbiblical history of Arabs follows, bypassing their legacy in biblical times since this will be developed more fully in the upcoming chapters.

Arab peoples today are native citizens of twenty-two countries belonging to the League of Arab States, where classical Arabic is the mother tongue and the official language of the people. These nations number in total no less than 250 million individuals. Although Islam is the religion of the majority of them, Arab countries include religious minorities of variable sizes, encompassing several Christian denominations, as well as a handful of Jewish groups. These nations today extend over the whole of the Middle East and North Africa in addition to the Arabian Peninsula.

However, in biblical times, Arabs were geographically restricted to the Arabian Peninsula and some of its outskirts. The term *Arab* originated from a mostly nomadic lifestyle. Genealogically, scholars generally agree that Arabs show up in three biblical lists. These are the descendants of Joktan (Gen. 10:25–30), accounting for the south Arabian stock; the descendants of Ishmael, Abraham's firstborn (25:12–18), accounting for the north Arabian tribes; and the descendants of Abraham through Keturah (25:1–6), which mostly populated central

Arabia.[4] A fourth line of genealogy through Cush, son of Ham, is sometimes suggested (10:7).[5] The obvious thing, however, is that by the end of the first millennium B.C., Ishmael and his line had become the dominant representatives of north and central Arabia.[6] Having started in the north, they managed over time to have most parts of the peninsula gradually identify with them, regardless of various ethnic bloodlines. What concerns us more in this introduction is how these Arabs—a population of nomads living in Arabia—spread geographically and became what they are now.

PRE-ISLAMIC ARABS

Islam as a religion did not appear in Arabia until the seventh century A.D. Until then, Arabs were under the influence of various political, economic, and religious trends.[7] Though the period is conventionally referred to by Arab Muslim historians as the "period of ignorance" *(Jahiliyyah),* this could not at all have meant that Arabs before Islam were ignorant.[8] Outstanding poets existed among Arabs during the period; many of them belonged to the Christian tradition. Analysis of their poetry yields evidence of tremendous wisdom literature and sophisticated metering as well as mature art and literary styles.[9]

Politically speaking, north and south in the peninsula, there were impressive monarchies in pre-Islamic times. The Sabaean kingdom of south Arabia displayed an elaborate civilization in the vicinity of today's Yemen. These people monopolized the production and distribution of frankincense and myrrh along with trading in other exotic goods for centuries before the rise of Islam. Living in secluded areas, they enjoyed long periods of peace, which helped them concentrate on trading and civic life. According to the historian Diodorus of Sicily (first century B.C.), the kingdom of Sheba in south Arabia surpassed "not only the neighboring Arabs but all other men in wealth and in their several extravagancies besides."[10] The Sabaean rule in the south was replaced by the Himyarite dynasty (115 B.C.) and continued until the early sixth century A.D., when the Ethiopians succeeded in taking control of their land.[11] However, the Ethiopian presence in south Arabia did not last long before the Sassanid Persians led a successful conquest aimed at controlling the crucial seaports of the southern part of the peninsula in A.D. 575.[12] Jewish presence, whether by conversion or from the diaspora, was significant in central and south Arabia by the sixth century A.D.

With the dawn of the Christian era, the remarkable Nabataean kingdom with its renowned capital of Petra established itself as the primary Arab power in the northern Arabian Desert. The Nabataeans' rise to political and economic glory started in the fourth century B.C., when they successfully defended themselves against the Greek leader Antigonus the One-Eyed, one of the commanders of Alexander the Great. Diodorus reports how Antigonus launched two attacks against the Nabataeans in 312 B.C.; both campaigns failed to subdue these nomads.[13] Having begun as a nomadic power, which replaced the Edomites over Mount Seir (Jer. 49:7–22; Ezek. 25:8–14; Mal. 1:2–5), they managed quickly to dominate major sections of the Arabian Peninsula for over four centuries. The Nabataeans reached the apex of their glory during the days of King Aretas IV (9 B.C.–A.D. 40), when New Testament events took place. The Romans had always had their eyes on the Arabian Peninsula, mostly to control the seaports that linked the south to India, until then monopolized by the Sabaeans.[14] The famous Roman expedition against Arabia under the leader Aelius Gallus (24–25 B.C.), which was somehow assisted by the Nabataeans, proved to be a total failure. Consequently, Rome changed its strategy to overcome the commercial monopoly of Arabia. Having replaced the Ptolemies over Egypt, the Romans revived the access to the Red Sea, and hence to Indian resources via the Nile.[15] Thus the trade monopoly of south Arabia was broken. This weakened the internal south-north trade system and affected all the states benefiting from south Arabian trade. The Nabataean economy gradually was destabilized as a result of that Roman breach.[16] The weakened Nabataean rule ended and their capital fell before the Syrian governor Cornelius Palma and was annexed to Rome in A.D. 106.[17] The magnificent city of Petra, lying in today's country of Jordan, became hidden for many centuries until its discovery by the Swiss explorer John L. Burckhardt on August 22, 1812.[18]

Other small kingdoms flourished in north Arabia in pre-Islamic Christian times. First among these were the Palmyrenes with their famous caravan city Palmyra to the northeast of Damascus. These Arabs were famous for their beautiful queen Zenobia, who dared to defy the Roman emperor by claiming to be "Queen of the East" and declaring her son Caesar Augustus.[19] Eventually, Zenobia's claim was seriously challenged by Rome, when Emperor Aurelian sacked Palmyra, destroyed the city, and led its queen captive in golden chains to Rome in A.D. 272.[20] That the Palmyrenes were Arabs is evident from their Arab names, though, like the Nabataeans, they used Aramaic in their official communications.[21] During the Palmyrene period an Arabian leader by the name of Philip, from the city of Shahba south of Damascus, rose to power and became emperor of Rome. "Philip the Arab," as he was conventionally called, ruled the Roman world from A.D. 244 to 249. There is impressive evidence that this Philip became the first Roman emperor to adopt Christianity, preceeding even Constantine, who is widely thought to bear that distinction.[22]

Finally, two later kingdoms are worth mentioning here: the kingdom of the Ghassānids, which was centered in the neighborhood of Damascus, and the Lakhmid kingdom, which was centered in Hira, southwest of the Euphrates. Both of these were vassal states, the first to Byzantium in the West, and the second to Persia in the East. Both peoples adopted Christianity as a state religion, though the first followed Monophysitism[23] and the second adopted Nestorianism.[24] The Ghassānids claim to have descended from a south Arabian tribe that converted to Christianity in pre-Islamic times. According to tradition, their ancestral tribe migrated to the north and populated Hauran south of Damascus in the early centuries A.D. Though these kingdoms yielded powerful kings, which were often rivals, both the Ghassānid and the Lakhmid kingdoms were weakened by mistreatments from suzerains Byzantium and Persia. At the eve of Islam, these kingdoms were ready for a shift of loyalty, especially if it came from Arabia.[25]

Arabia Under Islam

By the end of the sixth century A.D. the conditions in the Arabian Peninsula were discouraging on many levels. Hitti's summary of the situation is helpful to quote here.

> The national life developed in early South Arabia had become utterly disrupted; anarchy prevailed. . . . Vague monotheistic ideas had already appeared and developed into a cult. Christian and Jewish communities were established in Najran, South Arabia. Jewish tribes flourished in Yathrib (later Medina), Hijaz. From Syria and Abyssinia [Ethiopia] came Christian traders to the markets of Mecca. Christian influences had been increasingly felt, although the Christian idea had never caught hold of the Arab imagination. But the stage was set and the time had come for the rise of a great religious and national leader.[26]

In that atmosphere of social and religious disorder the prophet of Islam appeared. Arab traditions do not present a consensus on the details of his early life. However, it is widely held that about 570, a child was born in the tribe of Quraysh to a family living in Mecca. His father, ʿAbdullah, passed away before he was born. He became quickly known by the name of Muhammad, meaning "highly praised." Six years after his birth, his mother died and the child was raised by his grandfather Abd-el-Muttalib, and then by his uncle Abu-Talib.[27]

During his youth, the boy became involved in the trade business and built a reputation of integrity. Consequently, he was hired by a wealthy widow from Mecca by the name of Khadijah, to accompany her trading caravans. At the age of twenty-five, Muhammad married Khadijah, who was fifteen years his senior. "Her money provided him with the ease and independence needed to investigate and appraise the religious situation in Arabia."[28] Oftentimes, the young man Muhammad retreated to a cave in Mount Hira near Mecca for seclusion, meditation, and prayers. He frequently thought of the lawless and pagan condition of Arabs and compared it to the ordered life of Christians and Jews who each possessed a holy and inspired book.[29]

It was during one of these secluded times at the hill of Hira, when he was forty years old, that Muhammad encountered, according to Muslim tradition, the angel Gabriel, who called him to preach.[30] This was the beginning of his career as a religious reformer and prophet of Islam (611). Muhammad's early message was one of calling his people back to the one God *(Allah)*, the God of Abraham, of the Israelites, and of the Christians.[31] He preached a message of monotheism, of coming judgment for unbelievers and of reward in paradise for the believers.[32] However, his preaching found staunch opposition and very few listening ears in the trade city of Mecca. Converts to Islam were not many there.[33]

This indifference and rejection of the extravagant people of Mecca prompted Muhammad's family and a handful of families who converted to Islam to travel to the city of Yathrib (Medina). This event is called in Islam "the migration" (Ar. *Hijra*) and the year when it happened (622) became the first year of the Muslim calendar (Ar. *Hijri*). Medina was another caravan city located some 280 miles north of Mecca.[34] The city was mentioned in various ancient manuscripts, and at a certain stage of history became predominantly populated by Jews, both native and proselytes. There are reasons to think that the Jewish presence there may go back to the sixth century B.C.[35] Medina later attracted many Arabs, who eventually became the dominant power. Of primary importance among these were the rival tribes of *al-Aus* and *al-Khazraj.* The influential Jewish presence in the city played a decisive role in the power struggle there.[36] According to tradition, it was the Arab people of Medina who invited Muhammad to make their city his headquarters and to mediate among them.[37]

Muhammad gained many new converts to Islam among the people of Medina. Having started in Mecca as a religious leader and a prophet of Islam, Muhammad rose in Medina to political leadership. He quickly started consolidating the ranks of Muslims and getting rid of his enemies, whether Jews or pagan Arabs. It is in Medina that Islam became both religion and state.[38]

The year 624 was a decisive one for the followers of Islam. While a trade caravan belonging to the Meccan tribe of Quraysh was returning to Mecca from Syria, Muhammad and his followers attacked it and engaged it in battle at Badr. For the Meccan merchants this was a matter of life and death. They had a primary interest in keeping the trade routes safe, if income was to continue to flow from the northern regions. News of Muhammad's intent had already reached the Quraysh tribe, which dispatched around 1,000 men to fight the Muslims, who numbered about 300. The victory of Muhammad's followers in that battle was so overwhelming that it was believed to be a direct vindication from heaven of the new monotheistic religion.[39] This battle started a series of other campaigns in which Islam expanded its territories geographically and demographically. In 628 Muhammad signed a peace agreement with the Meccan people, but he soon terminated the agreement and took over the city in 630. At that time Mecca was purified from idols and paganism, thus becoming the spiritual center of Islam.[40]

On June 8, 632, Muhammad died in Medina as a result of a sudden grave illness.[41] By that time, the Muslim state had taken hold of many Arabian tribes, who converted to the new religion whether by conviction or from self-interest. Contracts with Christians and Jews in Arabia were made to protect them under Islam as "people of the book," belonging to the *dhimmi* category. The Qur'an with its Meccan and Medinese verses became the holy book of Muslim converts. In summary, Muhammad, at the head of the newly formed Muslim state, managed in a short period of time to make most of the Arabian Peninsula pledge allegiance to him. Muhammad's influence is summarized by Lewis in this way:

> To the pagan peoples of Western Arabia he had brought a new religion which, with its monotheism and its ethical doctrines, stood on an incomparably higher level than the paganism it replaced. . . . But he had done more than that; he had established a community and a well organized and armed state, the power and prestige of which made it a dominant factor in Arabia.[42]

Muhammad's death led to the period of the "caliphs," literally meaning "successors." However, the prophet of Islam left the scene of history without officially appointing anyone to take over his position as a Muslim leader. Abu Bakr, the prophet's father-in-law, was proclaimed as the next leader. With Abu Bakr started the institution of the caliphate.[43] The first five caliphs were among the closest circle of the prophet Muhammad, the first Meccan converts to Islam. These were Abu Bakr, Omar, Uthman, Ali (Muhammad's son-in-law), and Mu'awiyah. These caliphs ruled from 632 to 680. The period was characterized by conquest and expansion of the territories of Islam.[44] The first regions to fall under Arab Muslims were Syria and Iraq (633–637). Next came Egypt and Persia (639–643). Gradually North Africa fell under Arabian domination too. Thus both Byzantine and Persian realms yielded quickly to the newly rising Arab Muslim power.[45]

Whereas Ali left Medina and made Kufa in Iraq his capital, the Umayyad, Mu'awiyah, made Damascus the capital of the Muslim caliphate.[46] The years 710–714 witnessed an important development, as the Umayyad Arabs invaded Spain in the West and extended their control to the Indus valley in the East.[47] Arabs kept a foothold in Spain until the fall of Granada at the hands of Ferdinand and Isabella in 1492. With the defeat of the caliph Marwan II at the hand of Abbas in 750, the Umayyad caliphate ended and the Abbasid line started ruling over the Arab Empire from Iraq.[48]

In 762–763 the caliph al-Mansur founded the city of Baghdad and established it as the new capital of the caliphate.[49] The Abbasid rule stretched from 750 until 1258, when it fell to the deadly blows of the Mongols. During this long and golden period, the Fatimid dynasty (named after Fatima Ali's wife and Muhammad's daughter) rose in North Africa and Egypt. Their rule started first in Tunisia and moved later to Egypt, lasting from 909 until 1171. It was the Fatimids who built Cairo and established it as their capital in 969.[50]

By 1099 the crusaders, who started their march from western Europe, succeeded in capturing Jerusalem. The first Muslim reactions against these crusaders started being felt by the year 1127.[51] In 1171, Saladin ended the Fatimid caliphate, conquering Egypt and founding the Ayyubid dynasty in Syria and Egypt. Having succeeded noticeably in his military conquests, Saladin challenged the crusaders and defeated them at Hittin and captured Jerusalem in 1187.[52]

By the thirteenth century, Muslim Arabs in Spain began to give up territories as Christians succeeded in taking Cordoba back in 1236. Eventually European domination of Spain was restored as Ferdinand captured Granada in 1492. The Mamluk sultanate rose to power in Egypt and Syria between 1250 and 1260. Two centuries later (1453), the Ottoman Turks sacked Constantinople, defeating the Byzantines, and eventually destroyed the Mamluks in 1517, conquering both Syria and Egypt. After the fall of Iraq to Ottoman power in 1639, the Arab Empire faded away and gradually went into the shadows. Arabs were in some form subject to Ottoman domination until the Turkish Empire terminated at the end of World War I (1918). As a result of this global war, several Arab countries in the Middle East became controlled by the Allied nations under the French and the British mandates. Henceforth, many individual Arab states started struggling for their independence. By the middle of the twentieth century, most Arab states achieved independence, formed the Arab League of States, and eventually joined the United Nations as sovereign countries.[53]

Jews in the Arab World

To the Twentieth Century

The Arab-Israeli conflict continues to make the news headlines and attract major attention amid the events of the world today. A significant number of people have the impression that the enmity between Arabs and Jews is a pattern deeply rooted in history. However, a closer examination of times past reveals quite a different truth.

As far as biblical history is concerned, the testimony of the Jewish scholar Nahum Sarna is very significant. In his commentary on Genesis, he admits clearly what many Christians today are not predisposed to think.

> It is noteworthy that the image of Ishmael in the Bible, as distinct from later Jewish literature, is by and large *not a negative one. He is not an inveterate enemy of Israel.* In fact there seems to have been some *intermingling* between the tribe of Simeon and the Ishmaelites, for the clans of Mibsam and of Mishma are associated with both, as proved by Genesis 25:13 and 1 Chronicles 4:25. The Ishmaelites do not appear among the victims of David's raids into the south lands, even though these incursions encroach upon their habitat, as it is clear from 1 Samuel 27:8 and Genesis 25:18. David's sister married "Jether the Ishmaelite," according to 1 Chronicles 2:17, and among the administrators of crown property under David were "Obil the Ishmaelite" and "Jaziz the Hagarite," according to 1 Chronicles 27:30f. (emphasis added)[54]

This positive view of Ishmael will be explored further and evaluated in the following chapters. Interestingly enough, postbiblical history yields similar conclusions. Unlike the anti-Semitic waves that characterized Europe in the Middle Ages and in recent centuries as well, Arabs were not typically known for their anti-Semitism and hatred of the Jewish race. Conflicting interests may have triggered at some point a few hostilities between Arabs and Jews. However, under Arabs, "Judaism and its adherents," as Rosenthal expresses it, "had not to endure anything like the sustained, officially sponsored and relentlessly conducted attack of the Christian Church on Jews in Christian lands [i.e., Europe]."[55]

Under Islam, monotheistic groups like Christians and Jews were not forced to convert to the new religion, but could enjoy protection and religious freedom as *dhimmis,* that is, people of a covenant or contract.[56] In order to secure these rights, people belonging to the *dhimmi* category were supposed to pay poll taxes *(jizya)* and land taxes *(kharaj).* In many instances these taxes were more manageable than the heavier taxation that was previously imposed by the Byzantine and Persian rulers. This, according to Lewis, led a Jewish apocalyptic writer of the early Islamic period to communicate an angelic message of gratitude to God for raising Arab Muslims: "Do not fear, Ben Yõhāi," the angel said to a rabbinic seer, "the Creator, blessed be He, has only brought the Kingdom of Ishmael in order to save you from this wickedness [i.e., Byzantium] . . . the Holy One, blessed be He, will raise up for them a Prophet according to His will, and conquer the land for them, and they will come and restore it."[57]

However, those belonging to the category of *dhimmi* were considered to be second-class citizens, and as such, had several social restrictions put on them, and they were "forbidden from exercising control over Muslims, although these restrictions were sometimes ignored."[58] Power abuse and religious fanaticism led occasionally to conflicts, massacres, and attacks against the Jews, as well as against other groups of conflicting interests. Yet, despite these incidences, "no [Arab] Islamic ruler," as Bickerton and Klausner put it, "ever instituted a policy of wholesale expulsion or extermination of the Jews."[59]

For long centuries during the Middle Ages, the bulk of the Jews lived and prospered among Arab Muslims, whether in Spain, North Africa, or the Middle East.[60] P. Johnson summarizes the reasons for Islamic tolerance of the Jews.

> Jewish monotheism was as pure as Islam's. The Jews had no offensive dogmas. Their laws on diet and cleanliness were in many ways similar. There is, then, very little anti-Jewish polemic in Islamic religious writing. Nor had the Arabs inherited the vast pagan-Greek corpus of anti-Semitism, on which to superimpose their own variety. Finally, Judaism, unlike Christianity, never constituted a political and military threat to Islam, as did the Byzantine East and later the Latin West. For all these reasons the Jews found it easier to live and prosper in Islamic territories.[61]

They did significantly well in Iraq, where they had a substantial and successful presence in the newly founded city of Baghdad in Abbasid times. They also had a great social and academic life in Kairouan (Tunisia) between the eighth and the eleventh centuries.[62]

But the most flourishing Jewish settlement during that period was to be found in Spain.[63]

In Umayyad Spain, the Jews established a substantial presence and well-to-do communities in very many cities. The Jews provided the caliphs with court doctors, astronomers, and great scholars; they had many successful merchants and enjoyed a "gracious, productive and satisfying way of life" that they were not, "perhaps, to find anywhere else until the nineteenth century."[64] Only when Granada fell in 1492 at the hand of Ferdinand and Isabella did the Jews, among other groups, become subject to harsh persecution and ejection, and "many of them sought refuge in North Africa and in Arab Palestine."[65] The bonding that the Jews had with the Arab culture pushed Goietin to conclude, "Never has Judaism encountered such a close and fructuous symbiosis as that with the medieval civilization of Arab Islam."[66]

In the Twentieth Century

It was only with the end of the nineteenth century and the beginning of the twentieth that the relationships between Arabs and Jews started to become consistently characterized by tension and conflict. Historically speaking, the mutual relationships between the two groups in the past century have been shaped to a large extent by the rise of Arab nationalism and that of Jewish Zionism.

The Rise of Zionism

The word *Zionism* was "probably first used by Nathan Birnbaum in an article published in 1886; it has come to be understood to refer to a movement for the reestablishment of a Jewish nation in Palestine."[67] The rise of modern Zionism is often traced back to a specific event commonly known as the Dreyfus Affair. Alfred Dreyfus was "a Jewish officer of the French General Staff who in 1894 was convicted of treason and sentenced to a life term on Devil's Island."[68] A Hungarian-born Jew by the name of Theodore Herzl happened to cover the trial. Herzl believed with many others that Dreyfus was wrongly accused and racially abused. As a matter of fact, after a second trial in 1906, Dreyfus was acquitted and released from prison.[69] However, the anti-Jewish wave that the trial generated in France "confirmed in Herzl's mind the belief that anti-Semitism was an incurable Gentile pathology."[70] The only suggested solution for this chronic discrimination was that the Jews establish their own state. This proposal was outlined by Herzl in his book *Der Judenstaat* (The Jewish state) in 1896.[71] Though several thinkers before that date spoke of the Zionist dream, Herzl is still considered the father of political Zionism since only with him did this movement become popular.[72]

In August 1897, and under the leadership of Herzl, the first Zionist Congress in Basel, Switzerland, defined the steps toward building the nation of Israel in the land of Palestine. These included a regular sponsorship of settlements there, organizing all of the Jews, and strengthening their national feelings. The congress decided also to seek the consent of all governments able to make the goals of Zionism possible.[73]

Many Zionists at the beginning advocated Palestine as "a land without people for a people without land."[74] However, there were more realistic voices among them that recognized the intricacies of the situation. Asher Ginsberg, followed by Chaim Weizmann, acknowledged the Arab obstacle in Palestine. Thus Ginsberg in 1891 wrote an essay "attacking the 'mere' political Zionism of Herzl," warning against the neglect of Arab presence.[75] According to Ovendale, "in the late 1890s, Arabs warned the Zionist movement that its programme was not feasible. By 1914 there were 650,000 Arabs in Palestine who were already clashing with the Jewish colonists."[76] At the time, the Jewish population did not constitute more than 10 percent of the inhabitants of Palestine, according to the best estimate possible.[77] Thus facts on the ground were not as easy as theories pictured them to be.

Arab Nationalism and the Zionist Program

On the verge of the twentieth century, the Middle East was already a center of tension among world powers. Arabs were groaning under the

Ottomans and longing for a release from Turkish suzerainty. Engulfed in long-standing insignificance as subjects to the Turks, Arabs were about ready to be resurrected. This resurrection largely owes its beginning to the educational efforts of Christian missionaries. French Catholic and mainly American Protestant missionaries helped a great deal in spreading literacy and reviving the Arabic printed word, which contributed to the increase of knowledge and enlightenment among Arabs.[78] The Syrian Protestant College—now the American University of Beirut—founded by Presbyterian missionaries in 1866, influenced the Arab revival more "than any other institution."[79] Subsequently, in various places of the Ottoman Empire, secret societies were started that spread the concepts of Arab liberation and called for independence. The nascent Arab national movement had begun, and nationalistic leaders appeared on the scene. The seeds of Arab unity and revolt against the Turks were planted.[80]

On the other hand, Zionism benefited from the atmosphere of tension over the control of the Middle East to promote its own dream. After failing with the Ottomans, Herzl turned to England, which was eager to see the end of the Turkish domination over the Middle East. The Jewish leader was able to convince the British government that the Zionist aspirations in the land of Palestine would benefit Britain on two terms. First, it would serve well the English imperialist interests in the Middle East; second, it would ease the socioeconomic pressure caused by the growing Jewish migration to Britain.[81]

By 1914, World War I had started, and with it began the struggle between the Allied countries and their opponents. The Middle East was a crucial part of that struggle. In November 1917, the Zionist efforts in Britain led by Chaim Wizemann were crowned with the famous Balfour Declaration. Accordingly, the British prime minister, Arthur Balfour, promised the Zionists the establishing of a "national home for the Jewish people" in Palestine. Britain obtained in return the pledge of financial and political support of the Jews, support needed by the British in their war alongside the Allied countries.[82]

Prior to the Balfour Declaration, the British paved the political ground on two levels. First, they negotiated in 1915–16 the support of the Allies for the Arab revolt against Turkish domination in the famous Hussein-McMahon correspondence. Arabs would agree in return to side with the Allies and give Britain and France temporary control privileges over Iraq, Syria, Lebanon, Palestine, and the Transjordan.[83] On a second level, and in May 1916, the French and the British negotiated the partition of Middle East countries between them in what was conventionally called the Sykes-Picot agreement. Accordingly, the British controlled Palestine, the Transjordan, and Iraq.[84] In 1922, the League of Nations officially delegated Britain in their mandate over Palestine. The implementing of the Balfour Declaration was incorporated into the British mandate. Thus Western imperialism, according to Lesch and Tschirgi, "used the League of Nations to establish a new international order that they designed to fulfill their ambitions."[85]

Implementing the Zionist Vision

Over the next twenty years, the nationalistic feelings among Arabs and Jews increased significantly, each of them looking to establish their own nation on the same land.[86] Increasing immigration of the Jews into Palestine was faced with growing hostilities from Arab Palestinians in the land. The British mandate over Palestine became gradually objectionable to Arabs. An "Arab Revolt" against the mandate, lasting from April to October 1936, led to a British military deployment in Palestine to appease the situation.[87] England's yielding to Arab pressure angered the Jews as well.[88] It was not long before Jewish anger led extremist Zionist groups to wage "a campaign of terrorism against the mandatory administration" in Palestine.[89]

With the Nazis assuming power in Germany under the leadership of Adolf Hitler in 1933, Jewish resettlements in Palestine became more urgent. The dreadful Holocaust that the Jews endured at the hand of Hitler sealed the need to find a permanent solution to the Jewish Question.[90] However, the Holocaust created in the Jews a complex of powerlessness and engendered among them a "reprisal generation."[91] This generation determined to prove to the rest of the world its ability to defend itself and to protect the Jewish people and their interests. Ironically, the Jews expressed their revenge in an Arab context rather than in a European one.[92]

In November 1947, a plan for the partition of Palestine between Arabs and Jews was endorsed by the United Nations. The Arabs rejected the partition plan, insisting on having the whole of Palestine as an independent Arab state. The Jews reluctantly accepted the plan as "the indispensable minimum."[93] The Arab rejection of the proposed partition did not prevent the Jewish leadership six months later from proclaiming the State of Israel (May 1948).[94] International recognition of the Israeli state followed quickly. It seemed that the Zionist dream was finally fulfilled and that the Jewish Question was resolved once and forever. Yet that was far from being true. As a matter of fact, bloody clashes in the area have not stopped ever since.

The chronic anti-Semitic problem that the Jews endured over centuries in Europe was being solved but was creating a Palestinian crisis. Geddes informs us that by the beginning of 1949, the number of Christian and Muslim Arab refugees approached 950,000 as reported by the UN Palestine Conciliation Commission.[95] These "fled from the battle areas or had been expelled from the newly conquered Israeli territories."[96] Today, hundreds of thousands of them are still living in refugee camps in shocking conditions. Resolving the question of the Jewish diaspora created a Palestinian diaspora alongside. Foreign interests of major Western powers and political mistakes committed by local Arab leaders only complicated the dilemma in the area and contributed toward worsening Arab-Jewish relationships. Practically speaking, Herzl's political Zionism was wrong in ignoring the Palestinians in the land. Four major wars and endless skirmishes over the past fifty years confirmed Ginsberg's pragmatic concerns over the neglect of the Arab question. Shipler's words still ring true. "To draw the boldest outline of the past is to make Israel's basic case. To sketch the present is to see the Arab's plight."[97] While the past belongs to former generations, it is the present that our generation is shaping and thus accountable for.

Christians and the Arab-Israeli Conflict

Regrettably, today's world politics may be creating among Arab Palestinians another "reprisal generation." The rise of suicide bombers is a sign of chronic lack of communication in a world saturated with media. Moreover, Islamic fundamentalism and extremist fanatic groups are unfortunately becoming all the more appealing to oppressed people in the land. Voices of moderation are being silenced on both sides and violence is gaining more ground out of an atmosphere of despair. Anti-Semitism was an ugly phenomenon that engendered many atrocities against the Jews over many centuries in Europe. It desperately needed to be addressed. Today the world may be unconsciously replacing anti-Semitism with a different kind of racial favoritism—anti-Arabism. This only magnifies the problem and establishes a situation that will merely pass on the problems to the next generation. In a *New York Times* editorial on March 30, 2002, Yossi Beilin, a former member in Barak's cabinet in Israel, wrote,

> The Israeli war against the terrorist infrastructure will give birth to more terrorists because the terrorist infrastructure lies within people's hearts. It can be uprooted only if there is *hope for a different kind of life* in the Middle East. (emphasis added)[98]

Whatever Beilin's view on terrorism and its origin, he pointed out a crucial fact that recent history supports. The display of force cannot solve the Israeli problem, nor can violence vindicate the Arab cause. Jews as well as Arabs have the right to live in peace wherever they belong. Yet peace cannot coexist with oppression. Christ calls his followers in this world to uphold mercy and justice and be peace-makers (Matt. 5:7–9) rather than endorse controversial politics. It is a primary Christian task to offer hope to various people in the area. Only *hope for a different kind of life* would make peace possible.

Almost always, a different kind of life starts with a different way of thinking. This book is an attempt to stimulate this change of thinking, starting at a foundational level, that of the biblical text, and extending it to biblical history. Accordingly, it strives to achieve among Bible believers a more accurate understanding of sacred Scriptures related to Arabs. Moreover, it aims at resurfacing the Abrahamic heritage of the Arab people in order to bring them back to their biblical legacy and cause others to view them more fairly. Finally, it focuses on the positive Arab-Israeli relationships in biblical history, which will give us a framework to bring hope for the future of the Middle East.

THE PHILOSOPHY OF BIBLICAL HISTORY

Having sketched the Arab-Jewish relationships over the past two millennia, we now need to highlight the framework and philosophy of the discussion ahead. The present work explores in detail the Arab line of Ishmael in biblical history for the sake of drawing principles and establishing facts that will help ease contemporary tensions. Biblical history is the time frame assumed to stand behind the books of the Bible. Old Testament Scriptures will be divided into two main sections. The period starting with the call of Abraham and ending with Solomon's reign will be considered first. Since biblical history sketches basically the history of ancient Israel, this first period will be labeled, "The Light of Israel." The period beginning with the division of Israel's kingdom and ending at the eve of the first coming of Christ will be considered next, and will be referred to as "The Darkness of Israel." Ancient Arabs will be explored finally during the period of the New Testament, which will be called, "The Light of Christ."

The "Light" period was characterized by the nation's ascendancy to glory, which reached its apex in the Solomonic reign. Though there was a moral lapse during the period of the judges, it led to the consolidation of the different tribes and ended in the establishing of the united monarchy under King Saul. The period of "Darkness" started with the divided monarchy and was characterized by Israel's idolatry. The nation declined until the deportation of the northern kingdom in 722 B.C., followed by the exile of the southern kingdom in 586 B.C. to Babylon. Though a remnant of Israel returned to the land at the decree of the Persian emperor Cyrus (539 B.C.), the Davidic dynasty was never restored until the coming of Christ.

The suggested partition of history is not an arbitrary one, but rather based on the fact that Israel in biblical times was a nation elected for a missionary purpose. It was supposed to bear the light of the Lord to the nations around it and to act as a kingdom mediating between God and the kingdoms of the world (e.g., Exod. 19:6; Isa. 42:6; 49:6; Jonah 1–4; etc.). When this mission was successful, the nation was expected to become a blessing to its neighbors, causing conversions to the Lord among them. On the contrary, when ancient Israel failed to live up to the purpose behind its election it caused further alienation from God among the nations around it. In both cases Ishmaelite Arabs are considered as a study case to prove this cause-effect principle. This partition of Israel's history allows the scrutiny of the missionary role of the elect nation as it is applicable to the Israelites' closest theological kin, the Ishmaelites.

In covering the "Light of Christ" period, this book explores the Arabian line of Ishmael within the framework of New Testament Scriptures. Part 4 examines the Arabian origin of the magi involved in the worship of the Messiah-King of the Jews (Matt. 2:1–12). The period of "Light" yields evidence of conversions to the Lord among ancient Arabs. The period of "Darkness," marked by Israel's spiritual apostasy, results in spiritual darkness among the line of Ishmael, further alienating them from their Abrahamic heritage.

Establishing a foundation to build upon is necessary for our historical investigation of the line of Ishmael. Part 1 presents an in-depth study of Ishmael in Genesis 16, 17, 21, and Galatians 4:21–31. For centuries, interpretive difficulties involving these biblical passages have indirectly distorted the picture of Ishmael and have adversely affected the image of Arabs among Christians. Dealing with these portions of Scripture upfront clarifies the way to our exploration of biblical history.

By rightly dividing the word of truth (2 Tim. 2:15), this book attempts to revive the biblical profile of Ishmael. For long centuries, Ishmael has been appropriated and held in esteem by Muslims in general, and Arab Muslims in particular, regardless of their various bloodlines. In response, the Christian church has distanced itself from this biblical figure and espoused to a certain extent a negative attitude toward him. It is time to present Ishmael from a Christian perspective, and to reclaim him as part of biblical legacy. This will help build a bridge for dialogue with those who claim Ishmael as their ancestor. The biblical legacy of Arabs and Jews has the potential to reconcile both antagonistic parties under the Abrahamic umbrella and to offer the hope of the gospel of peace in an area tyrannized by war.

PART 1

BIBLICAL FOUNDATIONS

1

THE UNFORTUNATE BEGINNING (GEN. 16:1–6)

"WHAT DO YOU THINK OF THE spiritual condition of Ishmael, Abraham's firstborn?" The question came up in a doctoral seminar on the Pentateuch I attended while in seminary. The professor turned to one of the students in class, expecting an answer to this puzzling question. Well advanced in his doctoral work, the student confidently responded, "I think he is under a curse. Isn't he?" Most of the class did not have a clue about the matter. I felt that they sympathized with the answer. They started looking at each other and glancing at me. Fortunately, by that time I had dismissed the curse idea, which I used to believe. A major turnaround in my thinking happened at an earlier stage of my study. The professor then looked at me and said, "Tony, you might have a better answer for us, since you have studied the subject a little further. What can you tell us about Ishmael?"

I turned to my fellow student and challenged him to show me a Bible verse in the Old Testament that put Ishmael under curse. He was not ready to face that challenge and was embarrassed by my request. After a short discussion, he apologized for making a snap judgment.

His initial answer was not based on a serious study of the subject. Rather, it was grounded in a negative stereotype common in many evangelical circles today and among Christian leaders. Simply, it involves uniformed impressions.

Any serious change in our understanding of Bible-generated concepts has to be deeply rooted in Scriptures. Damage due to wrong interpretations of the Bible held over a long time cannot be mended by subjective treatment or shallow study. Only the light shining from a serious and objective handling of God's Word can brighten stereotypes darkened over centuries of biased tradition. There is no way out of the diligent study of Scriptures. There is no replacement for an inductive analysis of texts related to Ishmael in the Bible. It was my encounter with the text in its context that enlightened my mind and dispelled a myth I held for so long.

This part of the book lays the foundation for our study by examining the Word. It includes first a detailed exposition of Genesis 16, which is crucial to any exploration of Ishmael in the Bible. It also covers Genesis 21:8–21 and its New Testament counterpart, Galatians 4:21–31. The present chapter deals with the story from its beginning. It focuses on the circumstances that led to Ishmael's birth, highlighting the first six verses of Genesis 16, which are crucial to any correct understanding of the Ishmael narrative. Yet, before attempting to study the text itself we cannot avoid dealing with some preliminary issues.

Ishmael in Traditions

Ishmael's Relationship to Arabs

A widely held tradition in the Arab world associates Ishmael and his descendants with Arabs in general and Arab Muslims in particular. The eminent Arab genealogist, Hisham ibn Muhammad al-Kalbî (A.D. 737–819?), more commonly known as Ibn al-Kalbî, popularized the genealogical link supposed to exist between the prophet Muhammad and Ishmael. Ibn al-Kalbî quoted writers "who had access to biblical and Palmyrene sources," and he was well "informed of archaeological discoveries in the Yemen."[1] However, the bulk of his material came from ancient traditions transmitted orally throughout the generations of ancient Arabians.[2] This is why the link between Muhammad and Ishmael has been challenged and rejected by some as unscientific.[3]

However, older records clearly link ancient north Arabians to Ishmael, whether or not the tradition relating Muhammad to Abraham's firstborn withstands scientific scrutiny. By the time of Christ, there were strong attestations of this association. In this regard, the historian Diodorus of Sicily (first century B.C.) equates the Arabs of north Arabia with the Arabs of Assyrian time, who were associated in Assyrian inscriptions with prominent Ishmaelite tribes.[4] In his turn, the writer of the book of Jubilees (second century B.C.) makes interesting comments on Genesis 25. According to him, the children of Ishmael and those of Keturah intermarried, dwelt in north Arabia, and became known as the Arabs and Ishmaelites.[5] Furthermore, the Jewish historian Josephus (first century A.D.) makes many references to Arabia and his contemporary Arabs, the Nabataeans. He constantly equates these Arabs with the children of Ishmael.[6] Whether or not there is a strong ethnic basis for his classification,[7] no one can deny that Ishmael had become a great symbol for north Arabian tribes by the first century A.D.

As to where the Arabs originated from, the subject is still obscure. The common view popularized by medieval Arab genealogists is that they originated in the southern part of the Arabian Peninsula and then moved northward.[8] This view is largely based on the claim of Muslim Arab historians that their oldest ancestor is Qahtan, whom they identify as the biblical Joktan (Gen. 10:25–26). Montgomery finds it difficult to reconcile Joktan with Qahtan based on etymology. However, he sees in the names of the descendants of Joktan an Arabian identification, either "geographically or by etymology."[9]

It is fairly well known that Arab genealogists divide the Arabians into two ethnic stocks, the Arabian Arabs *(ʿaribah)* and the Arabicized Arabs *(mustaʾribah)*. The Arabian Arabs, according to this division, are the south Arabian stock associated with the Yemenites. They are descended from Joktan and form the original stock (Gen. 10:25–26). On the other hand, the Arabicized Arabs are the people of Hejaz and Najd in central Arabia, Nabataea, and Palmyra in north Arabia. These all descended from Adnan, one of the children of Ishmael according to Arab Muslim tradition. They are responsible for the spread of the classical Arabic language, while the southern stock spoke a dialect closer to Ethiopic than to classical Arabic.[10]

However, this view, though very common, is not uniformly held. There are those who suggest that the Arabs originated in the northern part of the peninsula.[11] Their view is based on the fact that, as early as the ninth century B.C., the Assyrian records mostly apply the term "Arabs" to north Arabian nomadic tribes.[12]

Nevertheless, Ephᶜal recognizes that the term also includes a reference to a variety of Arabian tribes as well.[13] A major argument advanced in favor of the northern origin of Arabs is the failure of thousands of south Arabian inscriptions to associate south Arabian tribes with the term "Arabs." In addition to that, the gradual appearance of a designation qualifying the south Arabian people as "Arabs" by the first century A.D. made Ephᶜal conclude that originally the term was a north Arabian concept. Later the bedouin territory expanded to the south and bedouins took over the land belonging to the sedentary population. Consequently the term started to be applied to the southern sections of the peninsula also.[14] Thus it would be hard to decide which of the views is correct because of the scarcity of the evidence regarding the origin of the Arabs. As Grohmann suggested, if the ancient five books of Uranius *(Arabica)* developing the history of Arabs had been preserved, scholars today would have more certain facts about this matter.[15]

The Muslim Ishmael

It is appropriate at this point to present a brief synopsis of the place of Ishmael in Islam.[16] Contrary to what is commonly thought, the Qurʾan does not contain much information about Ishmael. Only twelve Qurʾanic verses mention Ishmael by name. Nine of them list him among other holy men from ancient time. There, he is described among those having "preference above the worlds" (6:86). He is listed alongside Idris and Zul-Kifl as "one of constancy and patience" (21:85). He is commemorated together with Zul-Kifl and Elisha as "of the company of the good people" (38:48). All three references are found in Meccan Suras (i.e., early in Muhammad's life). In 2:125 (Medinan Sura, i.e., later life of Muhammad), God commands Abraham and Ishmael to purify his house *(Kaᶜba)* for those who want to use it as a place of prayer and worship. In 2:127–29 (Medinan), Abraham is shown together with Ishmael as raising the foundations of the house and asking God to make them submit to him (Muslims). In 2:133 Ishmael is described along with Abraham and Isaac as a monotheist submitting to one God. In 2:136 and 4:163 (Medinan), Ishmael is included among those who have received revelation from God.

The only place where Ishmael is mentioned by himself is in Sura 19:54–55 (Meccan), where he is described as "true to his promise," "a messenger," "a prophet," one who "enjoined upon his people the prayer and almsgiving," and "was in his Lord's eyes approved." Nowhere in the above-mentioned verses is Ishmael given a distinctive place. The only Qurʾanic reference that points to Abraham's relationship to Ishmael is a passing statement of thanksgiving, where Abraham praises God for giving him in his old age, his two sons Ishmael and Isaac (Sura 14:39). Other than that, the Qurʾan does not refer to the direct genealogical link between Abraham and Ishmael and does not speak of the family relationship between them as the Bible does (Gen. 16:1–16; 17:9; 21:8–21; 25:12–18).

Sura 37:102–7, which speaks about Abraham's attempt to sacrifice his son, is a controversial passage. Since it does not refer to the name of his son, many have assumed that Ishmael is implied there as the son offered to God, because it is not until verses 112–13 that Isaac's birth is announced. However, there is no unanimous agreement, and Muslim tradition is evenly divided between those who identify Isaac and those who see Ishmael as the sacrificed son. However, today, this is not a debated issue in Muslim circles, for it is generally assumed that Ishmael was the sacrificed son, hence the major Muslim holiday of *Adha* ("the sacrifice").

Post-Qurʾanic traditions supplement the picture of Ishmael in Islam. The following nine beliefs concerning Ishmael occur in Muslim tradition.

1. Abraham accompanied Hagar and Ishmael to Mecca in the desert, where he had to leave them and return to his wife Sarah.
2. Before leaving, Abraham, aided by Ishmael, laid the foundation of the temple and constructed its building.
3. Being left alone in the desert, Hagar and Ishmael became very thirsty. So Hagar started running back and forth between the hill of al-Marwa and al-Safa looking for water, a tradition that gave rise to the rite of Saʿy.
4. Ishmael was ordered by the angel Gabriel to dig in the sand with his foot. Thus the well of Zamzam sprang forth.
5. The Arabian tribe al-Djurhum settled close by with Hagar's consent, and later Hagar took a wife for Ishmael from that tribe.
6. It is believed that Abraham visited Ishmael twice in Mecca. The first time Abraham conveyed to his son a cryptic message that he should divorce his wife because she showed Abraham a lack of hospitality. The second time he asked him to keep his second wife because she was hospitable to him.
7. On his third visit Abraham called on Ishmael to help him build the Kaʿba.
8. Ishmael supposedly learned classical Arabic from the Djurhum tribe, and thus became the ancestor of the arabicized Arabs of the north (al-ʿArab al-Mustaʿriba) as opposed to the native Arabs of the south (al-ʿArab al-ʿĀriba). Arab genealogists make Ishmael the ancestor of north Arabian tribes through ʿAdnan, one of his early descendants. However, traditions present two main variations in linking ʿAdnan to Ishmael.
9. Ishmael was buried alongside Ḥagar in the Hidjr inside the Haram.[17]

This survey confirms the centrality of Ishmael in Islam. Muslim Arabs who do not belong to Ishmael's bloodline still associate with him theologically.[18] Whether or not linked to Ishmael ethnically or theologically, no Arab group can avoid a geo-cultural association. Any study of the rise and development of the Arabs must take into account this central figure and his line in history.

The Biblical Story (Chapter 16)

The appropriation of Ishmael by Muslims starting from Muhammad's time has indirectly led the church to avoid this biblical figure and look at him with suspicion. As a result, any defense of Ishmael, lightly considered, may be misunderstood as an apology for Islam. This work is an attempt to resurrect the Ishmael whom Christians have neglected and disdained over a long period of time. It is an effort to restore the biblical dignity of this character in order to bring back to the Bible a large section of people associated with this Arab patriarch. To accomplish this task, the biblical story of Ishmael must be considered from the beginning.

Inadequate Human Deliverance (16:1–3)

Abraham's Call in Perspective

Abraham's call as head of the elect nation (Gen. 12:1–3) occurs in the context of a corporate rebellion of nations against God (11:1–9). This rebellion was evidenced by the commitment of the nations to gather in one place at Shinar in disobedience to God's original command to fill the earth. This divine commission was given first to Adam and Eve (1:28) and renewed after the flood to Noah and his descendants (9:1). However, the nations' rebellion appeared in their intention to prosper independently from God by seeking to make "a name" for themselves, thus falling into the sin of national pride (11:4). As a result, God judged them by multiplying their languages and dispersing them from Babylon.[19] Afterward, the divine program for restoring his kingdom among the nations would be fulfilled through one individual, Abraham (12:1–3).

In the context of the Abrahamic covenant, the Lord commits himself to making Abraham a great nation that would act as a channel for God's blessing to the world (12:2).[20] Thus, beginning with chapter 12, the focus of the Genesis narrative shifts to Abraham and his descendants. However, as early as Genesis 11:30, the plot of the Abraham narrative is set with the declaration of Sarah's barrenness. This problem hindering the fulfillment of the seed promise leaves the door wide open for expectations of supernatural divine intervention as opposed to natural human reasoning.

Having received the promises of God and his calling to leave Ur of the Chaldees and go to the Promised Land (12:1), Abraham proceeded to Canaan after making a significant stop at Haran (11:31; 12:4–5).[21] Lot separated himself from the patriarch in Genesis 13, where God renewed his promise to multiply Abraham's seed and give him the land of Canaan as a perpetual inheritance (13:15–18). Subsequently, Abraham's military might was reflected in his victory over the coalition of kings led by Kedorlaomer in chapter 14. This chapter speaks also of his mysterious encounter with Melchizedek (vv. 18–19). In Genesis 15, the Lord ratifies his covenant with Abraham and predicts the slavery of his seed in Egypt and their eventual deliverance (vv. 12–17).

Sarah's Problem in Context

At the outset of the narrative in chapter 16 the focus of attention clearly shifts from Abraham to Sarah. The narrative presents Sarah in her relationship to Abraham (v. 1), his wife who was supposed to bear "to him."[22]

The prominence of Sarah's role at this point of the story is highlighted by two facts. First, Sarah breaks her silence for the first time since the beginning of the Abraham narrative.[23] Second, she addresses Abraham in the imperative mood and instructs him (v. 2b) to "go in to" her Egyptian maid named Hagar.

Jewish rabbinical tradition attempting to exalt the patriarchs held that Hagar was the daughter of Pharaoh.[24] However, there is no further support for this tradition. Acquiring a maid was part of a woman's dowry, as in the example of both Bilhah and Zilpah, the maids of Leah and Rachel (30:24, 29).[25] Nevertheless, it seems that the patriarchal family obtained Hagar while sojourning in the land of Egypt (12:16). As for the meaning behind the name "Hagar," speculations beyond the fact that it is a mere proper name are not needed for understanding the plot of the narrative.[26]

After a long silence since the beginning of the Abraham narrative, Sarah disclosed what was on her mind (16:2). She told Abraham, "Behold, Yahweh has refrained me from bearing." In saying this, she acknowledged that her barrenness was directly caused by God.[27] Her theological statement was immediately followed by her proposal to Abraham to resort to Hagar for children. Some people have looked at this action as an attempt by Sarah to counter God's restraining hand on her.[28] However, this may not necessarily be the case. Sarah's statement was an acknowledgment of God's sovereign control over the circumstances of her life, which may have suggested to her a certain course of action. She may have reasoned this way, "If the Lord has chosen to close my womb for so long until this old age, and he has promised Abraham a great posterity, might this mean that the seed would possibly be secured from another woman?"[29]

Though Sarah's reasoning seems immoral and sinful by New Testament standards,[30] and not according to God's perfect plan for marriage and for the promised seed, Sarah's action was very much in harmony with the social practices of the time. Contemporary legal customs related to the problem of a barren wife relate directly to the matriarch's proposal. Ancient texts shed some light on the cultural significance of her suggestion and Abraham's appropriation of Hagar as a secondary wife. Codes 144–147 of Hammurabi (eighteenth century B.C.) describe regulations related to marriage practices. Code 146 states:

> When a seignior married a hierodule and she gave a female slave to her husband and she has then borne children, if later that female slave has claimed equality with her mistress

> because she bore children, her mistress may not sell her; she may mark her with the slave-mark and count her among the slaves.[31]

A Nuzi text (fourteenth–fifteenth century B.C.) states:

> If Gilimninu (the bride) bears children, Shennima shall not take another wife. But if Gilimninu fails to bear children, Gilimninu shall get for Shennima a woman from the Lullu country (whence the choicest slaves were obtained) as a wife for Shennima [the bridegroom]. In that case, Gilimninu herself shall have authority over the offspring.[32]

Likewise, an old Assyrian marriage contract (twelfth century B.C.) says:

> Lâqîpum took [in marriage] Hatala, the daughter of Enisrû. In the country Lâqîpum shall not take [in marriage] another [woman], [but] in the city [of Ashshur] he may take [in marriage] *a qadishtum.* If within two years she has not procured offspring for him, only she may buy a maid-servant and even later on, after she procures somehow an infant for him, she may sell her where[soever] she pleases. If Lâqîpum divorces her, he will pay 5 minas of silver, and if Hatala divorces him, she will pay 5 minas of silver. Before Masâa, before Ashshuristikal, before Talia, before Shubbianika.[33]

A Neo-Assyrian text (middle first millennium B.C.) also states:

> If Ṣubētu does not conceive [and] (42) does not give birth, she may take a maidservant [and] (43) as a substitute in her position she may place [her]. (44) She [Ṣubētu] will (thereby) bring sons into being [and] the sons will be her [Ṣubētu's] sons. (45) If she loves [the maidservant] she may keep [her]. (46) If she hates [her] she may sell [her].[34]

These inscriptions reveal a practice allowed within marriages "spread over two millennia" in which a barren woman provides her husband with a surrogate wife, normally her maidservant, in order to secure children for herself.[35] It was a matter of utmost shame for a wife to stay barren in patriarchal and later Old Testament times (Gen. 29–30; Judg. 13:1–24; Ps. 113:9; Isa. 54:1; Luke 1:7, 25). Furthermore, it was imperative for a man to have children; otherwise he would be left without an heir to perpetuate his lineage, which was a matter of primary importance in the ancient Near East.[36] Some scholars feel that Sarah's act most likely was mandated, or at least expected, by social custom.[37] God in his sovereignty truly designed the circumstances that led to Ishmael's birth.

The Matriarch's Practical Theology

Sarah spoke to Abraham in verse 2b, saying, "Go in to my maidservant, maybe I shall be built up from her."[38] The expression "go in to" is used here as a "euphemism for sexual intercourse."[39] In Arab Muslim culture, the first night of marriage is called the night of *dakhlah*, of "going in to." It is not an easy thing for a woman to acknowledge the fact of her barrenness. It is even more difficult for her to jeopardize the uniqueness of her relationship to her husband by allowing another woman to compete with her. Therefore, the matriarch's scheme involved a reluctant attitude. It was her last resort to try to secure children for Abraham. Sarah's aim was "to be built up" from Hagar. The Hebrew verb she used derives from the root *banah*, meaning to build.[40] The basic idea of this verb is to be built up through the bearing of a son (Heb. *ben*) who will secure the continuity of the patriarchal line.[41]

Many people, including famous expositors, criticize Abraham and Sarah for their lack of faith. Somehow, specifically in this story, people tend to minimize God's sovereignty in designing history and to maximize the guilt of the patriarchal couple. It is true that Sarah's scheme was not in any sense in harmony with God's design for the promised seed. However, her proposal implemented by Abraham should not be attributed to a lack of faith and patience displayed by the patriarchal couple for several reasons.

First, Abraham initially received the promise of a seed while he was still in Ur of the Chaldees (Gen. 12:1–3; Acts 7:3). His wife was portrayed in earlier verses as barren (Gen. 11:30). Later, he settled in Haran for an extended period of time until his father died (compare Gen. 11:26 with Gen. 11:31–32 and Acts 7:4). The patriarch left Haran when he was seventy-five years old (Gen. 12:4). Then, after ten years of dwelling in Canaan, he took Hagar as a surrogate wife in compliance with cultural customs (16:3). Thus Abraham had already waited before the Lord for many years since he had first received the promise of land, seed, and blessing.[42] Not many believers could wait patiently that long under trial before attempting to take the initiative to help God. It is interesting in this regard that the New Testament bypasses the shortcoming of Sarah and attributes faith to her in the subject of the promised seed (Heb. 11:11–12).

Second, none of the promises given by God to Abraham prior to the birth of Ishmael clarified the way of fulfillment of the promised descendant. Abraham knew that the seed would come from his loins (Gen. 15:4). However, until then God did not specify to the patriarch that it would be through Sarah's womb, otherwise Sarah's controversial suggestion would not likely have been made. This is not to be taken for granted in light of the cultural practices. In fact, there is a progression in God's unfolding of details concerning the seed promise. First of all, the word translated "seed" is not used in 12:1–3. Instead, there is a general reference to making Abraham a great nation and a blessing to the nations of the earth. In 12:7, "seed" is used for the first time in relation to the Abrahamic promise after the extended stay in Haran is over. Abraham's seed will inherit the land of Canaan (12:7). Then in 13:15–16, God not only referred to Abraham's seed as inheriting the land, but also predicted the numberless multitudes of descendants that he will have. The Lord later specified to the patriarch that his seed would not be Eliezer, the chief servant of his household, but rather a seed from his loins (15:4). Later, the Lord predicted the future subjection of Abraham's seed in Egypt for 400 years (15:13–

17). After that, the Lord told Abraham that his son would be not only from his own loins but also from Sarah's womb (17:15–19).

However, the Lord did not specify Sarah's womb until Ishmael was around thirteen years old (17:25). Thus Abraham was purposely left to wrestle with the difficulty of fulfillment of the seed promise. He was fully aware of Sarah's barrenness, possibly of her dead womb being seventy-six years of age (16:15, 16; 17:1, 17, 24–25; Rom. 4:19). God so far had refrained from intervening in the matter. Since it is God who opens one womb and closes another, Sarah's proposal to have children through Hagar was not devoid of faith. By only hoping (saying, "perhaps") that she would be built up through Hagar, the matriarch again placed her faith in God for the provision of a seed. She acknowledged the fact that God is able to close the womb of Hagar, as he had prevented her all those long years from bearing children. Nevertheless, human ways of appropriating God's blessings will always fall short of divine supernatural provisions, and may generate complications that only a sovereign God is able to use for his decreed purposes.

Thus God's sovereign action in shutting Sarah's womb and opening Hagar's can possibly be explained in two ways. First, it may denote God's intention to set human natural efforts in contrast with divine supernatural interventions. The manner of Isaac's birth, bringing life out of death, is beyond human expectation (Gen. 17:17; 21:1–7). This divine supernatural intervention represents God's unmerited favor extended to the elect line in history and to the believer in general. Though God cared for Ishmael in a special way, as it will be shown later, it was through Isaac, whose birth was typical of heaven's intervention in history for salvation, that the seed promise leading to the Messiah was to be perpetuated (17:18–22). The symbolism of this picture is developed further in the New Testament and applied to salvation truths (Gal. 4). The second explanation accounts for the promise of multiplication of seed given to Hagar later in the narrative (Gen. 16:9). It is a fact that God not only designs the history of salvation, but also shapes the history of nations. Thus, besides the previous symbolism related to salvation, God's sovereign control over the circumstances accounted for the purpose he had for Ishmael and his descendants in his layout of human history (17:5–6).

Thus, Ishmael was not a sad mistake and an individual born through a sinful undertaking, as the casual reader might conclude. Rather, God in his sovereignty intended Ishmael's birth by allowing it, as much as he planned the supernatural birth of Isaac and executed it. He had already decreed to make Abraham the father of many nations (17:5–6), Ishmael's line included. It is important to note also that the typology in the stories of Ishmael and Isaac is not related to the nature of Ishmael as contrasted with that of Isaac. Rather it is related to the way each of these children was born and the circumstances of their births.

Expected Natural Complications (16:4–6)

Hagar's Sudden Exaltation (v. 4)

When Sarah took her maid and gave her to Abraham, the focus of the narrative shifted to Hagar (v. 3b). As a result of this move, the social status of Hagar changed to that of a wife. Formerly she was Sarah's maid; now she became Abraham's wife, though in a secondary sense. Reflecting Jewish rabbinical interpretations, Kasher notes that Abraham took Hagar "*to be his wife,* not his concubine. . . . She was to enjoy the full rights of a wife."[43] Hagar's status was to be distinguished from a mere concubine of Abraham. In Hebrew, she is called *ʾIššâ,* literally meaning "a woman," or "a wife" when in relation to a man. Yet she was not Abraham's wife in the primary sense of the word. She belonged to a middle class in between the concubine and the primary wife. In his discussion of women's legal rights in the ancient Near East, P. Cruveilhier notes an extrabiblical parallel situation, and observes the existence of a middle class, which is called the *esirtu* class.[44]

In Hebrew Scriptures, Hagar's status is also distinct from that of concubines in the later history of Israel. According to Hamilton, there were seven individuals outside of Genesis who had concubines: Caleb (1 Chron. 2:46, 48), Gideon (Judg. 8:31), a Levite (Judg. 19–20), Saul (2 Sam. 3:7; 21:11), David (2 Sam. 5:13; 15:16, etc.), Solomon (1 Kings

11:3) and Rehoboam (2 Chron. 11:20). In all of these instances the word used for concubine is *pilegeš*.[45] A comparison of the roles and privileges of a concubine *(pilegeš)* and a wife *(ʾiššâ)* shows that the two terms were distinct and not used interchangeably in later Hebrew narrative (cf. 2 Sam. 5:13; 19:6; 1 Kings 11:3; 2 Chron. 11:21).[46]

Unlike the rest of the Old Testament, in the patriarchal period the two words were used interchangeably. Thus Abraham's secondary wives, Hagar and Keturah (Gen. 25:1), were referred to as *ʾiššâ* and *pilegeš* (16:3; 25:1; 25:6; 1 Chron. 1:32). These two words were used together to refer to a category different from that of a wife, yet not similar to that of a concubine; this category may be called a "concubine-wife."[47] Hence, a noticeable shift in the social atmosphere in which Hagar would live occurred. With this change of status, a natural change in attitude and behavior can be expected. Trible notes the effect of this change in social structure: "In making Hagar Abram's wife, not concubine, Sarah has unwittingly diminished her own status in relationship to this servant. But she still retains full control over Abram."[48]

When Abraham "went in" to Hagar following Sarah's instructions, Hagar conceived as a result, and she became fully aware of her privilege, as "she saw" that she had conceived. Therefore, not only her social status changed but also her role, for now she prided herself in bearing the child who would become Abram's firstborn and heir. Being elevated to such a status and role, Hagar gained self-esteem. With this dignity newly bestowed on her, an inevitable devaluation of her mistress emerged as she was put in a place of rivalry with her. Nahum Sarna sees this as a "natural consequence of a situation in which barrenness is regarded as a disgrace."[49]

In Westermann's judgment, "the narrator is not describing a gross violation of law and custom by Hagar, but a conflict which was almost unavoidable, which in any case was the natural outcome of the situation, and which recurred again and again."[50] However, the action of Hagar is often inaccurately portrayed as "looking on her mistress with contempt,"[51] or "despising" her.[52] Such a translation suggests an attitude of hostility on Hagar's side against her mistress.[53]

Some have even suggested that there should be a connection between chapter 12 and chapter 16. In chapter 12, God promised to curse those who curse Abraham (v. 3). Hagar's eventual loss of the blessing, they claim, is in direct connection to this promise.[54] However, as Wenham puts it, "To disdain Abram was to bring oneself under the divine curse (cf. 12:3), and there is no evidence that Hagar is looked on this way in this story."[55] Furthermore, neither context nor grammar compels us to establish this link between both chapters of Genesis.[56]

The fact is that the Hebrew of verse 4 implies a milder situation. The original Hebrew literally translates, "and her mistress became little in her eyes," where the subject of the verb "became little"[57] is Sarah rather than Hagar.[58] Thus Sarah "became little in Hagar's eyes," that is, decreased in status in comparison with her previous position. This reveals an attitude of maternal pride on Hagar's part rather than an attitude of hatred or contempt.[59] However, with this shortening of distance between the two women, the scene becomes pregnant with potential conflict due to the ensuing rivalry and competition over marital rights.[60]

The Tragic Conflict (16:5–6)

When Abraham realized that Hagar was pregnant, he started treating her in a special way. After all, Hagar was carrying his firstborn baby. Feeling the great privilege, Hagar started taking advantage of her pregnancy after living for so long as a slave. Thus she may have refrained from doing some house chores she used to do for Sarah. Gradually, this new situation created tension between the mistress and her slave and triggered jealousy. As the days went by with Abraham's new attitude toward Hagar and the maid's new attitude toward her mistress, the situation became too tense to bear and Sarah was boiling mad. The matriarch's anger was displayed in three ways. First, she turned to Abraham instead of Hagar to blame him for the side effects of the scheme that she had initially orchestrated. As the head of the patriarchal family, Abraham had the authority to effect changes in the ensuing situation.

Second, Sarah was dismayed by the elevated position of Hagar that automatically resulted in her devaluation in the maid's eyes. Thus she magnified the problem, calling Hagar's attitude of pride "my wrong," or more literally, "my oppression."[61] Hamilton notes, "Sarah is now a non-child-producing *ʾIššâ,* and Hagar is a child-producing *ʾIššâ.* And this is what annoys Sarah and not any barbs that Hagar is throwing at her."[62] Wenham sees the term translated "wrong" (Heb. *khamas*) a bit strong to refer to Hagar's attitude. It is "used elsewhere in Genesis to describe the sins" of the people who perished in the flood judgment (6:11, 13) and the malicious vengeance of Simeon and Levi (49:5; 34:25).[63]

Sarah's anger may be justified in that while she turned to Hagar for help, the solicited help turned out to be costly for her privileged status. Yet one cannot think of any example of human exploitation that does not have harmful side effects. Only the Lord could have intervened on Sarah's behalf, providing her with a child without ever affecting her status.

The third aspect of Sarah's anger is displayed in the final words she says to her husband, "May Yahweh judge between me and you" (v. 5). The matriarch explains to Abraham the nature of Hagar's wrong: "I became little in her eyes" (literal translation). Thus she attributes to Hagar a heart attitude of pride that put Sarah's privileged status in jeopardy. So Sarah invites the Lord's judgment between her and her husband, thus holding Abraham responsible for allowing their marriage to be shaken, requesting from him a prompt action.

In his turn, Abraham places the matter back in the hand of Sarah (v. 6). By saying "behold your maid is in your hand," Abraham quickly dismisses his marital relationship to Hagar, calling her "your maid." Putting her back under Sarah's authority, the patriarch admits, without compelling legal reasons, that Hagar's servant-mistress relationship to Sarah will again supersede her relationship to him as wife *(ʿIššâ).*[64] Abraham here prefers to stay passive because of the delicacy of the situation. He plays "a rather unfortunate role between these two stubborn women."[65] Consequently he grants Sarah the freedom to do to Hagar whatever she sees fit.

Now as Sarah was belittled "in the eyes of her" maid, she is to do to her what is good "in your [Sarah's] eyes." It is Sarah's opportunity now to deal with the new condition as it pleases her. Feeling that her privilege as Abraham's primary wife is endangered, Sarah is now ready, as von Rad puts it, to "strike back."[66] Attempting to deal with the unwanted consequences of her proposal to Abraham, Sarah "afflicts" Hagar. The Hebrew verb used to refer to Sarah's treatment of Hagar stems from the root *ʿanah.* The verb form used here[67] suggests the idea of bringing someone under control and dominion by means of "harsh treatment" that may involve physical abuse.[68] According to Jewish interpreters, the verb implies physical and psychological abuse by Sarah aimed at subjecting Hagar.[69] As a result, Kasher notes that "Sarah sinned in afflicting" Hagar, "so did Abraham in permitting it."[70]

The same verb is used to refer to the Egyptians' oppression of the Israelites in the book of Exodus (1:11–12). In connection with that, Yahweh uses it in Genesis 15:13 to predict the Egyptian servitude of Israel. Hagar finds her way out of this oppression as she "fled from her presence" (literally, "from her face"). Hagar's flight *(baraḥ)* out of oppression *(ʿanah),* is paralleled by the Israelites' flight *(baraḥ)* to the wilderness out of the oppression *(ʿanah)* of the Egyptians (Exod. 14:5).[71] The reference to the oppression of Israel in Genesis 15:13 and in Exodus 1:11, 12 frames "Sarah's and Abraham's treatment of Hagar" and invites "the reader to compare their treatment of this Egyptian maid with Egypt's later treatment of the Hebrews."[72] The end of this first scene (Gen. 16:1–6) is quite sad: "Hagar lost her home, Sarah her maid, and Abraham his second wife" and his expected firstborn baby.[73]

2

HAGAR'S SONGS IN THE NIGHT (GEN. 16:7–16)

BLESSINGS IN THE WILDERNESS (16:7–9)

Fleeing the harsh subjection of her mistress, Hagar ends up in the wilderness. There she becomes the recipient of special divine attention. If fallen humans cannot help but sympathize with the helpless, how much more would a holy and gracious God do to comfort a young woman by herself in a barren wilderness, pregnant with the firstborn of Abraham, homeless, wandering with no aim, no food, and no one to rely upon. Her only security used to come from the household of her masters. Ironically, after becoming pregnant from her union with Abraham, marriage, normally designed to provide security and love for a woman, became a starting point for Hagar to lose everything. Having been lifted up by maternal pride and marital status to the extent that the woman who indirectly was the cause of her privilege became little in her eyes, Hagar was delivered by her husband back to a more severe subjection under her mistress. Fleeing became her only way out of abuse, yet with no aim or provision, no protection or security. Sin, as human failure to measure up to God's standards, always leads to complications that only God in his sovereignty is able to resolve.

The Strange Encounter (v. 7)

In the middle of Hagar's despair, the narrator tells his readers that "the Angel of the LORD found her by a well of water in the wilderness" (v. 7). The text gets more specific in pointing to the well "on the way to Shur." The Lord intervenes here on behalf of the afflicted one. Consequently, he reveals some of his feelings in the matter. Yet as he commissions Hagar to go back, he shows his concern for the whole patriarchal family. "As between Sarah and Hagar, there is no doubt," in Sarna's words, "as to where the sympathies of the Narrator lie. God, the guardian of the weak and the suffering, reveals Himself to the lowly Egyptian maidservant, bringing her a message of hope and comfort."[1]

A study of the use of the verb "find" (Heb. *matza'*) in the Hebrew Bible is significant here. In all parallel uses, when the subject of "find" is God and the direct object is impersonal, "the reference is normally to God's discovery of sin or evil in somebody" (Gen. 44:16; Pss. 10:15; 17:3; Jer. 2:34; 23:11).[2] However, when the direct object is a person with God as the subject, the verb *matza'* ("to find") "carries a technical meaning going well beyond connotations of the English verb: it includes elements of encounter and of divine election (cf. Deut. 32:10; Ps. 89:21; Hos. 12:5)."[3] This remark supports the conclusion that "Hagar was one of the nine righteous women proselytes of the Bible."[4]

The motif of divine appointment and potential marriage "at the well" favors the preceding conclusion, too. The well scenery comes back in Genesis 21:19. In 24:12–27, 42–48, God intervened on behalf of Isaac, providing him with Rebecca at a well of water. Moses also met his appointed wife at a well (Exod. 2:15–21). In the New Testament, Christ timed his meeting with the Samaritan woman at the well of Jacob and introduced himself to her as the giver of the living water (John 14). The mention of the Angel of Yahweh finding Hagar by the well of water may be a deliberate allusion by the inspired writer to the special attention that God gives to this used and abused woman.[5]

The "Angel of the LORD" here is most likely a reference to a theophany for the following reasons. First, in verse 10, the angel declares himself to be the one who will multiply Hagar's seed, a blessing that only the Lord could provide. He says, "I will multiply your seed exceedingly." Second, in verse 13 Hagar gives "the LORD who spoke with her" a name, "El Roi," and in verse 14 she gives the well a name, "the well of the Living One who sees," thus suggesting that she encountered the Lord himself. Third, in 21:17 it is God who hears the voice of the child, yet it is the Angel of God who calls Hagar from heaven, thus the same person is implied by this interchange. Fourth, in 22:11 "the Angel of the LORD" swears by himself, being the Lord of Abraham. Thus "the Angel of the LORD" who appeared to Hagar is very likely a reference to the Lord himself, probably a bodily appearance of the preincarnate Christ.[6]

However, whether one sees the Angel of the Lord as a theophany or as a simple divine messenger representing God himself, Hagar in both cases is the object of a special divine favor, revelation, and comfort. The narrator describes the place of the well as being "on the road to Shur." The word "Shur"[7] means "wall," normally of protection or separation.[8] Biblical references to Shur (Gen. 20:1; 25:18; Exod. 15:22; 1 Sam. 15:7; 27:8) point to a location on the southern border of Canaan close to the traditional location of Kadesh Barnea on the way to Egypt. It is likely that Hagar had traveled quite a distance before her encounter with the Angel of the Lord because Abraham was dwelling somewhere in Mamre near Hebron, which is about 60 miles north of Kadesh. A similar flight is seen in the story of Elijah, who fled to the wilderness of Sinai also before he met the Lord at Mount Horeb (1 Kings 19).

The Divine Interview (vv. 8–9)

After the Angel of the Lord found Hagar (v. 7), he called her by her name (v. 8), which implies a personal knowledge of her situation and a potential personal relationship. What a comfort it must have been for Hagar to be called by her personal name, even though she was quickly reminded of her status as the servant of Sarah. Until then, no one in the narrative referred to her by her name. She was always spoken of as the slave, even by her own husband Abraham. Yet the Lord saw her affliction, listened to her distress, and came to comfort her.

At first, the angel asked Hagar where she was coming from and where she was going (v. 8). As in Jacob's and Manoah's case (Gen. 28:22–32; Judg. 13:16–20), it is doubtful that Hagar realized at this point that the man talking to her was the Angel of the Lord. Yet, her short answer reflected humility and aimlessness. She answered, "From the presence of Sarah my mistress I am fleeing." By describing Sarah as her mistress, Hagar indirectly admitted her lowly status.[9]

In that sense, Hagar was humbly admitting to an unknown person that she was fleeing from the presence of the lady who had power over her and who was exercising this power unfairly. By acknowledging that power belonged to Sarah and that she was fleeing from her, Hagar was indirectly confessing her powerlessness. Yet the slave woman stopped short of telling where she was going. She failed to answer the second half of the angel's question—"Where are you going?"—for she was aimless though she was wandering on the desert road leading to her native land, Egypt.

The Angel of the Lord asked Hagar in verse 9 to go back to her mistress and submit again "under her hand." The imperative verb "submit" used in this request has the same Hebrew root *(ʿanah)* as the verb used in reference to Sarah's affliction of Hagar. The difference resides in the middle reflexive voice, yielding a meaning of "subjecting oneself voluntarily."[10] The angel was exhorting Hagar—as strange as it may seem—to go back and submit again to her mistress, apparently under the same conditions. Most likely, her return was still necessary since Ishmael was to be born in the house of Abraham, reared in the godly patriarchal family, and circumcised in Abraham's home (17:22–27) before being ultimately led to his divinely appointed land. In Jacob's terms, Hagar's "submission is not asked because God approves of [her] oppression; but it is necessary for his plans."[11]

However, Hagar's command to return to her mistress and submit to her was not devoid of divine compensation. Only fountains of spiritual blessings can empower a person to endure in the midst of adverse conditions. This has been the case for many of God's called people. It was after his vision of God's power and glory that Moses became compelled to return to Egypt and face Pharaoh (Exod. 3–4). Depressed Elijah was enabled to return and face Jezebel only after his vision of the Lord almighty on Mount Horeb (1 Kings 19). Similarly, Isaiah's vision of the exalted Lord in the temple was the starting point for his commission to a tough ministry (Isa. 6:1–13). In New Testament times, Paul's unique endurance in the midst of multiple adversities was energized by the glorious visions he received from the Lord of glory (2 Cor. 11–12).

Likewise, meeting the Lord face to face and hearing promises of blessings from him were surely enough to empower this young bondslave to accept her circumstances and subject herself voluntarily to her mistress. This may be the reason why after her encounter with the Lord and her subsequent return to her mistress, the narrator does not relate any flaw in Hagar's behavior. This maidservant ends up being expelled from Abraham's house, not for any wrong she has done herself (Gen. 21) but because of the natural tension over inheritance rights that would surface between Ishmael and Isaac. Having been the recipient of a special revelation from "the God who sees" everything and cares for everyone, it would become much easier for Hagar to accept her circumstances.[12]

God's Listening to Hagar (16:10–12)

A Numberless Offspring (v. 10)

After asking her to return to her mistress Sarah, the Angel of the Lord gave Hagar a message of comfort that would help her endure the hard circumstances of slavery.[13] He promised to multiply her seed exceedingly (v. 10). In so doing, God gave the slave woman a promise parallel to the promises given to the patriarchs (cf. 17:2; 22:17; 26:24) though it may be lacking "the covenant context."[14] Thus Hagar becomes the only woman in the Bible to whom God gives such a promise of multiplication of seed. If one is inclined to see an inclusion of the seed of Hagar in the promise given to Abraham concerning his numberless seed, then this promise given to her would be a development of one aspect of the Abrahamic covenant. If, on the contrary, there is no reference to the Ishmaelite line or to the Keturahite line (25:1–6) in the initial Abrahamic promises, then this promise would be an independent one. In both cases, Hagar stands by virtue of this promise as a recipient of divine blessings bestowed only on those who receive favor in the sight of the Lord.

A Blessed Name (v. 11)

Having decreed the numberless multitude of her descendants, the Angel of the Lord goes on, announcing to Hagar, "Behold you are pregnant and you will bear a son" (v. 11a). Hagar already knew she was pregnant (v. 4). Yet the newness of this declaration relates to the specifics of the child she was bearing. She will have a "son," and she will call him "Ishmael," meaning "God hears."[15] A rabbinical tradition says: "Four were named before they were born, viz., Isaac, Ishmael, Josiah and Solomon. Ishmael we see in our text. This applies to the righteous."[16] The reason the angel gives for this designation is that Yahweh has listened to Hagar and paid attention to her affliction. Luther thinks that Hagar and her descendants should have been proud of this beautiful name that neither Isaac nor Jacob received. In fact, it spoke of the Lord's sympathy toward them in their unfavored status.[17]

Interestingly enough, this is the first birth annunciation from heaven in the history of Israel. Raymond Brown draws a comparison between the various annunciations of birth in the Bible, seeing in them several common features. This comparison shows that the announcement of Ishmael's birth by the Angel of the Lord and the name God bestowed on him reflect divine grace that put Ishmael in the company of the saints.[18] Thus God offsets social classes by giving special divine favor to the lowly.

A God-Ordained Lifestyle (v. 12)

Subsequently, the Angel of the Lord gave Hagar three characteristics that would portray her son Ishmael. As pointed out earlier, these predictions have sometimes been mistakenly considered as negative factors in Ishmael's birth annunciation. However, each part of the prediction made by the Angel of the Lord was meant to comfort Hagar in a certain way. The best understanding of these traits of Ishmael must account for two facts: first, the syntactical structure of the composite prediction (v. 12a–c); second, the contribution of each individual prediction to the comfort theme of the revelation.

The Structure of the Prophecy

Syntactically, it is important to notice that the first two traits of Ishmael[19] are closely dependent on each other, with no conjunction separating them in the original Hebrew. Both of them are nominal clauses, the first functioning as an attributive predicate of the equative verb "will be," and the second likely acting as a relative clause without a relative pronoun (i.e., an asyndetic relative clause).[20] The second clause ("his hand against everyone and everyone's hand against him")[21] adds further explanation to the attributive predicate ("a wild donkey of a man"),[22] which functions as its antecedent.[23] Thus the first two predictions describe a set of life conditions of Ishmael. They are ontologically stemming out of each other, the second being a logical implication of the first. Meanwhile, the third prediction is dependent on the verb "will dwell," not on the equative "will be." Furthermore, it is separated from the first two by the conjunction "and" (Heb. *waw*). The disjunctive nuance of this *waw* is further supported by the insertion of an athnach at the end of the second statement in the Hebrew Masoretic Text. The athnach points to a major rest and a principal divider in prose.[24] Whether this *waw* is to be translated "and," "now," or "however," all of the above considerations seem to favor a break in the flow of interdependence of the traits with the introduction of an additional independent fact about Ishmael. By virtue of these considerations, the *waw* seems to link the third oracle on Ishmael to verse 11 rather than to the second prediction.[25] As such, the action verb "dwell" (Heb. *yishkon*) with its modifying clause (Heb. *al-penê kol akhayô;* literally translated, "in front of all his brethren") should be interpreted in light of the parallel use of the same verb in Genesis 25:18, where the prediction is stated as fulfilled.[26]

The Comfort Factor

In addition to syntactical structure, the comfort motif should also govern any correct interpretation of the Ishmael oracles (v. 12). This assertion is based on four considerations.

First, Hagar was exhorted by the Angel of the Lord in verse 8 to go back to Sarah and subject herself under her hand in light of the message of encouragement he was about to share with her. Negative statements concerning her son will not enable this slave mother to endure the unfortunate life conditions that transpired after Abraham's union with her. Therefore, the encouragement theme should not stop at verse 11. Rather, it governs verse 12 as well.

Second, the prediction of Ishmael's birth by itself hardly exhausts the comfort motif of the text. The consolation in the angel's message to Hagar does not come from the annunciation of the childbirth and naming only. Ishmael's name reflects God's care, but this will be insignificant to a mother if her son's life conditions reflect God's curse. The logical continuation of the comfort motif is supported by the conjunctive *waw*[27] linking verse 12 to verse 11. This conjunction makes verse 12 a logical implication of God's "hearing" of Hagar's affliction and may be working as an explicative *waw.*

Third, the hearing of God is not a passive one. The motif of affliction under slavery is paralleled, as pointed out earlier, in Israel's experience under the Egyptians described in the book of Exodus (chaps. 1–2). There, God heard the groaning of the sons of Israel under bondage (2:23–24). His hearing of their cries was an active one. Thus he immediately called Moses to reverse their situation and set them free (3:1–4:31). Likewise, God's hearing of Hagar's affliction is expected to be as active as his hearing of the groaning of the Israelites under bondage. This is why Yahweh's action to reverse Hagar's circumstances of slavery is only started at the prediction of the childbirth of Ishmael. This reversal of slavery-related circumstances is to be primarily embedded in the Ishmael oracles delineated in verse 12. Only then will Hagar be able to go back to the state of slavery and set of circumstances she has run away from,[28] awaiting the time appointed by God for the fulfillment of his promises to her.

Fourth, a final evidence of Hagar's finding positive elements in the predictions concerning her son is her exaltation of the Lord immediately following this prediction (v. 12) by giving him the name "El Roi "(v. 13). Her reaction supports the fact that the motif of comfort governed verse 12.[29] With the above syntactical and theological details in mind, the exegetical task becomes a little easier to undertake.

Reversing Hagar's Slavery (16:12a)

It goes without saying that the traits of a man in divine predictions, especially those made in Genesis, are reflected in his descendants. Thus the predicted traits of the sons of Noah (Gen. 9:25–27) were a forecast of their future makeup. Likewise the future profile of the twelve tribes of Israel was predicted by their father Jacob in Genesis 49. In a similar fashion, the traits of Ishmael as described in verse 12 apply to Ishmael's life and predict that of his descendants as well.

Ishmael is said to be *peré adām.* To start with, there is a wide agreement among commentators that this expression should be rendered, "a wild donkey of a man" or "a wild colt of a man."[30] This controversial prediction has often been misunderstood and has prompted many unwarranted conclusions concerning Ishmael. Many people think that "the second half of Hagar's 'blessing' did not portend well for her son: he would be a 'wild donkey of a man.'"[31] The Lord comforted Hagar in verse 11 by predicting the birth of her son Ishmael, yet in verse 12 he told her how obnoxious this son of hers will be. However, there is no need to look at this trait of Ishmael as negative. Otherwise justice would not be done to the comfort context of the message.

This verse does not portray Ishmael, as some put it, as "the father of a great tribe of *wild,* hostile people" [emphasis original].[32] While in the present-day culture referring to someone as a "wild donkey of a man" seems to be a negative attribute, in the context of this narrative it was not a bad statement at all. Animal imagery was used extensively in the nomadic culture of patriarchal times (see Gen. 49; Deut. 33). In fact, Jacob gave five of the tribes of Israel animal by-names (Gen. 49). Thus, Judah was called a lion's cub; Issachar, a sturdy donkey; Dan, a viper or hornet serpent; Gad, a rampant lion; Benjamin, a wolf. There is even a possibility according to the Hebrew scholar Speiser that Genesis 49:22 portrays Joseph as "a wild colt by a spring."[33]

Consequently, it is not strange to portray Ishmael as "a wild donkey of a man." In fact, the wild donkey was a valued and admired animal in the ancient Near East. Shehadeh summarizes the traits of a wild donkey as presented in the Bible:

> (1) Strong willed, choosing his own way, and getting what he desires (Job 39:8; Jer. 2:24; Hos. 8:9); (2) his habitat is the desert, and it is given to him by God; he escapes from none, but rather he is set free (Job 24:5; 39:6, 8; Jer. 2:24); (3) free moving and having a nomadic life style (Job 38:9:39:5; Jer. 2:24; (4) he scorns civilization (Job 39:7).[34]

Commenting on Job 39:5–8, Francis Andersen writes about the wild colt, saying:

> He has his own life, wide-ranging (8), and his place in the purposes of God is not to be explained by the service he renders to men (like his domesticated cousin) . . . the poem seems to express a certain envy of his freedom notwithstanding the hardship of rough terrain, *steppe* and *salt land* he lives in.[35]

The above-mentioned characteristics of the wild donkey match perfectly the description of the nomadic lifestyle of Ishmael and his descendants, which they would lead in the desert. Expressing a similar conclusion, Shimon Bar-Efrat correctly notes: "This *[peré adām]* is usually taken to mean 'a wild man', but the angel, whose object was to comfort and encourage Hagar, clearly meant something different, namely, that the son would be a free man, independent like the nomadic tribes of the desert, not a slave like his mother."[36]

Hagar is told to go and subject herself under the hand of her mistress as a slave, yet she is promised a son who will be free, independent, and not subject to anyone. He will never experience bondage, rather, "he will be among the families of mankind what the wild donkey is amongst animals."[37] This is "a fine image of the free untractable Bedouin character which is to be manifested in Ishmael's descendants,"[38] and of "individualistic lifestyle untrammeled by social convention."[39] Based on the use of the imagery of a wild donkey in nomadic culture, M. Seale argues persuasively that this expression is a by-name for a tribal head as bedouin poetry reveals it. He suggests that the prediction should be rendered "and he will be a tribal chief."[40] This interpretation fits very well in the context of comfort, and adds some explanation to the promise of multiplication of Hagar's seed (v. 10) by making Ishmael the "head of a multitude."[41] Thus Ishmael is predicted to be free as a nomad and prominent as a father of many (17:20).

Reversing Hagar's Powerlessness (16:12b)

Ishmael's second trait stems from the first prediction concerning him. He will have *yadô bekol weyad kol bô*. This phrase is generally translated, "his hand upon (or against)[42] everyone and everyone's hand upon him."[43] In order to understand it correctly, this expression should be closely tied to and dependent on the first oracle predicting Ishmael's bedouin lifestyle. As noted above, the syntactical structure of this verse with no connective particle between the first two clauses governed by the Hebrew verb "to be" implies that the second is a direct implication of the first. Therefore, since the first attributive predicate speaks of the free nomadic life in the desert, the meaning of the relative nominal clause that follows should be a qualifier of this nomadic life. Thus "his hand upon (or against) everyone and everyone's hand upon him" most likely predicts the incessant struggle characteristic of the bedouin life, and "the unceasing tension existing between the sedentary and nomadic populations in the Near East."[44] Constant roaming of the bedouin tribes in the desert, with no established legal system and clear civil law code, put them in a state of conflict with each other, and set others against them for fear of their raids, since nomads dislike the settled life (Job 39:7). This is what characterized the life of bedouin tribes in ancient history and more recent times as well.[45] By using the general term *everyone (kol)*, this prediction describes a general lifestyle of Ishmael and his descendants in the desert, and does not focus on hatred and conflict with any specific group of people. As Gispen put it, "Ishmael's love of freedom will bring him into mutual conflict in his dealings with all other men."[46] Since the expression "wild donkey of a man" predicted the freedom characteristic of Hagar's descendants, the idiomatic relative clause "his hand upon everyone and everyone's hand upon him" predicts their ability to fight for the sake of conserving that freedom. This has resulted in the survival of the Ishmaelites as a people by God's providence, alongside their kinfolk the Hebrews. Margoliouth comments on the survival of the Arabian line.

> We hear of no immigrations into Arabia, whereby successive settlers have ousted or submerged each other, as has been the case in most of the countries of which we have chronicles, such as India or Persia, Greece, Italy, or England. Invaders have rarely succeeded in penetrating the deserts which guard the country, and such success as they have had has been ephemeral. The peninsula has sent out conquering hordes, perhaps more than once on the scale which followed the rise of Islam; its own population, the inhabitants of its oases, have never been swamped or forced back by conquering immigrants. Ethnologically speaking its population has remained the same through the ages.[47]

Thus an enslaved and powerless Hagar, fleeing from the harsh subjection of her mistress, is so far given a promise of a son who will be free and strong, able to fight against all who desire to subdue him and to preserve his freedom as a nomad.

Reversing Hagar's Alienation (v. 12c)

An often misunderstood and controversial oracle on Ishmael is found in Genesis16:12c , which says that Hagar's son shall dwell *al-pené* all his brethren. There has been a debate over the meaning of the expression *al-pené.* The NASB translates the term, "he will live *to the east of* all his brothers"[48] while the KJV translates it, "and he shall dwell *in the presence of* all his brethren."[49] However, more recent translations of the Bible have seen a nuance of adversity in the prediction. Thus, a very popular translation, the NIV, renders the expression, "he will live *in hostility toward* all his brothers."[50] Meanwhile the NRSV translates the verse, "he shall live *at odds* with all his kin."[51]

However, Hebrew translators since the postexilic era did not see any hostility or enmity in the term *al-penê* used here. Consequently, Targum Pseudo-Jonathan renders the term in 16:12c "he shall dwell *alongside* all his kinsmen *and he shall be mixed (with them),*" and in 25:18 where the prediction is stated as fulfilled, "he dwelt *opposite* all his brothers *in his inheritance.*"[52] Similarly, Targum Onqelos translates 16:12c, "and *in the presence* of all his brethren he shall dwell," and 25:18, "he dwelt *in the presence* of all his kinsmen."[53] Not only did Hebrew translators of old fail to detect a sense of enmity and hostility in that expression, but also modern Hebrew translators did not reflect it either. A fairly recent Jewish translation renders 16:12c, "he shall dwell *alongside* all his kinsmen" (16:12); and 25:18, "they camped *alongside* all their kinsmen."[54]

The expression *al-penê* literally means "before the face of" or "in front of." Rendering it "at odds with," or "in hostility with" has to depend heavily on contextual considerations.[55] That the primary meaning of *al-penê* in 16:12c is the geographic one—granted the possibility of a collateral meaning of challenge—is supported by the following reasons.

First, the immediate fulfillment of this prediction is indicated in

25:18 and is decisive in determining whether the idea is hostility or geographic location.

Second, 25:12–18 lists the twelve sons of Ishmael, gives the death account of Ishmael, and tells about the respective desert dwelling places of the twelve sons of Ishmael. The parallel use of the Hebrew verb "dwell" *(yishkon)* in 25:18a denotes geographical locations extending from Havilah to Shur.[56] Therefore, the same verb used in 16:12 should be pointing to a geographical place rather than an attitude of hostility.

Third, the immediate context of the parallel fulfillment statement does not reflect any tension or hostility. The narrator ends the text of the generations of Ishmael with the following summary statement, "*al penê kol akhayô nafâl.*"[57] This statement summarizes the previous one, which speaks about the extended geographical distribution of the Ishmaelite tribes. Introducing the idea of hostility (cf. NIV) at this late stage of the generations' account is foreign to the immediate context.[58]

Fourth, the larger context of fulfillment of the prediction (25:18) is definitely not a hostile one. Ishmael is portrayed a few verses earlier in the same chapter as burying his father Abraham together with his brother Isaac (25:9). Furthermore, Isaac is said to have settled by the well of Lahai Rôî (25:11), which is the sacred memorial place of Hagar, as we will see in 16:13–14. Additionally, no conflict, whether direct or indirect, is mentioned between the sons of Ishmael and the sons of Israel, neither in the immediate context nor in the larger context of Genesis and the Pentateuch as a whole. The unfortunate tension which was an expected result of Abraham and Sarah's use of Hagar (16:1–14) was resolved by God in freeing the slave and her son and leading them to their inheritance appointed to them by the Lord (21:8–21). The Pentateuch does not reflect a continuation of the initial tension at all, implying that God's blessings upon Hagar and Ishmael played a healing role in the shaken relationship caused by rivalry in Abraham's household. There are only two references to Ishmaelites in Genesis after chapter 25. The first is with regard to the daughter of Ishmael,[59] whom Esau married in order to please his parents (28:9). The second is with regard to the selling of Joseph to the caravan of Ishmaelites that took him down to Egypt (37:25–30).[60] In both cases the narrator does not portray the Ishmaelites in a negative way. In the first, they were, in Isaac's and Rebecca's eyes, better in-laws than the Hittites; in the second, they acted as the means of carrying Joseph to the land of Egypt instead of being left to be killed by his brothers.[61]

Fifth, those who translate the term *al-penê* "in hostility with," "at odds with," or "in defiance of"[62] put the third prediction in logical dependence on the second oracle and thus come up with defiance as a primary interpretation.[63] However, the structural independence of the third prediction has been established earlier together with the connection of the third prediction to verse 11, rather than being a development of the second prediction.

Sixth, since the first two predictions about Hagar's son are attempts to reverse the life conditions of this slave mother and comfort her by foretelling the future makeup of her son, the third prediction should logically follow this line of reasoning. The first predicted his freedom, the second his power, and the third is a designation of Ishmael's God-appointed place of dwelling.

Thus the reversal of Hagar's slavery conditions becomes obvious throughout verse 12. In 12a, her son is portrayed as a wild donkey of a man, a prediction of a free nomadic lifestyle. This reverses Hagar's situation, who is pictured as a mere instrument in service of others.[64] Furthermore, the statement "his hand upon everyone and everyone's hand upon him" in 12b plays on the term translated "hand" as a metonymy for power. Powerless Hagar was delivered by her husband to the power of Sarah her mistress—"in your *hand*" (v. 6). In the wilderness the angel tells Hagar to go back and subject herself again to the power of Sarah—"under her *hand*" (v. 9). For Hagar to be fleeing from confrontation is a sign of powerlessness. Consequently, this powerless slave mother was promised a son who will have power to fight for his freedom. He will not be under the *hand* of anyone. Although many would like to subdue him ("everyone's hand upon him"), he will always be able to maintain his freedom ("his hand upon everyone"). Third, dwelling "before the face of" all his brethren (v. 12c) plays on the motif of "face," in the sense of presence. Sarah afflicted Hagar because her *presence* in Abraham's household was a continuous challenge to her privilege as the primary wife. She wanted to do something to get rid of the ensuing situation. She afflicted Hagar, and Hagar fled from her presence (literally, "from her face," v. 6). Later, Hagar confirmed, "from the *face* of Sarah, my mistress, I am fleeing" (from Sarah's presence, v. 8). Now Hagar is told that her son will be continually dwelling in the presence—"before the face of"—all his brethren.

Thus the geographical presence of the sons of Ishmael alongside the sons of Isaac is established by the Lord. This will be a reversal of the effects of Sarah's affliction of Hagar in the future because of God's hearing. Ishmael will always be there, dwelling in proximity of his brethren. After her so-called "wrong," Sarah may have wished she had never delivered her slave to Abraham. Yet, this proves to be an irreversible action. The elect line cannot get rid of Ishmael and his descendants. God has chosen to bless them, listen to their cries, prosper them, and maintain them in the neighborhood of their kin, the Israelites. Ishmael will be deprived of his share in Abraham's land inheritance. It will be kept for Isaac, in whom God's redemptive plan is to be accomplished. Still, Ishmael would have a land appointed to him by the Lord. Thus it is not strange that Hagar would marvel at this theophany and call the Lord who spoke to her El Roi (v. 13). A subject, powerless slave mother fleeing from the presence of her mistress without compensation feels compensated by the Lord promising her a son, free, powerful, and dwelling in a land designed for him by God in the presence of his kin (v. 12).

Theologically, the Ishmaelite line is designed by God as a reminder for Israel that the Abrahamic blessings have to be enjoyed by faith alone. Mere blood relationship is not enough; Ishmael is the firstborn of Abraham. Circumcision in the flesh is also not enough; Ishmael is circumcised (17:23–25). Only faith can make Isaac and his descendants as well as Ishmael and his descendants enjoy the blessings of Abraham since "in him" (12:3) and "in his Seed" (Gal. 3:16) all the nations of the earth would be blessed (Gen. 22:18).

On the other hand, may it be that this geographical proximity of the sons of Ishmael involves a theological blessing for them instead of an alleged unwarranted hostility? After all, they would be closer to the missionary community of the Old Testament. May it be that God has meant to keep the sons of Ishmael in the presence of the sons of Isaac so that they will be close to the unfolding of his redemptive plan? After all, God's purpose was to bless all people through Abraham, so why not his firstborn (17:18–20; 21:13)? May it be that Israel's outreach program will prompt a faithful remnant among the Ishmaelites to put their faith in the God of Israel and of their father Abraham, whose covenant they display in their circumcision in the flesh? Such things should be expected; otherwise the missionary heart of God and his purpose for electing Abraham would have been totally missed.

This study explores the evidence for positive answers to these questions throughout biblical history. Many slaves were around in the time of Hagar. Yet only she and her son were directly blessed by the Lord, though through unfortunate circumstances. It is true that Sarah's program for building a family was inconsistent with God's plan for the promised seed. However, only God can turn his children's shortcomings into a potential for more blessings. Otherwise, how would Hagar have become the subject of two theophanies and divine promises of blessings if this seemingly sad story had never happened? The same principle is true of the believer today who may become the recipient of much hardship in the process of becoming a channel of blessing to others.

THE GOD WHO SEES (16:13–16)

Marveling at this encounter with the man at the well, and comforted in the promises she heard, Hagar fully realized she was highly privileged to be in God's presence. Tsevat summarizes the progress of Hagar's awareness of God:

> During the encounter, the words of the man have become progressively more wonderful and impressive: he knows Hagar's name and station, he commands, he utters a birth annunciation; at the end she knows who he is. In terms of an

> actor-audience analysis of the narrative, in vss. 7–12 the reader knew more than the protagonist, since the speaker was identified for him as a "messenger of the LORD" and was not identified for her; in vs. 13 both have achieved a similar measure of awareness. As for the reader, the narrator drops the "messenger" and says simply "(the name of) the LORD (Who talked to her);" as for her, she calls him "God." At this moment, he vanishes. As man comes to realize the presence of God, as he recognizes Him, God has disappeared.[65]

Thus she calls the name of the Lord who spoke to her, "you are a God of seeing" (v. 13). It is not quite clear whether "Roi" is to be taken as a subjective genitive, "a God *who sees*," or as an objective genitive, "a God *who may be seen.*" This ambiguity leaves room for both possibilities without theological problems.[66] At any rate Hagar, the slave woman, stands out as the only person in the Bible to confer a name on deity. It is quite normal that people "give names to family members, to animals, to sacred sites, but never to one's God, with the exception of Hagar."[67] It is not that God was nameless, but for Hagar he became a personal God. It is as if she were saying, "the one who came to my aid in my distress," he is the "God who sees me."[68] The reason she gives for her naming of the Lord by this name can be found in the rest of verse 13.[69] Whether Hagar here was wondering how she survived after seeing God, or how she met the One Who looked after her,[70] or was delighted for seeing the back, that is, the glory of the God who sees her,[71] she surely must have felt privileged, exalted, and comforted by the glorious presence of the Lord in her life. Thus she called the well "the well of the Living One Who sees me" (v. 14), which the narrator locates between Kadesh and Bered.[72]

This was a definite turning point in the life of Hagar. Verse 15 assumes that she went back to Abraham's house. Her son had to be born not in the wilderness, nor in Egypt, but in the house of Abraham his father, where he had to be brought up until the appointed time. Hagar surely shared with the patriarch and the matriarch the details of her encounter with the Lord. Having heard from Hagar how the Lord promised to multiply her seed, Sarah and Abraham may have felt that Ishmael was after all the promised seed. Thus Abraham, at the age of eighty-six years, ended up appropriating the child that Hagar bore to him by naming him "Ishmael" (vv. 15b–16).

Still, the promises given to Hagar are pregnant with possibilities and full with expectations. Ishmael eventually has to be led by God to his designated dwelling place, the desert. The fulfillment of God's promises to Hagar will not come the easy way. Another trauma and yet another theophany and set of promises await the "son of the flesh" and his mother to establish the fact that "God hears" the cry of the afflicted wherever he is (21:8–21). In the meantime, Ishmael has to live his childhood with his father Abraham, learn about the Lord further in that godly home, and eventually be circumcised before being led to the Arabian Desert dwelling.

3

THE PURSUIT OF DESTINY (GEN. 17; 21:1–21)

THE HAGAR/ISHMAEL NARRATIVE IN the foundational chapter of Genesis 16 sets the stage for the unfolding of God's oracles concerning Ishmael in biblical history. However, with Abraham's firstborn still at his house, the situation remains full of expectations in light of God's alternative plan for the son of the promise. This chapter looks at Ishmael in Genesis 17, and deals in particular with the circumstances of the exit of Hagar and her son to the wilderness described in Genesis 21.

ISHMAEL UNDER THE ABRAHAMIC COVENANT

A careful exegesis of Genesis 16 in its historical, literary, and theological contexts showed how Ishmael and his mother were the objects of God's special care, despite the unfortunate circumstances that accompanied the revelation of his purposes for the "son of the flesh" in history. The Lord promised Hagar a son who would be free as a nomad, who would be powerful enough to maintain his freedom through continuous struggle for survival, and who would dwell in the neighboring Arabian Desert with its entire animal and mineral riches. He would always live near his kinfolk with all that that implies in terms of blessing and challenge (16:12). Since the implementation of these promises cannot take place with Ishmael being in Abraham's home, the narrative leaves the door wide open before the development of particular circumstances that would accompany their fulfillment. This expectation becomes evident in view of God's alternative plan for "the son of promise" revealed in 17:15–22.

Isaac, Not Ishmael

After renewing his covenant with Abraham (17:1–9), and promising to make him the father of many nations (17:4–5), the Lord proceeded to give the patriarch a material sign for the covenant he established with him: the circumcision in the flesh of all males in Abraham's household (17:10–14). Every male born in the patriarch's house, as well as all who were bought with money, were to be circumcised. Further, God revealed his plan to Abraham concerning the promised seed: Sarah was to bear him a son supernaturally (17:15–16), one who would carry on God's covenantal promises in history (17:19, 21). This contrary-to-nature prospective birth prompted the patriarch to fall on his face and laugh (17:17). From this point forward the narrator employs the motif of laughter in the patriarchal narrative.[1]

Both Ishmael and Isaac

Abraham's first reaction to God's revelation after his laughter was a prayer for Ishmael his firstborn: "O that Ishmael might live before you" (17:18). The patriarch had likely believed for thirteen years that Ishmael was the promised son. This conviction might have been reinforced by Hagar's narration of the extraordinary encounter with the Angel of the Lord and the revelations she heard from him concerning Ishmael. God's reply to Abraham in verse 19 supports this conclusion as well. It is unfortunate that many English translations of the Bible miss God's favorable response (v. 19) to Abraham's request concerning Ishmael. They translate the Hebrew term *ebâl,* "no"[2] ("No, but Sarah your wife shall bear you a son . . ."), and are thus inconsistent with the more positive nuance the same term is given all throughout the Hebrew Bible and in the Septuagint. Interestingly, the NIV translation is more congruent this time with the text and with the next verse (17:20), where Ishmael receives from God great blessings and promises. It renders the Hebrew term *ebâl*, "yes." "Nevertheless" (NAV) is an acceptable translation that conveys the idea of God's heeding of Abraham's prayer for Ishmael and providing room for the alternative plan concerning Sarah's son.[3]

Though God was getting ready to pronounce blessings on Ishmael (17:20), the son of supernatural conception was the one meant to perpetuate his redemptive dealings in history. Divine intervention, not human arrangement, would sustain redemption. Isaac was not the only seed of Abraham; Ishmael was, too (21:13). However, Isaac was the only son of Sarah. In that sense, he was the seed of the barren woman, or simply speaking, the "seed of the woman" foreshadowing the coming "Seed of the woman" (3:15). Thus Isaac's birth set the pattern that would be ultimately fulfilled in the virgin birth of Christ (Matt. 1:16–25).

However, while confirming his covenantal plan for Isaac, God assured Abraham that Ishmael would not be neglected in the process. The patriarch's prayer concerning Ishmael was that he might "live before God," that is, under God's blessing and care. God heard this prayer and promised to bless Ishmael, make him fruitful, and multiply him exceedingly, with twelve princes being the fruit of his loins (Gen. 17:20). Sailhamer makes an interesting comment on this divine promise:

> In this final speech, . . . the author is careful to show that although Ishmael has been excluded from the covenant with Abraham, he and his descendants were still to live under the blessing of God (v. 20). In fact, in God's blessing of Ishmael (v. 20), he reiterated both his original blessing of all humankind in 1:28 ("I will surely bless him; I will make him fruitful and will greatly increase his numbers," 17:20) and his blessing to Abraham in 12:2 ("I will make him into a great nation," 17:20b).[4]

Thus 17:20 establishes the fact that the election of Isaac to administrate God's kingdom purposes in history did not automatically alienate Ishmael from God's spiritual and material care.[5] For in view of the corporate terminology used by God in verse 13 with reference to the sign of the covenant ("And my covenant will be in your [pl.] flesh, an everlasting covenant"),[6] the exclusion of Ishmael from that covenant has to be qualified. The command of circumcision given to Abraham (17:10–14), which was carried out in verses 23–27, included Ishmael as part of the patriarch's household. Consequently, Abraham circumcised himself at the age of ninety-nine, his firstborn Ishmael at the age of thirteen, as well as the rest of his household (17:23–27). Kidner's remarks highlight the universal blessings of the Abrahamic covenant:

> Verses 26, 27 bring out the main emphasis of the paragraph, which is on the diversity of men, in age, status and spiritual experience, who were gathered into the one covenant. For Abraham it sealed an old transaction (Rom. 4:9–12); for others it was a sudden introduction (*that very day,* 26, RSV) into a bond with God and each other, whose implications must now be grasped and lived out. In the sense that Pentecost was the birthday of the church, this was the birthday of the church of the Old Testament.[7]

It is true that Ishmael cannot be the seed in whom the gracious implementations of God's covenant will take place. However, his obedience to circumcision put him under the spiritual blessings promised to Abraham. "He too is to walk as one of Yahweh's children."[8] The sign of the covenant in Ishmael's flesh makes him a primary example of the many people who were blessed through Abraham (12:4–5; 17:23–27).

Arabs Under the Covenant Sign

Other Semitic peoples and Canaanites practiced circumcision for different reasons, mostly related to fertility cults.[9] However, for those related to Abraham, circumcision was a practice initially linked to the Abrahamic covenant. Interestingly, this rite was maintained as a custom among the descendants of Ishmael in north Arabia, as much as it continued to be observed among Jews in later history. Josephus and Origen noted that the age of circumcision among the Arabs of old was thirteen years.[10] However, this age varied significantly among different Arab groups in the peninsula.

Circumcision is still practiced today among Muslims in general and Arab Muslims in particular. However, this rite is not mandated or even explicitly mentioned in the Qurʾan. Muslim tradition *(Hadîth)* establishes it based on earlier customs among Arabians that go back to Abraham.[11] Thus, no matter what different generations throughout history thought of the practice, the sign of God's covenant with Abraham was perpetuated among the patriarch's Arabian line.

As part of the blessings of being related to Abraham, God gave Ishmael beautiful promises in 17:20. These promises, together with those given earlier to Hagar (16:11–12), make the narrative once again pregnant with anticipations of fulfillment. This is especially true in light of the terms of the covenant developed earlier (12:1–3, 7; 13:15–17; 15:12–21), in which God restricted its perpetuation to Isaac to the exclusion of Ishmael (17:18, 21). Earlier in the narrative, God comforted the slave woman by making her the subject of special divine attention (16:7–14). Feeling spiritually compensated, Hagar more readily accepted her life circumstances after returning to Abraham's home. Would Ishmael be, in his turn, the recipient of similar compensation from the Lord? Would God extend to him a special favor in light of his inevitable deprivation from Abraham's inheritance implied by God's election of Isaac? Genesis 21 answers this question.

Ishmael's Desert Exit (21:1–21)

God fulfilled his promise to Abraham and Sarah and provided the barren woman with a son contrary to all natural expectations (Gen. 21:1–5). His unexpected ways of redemption generated joy and laughter (Ps. 126:1–2; Isa. 54:1–2). Thus Sarah and all who heard of her exaltation by the Lord rejoiced, laughing (Gen. 21:6–7). The circumstances that led to Ishmael's birth (16:1) were removed, and Sarah's dignity as a fruitful woman was restored. However, the results of the initial proposal to Abraham to secure Hagar as a surrogate wife weighed more heavily on Sarah. When she was accepting the fact of her barrenness, Sarah secured a child by appropriating Hagar's son as her own, having said, "Perhaps I shall be built from her" (16:2). Now that Isaac is born, Ishmael is no longer considered as her son. Rather, she sees him as "the son of this slave woman" (21:10).

Ishmael's presence in Sarah's home created a natural rivalry over home and inheritance privileges. It threatened the role of the matriarch's son, Isaac, whom God called to become the recipient of the covenant he established with Abraham, and by this token, the heir of Abraham's estate.[12] Was there a way for Sarah and her son to remove themselves from this situation created by Sarah's initial suggestion? Could Hagar and her son be set free to see the promises of God for them fulfilled? Yes, but not without human tragedy.

A Memorable Ceremony (Gen. 21:8–13)

The weaning of Isaac eventually became the situation used by God to remove the rivalry from Abraham's house and free both of his sons to pursue their respective destinies. Breast-feeding lasted an average of three years in Israel (2 Macc. 7:27), as well as in Egypt and Assyria, at the end of which a major celebration was observed.[13]

Ishmael's Unfortunate Laughter

During the weaning celebration that centered on Isaac, "Sarah saw the son of Hagar the Egyptian whom she had born to Abraham *joking*" (Heb. *metsakhêq*, v. 9).[14] It is important to note that the narrator presents the facts from Sarah's perspective. Not only did Sarah see Ishmael as "the son of Hagar the Egyptian," but she also saw him as the son that the slave woman had "borne *to Abraham*." Thus Sarah distanced herself emotionally and socially from Hagar and her son.

This was the inevitable outcome of the rivalry that had originated much earlier between the two women (16:4). Somehow, the birth of Isaac rekindled the conflict that was quieted for a while by the intervention of God on Hagar's behalf in the wilderness (16:7–14).

The initial conflict between the two women started when Hagar "*saw* that she was pregnant" (16:4), and the link to the final conflict was also highlighted by the fact that "Sarah *saw* Ishmael joking" (21:9). The object of seeing in both cases was not necessarily a provocation, yet it became significant enough for each of these women to initiate a conflict. While the first conflict started with Hagar's seeing of her privileged condition, which resulted in her competition with Sarah over Abraham's favor, the final conflict started with Sarah's seeing of the future competition between Ishmael and Isaac over Abraham's inheritance. The first seeing established the rivalry, and the second would remove it, but not without much pain accompanied by gracious intervention from the "God who hears."

What Sarah saw Ishmael doing has become a matter of great speculation. Targum Pseudo-Jonathan[15] and Targum Neofiti[16] portray Ishmael as practicing idolatry. Yet, these traditions do not attribute to Ishmael a direct conflict with Isaac at this point. However, rabbinic literature covered the whole spectrum of possible interpretations in trying to determine the nature of Ishmael's action.

> And Sarah saw the son of Hagar the Egyptian, etc. (xxi, 9). R. Simeon b. Yohai said: R. Akiba used to interpret this to his [Ishmael's] shame. Thus R. Akiba lectured: And Sarah saw the son of Hagar the Egyptian, whom she had borne unto Abraham, making sport. Now making sport refers to nought else but immorality, as in the verse, *The Hebrew servant, whom thou hast brought unto us, came in unto me to* make sport *of me* (Gen. xxxix, 17). Thus this teaches that Sarah saw Ishmael ravish maidens, seduce married women and dishonour them. R. Ishmael taught: This term Sport refers to idolatry, as in the verse, *And rose up to* make sport (Ex. xxxii, 6). This teaches that Sarah saw Ishmael build altars, catch locusts, and sacri-

> fice them. R. Eleazar said: The term sport refers to bloodshed, as in the verse, *Let the young men, I pray thee, arise and* sport *before us* (ii Sam. ii, 14). R. ʿAzariah said in R. Levi's name: Ishmael said to Isaac, 'Let us go and see our portions in the field'; then Ishmael would take a bow and arrows and shoot them in Isaac's direction, whilst pretending to be playing. Thus it is written, *As a madman who casteth fire-brands, arrows, and death; so is the man that deceiveth his neighbour, and saith: Am not I in sport* (Prov. xxii, 18f.)?[17]

Such views attempt to match Ishmael's action with the magnitude of Sarah's demand. In view of the rabbinical tendency to picture Ishmael in a negative manner,[18] and based on the grammatical considerations developed later in this chapter, these interpretations seem to reflect unwarranted conclusions since "elsewhere Ishmael appears in a quite positive light."[19]

On the other hand, a host of scholars consider the scene to be a neutral one. Thus Skinner sees that what "excites Sarah's maternal jealousy and prompts her cruel demands," is "the spectacle of the two young children playing together, innocent of social distinctions."[20] Sarna agrees that Ishmael was either "amusing himself" or "playing with Isaac."[21] Highlighting the fact that the narrator emphasizes "Ishmael's inferior rank" in the eyes of Sarah,[22] von Rad argues, "What Ishmael did need not be anything evil at all. The picture of the two boys playing with each other on an equal footing is quite sufficient to bring the jealous mother to a firm conclusion: Ishmael must go."[23] Speiser believes "traditional 'mocking' would require the preposition *b-* to designate the object."[24] Thus he concludes, "his playing with Isaac, need mean no more than that the older boy was trying to amuse his little brother. There is nothing in the text to suggest that he was abusing him," something that would be deduced by "troubled readers" trying to "account for Sarah's anger."[25] Westermann, based on the grammatical observation noted earlier by Speiser concerning the use of *metsakhêq*, settles with the meaning of innocent "playing," since "it is a peaceful scene that meets Sarah's gaze."[26] F. Lenormant translates the verse, "And Sarah saw the son of Hagar the Egyptian, which she had born to Abraham, laughing,"[27] taking the action of Ishmael as a simple laughter.

Between both ends of the pendulum, Wenham,[28] Hamilton,[29] and Coats[30] present a middle ground position. Wenham rejects the rabbinical interpretations.[31] However, he thinks that the understanding of a peaceful scene of children's innocent playing, advocated by Skinner, Speiser, von Rad, Sarna, and Westermann "puts Sarah in a dreadful light and, indeed, reflects badly on the Lord and Abraham for acceding to her demand, if this is the context."[32] Thus "something like 'mock,' 'jest,' 'make fun of' would seem" to him "an apt English translation."[33] Hamilton is inclined to take the action as referring to "fondling" or "horsing around,"[34] and Coats settles with "mocking," saying,

> The threat of Ishmael throughout the narrative is that he would replace Sarah's son . . . as the heir of Abraham. Now the wordplay so crucial for the whole story sets out the weight of the conflict. It does not imply that Ishmael has done something amiss with Isaac. It suggests on the contrary, that Sarah saw Ishmael *mĕṣaḥeq*, playing the role of Isaac.[35]

This middle ground is supported by one Jewish tradition that sees the term as referring to mockery with reference to the inheritance. "For when our father Isaac was born all rejoiced, whereupon Ishmael said to them, 'You are fools, for I am the firstborn and I receive double portion.' You may infer this from Sarah's protest to Abraham."[36]

To conclude this survey of views on the nature of Ishmael's action, we need to highlight several facts that help us in making a fair judgment.

First, earlier Jewish traditions seem to support the neutrality of Ishmael's action. Thus the Greek text of the Septuagint (third century B.C.) indicates that Sarah saw Ishmael "playing" (Gr. *paizonta*), adding to the Hebrew text, "with Isaac her son."[37] Furthermore, the second-century B.C. book of Jubilees maintains that "Sarah saw Ishmael playing and dancing and Abraham rejoicing very greatly. And she was jealous of Ishmael and she said to Abraham, 'Drive out . . .'"[38]

Second, as pointed out earlier, the use of the participle *metsakhêq* without the addition of a preposition implies neutral laughter or playing.[39] The only other place where this participle is used in an absolute form is in reference to Lot's preaching to his sons-in-law, when he appeared to them as "joking," saying funny things (Gen. 19:14).

Third, even if the interpreter settles with the sense of mocking for the sake of defending Sarah's tough response, Ishmael's action by itself still falls short of justifying her demand. The harsh dismissal of Hagar and her son outweighs by far the magnitude of the action. In fact, Hagar did not do anything at that point to deserve the treatment she was about to get, and Ishmael's playing, joking, or even mocking is hardly enough reason to be banished from the house of his father.

Fourth, Sarah's demand is prompted by a future fact, rather than by a present act. Ishmael is much older than Isaac, she may have thought, and having been the object of fourteen years[40] of paternal love and affection without a rival, he would inevitably grow stronger and later divide the inheritance with her son Isaac.[41] Seeing far ahead, Sarah decided not to allow that to happen in view of God's covenantal promises made solely available to Isaac, and possibly to settle an old account with "this slave woman" (21:10).

Fifth, God's sanctioning of Sarah's demand does not necessarily reflect badly on Ishmael's action. The sons of Keturah, Abraham's third wife, were dismissed later from their father's house without any conflict with Isaac (25:6). In fact, they were born to Abraham after Sarah died. This establishes the case that God's plan for Isaac cannot be fully implemented with the presence of other children in the house of Abraham besides him. In that sense, even if Ishmael would have done nothing wrong, he would still have been somehow dismissed to the desert. The reason is that the patriarch's estate, by virtue of its close link to the Abrahamic covenant, was to be appropriated solely by the elect seed of Abraham—Isaac (17:21). Moreover, God's historical purposes for Ishmael (16:12; 17:20) cannot be implemented in Abraham's house.

Sixth, God's bypassing of the methods used by the matriarchs to preserve the patriarchal blessing for the elect seed does not imply that these means were blameless. In fact, Rebecca used lying and deception with her husband Isaac in trying to secure the Abrahamic blessing to the chosen line of Jacob (25:23). The narrator does not directly show God's displeasure with her ways (chap. 27). This implies that the focus of the narrative was to show how the covenantal blessings flowed to the elect administrator of God's kingdom, rather than to sanction any doubtful means used by his human agents to secure that end.

Finally, the narrator's vivid description of Abraham's rage over Sarah's demand seems to minimize the seriousness of Ishmael's action. The fact that the angel of God listened to the voice of dying Ishmael in the wilderness (21:17) is another deliberate allusion from the narrator to an earlier parallel situation, where God listened to Hagar's unfair affliction under Sarah's hand and intervened to comfort her (16:10–12).

The above considerations favor the fact that the action that prompted Sarah to send away Ishmael was not moral failure. "Sarah saw Ishmael joking"[42] seems to the writer to be an acceptable English translation. Ishmael's action may have been geared toward drawing social attention to him as the firstborn of Abraham in a celebration that highlighted the newly weaned child, Isaac. This sparked the insight of Sarah into the future competition. The New Testament reference to Ishmael's "persecution" of Isaac in Galatians 4:29 should not affect this understanding of the term as will be shown in the brief discussion of Galatians 4:21–31 in the following chapter.

Sarah's Controversial Request

The high death rate among children in their early years of life made the survival of any child a matter of major concern. This is why Isaac's weaning was a time of joyful celebration. When the child reached the weaning period, he was considered to have overcome a major hurdle, and the future became surer for him.[43] This is likely why Sarah, at that specific time, considered Isaac's future more seriously. On the other hand, the matriarch regarded Ishmael as the "son," not of *her* maidservant, but rather "of *this* (as disowned) slave woman," and as the one whom Hagar "had born to Abraham," not to her. Thus she distanced herself from both, the maidservant and her child. With this mind-set, upon seeing Ishmael "joking" and having fun on equal ground with Isaac, Sarah's foresight prompted her to make a bold demand.[44] "Cast out *this slave woman* and *her son,* for *the son of this slave woman* shall not inherit with *my son,* with *Isaac*" (21:10).

Commentators describe the matriarch's language here as a contemptuous speech,[45] a "harsh demand,"[46] suggesting a "mean belittling of Hagar and Ishmael."[47] For Sarah deliberately avoided using their proper names. She called them "this slave woman" (twice) and "her son," contrasting them to "my son, Isaac."[48] The similarity between Sarah's demand and Pharaoh's, later, is highlighted by the use of the verb "cast out" (Heb. *grš*).[49] Trible notes that Pharaoh in Exodus, being threatened with the death of his firstborn, "cast out *[grš]* the Hebrew slaves from Egypt."[50] Here Sarah "wants the slave cast out *[grš]* to protect the life of her firstborn son."[51]

Thus Sarah's request, no matter how bold it was, aimed at safeguarding Isaac by preventing Ishmael from partaking in his father's estate. This raises a legal question. Did Ishmael have any legal right to the inheritance, even after Isaac was born? Sarna's comments are helpful.

> Sarah's formulation of her demand and the extreme length to which she was prepared to go point to an affirmative answer. The laws of Hammurabi (par. 170f.) and the still earlier Lipit-Ishtar (par. 25) implicitly make *inheritance rights a consequence of the father's acceptance of the infant as his legitimate son.* There is no doubt that Ishmael was entitled to a share of Abraham's estate. The key to Sarah's demand lies in a clause in the laws of Lipit-Ishtar where it is stipulated that the father *may grant freedom to the slave woman and the children* she has borne to him, in which case *they forfeit their share of the paternal property* (cf. Judg. 11:1–3). Sarah is asking Abraham to exercise that legal right (cf. 25:6).[52]

Thus, contemporary legal codes make Sarah's "harsh demand" understandable in that archaic society, for the future of a woman was intimately linked to the future welfare of her son.[53] As long as the presence of Ishmael threatens her son's future and her own as well, Sarah feels compelled to act quickly,[54] even though Ishmael's legal position as a son of Abraham is very clear. In fact, Abraham clearly "recognized Ishmael as his legitimate son" (16:15; 17:23, 25; 21:11; 25:9, 12).[55] Yet, since he is no more claimed as the son of Sarah, his privileges are diminished in the house. From the matriarch's perspective, now that Isaac is here, Ishmael must depart.

However, Abraham's first reaction to Sarah's demand was great displeasure (21:11). This short description of his dismay leaves the door open to the reader's imagination. Most likely, the patriarch had quite an argument with Sarah over this question. Abraham was mostly upset "for his son's sake." God's words to Abraham later reveal that he was also concerned "for his slave woman" (21:12). For Sarah, Ishmael was "the son of this slave woman." For Abraham, Ishmael was "his son." This little phrase, deliberately inserted by the narrator, reveals some of Abraham's strong attachment to Ishmael as a father.[56]

From God's perspective, his plan for Isaac is incompatible with his purposes for Ishmael. No matter how severe Sarah's demand was, and no matter how serious Abraham's concern for his firstborn, God saw it better for Hagar and her son Ishmael to be dismissed to the wilderness and live under his care than to be kept in Abraham's house and live in rivalry with Sarah and her son Isaac. The patriarch had a limited inheritance, and it was ordained to go to the promised seed (12:7; 13:15; 17:10–14). However, God has plenty for every one of his children (17:20). This is the primary reason for his summoning Abraham to listen to Sarah's voice, and not because of any cursing of Ishmael, as it may occur to the casual reader. Thus, in order to "remove any suggestion of moral taint," God justified his request on two grounds related to the different plans he had for Abraham's two sons.[57] First, Abraham's elect line is to be perpetuated exclusively through Isaac (21:12c).[58] Second, Hagar and her son will be cared for by God in the wilderness and "a great future awaits Ishmael"[59] according to God's purposes for him (16:12; 17:20; 21:13).

Ishmael Desert-Bound (21:14–21)

"Early in the morning Abraham took bread and a skin of water and gave them to Hagar putting them on her shoulder and the child and sent her away" (21:14). This last sentence does not mean that Abraham put Ishmael on Hagar's shoulder, too,[60] for the boy was a teenager by then.[61] The concern of Abraham was not only indicated by the reference to his provision and his early rise, so as to avoid the heat of the day, but also by the fact that "he dismissed her"(Heb. *shlkh*), which is a verb less strong than Sarah's demand of casting her out *(grš)*.[62] This difference of nuance may also imply a dismissal with blessing.[63]

Having left Abraham's house with her son Ishmael, Hagar wandered in the wilderness of Beersheba.[64] Possibly, the tears in her eyes and the sad circumstances of her departure contributed to her loss of direction. To make things worse, she ran out of water (21:15a), and ended up casting her son under a tree (21:15b). Her action proves that she was exhausted. Since Ishmael is at death's door, casting him under a tree would at least allow her son to "die in the shade."[65] Trible's notes on this deplorable situation are to the point.

> No divine messenger finds her by a spring of water. In fact, unlike the region of Shur, the territory of Beersheba provides no water at all. Furthermore, it does not border Egypt. Receiving Hagar in forced exile rather than voluntary flight, this wilderness is an arid and alien place. It supplies only a deathbed for the child."[66]

No one can read this sad story without being moved and filled with compassion for this homeless single mother and her dying son. Hagar withdrew herself from the scene of agony, uttering a sad prayer request, "Let me not see the death of the child" (21:16b).[67] She sat "far enough away to be able to let her tears run freely."[68] Naturally speaking, there was no more hope for Abraham's firstborn, and a fading one for his slave-wife. Ironically, this maidservant was set free against her will, only to face death in the wilderness of Beersheba. She left her slavery within the circle of blessing to become sovereign in a land of thorns and thistles. Nothing else can rescue Hagar and her son other than a display of God's redemptive work. Only a divine irruption in time can change the course of things.

Having promised repeatedly to make Ishmael a great nation (16:10–11; 17:20; 21:13), God could not have led Hagar and her son out of Abraham's house only to let them perish in the wilderness. However, since the shadow of death allows salvation's light to shine brighter, God heard from heaven the agonizing voice of the dying child (21:17a). When Hagar was not able to bear the cries of her son, God heard him "where he [was]" (21:17c). This indicates that Ishmael was not forsaken or forgotten by God. In fact, his name indicates the contrary. Thus God called to Hagar from heaven, and exhorted her to lift her son up with a strong hand, and reassured her of the great future that awaited the lad (21:18). This is the only time since the Hagar/Ishmael narrative started where Hagar is referred to by her name without any qualification. The last time the Lord spoke to her (16:7–8), he called her name but immediately reminded her of her status as Sarah's slave, and encouraged her to go back to her mistress. Ishmael had to be born and reared in Abraham's house. However, in the present scene, God addresses the former slave purely by her name, "Hagar," with no more qualification. Finally, she is sovereign, but not without much suffering.

The Lord opened the eyes of the freed slave to see the well of water (21:19a). Fortunately, Hagar's wilderness once again is coupled with a well of water that illustrates the divine grace extended to the lost. In chapter 16, the well was the place of her meeting with the Lord (16:7). Here she did not see his provision. Possibly the gloominess of the situation and the tears that filled her eyes prevented the freed slave from seeing the well even though it was always there. Despair stops the bereaved from seeing God's blessing.[69] Thus, with divine intervention and assurance, Hagar hurried and filled the skin of water and gave her child a drink (21:19b).

For some reason, Ishmael's name is not mentioned explicitly in this narrative. Nevertheless, the motif of God's hearing is still present.[70]

God's intervention on behalf of Ishmael did not stop at just providing water for his survival. For the narrator deliberately notes the presence of God with Ishmael to prosper his life. "And God was *with* the lad, so he grew up, and dwelt in the desert, and became a bow hunter" (21:20). Thus "'from heaven' gives way to *with,* and a celestial theophany is replaced by the imminent, divine presence."[71] A rabbinical tradition comments on "with him," saying that this "means with him, his ass-drivers, and his camel-drivers and his household."[72] So Ishmael settled in the wilderness of Paran, and his mother took him a wife from the country of Egypt. Habakkuk highlighted the fact that "God came from Teman and the Holy one from the mount of Paran" (Hab. 3:3). It seems that God compensated those who were forced to depart from the circle of blessing in Abraham's home by making them the object of a special spiritual care because they are also Abraham's seed. If this is the case, it would be another evidence of God's implementation of his promises to bless Ishmael (Gen. 17:20), by making his presence counterbalance Ishmael's deprivation from inheritance.

While the focus of the Angel of the Lord in chapter 16 was on Hagar to comfort her, and the promise of multiplication was concerned with her seed, in chapter 21 the Angel of God focused on the deprived son of Abraham, and the promise of multiplication was concerned with him. The narrator deliberately highlighted Ishmael in the last section of the story. Thus God promised Abraham, "the son of the slave, I will *make him a nation* also because *he is* your seed" (21:13). Also, when Hagar cast her son under a tree and lifted her voice and cried, instead of hearing her voice, 21:17 says "and God heard *the voice of the lad,* and the angel of God called Hagar . . . *I heard the voice of the lad* where *he is.*" Again, God encouraged Hagar to lift Ishmael and grab him tightly by hand "since *I will make him* a great nation." Soon after her filling the skin of water, Hagar "gave *the child* to drink" (v. 19). Then "God *was with the lad* so he grew up" (v. 20). This emphasis on Ishmael established the fact that, while chapter 16 emphasized the two women, chapter 21 focused on the two sons. The welfare of the two women is portrayed as genuinely depending on that of their sons. The first section portrayed Sarah's concern for Isaac's welfare (21:1–12). The second revealed Hagar's concern for Ishmael and God's faithfulness in protecting him and providing for him (21:13–21).

While Hagar became the object of a theophany in chapter 16, and hence felt spiritually compensated, Ishmael became the focus of the "theophany" from heaven in chapter 21. Thus God compensated Ishmael, when he was deprived of Abraham's inheritance, by blessing him with his presence and his material provision. Sarah felt vindicated and Hagar ended up exalted, too. The rivalry was removed from Abraham's house, and the tension was cured by divine intervention. Only a God "who hears" can remedy human failures, and create blessings out of misery.

4

THE JEWISH ISHMAEL (GAL. 4:21–31)

PAUL'S TYPOLOGICAL USE OF ISHMAEL

It is almost impossible to look at Genesis 21:8–21 without automatically thinking of its New Testament counterpart in Paul's epistle to the Galatians. Though Genesis does not necessarily convey a negative picture of Ishmael, Galatians 4:29 seems to portray him in a negative way. It presents him as "the one born according to the flesh"[1] who persecuted "the one [born] according to the Spirit." This controversial verse and its immediate context have shaped the view of many people concerning Ishmael. A casual reading of Galatians 4:21–31 gives a gloomy impression of Isaac's stepbrother. However, in that passage, Paul clearly alludes to the incident that accompanied Ishmael's dismissal from Abraham's house. It was shown that the description of Ishmael as *metsakhêq* meant primarily something like "playing," "laughing," or "joking." Even if someone admits that it may mean "mocking," none of these meanings has the sense of persecuting. How then can the interpreter account for Paul's portrayal of Ishmael as a persecutor of Isaac? In the following discussion, we will first reflect briefly on the epistle as a whole. Afterward, we will discuss the role of Galatians 4:21–31 in the argument of the epistle and explore proposed solutions to the problem of Galatians 4:29.

Galatians: The Epistle of Liberty in Christ

The Galatian believers, won to Christ by Paul (1:8; 4:13–14) through the preaching of salvation by grace through faith (3:2), became the target of the wrong teaching of the Judaizers.[2] Most commentators view these false teachers as Jewish Christians who adopted a separatistic attitude toward Gentile believers.[3] Consequently, these Judaizers proclaimed a false gospel (1:6–10) consisting of adding circumcision and observance of the law to the initial faith in Christ for the sake of salvation and perfection (2:21; 3:2–3; 4:8–11, 21; 5:2–4, 11; 6:12–13).

C. K. Barrett keenly summarized their argument:

> The true descendants of Abraham are the Jews, who inhabit Jerusalem. Here are the true people of God; and it will follow that Jerusalem is the authoritative centre of the renewed people of God, now called the church. Those who are not prepared to attach themselves to this community by the approved means (circumcision) must be cast out; they cannot hope to inherit promises made to Abraham and his seed.[4]

In fighting the erroneous teaching of the Judaizers, the apostle Paul divided his argument in Galatians into three parts. First, biographically, he attempted to establish his authority as an apostle of Jesus Christ, and consequently the authority of his gospel of grace (chaps. 1–2). Second, doctrinally, Paul defended the gospel of justification by grace through faith against the false teaching of the Judaizers (chaps. 3–4). Third, practically, Paul pointed out the implications for the gospel of grace on the Christian's daily life (chaps. 5–6).

A Crucial Yet Controversial Allegory

The allegorical nature of the last part of Paul's doctrinal piece of argumentation (4:21–31) has given rise to criticism regarding its historicity.[5] J. Montgomery Boice summarizes the different purposes for this section in the development of the epistle's argument.

> (1) The allegory allows Paul to end on a final citation of the law and, in particular, on a passage involving Abraham, who has been his primary example; (2) it allows him to use a method of argument which, we may assume, had been used by the legalizers, thus turning their own style of exegesis against them; (3) it illustrates and reviews all his main points, the radical opposition between the principle of law and the principle of faith, the fact that life under law is a life of bondage and the life of faith is freedom, that the life of faith is a result of the supernatural working of God by means of the Holy Spirit; (4) the story contains an emotional overtone suited both to a wrap-up of the formal argument and to a final personal appeal; and (5) it gives Paul a base upon which to suggest what he had undoubtedly thought but had apparently been reluctant to say previously that the Galatians should obey God by casting out the legalizers (v. 30). Therefore, the allegory effectively ties together both the doctrinal section of the letter and the appeal based on it, while at the same time leading into the ethical section that begins in chapter 5.[6]

Thus 4:21–31 is the climax of Paul's doctrinal argument developed in chapters 3–4. First, this section establishes faith as a principle of Christian living, which the Old Testament itself testifies is superior to the law (3:1–9). Next, it clarifies how Christ removed the curse as incurred by humanity because of their disobedience to the law (3:10–14). Then, it shows how the law, which was given to prepare the way to Christ, could not annul the promises appropriated by faith (3:15–29). In fact, tutelage under the law was terminated because maturity through sonship in Christ had come (4:1–7). Finally, being perplexed at the return of the Galatians to rituals (4:8–20), Paul culminates his reasoning by rehearsing the Old Testament story of Abraham's two sons. He uses that story to argue for the superiority of Christian freedom over legal bondage (4:21–31).

Within this allegorical section, the apostle first presents the historical facts related to that story in the Old Testament (vv. 21–23). The details of the story have already been established in the previous chapter. After that, Paul explores the symbolism behind the story (vv. 24–27). The two women, in their relationship to Abraham, symbolize the two covenants of God. The slave woman, Hagar, is a symbol of the Sinai covenant, under which the person attempts to appropriate divine favor, primarily by means of works, only to end up in bondage to the legal system (vv. 24–25). The free woman, Sarah, is a symbol of the new covenant, under which the person appropriates the promised blessings by faith. Faith frees the believer from bondage to the law through imputed righteousness effected by the Holy Spirit (vv. 26–27).[7]

Finally, Paul applies the story to his contemporary readers (vv. 28–31). The Galatian believers are like Isaac, children born by faith in the promise (v. 28). However, just as Ishmael's presence in the house of Abraham was incompatible with Isaac's privileges in that house (v. 29), Ishmael, whose birth came by natural means, had to be dismissed. Consequently, the Judaizers who are attempting to inherit the Abrahamic promises through human efforts must be cast out (v. 30). The Galatian Christians are not children of slavery (i.e., of bondage to the legal system) because they were born into the family of God by faith in the promise, effected by the Spirit. Therefore, they should live their freedom from the law and get rid of the false teachers trying to drag them back under the legal system (v. 31).

Did Ishmael Really Persecute Isaac?

What did Paul mean when he wrote that Ishmael persecuted Isaac (4:29)? Was he interpreting the Hebrew *metsakhêq* of the old text (Gen. 21:9)? Was he using a common Jewish tradition portraying Ishmael negatively to reflect on his and the Galatians' experience with the Judaizers? Or was he associating himself with Sarah and picturing Ishmael as the matriarch may have?

The first option is the most natural and spontaneous interpretation. However, the majority of New Testament commentators think that Paul's picturing of Ishmael as the one who "persecuted" Isaac is incongruent with the exegesis of the Old Testament incident. For

D. Guthrie, "no such incident is specifically mentioned in Scripture."[8] R. Longenecker sees Paul as presuming "a more developed account of the story of Ishmael and Isaac than the one presented in Scripture, for the Old Testament does not record anything about Ishmael's persecution of Isaac."[9] F. F. Bruce believes that "biblical substantiation for the statement that Ishmael persecuted Isaac is not forthcoming, so far as the two individuals are concerned."[10] Commenting on Sarah's demand (Gen. 21:10), Bruce adds, "the sight of Ishmael playing with her baby son reminded Sarah that Isaac had this older brother who had been since his birth the apple of his father's eye and she felt that Isaac's position was insecure so long as Ishmael was around."[11] Thus it is generally agreed upon that Paul was not exegeting the text of Genesis 21:9–10. Our previous dealing with the Old Testament text strongly endorses this conclusion as well.

Was Paul building on the negative Jewish tradition of his time (pointed out earlier), which the Judaizers were possibly familiar with? Rabbinic Midrash surveyed earlier in the study portrayed Ishmael as a persecutor of Isaac.[12] Many commentators think that Paul may have taken advantage of this tradition to reflect on the bad behavior of the Judaizers.[13] However, while this possibility is granted, I find myself in agreement with Bruce, who notes: "These observations [rabbinic views] are all later than Paul's day: whether there were earlier forms of any, specifically of the last (Ishmael's shooting arrows toward Isaac),[14] which he knew we cannot say."[15] Thus Paul's dependence on Jewish tradition, although possible, is not certain.

We are left at this point with a third alternative. Was Paul interpreting Ishmael's action from Sarah's futuristic perspective? The answer to this question is probably yes for the following reasons.

First, the apostle's doctrinal concern parallels Sarah's historical concern viewed typologically. Paul's highlighting of the believer's faith inheritance throughout his doctrinal argument (Gal. 3:14, 18, 29; 4:1–7, 30–31) indicates that the issue that preoccupied his mind was the same one that concerned Sarah when she reflected on Ishmael's presence alongside Isaac. Who would inherit the promised blessings of Abraham? As long as Ishmael was the only son in Abraham's house,

Sarah conceded that he would become the heir of his father's estate, thinking that he may be the son of promise, though his birth resulted from human reasoning. However, the supernatural birth of Isaac ended up displacing the son born the natural way. Sarah could no longer allow Ishmael to jeopardize the promised inheritance. In her mind, Ishmael constituted a continuous threat to her son's future welfare; therefore, he should depart. In Paul's mind, Isaac's pattern, as a child of the supernatural fulfillment of the promise, established faith as the only means of securing Abraham's spiritual blessings. As the supernatural birth displaced then the naturally born, thus also faith now displaces legal works. Therefore the Judaizers must be cast out.

Second, treating the command of Sarah as authoritative "Scripture" (4:30) is another indication that the apostle was looking at Ishmael's presence alongside Isaac from the matriarch's angle. Even though God encouraged Abraham to listen to the harsh demand of Sarah, Ishmael's ejection was not by God's direct command, but through concession to Sarah's request. While the matriarch's vision may have been limited to the near welfare of Isaac, God foresaw the implementation of his plan behind election and his historical purposes for Ishmael. As far as redemptive typology is concerned, Sarah's demand becomes authoritative "Scripture" since it reflected a basic gospel truth: "legal bondage and spiritual freedom cannot coexist."[16]

Third, the majority of translators render the Greek verb *ediõkên* in Galatians 4:29, "persecuted."[17] Thus it is beyond doubt that this is a legitimate translation. However, at least one translation, that of Wiclif (A.D. 1380), articulates the nuance of "pursuing," rendering the same verb "pursue,"[18] that is, "go after." Though "persecuted" can be maintained as a translation, the verb should be understood with this latter nuance in mind. There are approximately forty-three uses of the Greek verb *diõkõ* in the New Testament. Eleven of them are used in the sense of "pursue" and eight of these eleven uses are in Pauline literature (Rom. 9:30; 14:19; 1 Cor. 14:1; Phil. 3:12, 14; 1 Thess. 5:15; 1 Tim. 6:11; 2 Tim. 2:22). The nuance of pursuing, which is milder than physical persecution, seems to fit better the context of the underlying Old Testament passage.

Thus, Genesis 21:9 does not present Ishmael as a persecutor of the three-year-old child, Isaac. Nonetheless, in the mind of Sarah, Ishmael's presence in Abraham's house on equal social level with Isaac would result in his future pursuing of Isaac's inheritance. Regardless of what Sarah saw Ishmael doing, she built her demand on a future perception rather than on a present action. Therefore, the threat was not so much physical as it was social. Similarly, by insisting on the necessity of observing the law in addition to faith in Christ, the Judaizers were in a sense discrediting the social status[19] of the Galatian believers based on faith alone and thus chasing their privileges in Christ. In Ridderbos's terms, "the word persecuted means—as it is evident from the command so also it is now—not so much a threat of life as one to freedom and security."[20] This nuance of the term seems more in congruence with exegetical and historical facts.

Thus it appears that Paul's description of Ishmael as a social "persecutor" of Isaac reflects Sarah's foresight. However, the apostle replaced the matriarch's perception of a future likelihood with the present reality materialized by his experience with the Judaizers; hence the forcefulness of the terminology.

It is appropriate to end this discussion with a needed disclaimer. In his use of typology in Galatians 4:21–31, the apostle Paul was not motivated by racial distinctions. In fact, as an apostle to the Gentiles he was the one blamed for having destroyed all racial distinctions "in Christ" (cf. 2:6–21; 3:27–29). Many Arabs today, because of their traditional association with Ishmael, are embarrassed by this allegory in Galatians, especially by verses 29–30. These verses cannot be used as an indication of an ordained enmity between Arabs and Jews. The words of Thomas are to the point here.

> The intent of the allegory is not to denigrate Hagar and Ishmael, or her descendants the Arabs: Rather Paul is referring to God's provision of freedom from bondage to the law. In fact, he turns the literal interpretation on its head. "The Hagar-Ishmael line, leading historically to the Arabs, now leads to the Jews; the Sarah-Isaac line, however, from which the Jews

> trace their descent, leads to the Christians" (Gerhard Ebling, *The Epistle to the Galatians,* 234). The recognition of this reversal serves as a warning not to read interpretation based on tradition back into a text; in this case, we should not read Hagar and Ishmael as representing Arabs or Muslims back into this passage.[21]

Summary of Part 1 Findings

Because we focus so intently on God's faithfulness in the supernatural provision of the promised seed, we tend to forget how divine mercy is displayed toward those who stumble with their limited social privileges. We rarely hear messages preached on Hagar and Ishmael and God's gracious dealings with them. Oftentimes, when the Hagar/Ishmael story is remembered, it is used to highlight human failures on the part of Abraham and Sarah. Yet the narrative is loaded with lessons and principles emphasizing God's grace and love displayed on behalf of lowly humanity. The narrative in Genesis 16 is a very nicely woven story. Although only sixteen verses long, the chapter is full of action, drama, and favorable and unfavorable events. Much has been said about the unbelief of Abraham and Sarah and their lack of patience in the matter of Ishmael's birth. However, a closer look at their circumstances and the cultural customs of their time makes the informed reader sympathize more with the couple in their difficult ordeal. This is especially true in light of the divinely caused problem of Sarah's chronic barrenness, leaving the couple to wrestle with the possibility of a cultural alternative for appropriating the seed promise in light of their advanced age and the limited revelation they had from God.

Thus God's sovereign action in shutting Sarah's womb for so long and opening Hagar's is explicable in view of his intention to set human natural efforts in contrast with divine supernatural interventions, and in light of the plan he had for Ishmael and his descendants in secular history. Human reasoning prompted Sarah to resort to Hagar for children. Yet from a divine perspective, this scheme was short of

God's plan for the birth of the "son of the promise." However, this ordeal proved to be his unique plan for blessing Hagar and her descendants in history. Enduring the terrible consequences of Sarah's proposal and Abraham's implementation was the only way prideful Hagar could have her unique personal encounter with the Lord. Affliction and powerlessness under slavery paved the thorny road to blessing from a God who "hears" and "sees." Trible sums up the privileges of Hagar's unique profile as it is reflected in this biblical drama:

> Besides symbolizing the various kinds and conditions of people in contemporary society, Hagar is also a pivotal figure in biblical theology. She is the first person in scripture whom a divine messenger visits and the only person who dares to name the deity. Within the historical memories of Israel, she is the first woman to bear a child. This conception and birth make her an extraordinary figure in the story of faith: the first woman to hear an annunciation; the only one to receive a divine promise of descendants; and the first to weep for her dying child. Truly, Hagar the Egyptian is the prototype of not only special mothers but of all mothers in Israel.[22]

As far as Ishmael is concerned, the nomadic lifestyle of his descendants will set them against many and set many against them. Yet the name of Hagar's son, Ishmael, became an indication that God will listen to their affliction as an unfavored people.

From God's perspective, Ishmael is another potential for blessing through Abraham and his promised seed. His promises concerning Ishmael were a source of comfort for the helpless enslaved woman. Her son will be free and powerful as a nomad. Plus he will have inherited his own land from the Lord. Yet this dwelling place will be close by. As such it will serve a double purpose. First, it will be a potential for blessings through the elect seed. Jeremiah expresses this blessing with the following statement from the Lord. "Then it will come about that if they will really learn the ways of My people, to swear by My name, 'As the Lord lives,' . . . then they will be built up in the midst of

My people."[23] Second, it will be a challenge before Isaac's descendants, reminding them that faith and not mere blood relationship is the way to enjoying the Abrahamic promised blessings.

Chapter 3 showed that though Ishmael was not chosen to carry out God's covenantal promises given to Abraham, he was still the object of a special care and attention from God. His circumcision (Gen. 17:23–25) and the gracious promises of blessings he received (17:20) were signs of divine favor bestowed on him as a seed of Abraham (21:13), and as one of the children of the Lord. God's permission for the dismissal of Ishmael and his mother to the wilderness was proven not to be indicative of divine judgment on them, as much as the only way to see his plan for Isaac and his purposes for Ishmael fully implemented in history (21:8–21).

A closer look at Paul's use of the Old Testament account of Ishmael's dismissal to the wilderness showed that the apostle's concern for preserving a gospel truth led him to look at Ishmael's presence in Abraham's home with Sarah's foresight. Ethnologically speaking, Paul's use of typology cannot be employed to support any hostility between the Ishmaelites in history and the descendants of Isaac for two reasons. First, the rivalry between the brothers was resolved by God's choosing to bless both of them in two different realms: Isaac in Abraham's house and through his inheritance, Ishmael in the wilderness. Second, Paul's symbolism inverted the ethnic order, with Ishmael being made the representative of the Jews and Isaac of the believing Gentiles. With Ishmael finally restricted to his dwelling place, where God chose to bless him, the stage is set to trace what became of him in the remainder of biblical history.

PART 2

ARABS IN THE LIGHT OF ISRAEL

5

SUNRISE OF ABRAHAM'S CHILDREN

SINCE TRADITION LINKS MUSLIM ARABS to Ishmael ethnically or through theological association, many inadvertently interpret the Genesis oracles on Ishmael in light of Islam. Consequently, some people directly tie the Arab glory under Islam with the fulfilling of God's promise to make Ishmael a great nation (17:20; 21:18). That biblical prophecy has implications for postbiblical history, especially end-time events, is a fact hard to deny. The preservation of the Jews as a distinct ethnic group until today is an implication of Old Testament prophecy. Similarly, the survival and prospering of the Arabian line of Abraham until today has its roots in God's purposeful design of the history of Ishmael as outlined in the Bible. However, one can hardly accept that God had to wait for more than two and a half millennia to fulfill his promises to Hagar concerning her son. Hence, evidence of fulfillment of the Ishmael oracles has to be traced in biblical time. Accordingly, the remainder of this book attempts to find out what became of Ishmael in the 2,000 years of history following his birth. For that reason, biblical and extrabiblical material will be examined mutually.

Having considered in the previous chapters the texts pertaining to Ishmael's birth, his childhood, and his exit to the wilderness, part 2 endeavors to trace the history of Abraham's firstborn in the period defined earlier as "The Light of Israel." This period covers the time span from Abraham until the end of the Solomonic reign. During that time Israel was fulfilling to a certain extent God's missionary purpose behind its election as Light to the Gentiles (Exod. 19:6; Isa. 42:6; 49:6 etc.). In that sense, the nation was moving uphill toward glory as a theocracy.[1] Thus, Old Testament books written against a historical background culminating in the united monarchy under Solomon will be examined.[2] Historical narratives will be surveyed first. Wisdom literature will be considered next, with special attention given to the Arabian flavor of the book of Job and the identity of Agur and Lemuel in Proverbs 30 and 31.

Exploration Highways

Before trying to trace the line of Ishmael developed in ancient history, we need to define the criteria of our search. The primary method of conducting the survey will be to look for the different occurrences of the names of Ishmael and his twelve sons[3] and related designations, first in the Bible and then in extrabiblical material. When available, extrabiblical information is mostly helpful in assessing the political, social, and religious conditions of the Ishmaelites. Biblical material helps to trace the Abrahamic heritage of the Ishmaelites and evaluate their relationship with Israel. For the sake of clarity in the use of terms, it will be helpful at the outset of this survey of historical Ishmael to define the designations that involve the children of Ishmael.

Beside the direct reference to Ishmael and to his twelve sons, there are at least two other designations that should be considered in relation to the Ishmaelites in biblical history. The first one is the designation of "Arabians."[4] The second is that of the "children of the east" (Heb. *benê qedem*).[5]

The Ishmaelites as "Arabians"

To begin with, it is important to determine how *Arab* was defined in times past. Arabists are familiar with the fact that the first clear occurrence of the word "Arab" in extrabiblical texts is found in an Assyrian record mentioning the battle of Shalmaneser III at Qarqar north of Hamath during the sixth year of his reign (853 B.C.).[6] At the end of the list of his adversaries at Qarqar, Shalmaneser mentions "Gindibu" (Ar. *Jundub*)[7] "the Arabian" and his "1,000 camels."[8] The western coalition facing the Assyrians included Ahab of Israel, the king of Aram, and the Arabian leader Jundub. Hitti finds it very appropriate that "the name of the first Arabian in recorded history should be associated with the camel."[9] As a matter of fact, Arab nomads domesticated the camel centuries ago. Camels are heavy-duty animals that can travel long distances in the desert without the need for water, and can run as fast as horses and carry heavy loads at the same time. Thus they served as the primary means of transport for caravan trade across the Arabian Desert.[10]

Arabs appear frequently in the records of Assyrian kings, from Tiglath Pileser III through Ashurbanipal (745–627 B.C.), both as allies and as enemies.[11] Sargon II claimed to have resettled some Arab nomadic groups in Samaria as part of the Assyrian deportation policy applied to the areas conquered by them.[12] If this is true, it makes it very likely that the Samaritan woman, whom Christ met at the well (John 4), had Arabian blood. Also the Samaritan leper, who was the only one to come back and give glory to God for being healed, may be related to Ishmael.[13]

Etymologically speaking, the word *Arab* refers to nomadic desert dwellers without allusion to ethnic descent or nationality.[14] Most of the time, Assyrian inscriptions mention Arabians in reference to the nomadic tribes that dwelt in north and central Arabia. The Ishmaelites were a prominent section of these nomads and assumed a leadership role in the north Arabian Desert. Though nomadic life today is not highly regarded among people of different ethnicity, even among Arabs themselves, the Bible does not portray this lifestyle in a negative way. On the contrary, it reflects a simple lifestyle prompting one to rely on God for sustenance and blessing. In fact, Abraham in Canaan, Moses in Midian, and Israel in its early life all led a nomadic and seminomadic life and could be technically labeled as "Arabs."[15]

Thus we see that the designation of "Arab" was applied first to nomads who dwelt mainly in the Arabian Peninsula, the Sinai Peninsula, and the Syro-Arabian Desert.[16] Grohmann rightly suggests that "'the Aramaean Bedouins,' who in 880 B.C. interfered in the affairs of Bet-Zamāni on the upper Euphrates and helped to overthrow the local vassal of the Assyrian king Assur Nasirpal, were predecessors of the Arabs."[17] Rosmarin, who classified the references to Arabians in Assyrian and Babylonian sources, makes an interesting observation: "Most likely, in most ancient times, there was not a clear difference between Arabs and Arameans, since both ethnic groups were Bedouins. Also the Assyrian kings made no sharp distinction between Arabs and Arameans."[18]

On the other hand, though the Old Testament sporadically used the term *Arab* as an indication of nomadic individuals (Isa. 13:20; 21:13; Jer. 3:2), the first clear biblical use of the appellation *Arabs* as a corporate unit occurs in Jeremiah 25:24.[19] Jeremiah's official ministry covered the period from 627 B.C. to 586 B.C. Among the kings and peoples against whom he prophesied were the "kings of the Arabs." Most likely, the reference was to north Arabian tribal leaders (sheikhs) who dwelt in the Syro-Arabian Desert.[20] In that sense it included the Ishmaelite tribes that dwelt in most parts of that desert (Gen. 25:12–18). However, later the term *Arabian* was applied in a more general sense as a reference to any inhabitant of the Arabian Peninsula.[21]

Thus it becomes clear that the oldest application of the term *Arab* concerned the dwellers of the Sinai and Arabian peninsulas, who led a nomadic and later seminomadic life, without reference to their nationality. Though references to "Arabs" or "Arabians" in the collective sense did not occur until about the ninth century B.C., there were earlier references to individual nomadic (Arabian) tribes.

The Ishmaelites as "Children of the East"

The second designation related to the Ishmaelites is that of *benê qedem,* translated "children (people or sons) of the east." It is generally maintained that the Qedemites of the Old Testament *(benê qedem)* are to be identified with nomadic (Arab) tribes that were allotted by Abraham a dwelling place in the desert of Transjordan, east of Palestine (Gen. 25:6, 13–18).[22] This identity is attested in later biblical uses of the term. In Judges 6:3, 33; 7:12; and 8:10, the children of the east," or Qedemites,[23] are coupled with Midian and Amalek, while in Jeremiah 49:28 they are associated with Qedar. The mention of their bedouin encampment in Ezekiel 25:4, 10 associates them with the sons of Ishmael, of whom the same term is used.[24] Reference is made to their proverbial wisdom in 1 Kings 4:30 and Isaiah 19:11, and the Old Testament figure of Job is reckoned as the greatest among the "children of the east" (Job 1:3).[25] In his study of the issue, Ephᶜal concludes:

> This . . . reveals that in the historical and literary parts of the Bible there are radical changes in names of the nomad groups, the turning-point occurring in the mid-tenth century B.C.: thereafter Hagarites, Ishmaelites, Midianites and Amalekites do not appear (nor, it should be noted, do they figure in extra-biblical sources, either of the period of this study or prior to it). Instead, the collective noun "Arab(s)" begins to be used, and various groups (Buz, Dedan, Dumah, ᶜEphah, Massa', Nebaioth, Qedar, Sheba and Tema') not in the sources for the earlier period are referred to. *Only the designation "People of the East" . . . spans both periods.* (emphasis added)[26]

Thus it becomes clear that the expression of *benê qedem* designates the north Arabian nomadic tribes, of which the Ishmaelites were a major part and by virtue of this truth, this expression is directly relevant to the present study.

ISHMAEL "WHEN ISRAEL WAS A CHILD"

Our exploration of historical Ishmael starts before the establishing of Israel as a nation. This period of biblical history is commonly known as the patriarchal period. It covers the time span from Abraham until the exodus of the Hebrew people out of Egypt. We will explore what happened to Ishmael and his children during that stage of history. Most of our information for this period comes from the biblical text. There are almost no extrabiblical sources of information on Arabs before the beginning of the first millennium B.C.

The first mention of Hagar's son after his dismissal to the wilderness occurs in Genesis 25:9, which pictures Ishmael together with Isaac burying their father Abraham. No wonder they were performing that family duty together. In fact, after God blessed Isaac, he dwelt at Beer Lahai Roi, the sacred Ishmaelite well (25:11), alongside his half brother Ishmael. Later, the writer of Genesis gives us an idea of the widespread geographical area of settlement for the children of Ishmael (25:12–18). The twelve Ishmaelite tribes dwelt in the Syro-Arabian Desert between Sinai and the western borders of the Euphrates.[27] The marriage of Esau to the daughter of Ishmael (28:9; 36:3–4, 13, 17) is an indication of an early intermixing between Edomites and Ishmaelites. A similar early intermingling occurred between the descendants of Ishmael and their kin, the descendants of Keturah, led by the Midianites.[28] Besides the mention of Ishmaelites in connection with the selling of Joseph and his descent into Egypt, there is no other direct reference to them in the Pentateuch. The rest of the Pentateuch deals with the period that just preceded Israel's conquest of the land of Canaan.

Very little is known about the history of the Ishmaelites during the 400 years while Israel was in Egypt since no biblical records cover that time span. Likewise no extrabiblical manuscripts provide any significant information about them. The lack of sedentary life of various Ishmaelite tribes makes it very difficult to trace the chronological history and cultural development of these nomads. Historians have to rely mostly on what others say about them, though it may not always be an objective presentation.[29] Nevertheless, the book of Job, likely written against a patriarchal background,[30] may yield relevant information about the Ishmaelites during that early period of Israel's history.

Early after Israel's settlement in the land of Canaan, there seems to have been some intermingling between the closer Ishmaelite tribes and the children of Israel. In fact, two of the tribes of Ishmael, Mibsam and Mishma (25:12–18), seem to have merged under the tribe of Simeon, since these two tribes appear in the genealogical list of the Simeonites who lived close to the Ishmaelites in the south (25:13; 1 Chron. 4:25).[31] It is of significance in this regard that these two tribes are among the only three of the descendants of Ishmael that cannot be identified in later history, neither in cuneiform texts nor in biblical records.[32] Though this genealogical merging seems puzzling to the modern reader of biblical genealogy, in nomadic culture this practice was perfectly understandable. De Vaux makes some helpful observations related to the customs that characterized the Arabian tribal life as well as the early life of the Israelites.

> In practice, other factors beside common descent may help to constitute a tribe. The mere fact of living in the same region leads groups of families to join together. Weak elements are absorbed by stronger neighbours; alternatively, several weak groups combine to form a body capable of remaining autonomous, that is, of standing up to attack. Individuals, too, can be incorporated into a tribe either by adoption into a family (as often happens with freed slaves), or through acceptance by the sheikh or the elders. But even here the principle is safeguarded, for the newcomer is attached "in name and in blood" to the tribe; this means that he acknowledges the tribe's ancestor as his own, that he will marry within the tribe and raise up his family inside it. The Arabs say that he is "genealogized" (root: *nasaba*). With a whole clan the fusion takes longer, but the result is the same, and the newcomers are finally considered as being of the same blood. A text of Al-Bakri puts it neatly: "And the Nahd ben Zaïd joined the Bené al-Harith, became confederate with them and completely united with them; and the Jarm ben Rabbân joined the Bené Zubaïd, attached themselves to them and lived together, and the whole tribe with its confederates was attached to the same ancestor *(nusibat)*."[33]

With this background in mind the genealogical list becomes more significant. In fact, the listing of Ishmaelite elements in blood relationship with indigenous Israelite tribe members, under the same ancestor, reflects the depth of social, cultural, and religious unity between both merged and natural elements.[34] This phenomenon sheds some light on the intensity of social relationships that existed between the two groups at an early period of Israel's history.

The time of the judges indicates a period of seven years of hostilities between Israel and different nomadic tribes of the Transjordan that included the "children of the east" (Heb. *benê qedem*). The preceding expression occurs several times in the book of Judges (6:3, 33; 7:12; 8:10). It points there to a group of people associated with the Midianites and the Amalekites in their fight against the sons of Israel led by Gideon. Since the Ishmaelite tribes covered a geographical area that extended from Paran to Babylon across the Syro-Arabian Desert (Gen. 25:12–18; Jubilee 20:11–13), it is unlikely that the children of the east mentioned in Judges included all the Ishmaelites.[35] Only the tribes that lived in the neighborhood of Canaan were likely involved.

It is very probable that the term *Midian* is used in the narrative's context as a collective reference to the Midianites, Amalekites, and the children of the east (Judg. 6:3, 33; 7:12, 13, 14, 23, 24; 8:28). By this token, and from an ethnic standpoint, the Midianites who descended from Keturah (Gen. 25:1–6) were apparently at the head of a large tribal confederation.[36] According to Dumbrell, that confederation controlled the area surrounding Canaan eastward to the Transjordan and southward to Edom and Sinai.[37] The defeat of the Midianites by Gideon became the starting point for their decline as a dominant political entity. This decline of the Midianites gave rise to the prominence of the Ishmaelites as a nomadic group and dominant political power.[38] Most specifically "the sons of Qedar" presided over north Arabian tribes until late in the Persian Empire, when somehow the Nabataeans assumed control over north Arabia.

We cannot avoid at this point addressing a minor detail concerning the children of Midian. According to biblical data the Midianites appear in two different pictures, a good one and a bad one. The good

Midianites included the descendants of Jethro, Moses' father-in-law (later called the Kenite, Judg. 1:16), and all the Rechabites who are directly related to them (Jer. 35). These people from Arabian descent apparently became the scribes in the temple of God and were associated with the people of the city of Jabez, suggesting that Jabez may likely have been one of the descendants of Jethro the Kenite (1 Chron. 2:55). Among these descendants of Jethro is Jael, the wife of Haber the Kenite, who killed Sisera, the enemy of Israel, in her tent, and was greatly praised by Deborah the judge in her song (Judg. 4:18–21; 5:24ff.). She was an Arabian woman, too. On the other hand, the Bible points to some bad Midianites. They seem to have dwelt in a different place since they seem to have come from an area in the Transjordan instead of the land of Midian in Northwest Arabia (Judg. 7:33). Besides their association with the stumbling of Israel at Peor (Num. 25; 31), they were among the oppressors of Israel faced by Gideon, when God disciplined his people for idolatry. In that sense a section of the Ishmaelites may have associated with them under the designation of "the children of the east."

One more attested conflict between Ishmaelite tribes and the Israelites in the period under consideration is described in the genealogical listing of Reuben, Gad, and half of the tribe of Manassah (1 Chron. 5:10, 19–22), which are the tribes that dwelt in the Transjordan (Josh. 13:15–32). The fight happened during the days of Saul between the Hagarenes (1 Chron. 5:10), Yetur, Naphish, and Nodab (5:19–22) on the one hand, and the Reubenites, the Gadites, and half of the tribe of Manassah on the other hand.[39] It seems that the direct cause of that struggle was the increased size of the flocks on both sides (5:9), and the proximity of the different tribes that limits the grazing land available for each one of them.[40] The Israelite tribes came out of this fight victorious, and this was God's disciplining hand against the Ishmaelite tribes (5:22).

Besides the seven years of hostilities against Israel, which occurred early in the period of the judges (Judg. 6:1), and the fight during Saul's time in the Transjordan, historical narratives do not refer to any other contact between the Ishmaelite tribes and Israel until the united monarchy. This may imply that the relationship between the two groups was peaceful and their contacts involved social relationship and trade,[41] since the Ishmaelites are not mentioned in any later raid against Israel during that period.

During the united monarchy, Israel's golden age of prosperity under the Lord, there is also evidence of positive relationships between the sons of Israel and the sons of Ishmael. As previously mentioned, David's raids on the Negev during the reign of Saul did not involve the Ishmaelites. They were not listed among his victims, even though his raids "encroached upon their habitat, as is clear from 1 Samuel 27:8 and Genesis 25:18."[42] David's sister was married to "Jether the Ishmaelite,"[43] the father of Amasa who was to replace Joab as a later leader of Israel's army (2 Sam. 20:4–13; 1 Chron. 2:17). Furthermore, among those who administrated "crown property" under David were "Obil the Ishmaelite" and "Jaziz the Hagarite" (1 Chron. 27:30).[44]

Under Solomon there was evidence of ongoing friendly relationships with the Arabians. First Kings indicates that "all the kings of the Arabs" used to offer Solomon great gifts of gold (10:15). According to Herodotus, subdued vassal kingdoms used to pay tributes to the Persian king, while friendly vassal kingdoms brought him yearly gifts instead.[45] By bringing gifts to Solomon, these Arab kings asserted the friendship of their kingdoms to Israel and its king. Befriending Yahweh's theocratic kingdom inevitably had a religious and spiritual impact. In that regard, the visit of the Arabian queen of Sheba to King Solomon is of great significance. This queen was praised by Christ as a believer (Matt. 12:42; Luke 11:31). According to Ephʿal, "recent research on South Arabia has removed all doubt about the existence of the kingdom of Sheba" in the south as early as the eighth century B.C.[46] If in fact this queen came from north Arabia instead, as many historians now contend,[47] she would represent the confederation of other petty Ishmaelite tribal kingdoms.[48]

Additionally, one of the only two daughters of Solomon mentioned in Scripture was named Basma (1 Kings 4:15). This name has no Hebrew root, but is of Arabic origin (*basmah* or *bāsimah,* meaning, "smile" or "the smiling one").[49] The only other place in the Hebrew

Bible where the proper name *Basma* occurs is with reference to the daughter of Ishmael, sister of Nebayot, whom Esau married (Gen. 28:9; 36:3–4, 13, 17).[50] With that in mind, this naming of Solomon's daughter may imply that he had an Ishmaelite wife. This should not be a strange inference in view of the fact that Solomon married many wives from the nations surrounding Israel (1 Kings 11:1–3), and that Abigail, David's sister, was married to "Jether the Ishmaelite," the father of Amasa (1 Chron. 2:17). No further information about Ishmaelites can be drawn from the historical narratives from the period under consideration.

However, since Solomon's reign was characterized by a great interest in wisdom sayings (1 Kings 4:30), with kings from the surrounding nations visiting Solomon to listen to his wisdom and share their own heritage (4:34; 10:1–11), it is safe to conjecture that wisdom traditions of non-Hebrew origin were integrated into Hebrew culture during the Solomonic era. This makes the book of Job and Proverbs 30–31 relevant to this study.[51]

6

Job, Son of the Arabian Desert

Hagar's Children Wisdom Seekers

The vast amount of ancient material that is generally recognized as wisdom literature indicates that the Old Testament wisdom books were not produced in a literary vacuum.[1] Most extant literature from the ancient Near East is Egyptian wisdom.[2] However, the Bible highlights both the wisdom of the children of the east and Egyptian wisdom in comparison to Solomon's wisdom (1 Kings 4:30). The book of Baruch (third century B.C.) describes the children of Hagar as those "who seek wisdom upon the earth" (3:23). Non-Israelite wisdom sayings were always available to the Hebrew nation by virtue of its regular contacts with the peoples around them. Nevertheless, a dramatic escalation of this exchange of wisdom material was witnessed in the days of Solomon. The Bible relates how many kings from the surrounding nations came to Israel to hear Solomon's wisdom (1 Kings 4:34; 10:1–13). Therefore it may be conjectured that, regardless of dates of writing, non-Israelite wisdom traditions, and Ishmaelite wisdom in particular, became part of Israel's life during the prominent rule of Solomon with its significant international outlook.

The nomadic and seminomadic lifestyle of the children of the east accounted for the scarcity of their written remains. However, some of their wisdom traditions may have been preserved in Hebrew literature. In this chapter, we examine the evidence for such a claim. The geo-ethnic background to the book of Job will be considered in detail in order to reflect on its relevance to Ishmaelite culture. The high theology of Job will be examined in terms of its significance as far as the early Arab religious atmosphere.

ISHMAEL AND JOB

The Arabian flavor of the book of Job stems out of cultural, historical, and literary backgrounds. What is the identity of Job, the location of the land of Uz, and the origin and theological atmosphere of the book? The following is a survey of these issues, aiming to determine what the book of Job can convey about Ishmael.

The Identity of Job

Job's name is attested outside of Israel. The letters of Tel el-Amarna contain a name that closely resembles his. The name "Job" is attributed there to a certain king of Pella, and assumes the form *A-ia-ab.*[3] According to Dhorme, this name "belongs to the West Semitic group of names, as is confirmed by the uninflected form A-ia-ab; the transformation of *Aiâb* into *Ayôb* and finally into *ʾIyôb* is paralleled by the changes of *qattâl* into *qittôl* known to grammarians."[4] Since the name "Job" (Heb. *ʾIyôb*) is not attested in Hebrew literature except here,[5] it has been proposed that it is better explained as a form of the Arabic *ʾawwāb* ("the returning one," or penitent), stemming from the root verb *ʾāba* ("to return").[6] Dhorme, while acknowledging this possibility, still sees some difficulty in portraying Job as the "penitent one."[7] However, this difficulty is resolved if one sees in Job an additional picture of returning. As a matter of fact, in the community, Job's "coming back" is more of a return to social and material blessing (Job 42:12). This would likely be the case especially if Job's name was given to him later by his community, as the Septuagint tradition maintains.[8]

Job's historicity is further attested by Ezekiel, who places him alongside Noah and Daniel among the righteous biblical characters (Ezek. 28:3).[9] He is described by the author of his book as the greatest among the children of the east (Job 1:3). This automatically puts him outside the Israelite line. Furthermore, it places him in the Transjordan, a little beyond the land of Ammon, Moab, and Edom.[10] As noted previously, the expression "children of the east" generally refers to nomadic dwellers of the Syro-Arabian Desert. Though Genesis 29:1 may be interpreted as including Aramaeans with them,[11] all the rest of biblical references argue, as Pfeiffer notes, that these easterners "are not Arameans but Bedawin."[12] The Egyptian tale of Sinuhe points also to a land of Qedem, which the traveler approached as he moved eastward out of Byblos. As vague as it may sound, this reference may allude also to the Syrian Desert, as most biblical references point out (Judg. 6:3, 33; 7:12; 8:10; Jer. 49:28; Ezek. 25:4, 10).[13]

The Greek text of the Septuagint adds an appendix to the book of Job (42:17), which is a translation of "the Syriac book."[14] This appendix reflects an Aramaic tradition about the identity of the biblical character of Job. That tradition assumes several things about this hero. First, the name of Job was first Jobab, who appears in Genesis 36:33 as one of the descendants of Esau from his marriage with Basma the daughter of Ishmael. Second, Job lived in the land of Uz, which this tradition locates "on the borders of Idumea and Arabia." Third, he married an Arabian woman who gave birth to a son named Ennon. Fourth, Job's father was Zerah and his mother was Bosorras; thus he was the fifth from Abraham. Fifth, Job's friend Eliphaz is one of the sons of Esau, king of the Teimanites. Baldad is king of the Shuhaites and Sophar "king of the Minaeans," which is a south Arabian kingdom.

Objections raised against this tradition are not serious enough to dismiss it as useless,[15] and the identification of Job with Jobab deserves some attention, especially since it does not contradict the internal evidence of the book of Job and other Scriptures, as it shall be seen. Though this tradition may be possible, it may not be accurate in every single detail. For example, mentioning only one son for Job, Ennon, seems to contradict scriptural data (Job 42:13–15). Therefore, the relevance of the book of Job to the study of the early history of the Ishmaelites is reinforced by this tradition, though it does not depend on it.

The Date of Job

Dhorme established the patriarchal setting of the events of Job based on internal considerations:

1. Job's wealth (Job 1:3) is described in terms of the magnitude of his livestock like in the portrayal of "the prosperity of Isaac" (Gen. 26:13–14).
2. Job was the tribal head of his family, offering sacrifices for his children (Job 1:5).
3. According to a nomadic cult, Job offered seven bulls and seven rams, and sacrificed on behalf of his friends (compare with the sacrifice of Balak and Balaam in Num. 23:11–14 and with Abraham and Abimelech in Gen. 20:7).
4. The currency used in Job's time is the *kesîtāh* (Job 42:11), as in Jacob's time (Gen. 33:19).
5. Job lived about 210 years (42:16), and saw his grandsons up to the fourth generation (Joseph lived only 110 years, according to Gen. 50:23).
6. Job's death formula is exactly the same as that of Abraham and Isaac (cf. 25:8; 35:29).[16]

Zuck presents two more arguments for the patriarchal setting. First, the names of places used in the book are patriarchal. Second, the use of *šadday* (thirty-one times in Job) as a reference to God is certainly patriarchal, since this term is used only seventeen times in the rest of the Old Testament.[17]

However, the association of Job's friend Eliphaz with Teiman puts the events of the book in the latter part of the patriarchal age. The name *Teiman* is mentioned for the first time in the Old Testament as a son of Eliphaz, son of Esau (Gen. 36:11).

The events of the book of Job, though patriarchal in setting, should not be thought of as contemporary to Abraham. They should be put late in the patriarchal age, at least as late as the birth of Esau's grandson Teiman. Anachronism may not be likely here, since Taymāʾ appears in the book of Job to be a fully established caravan oasis (Job 6:19), which means that an extended time elapsed since the birth of Taymāʾ, Ishmael's ninth son (Gen. 25:15). In order for Job's friend to have Teiman as his homeland, at least one generation has likely passed so that the dwelling place of Teiman becomes associated with his name, since Teiman was the first Edomite prince to rule his area (36:15). So Eliphaz the Teimanite is most likely a grandson of Eliphaz, Esau's firstborn (36:11). Therefore, identifying Job with Jobab, son of Zerah, son of Reuel, son of Esau (from Ishmael's daughter), is possible. In any event, the presence of Eliphaz the Teimanite among Job's friends puts the events of Job's book in the period of the early existence of Ishmaelites and not before them, and makes the book relevant to the study of their early history.[18]

The Land of Uz

The South Tradition

Two main traditions are normally highlighted in regard to the land of Uz. The first one puts Uz in an oasis somewhere between Idumea and Arabia. This tradition conforms to many biblical references to the land of Uz. Jeremiah (25:20) refers to "all the kings of the land of Uz," suggesting an extended geographical area, rather than a limited one. In the same text, the prophet seems to distinguish between Edom and "the land of Uz" by mentioning each one of them separately in his extended list of kingdoms under God's judgment (25:18–26). However, the same prophet (Lam. 4:21) describes "the daughter of Edom" as dwelling in the "land of Uz."[19] Thus the "daughter of Edom" may be a reference either to Edomites dwelling in Uz, or, as Owen suggests, to a colony of Edom.[20] The genealogy of Esau-Seir lists Uz as one of the sons of Dishan, the son of Seir the Horite (Gen. 36:20, 28). Seir, whose children's names display clear Arabic structure,[21] is not to be confused with Edom, since Esau (that is, Edom) inherited the Mount of Seir (Deut. 2:5). The Septuagint tradition (Job 42:17), depending on "the Syriac Book," is in harmony with Jeremiah's view of the land of Uz.[22]

The North Tradition

The second tradition puts the land of Uz in the Hauran area, south and southeast of Damascus.[23] According to Josephus, Uz, one of the children of Aram (Gen. 10:22–23), founded Damascus and Trachonitus.[24] Similarly, one of the sons of Nahor, Abraham's brother, is also called Uz (22:21). This makes "the Aramean connections of the name very strong,"[25] and harmonizes with the Arab and Byzantine tradition, which places the land of Uz in *Nawā* and its vicinity near *Sheikh Meskîn* in the Hauran area and *al-Bathaniyyah* provinces.[26] The monastery called *Deir-ʾAyyûb,* in the vicinity of Damascus, has been added as "another witness to this tradition."[27] On the other hand, there is in the lower part of the Kidron Valley in Palestine (just beyond the place where the pool of Siloam is located) a well named *Bîr-ʾAyyûb.*[28]

Traditions Reconciled

Positions vary significantly between these two conflicting traditions. Tur-Sinai reconciles the two by arguing that Job lived initially on the borders of Edom, and later moved to the neighborhood of Damascus.[29] Pope thinks it is "impossible to reconcile the conflicting evidences and opinions as to the exact location of Uz."[30] Dhorme settles for a place on the "borders of Edom and Arabia," saying, "we cannot legitimately argue from tradition in order to adopt a different location from that which is suggested by the O.T. texts [Jer. 25:20; Lam. 4:21]."[31]

That there was a distinct geographical area called the land of Uz is also made clear from Assyrian inscriptions. In his chronicles, Shalmaneser III refers to collecting tribute from Sasi, "the Uzzite,"[32] but gives no further information about the location of the land of Uz.[33] Musil points out a place by the name of *Khirbet el-ʿIṣ,* which he identifies with the land of *ʿUṣ,* and places it at about 3 kilometers south southeast of *aṭ-Ṭafîle,* some 50 kilometers southeast of the Red Sea north of Aqaba.[34] Owens identifies the land of Uz with Wādî Sirhān, which is a "great shallow plain-like depression some 210 miles long and averaging 20 miles wide,"[35] stretching east and southeast of Amman on the way to *Dumat el-Jandal* (biblical Dumah, Assyrian *Adummatu*). It is situated on the major caravan trade route linking the oasis of Dumah to the Kings Highway.[36] At some points *Wādî Sirhān* is "only 40 to 100 miles from the eastern borders of Edom."[37]

Owen's identification[38] may be an acceptable geographical compromise. The situation of *Wādî Sirhān* midway between Hauran in the north and Edom in the south makes it close enough for Job to have access to both lands. The immense livestock that Job had (Job 1:3) and his eminent situation among all the children of the east are indications that he most likely was not only a chief of his own tribe, but also of several tribes. In bedouin terms, Job may be called *shaykh mashāyekh,* that is, an "elder of elders."[39] By this token, his social impact, as the wisest leader in the land, was not restricted to his immediate neighborhood only, but stretched to all the families in the farther neighborhoods too (Job 4:3–4; 29:7–25). Therefore, it should not be strange if people from north and south identify with him in their own traditions. Furthermore, the *al-Jawf* area (meaning "cavity" or "basin") of *Wādî Sirhān* may be an exemplary place for pasturing the extended flock that Job had, and for renting his camels for caravan trade (6:19). Being a fertile land in the middle of the Syro-Arabian Desert, it offers the possibility of the seminomadic lifestyle that characterized the patriarch.[40]

Though identifying Uz with the al-Jawf area seems to fit most data, it is still safer to leave the question open and await further information. What seems unquestionable, though, whether the land of Uz is to be located on the borders of Edom and Arabia or in Hauran, is that Job lived in Ishmaelite territory in north Arabia. As Clines put it, "the importance of the name Uz lies not in where such a place is, but in where it is not," and it is clear that it is "not in Israel,"[41] but among the desert dwellers, the children of the east.

The Literary Origin of Job

Difficulties in the language of the book of Job[42] have led some scholars to search for an Aramaic or Arabic literary origin for it. Ibn Ezra, the famous Jewish scholar of the twelfth century, was the first known to suggest that the book of Job is a translation done by Moses.[43] Possibly Ibn Ezra might have believed that Moses came in contact with the original Job in the northwest Arabian district of Midian where he spent forty years (Exod. 3; Acts 7:30). Tur-Sinai suggested that a disciple of Ezra or some other scribe of the same period might have translated the poetic parts of Job from an Aramaic original.[44] Albright follows Tur-Sinai's theory of translation but qualifies the original as being Edomite Aramaic.[45] However, the cases of Aramaisms in the book have been increasingly challenged since then.[46] On the other hand, after considering the Arabic affinities of Job, Margoliouth concluded:

> The impression left by many chapters of this book on those who see little or no evidence of serious textual corruption is that of inadequate translation. This would account for the difficulty of assigning a meaning to many (or most) of the verses in various chapters. And since the problems discussed seem to be no better suited to Arabia than to any other land, it is hard to find a reason why if the work were not originally Arabian it should be located in that country.[47]

Drawing on Schultens's[48] extensive philological treatment, Foster reconsidered favorably the Arabic origin of the book of Job. He found in it many Arabian proverbial sayings and clarified alleged mistranslations based on Arabic literature and Qurʾanic considerations.[49] As an example of Arabic proverbial similarities found by Foster, Job 8:13–15 says:

> Such is the destiny of all who forget God; so perishes the hope of the godless. What he trusts in is fragile; what he relies on is a spider's web. He leans on his web, but it gives way; he clings to it, but it does not hold.

Compare with Qurʾanic Sura 29:41, which says:

> The likeness of those who take rulers *(ʾAwliyāʾ)* other than Allah is as the likeness of a spider who builds a house, but the frailest of houses is the spider's house-But if they knew.[50]

Furthermore, Job's saying in 7:19, "Let me alone until I swallow my saliva," is a clear Arabic proverbial expression meaning "the briefest possible space of time."[51] Many similar parallels are also established by Foster between Arabic sayings and Job 2:5; 5:5; 11:15–17; 17:4; 19:20–22; 23:7; 30:11, 13, 22.

According to the same writer, several verses in Job remain obscure if they are not understood against a desert setting. Thus the reference to his friends' deception "as a torrent" in a desert valley (6:15), freezing by night and drying with the coming of the next day's heat (6:16–17); and the allusion to desert hospitality (31:32), the wasteland having no roads (12:24), the solitary wilderness "wherein was no man" (38:26), and wilderness animals including the wild donkey and the ostrich (39:5–18), all indicate an Arabian Desert setting.[52]

More recently, A. Guillaume[53] has further developed the hypothesis of an Arabian origin. Having established the desert mise en scène of the book, and drawn significant literary parallelism between Qurʾanic verses, Arabic literature, and the text of Job, he concluded that the best explanation for the origin of the book is that Job himself wrote it during the reign of Nabonidus, who ruled in Taymāʾ for ten years.[54] Seeing a strong Hebrew settlement in the Arabian district of Hejaz in general, and in Taymāʾ in particular, he deduced that Job was a Hebrew living in the northwest district of Hejaz. Job is further believed to be competent in both Arabic and Hebrew. Thus he wrote his own book in the latter part of the sixth century B.C.[55] Guillaume went on to clarify that the concept of Arabic language should not be restricted to classical Arabic, which is the language of the poets of Najd, but should include also all the dialects of the different Arabian tribes that were distributed in the large area of the peninsula. This would explain the presence of dialectical forms in Job unaccounted for in modern classical Arabic.[56]

Against the theory of a translation from an Arabic original is the fact that so far no such work has been found in any part of the Arabian Peninsula.[57] Until the recovery of such evidence, this theory remains a mere hypothesis, despite the important cases of Arabism and parallelism with Arabian literature it surfaced. Moreover, it has been noted how the author of Job shows great familiarity with Egypt and Mesopotamia,[58] and Dhorme has already pointed out the affinities of Job with other books of the Old Testament.[59] Thus as Lévêque put it, "the hypothesis of a translation of Job from an Arabic original must, in order to be accepted, present other letters of credentials."[60] Meanwhile, for Montgomery, despite its seduction, that theory is "not only unproved but also unnecessary."[61]

While a translation from an Arabian original seems beyond proof at this point, a late-sixth-century B.C. setting in the Hejaz also seems a remote possibility. For, though it does account for many historical and literary elements, Guillaume's theory ignores the idolatrous theological atmosphere that pervaded the Arabian Peninsula during that period. Since Job's friends come from different geographical areas, the book portrays a widespread monotheism in north Arabia, which did not exist in the sixth century as the present chapter will show. A Hebrew ethnicity for Job does not overcome this difficulty. Israel and Judah were also long immersed in idolatry, and only a deportation from their land could cure their apostasy. On the contrary, the patriarchal setting of Job has been established,[62] and "the monotheistic atmosphere of the speakers [in the book of Job] is serener than that of the Prophets; the latter are troubled by an idolatrous environment, whereas to the speakers in Job *the alternative to monotheism is atheism*" (emphasis added).[63]

Several facts are evident after this short consideration of the literary origins of Job. The setting of the book is clearly in the land of the children of the east and the characters of the book are non-Israelites, the events of the book have taken place in the patriarchal age. Therefore, regardless of the date of writing, the writer of Job had to rely on an Arabian[64] tradition as a primary source of information for his writing.[65] Furthermore, if Job was an Arabian-Edomite,[66] this implies that the dialect used in the transmission of the oral tradition of his story would account for both the Arabic and Aramaic affinities in it.[67] Aramaic influence is expected to come through the line of Esau, son of Isaac (Deut. 26:5), and Arabic might be assumed from the legacy of Basma, daughter of Ishmael (Gen. 36:3–4, 17, 33), or through the Horite culture, which was replaced by the Edomites (Deut. 2:12, 22).[68]

Be that as it may, holding to a north Arabian tradition for the book of Job should not be viewed as "a penchant for denigrating" the "creators" of Hebrew literature.[69] The opposite is definitely true. By including in the Hebrew Bible wisdom traditions that originated among the non-Israelite Abrahamic stock, the "creators" of the Hebrew literature testify that Yahweh's calling of Abraham and his descendants to be a blessing to the nations (Gen. 12:1–3) was at work in the Old Testament. This truth puts Israel's role as "Light to the Gentiles" in perspective (cf. Isa. 42:6; 49:6).

Job and Early Ishmaelite Monotheism

The background study of Job aimed at highlighting one point with regard to Ishmael and his descendants during the patriarchal age. This Old Testament universal drama unveils a truth related to the theological atmosphere that reigned among the children of the east before the establishment of Israel as a nation. It is true that Ishmael was dismissed from Abraham's home and settled in the wilderness of Paran, where his children multiplied according to God's blessings on them (Gen. 17:20). It is also true that these descendants occupied a major part of the Syro-Arabian Desert (25:12–18). However, it becomes clear that much of the Abrahamic spiritual heritage characterized by a monotheistic faith survived also within the early history of the so-called nonelect children of Abraham.[70] In fact, the widespread geographical distribution of the key players in Job's story[71] put the early Ishmaelites in the middle of its sphere of action. The presence of a resolute monotheism among the early children of the east, among whom Job was the greatest leader, is further supported by the study of early Semitic religions and by other biblical evidence.

Early Semitic Religions

As highlighted earlier, the bulk of evidence puts the events of the book of Job in a patriarchal setting. It is therefore interesting to compare the religious atmosphere of that book to the one that prevailed in the same area during that period of history. In this regard, one must note the terminology used for deity in Job. According to Lévêque, the name *El* is used fifty-five times in the poetic dialogue of the book of Job, while it is used in the whole Pentateuch only forty-seven times and in the Prophets thirty-one times; the name *Elô(a)h* is used forty-one times in Job and fifty-seven times in the rest of the Old Testament (the plural *Elohîm* is used more than two thousand times), while */adday* is used thirty-one times in Job and seventeen times only in the rest of the Old Testament.[72] Thus the author of Job insisted on using the Hebrew word *Elô(a)h* in reference to God. By doing that, while scarcely using the name *Yhwh* or even the plural form *Elohîm,* the author of Job deliberately asserts the non-Israelite and patriarchal religious atmosphere of the story.

The deity *El* is equivalent to Arabic *Ilāh* and to Hebrew *Elô(a)h.* It is interesting to note that the Arabic term *Allah,* meaning God, is a contraction of *al-Ilāh* (the god).[73] Different representations of the deity *El* "were known through the Arabian world, as inscriptions from South Arabia to the Land of Midian show."[74] Hence, there are reasons to believe that the concept of the deity *El,* worshiped by the patriarchs and among their contemporary children of the east, may have had an Arabian origin,[75] and therefore is different, as Cazelles suggests, from the Canaanite *El* with all his sexual problems.[76] In fact, Père Starcky affirms that "the epithet of *most high* (*tʾly,* cf. *ʿelyôn* of the Bible) that several inscriptions [from south Arabia] give him harmonizes perfectly with *El* of antiquity."[77]

Starcky concludes his discussion of early Semitic religions by noting that the religion of ancient Semites went through three stages. The first Semites were monotheists and worshiped the supreme deity *El.* However, soon after that, they personified the major stars, primarily the Moon and Venus, which were very important for the nomads. Thus they associated with their personal God some object-deities. The third phase was characterized by contacts with sedentary culture, and thus the Semites adopted sedentary deities, which personified the forces of nature.[78]

Backing the same conclusion suggested above, Gibb developed from Qurʾanic verses the underlying concept of monotheism assumed among apparent polytheists in Arabia in Muhammad's time. He pointed out the presence of monotheistic groups referred to by the Qurʾan, called *hanifs,* who were independent from the organized churches. They were not adherents to Judaism at the time, but continued a monotheistic tradition that went back to Abraham's time.[79] Montgomery argues similarly, saying:

> At all events in putting a high theology into the mouths of his actors [in Job] the poet was not deserting the color of his stage, and the work may be early evidence for considerable theological advance among ancient Arabs. . . . *Allah* did not arise out of Mohammad's original summation of all gods into one God. This was already posited in the Arab consciousness, and Mohammad's diatribes against polytheism are similar to those of the Prophets against the cult of strange gods; their polytheism, he argued, was illogical in view of their fundamental belief in One God.[80]

Arabian Monotheism and Scriptures

Monotheism among early Semites in general and early Arabs in particular is also in agreement with biblical evidence. In the Genesis account Noah blesses Yahweh as the God of Shem (Gen. 9:26), and the first theophoric names that include the deity *El* in their structure are found among the south Arabian descendants of Joktan (10:26). The name "Elmodad," which combines the name *El* with the epithet derived from the Arabic verb *wadada* ("to befriend" or "to love") means "God is a friend."[81] The name "Abimael," reflecting an "Amoritic-Babylonian" structure, means "God is a father" or "God is my father."[82] Thus by worshiping *El,* Job, his friends, and his Edomite-Ishmaelite neighbors not only inherited the Abrahamic spiritual heritage, but they also were at home with this concept of monotheistic worship, especially in Arabia.[83]

An additional line of evidence is also found in three biblical texts: Deuteronomy 33:2; Judges 5:4; and Habakkuk 3:3, 7. These portions of Scripture support Job in asserting the fact that the knowledge of *El* was common among the children of the east early in biblical history. Each associates El and Yahweh[84] with the vicinity of Seir-Midian. While the first two relate a tradition that makes Yahweh come from Sinai-Seir to do battle on behalf of his people, Habakkuk 3:3, 7 makes El come from Midian-Teiman-Paran. Knauf[85] suggested reconciling the different geographical data by making the land of Midian, which is biblically associated with Sinai, the land where God came from to lead his people in the conquest of Canaan.

Current discoveries seem to harmonize well with the above suggestion. The land of Midian, which is traditionally located east of the Gulf of Aqaba in the Hejaz area, presents a difficulty with regard to locating Mount Sinai by St. Katherina Monastery in the Sinai Peninsula. It seems that a mount on the eastern side of Aqaba agrees better with biblical data. For while Moses was dwelling as a refugee in the land of Midian, he met Yahweh at Mount Horeb there (Exod. 3:1–2), which Paul puts in Arabia (Gal. 4:25). It took Elijah forty days from Beer Sheba in the Negev to get to Mount Sinai (1 Kings 19:8). However, Deuteronomy seems to suggest that it took eleven days to travel from Mount Horeb to Kadesh Barnea (Deut. 1:2). Recent findings by Williams and Cornuke at Jabal al-Lawz on the eastern side of the Gulf of Aqaba have revived the quest for Mount Horeb in Midian. Though not moved by scholarship, these two adventurers found by Jabal al-Lawz (called by locals, Mount of Moses) evidence suggesting that this is where Mount Horeb is to be located. This view is becoming increasingly plausible to scholars as an alternative to Jabal Moussa in the Sinai Peninsula.[86]

The view that Mount Sinai stood in Midian was proposed by Charles Beke and by the pioneer explorer of north Arabia, A. Musil.[87] Subsequently, Phythian-Adams adopted Musil's suggestion and developed it further, associating Kadesh-Barnea of Numbers 13–14 with Petra.[88] The eastern part of the Gulf of Aqaba also seemed plausible to Montgomery.[89] At any rate, the conjecture that these texts associate Yahweh's presence with Midian-Seir prior to Israel's conquest of Canaan[90] appears to be warranted by two more arguments, one biblical and another extrabiblical.

God's dealings with the Edomites present biblical support for the above conclusion. In Deuteronomy 2:5, Yahweh warns the children of Israel, who are on their way to Canaan, not to hurt the sons of Esau in any way for he has given them the land of Seir as an inheritance. Furthermore, verses 12 and 22 of the same chapter indicate that God drove out the Horites who lived in Seir and annihilated them before the children of Esau, just as he did for Israel in Canaan. This seems to indicate that though Esau was not elected to play a direct role in God's unfolding of the history of redemption, still he and his children were not left out by God. By driving the Horites out of Seir miraculously as he did for Israel later (Deut. 2:12), God revealed himself to the Edomites and his presence and worship would have been expected as a result of this special dealing with them.

On the extrabiblical level, it has been pointed out that Egyptian topographical lists from the fourteenth and thirteenth centuries B.C. mention a country of *Yhw*-nomads under the title of "country of Seir-nomads."[91] According to Knauf, the most ancient biblical and extrabiblical sources connect Yahweh with Seir, southeast of Canaan.[92] Furthermore, Ahlström believes that the mention of Yahweh of Teman and his Asherah in the inscriptions of Kuntillet ʿAjrud (ca. 800 B.C.) "confirms an Edomite provenience for Yahweh."[93] These areas of extrabiblical studies will surely be subject to further research, and no hasty conclusion should be made from them. Yet one thing remains clear from the biblical text. The area of Edom-Midian, prior to Israel's exodus from Egypt, was not left out by Yahweh-El, but rather the people who lived there were monotheists. This becomes a further confirmation that the knowledge of God was common among the children of the east, whether Edomites or Ishmaelites, during the patriarchal age. This should not be strange since both lines are descendants of Abraham.

This background study of the book of Job revealed, among other things, a crucial religious fact belonging to ancient Arabs. The high theology of Job and his friends presents strong evidence of the monotheistic atmosphere that spread over the Syro-Arabian Desert *(Qedem)*, where the Arabian children of Abraham dwelt. Thus, while Israel was gestating in Egypt's womb, being prepared for delivery, the godly Abrahamic heritage was in display in Arabia. It was to the Arabian shelter in Midian that Moses was led by God for forty years before he was called to rescue the people of Israel from bondage. It is in that sanctuary that his view of God was shaped. The relationship between Arabia and Israel was intimate from Israel's beginnings.

7

AGUR AND LEMUEL, WISE MEN FROM ARABIA

SOLOMON'S WISDOM IS SAID TO have surpassed the wisdom of all Egyptians and all the children of the east (1 Kings 4:30). While the book of Proverbs that contains the wise sayings of King Solomon has received much attention in terms of its relationship to Egyptian wisdom literature,[1] less attention has been given to the special Semitic contribution to the book.[2] Having explored the Arabian tradition behind the book of Job, we will now focus on the Ishmaelite tradition behind the appendix to the book of Proverbs (chaps. 30–31).[3]

*Massā*ʾ: An Oracle or a Kingdom?

A quick survey of different translations of the Bible reveals that Proverbs 30:1 and 31:1 have been translated in various ways by different translators. The Hebrew term *massāʾ* in both verses accounts for various peculiar translations. Should this term be understood as a reference to a prophetic oracle, or should it be taken as a proper name? Textual corruption in 30:1, and the pointing of the Masoretes in 31:1,[4] together with ignorance concerning the kingdom of Massa, contributed further to this confusion over the appropriate translation. As the

Hebrew text of 30:1 stands in its MT form, and assuming that the word *massāʾ* is to be translated "burden" or "oracle," a literal translation might be: "the words of Agur, the son of Yakeh, the burden (or prophetic oracle), oracle of the man to Ithiel." For 31:1 a literal translation would be, "the words of Lemuel, a king; a burden that his mother instructed him."

In order to overcome the awkwardness of the grammatical structure in 30:1,[5] the NRSV and the NIV replace "*the* oracle" *(hammassāʾ)* by "*an* oracle" (neglecting the definite article *ha*). The NRSV also paraphrases "oracle of the man" (Heb. *neʾûm ha-geber*) into "thus says the man" in order to remove the redundancy. For the same reason, the NIV renders these words, "This man declared to Ithiel." On the other hand, the KJV adds "even" before "the prophecy" *(hammassāʾ)*, and also paraphrases the construct phrase "oracle of the man" *(neʾûm ha-geber)* into "the man spake" in order to avoid repetitions.

The revised French translation of Louis Segond[6] ignores one of the two terms in 30:1 *(ha-geber* or *neʾûm)* completely, and thus restores the symmetry between the two coli and removes the redundancy as well. It gives an even better grammatical structure for the translated verse, rendering it, "Words of Agur, son of Yaqeh. Oracle of this man for Ethiel."[7] Possibly influenced by rabbinic tradition, the Targum of Proverbs renders 30:1a, "the words of Agur son of Yaqeh, *who received* the prophecy."[8] Alternative ways of dealing with this difficulty abound and are too many to cite here.

With respect to Proverbs 31:1,[9] the Septuagint text renders it, "my words spoken by God; an oracle of a king, which his mother taught him."[10] Thus it fails to recognize a Hebrew proper name in *Lemûʾêl*, but renders it "for God," and takes the Hebrew *melek* ("king") as genitive of *massāʾ* (translated "oracle"). Again, the Aramaic Targum renders Proverbs 31:1a, "the words of Lemuel the king: the Prophecy,"[11] turning the two indeterminate Hebrew words, *melek massāʾ*, into a determinate form "the king; the prophecy" for the sake of grammatical and syntactical soundness.

The Case for Ishmaelite Wisdom

A Better Translation

By failing to recognize *massāʾ* as the proper name of an Ishmaelite kingdom, the above translations have sentence structures that involve many grammatical and stylistic compromises. This writer prefers a view favored by a majority of scholars today,[12] opting to translate *massāʾ* in Proverbs 30:1 and 31:1 as a proper name. This translation is attested in the medieval version *Graecus Venetus*,[13] the Arabic Van Dyke version,[14] and many modern English translations.[15]

The alternative translation suggested here renders the MT into the following in 30:1: "The words of Agur, son of Yakeh the Massaite; the saying of the man to Ithiel."[16] It then translates 31:1 as, "the words of Lemuel king of Massa, which his mother taught him." The arguments for this view will be divided into textual considerations and ethnic considerations.

Textual Considerations

With regard to the textual argument the main points are as follows. First, rendering *massāʾ* "a prophecy" or "an oracle" is very inappropriate for the context of Proverbs 30 and 31.[17] The word is a verbal noun from *nassāʾ*, meaning "to lift," or "to raise," with the nuance of lifting the voice in a solemn oracle,[18] and is almost always used as "the message of God as the avenger."[19]

Second, rendering *hammassāʾ* in 30:1 "the oracle" corrupts the elements of symmetry between the first two coli of the verse. There is a striking similarity between the opening statement of Agur and the opening statement of Balaam's oracles in Numbers 24:3 and David's in 2 Samuel 23:1. For example Balaam says:

"**Saying** *of Balaam* the son of Beor—**Saying** *of the man* with open eyes" (Num. 24:3).

David also introduces his speech saying:

"**Saying** *of David* the son of Jesse—**Saying** *of the man* who is lifted up" (2 Sam. 23:1).

Compare Agur's opening statement:

"**Words** *of Agur* son of Yakeh *hammassā̲ʾ(i?)*—**Saying** *of the man* to Ithiel" (Prov. 30:1a–b).

A simple comparison of the oracles shows that the parallelism involved in the two opening coli is as follows: **Saying** (in construct structure) + *name* of the speaker (in subjective genitive structure) + a statement of origin. The two ending coli would have: **Saying** (in construct structure) + *the man* (in subjective genitive structure) + a descriptive statement.

If the word *hammassāʾ* is to be translated as "the oracle," it not only looks odd for Semitic syntax,[20] but it also corrupts the parallelism between the coli. The symmetrical elements would then become as follows: **Saying** + *name* + a statement of origin + **oracle**—**Saying** + *man* + a descriptive statement. It is obvious, as it stands, that "the oracle" is an unwanted addition, since it affects the symmetrical structure, to say nothing of the redundancy caused by the immediate mention of "saying" after the word *hammassāʾ*.[21] However, the solution, as good as it looks, does not involve dropping one of the two terms, as the French translator Segond did (see above). The simplest solution is to translate the term as "the Massaite" or "from Massa," which are possible emendations of the Hebrew text.[22] Only then is the awkwardness removed and parallelism preserved.[23]

Third, K. Kitchen goes into great detail in comparing the structure of the different collections of sayings in Proverbs with extrabiblical wisdom literature. By comparing different title structures, he concludes that the phrase *Lemuʾel melek massā* should be translated "Lemuel, king of Massa," exactly as the title "Solomon (son of David), king of Israel" in Proverbs 1:1.[24] In a similar fashion, Agur's descriptive title should also introduce his origin as the Massaite, since his, Yakeh's, and Lemuel's names are all foreign to Hebrew literature.

Fourth, translating *lemûʾel melek* in 31:1a as "Lemuel the king (or king Lemuel)" is a "linguistic impossibility."[25] In order for *melek* to become a title for Lemuel, it should be determinated *(lemûʾêl hammelek)* as the Targum renders it, *lemûʾêl malkāʾ*.[26] Though the Masoretes' spacing implies an ending of the first colon after *massāʾ*, the athnach associated with *melek* instead breaks the sentence before *massāʾ*, thus isolating it from *melek* and combining it with *lemûʾel*, likely because they saw in Lemuel a *nom-de-plume* for Solomon, as many medieval rabbis believed.[27]

However, keeping the athnach under *melek* rather than shifting it to *massāʾ* makes the verb *yisserattû* (meaning, "instructed him") refer to *massāʾ* rather than to *dibrey* ("words"). As Crenshaw articulated it, "*massāʾ* in the sense of prophetic oracle . . . one 'proclaims' rather than 'instructs.'"[28] Therefore, the indeterminate form of the two terms *melek massāʾ* strongly argues for shifting the athnach to *massā*, taking both terms as a construct-genitive structure to be translated "king of Massa" in accord with sound Hebrew grammar.[29]

After highlighting literary and textual issues, it becomes necessary to consider the following arguments for the non-Israelite nature of the sayings of Agur and Lemuel.

Ethnic Considerations

There is wide agreement that the sayings of Agur and Lemuel, though Semitic, are non-Israelite in their origin.[30] It seems that this fact is also recognized by the Septuagint, though it failed to identify the proper names of Agur and Lemuel. In fact, the LXX puts the sayings of Agur and Lemuel immediately after 24:22, which is the verse that terminates the "sayings of the wise" (22:17–24:22). As pointed out earlier, that is a section of Proverbs in which scholars see a clear dependence on Egyptian wisdom.[31] Thus this may indicate recognition by the LXX translators of the non-Israelite tradition behind the sayings of Agur and Lemuel. By putting these sayings after the Words of the Wise, the Septuagint sees in the book of Proverbs a fair representation of Egyptian wisdom and that of the children of the east, both admired by the Israelites.

As far as the names are concerned, Agur[32] and Yakeh are not attested in Old Testament literature. However, they have been attested in the onomasticon (body of names) of south and north Arabia.[33] Lemuel also does not occur anywhere in Hebrew literature. Jirku, based on the Mari texts, has proposed for Lemuel the meaning "Lim is God."[34] However, it is better to see it as meaning "belonging to God."[35] The name *moʾêl* occurs also in south Arabian inscriptions as a woman's proper name, and it is similar to Lemuel of chapter 31.[36] Since Proverbs 31 introduces the words of Lemuel as those *which his mother taught him,* "the suspicion occurs that this name is not to be interpreted 'belonging to Il', but 'belonging to Mau'il.'"[37] Massa is not an unidentified kingdom; in fact, he is one of the children of Ishmael (Gen. 25:12–18), and his kingdom is the URU*Maas-ʾa-a-a* that Tiglath Pileser received tribute from around 735 B.C.,[38] which was probably referred to by Ptolemy as the *Masanoi* of the Arabian Desert,[39] and Winnett locates somewhere between *Taymāʾ* and *al-Jawf.*[40]

Internal Ethnic Evidence

Arabic Influence

It has been noted by scholars that there are several affinities in the section belonging to Agur and Lemuel with Aramaic and Arabic languages, in addition to a clear dependence of the first statements of Agur on Job 38. In this regard, Tur-Sinai argued that Agur's inquiries and their answers are understandable only in light of Job's conditions, since the dilemma that Agur was facing is very similar to that of Job when he questioned the justice of God and his power.[41] Furthermore, Margoliouth pointed out the existence in Proverbs 30:31 of the word *ʾel-qom,* which most probably has to be identified with north Arabic *ʾal-Qawm,* meaning "the men," referring here to the troops.[42] In his description of the structure of society among the Rwala bedouins, Musil notes:

> The word *ḳowm* indicates the Bedouins ruled by a chief. Thus it is possible to say: "*Ḳowm eben shaʿlān*, he is of the *ḳowm* of Eben *shaʿlān;*" "the *ḳowm* of Eben Meʾjel are encamped there; the *ḳowm* of Eben Jandal also took part in the raid"; but such a phrase as: "That is the *ḳowm* of the Rwala" or "He is descended from the *ḳowm* of the Freje" will never be heard.[43]

Thus Musil's remarks suggest a close link between the bedouin use of the term and the troop of men led by their tribal leader (king), as Proverbs 30:31 suggests.

It is also significant to note that Rabbi Saadia, in his Arabic translation of Proverbs, refers to King Hezekiah's men (25:1) as *qawm* Ḥazaqiyyā al-malik.[44] Since the parallel expression of this word is the usual Hebrew word for troop *(gedûd)*, used in Job 29:25, this "seems to render this interpretation of the text in Proverbs certain; for in both the confidence which the presence of his army confers upon the king is noted."[45]

Aramaic Influence

According to E. Lipinski, the word *makhôt* in Proverbs 31:3 is definitely of Aramaic origin, and *malakîn* is an Aramaic plural. Therefore, he believes the expression *makhôt malakîn* should be translated "the kings' female diviners."[46]

All the evidence cited above, whether textual or ethnic, argued clearly for identifying Agur as "son of Yakeh of Massa (or the Massaite)" and Lemuel as "king of Massa," where Massa is one of the Ishmaelite tribal kingdoms of north Arabia, and should not be translated in this context as "a burden." Thus Agur and Lemuel were Arab sages from the "descendants of Hagar who seek wisdom on the earth" (Baruch 3:23). They must have found the truth in God's revelation through their Hebrew kin.[47] Delitzsch concludes his discussion on the identity of these biblical figures by saying, "We regard it as more probable that King Lemuel and his countryman Agur were Ishmaelites who had raised themselves above the religion of Abraham [*Dîn Ibrâhîm*, a belief, which along with Mosaism, continues among nomadic tribes in north Arabia] and recognized the religion of Israel as its completion."[48]

The significance of this conclusion lies in the fact that the wisdom of the children of the east (1 Kings 4:30) becomes once again a part of the Hebrew canon. Not only does the book of Job rely on north Arabian tradition, the sayings of Agur and Lemuel do also. By displaying strong piety and a knowledge of God and Yahweh (Prov. 30:2–9; 31:1, 8), these two sages are a clear example of conversions to Yahweh among the Gentiles due to Israel's "light." This light impacted primarily Israel's closest kin, the Arabian descendants of Abraham through Ishmael.

The united monarchy, a period of climactic glory for Israel and an embodiment of Yahweh's presence among the nations, was the time when non-Israelite godly literature was integrated into the Hebrew canon. It is likely that Solomon, with his international outlook and deep love for wisdom, promoted an intense exchange of wisdom literature (1 Kings 4:30–34). If the "Words of the Wise" were the reminiscences of a godly Egyptian scribe in the court of Solomon, as Ruffle proposes, could the sayings of Agur and Lemuel be introduced by the Ishmaelite officials who ministered in the cabinet of David and Solomon (1 Chron. 2:17; 27:30–31)?

Ishmael in the Song of Songs

At the end of this survey of "Arabs in the Light of Israel" a word should be said about the Song of Songs. Hitti has suggested an Ishmaelite origin for the Shulammite in the book.[49] With her being "black" (or "dark"), associated with "the tents of Qedar"[50] (Song 1:5) from extensive exposure to the sun in the wilderness (1:6), and coming from the desert as a bedouin perfumed with all the spices of Arabia (3:6; cf. Ps. 72:10–15; 1 Kings 10:10; Isa. 60:6–7), there may be some evidence that Solomon's beloved was an Arabian Ishmaelite. Moses' wife was an Arabian from Midian (Exod. 2). Furthermore, the great affinity of the descriptive similes used in the book with nomadic hymns of love and Arabian erotic poetry may be a further indication for such a proposal.[51] However, the book also presents affinities with other ancient Near Eastern literature,[52] and Hitti's suggestion for the Ishmaelite origin of Solomon's bride, the Shulammite, though it may offer an explanation for the Arabic name of his daughter (Basma), is beyond proof. However, a case may be made, as Seale argues, for the literary affinity existing in the book of Songs with desert Ishmaelite culture.[53] Thus this piece of inspired Hebrew poetry reflects, together with Job and Proverbs 30–31, a positive atmosphere between Israel and Ishmael during the united monarchy.

Summary of Part 2 Findings

Part 2 surveyed the period starting from the time of Abraham's dismissal of Ishmael and his mother until the end of the united monarchy. One aim of the survey was to find out how God fulfilled his oracles on Ishmael given to the slave woman in the wilderness (Gen. 16:12). A related goal was to trace the relationships that existed between the line of Abraham's firstborn and the Israelite line during that period of history.[54] The historical narratives revealed an extended period of positive relations between both groups, interrupted only by seven years of hostilities between Israel and the surrounding nomadic tribes led by the Midianites. The children of the east appeared in the book of Judges to be plagued with idolatry as Israel struggled with syncretism (8:2–28; 21:25) before its consolidation as a kingdom. A second incident of deadly fighting over grazing land happened during the days of King Saul and is mentioned in 1 Chronicles 5:10, 19–22. After that no hostilities were related between the Israelites and their kin the Ishmaelites. During the period of the united monarchy, the overall relationships between both groups were friendly, to such an extent that Arab Ishmaelites shared ministerial responsibilities under David and Solomon and were part of the closer family circle (1 Chron. 2:17; 27:30–31).

God chose Abraham, as Scriptures tell us, in order for him to instruct his children after him to keep the ways of the Lord in their generations (Gen. 18:19). The book of Job, written against a late patriarchal background, revealed the high theology and sweeping monotheism that characterized the children of the east during that time period. The monotheistic atmosphere that reigned in the Arabian Desert among these other children of Abraham was part of the godly heritage inherited by Arab Ishmaelites from the great patriarch. This heritage was reflected early on in their history, as the book of Job makes evident.

The Song of Solomon only reflected affinities with desert culture and Arabian love poetry. However, the appendix to the book of Proverbs showed that Agur, Lemuel, and his mother were north Arabian Massaite sages who came to full knowledge of the Lord through Israel's light, likely during the united monarchy. Thus the book of Job, along with the sayings of Agur and Lemuel, were examples of Ishmaelite wisdom literature "thought worthy of a place in the religious literature of the Jews."[55] This integration of the eastern wisdom tradition may indicate that our biblical heritage includes Arab elements in it alongside the Hebrew legacy, which forms the bulk of its corpus. This should be considered from a positive perspective. Israel's testimony during the period of "Light" may be likened to that of the apostolic church, which may have led to the integration of Gentile-inspired writings in the Jewish New Testament. In fact, it is widely accepted that Luke, a Gentile physician (Col. 4:10–14), wrote the books of Luke and Acts, which comprise about 28 percent of the New Testament. If this was true in the church era, why should it not be expected during Israel's glorious period, when the Solomonic reign displayed Yahweh's glory among the nations around as a testimony for the true God (Isa. 42:6; 49:6)? Furthermore, who more than Ishmael should be expected to be integrated into the Abrahamic legacy of the Hebrew people? After all, Hagar's son was predicted to dwell in "the proximity," "alongside," or "in the presence" of all his brethren as decreed by God (Gen. 16:12c). Evidence confirms this to be a word of integration rather than as a word of alienation and hostility as is often believed.

PART 3

ARABS IN THE DARKNESS OF ISRAEL

8

WHAT BECAME OF ISHMAEL?

GREATER PRIVILEGES NORMALLY COME WITH greater responsibilities, which, when ignored, may lead to failure. Accordingly, it is ironic, yet commonly experienced in the Bible, that spiritual peak and physical prosperity are often coupled with a threat of apostasy, pride, and peril. That is true on individual level, and when the individual is Israel's king it becomes true on a national level as well.

Thus the glorious kingdom of Solomon, which constituted the golden age of the theocratic nation, also started Israel's spiritual apostasy and national decline. After Solomon's apostasy in his last years (1 Kings 11:1–13) the monarchy split into two political entities in the days of his son Rehoboam (1 Kings 12). The northern kingdom consistently yielded wicked kings who did what was evil in the sight of Yahweh. Consequently, their capital Samaria fell to the Assyrians and the citizens suffered deportation to Assyria in 722 B.C.

The southern kingdom itself produced only a few kings who pleased the Lord; the majority of its rulers followed the evil pattern of the northern kings. Eventually, the kingdom of Judah in its turn underwent grievous discipline and many of its people were deported by the Babylonians in 586 B.C. Though restored to the land after serving in exile, the Jews never again functioned as a Davidic kingdom. True, they were sovereign during the Hasmonean rule (143–63 B.C.), but they did not have any ruler from the Davidic line (2 Sam. 7:12–16). Thus their testimony as "light to the Gentiles" was obscured during the "Darkness of Israel" period, which covers a big chunk of the first millennium before the first coming of the Messiah.

Part 2 dealt with historical Ishmael in Israel's life during its uphill history. Part 3 considers Ishmael during the following downhill period. From Israel's standpoint, this period is covered in biblical books written against the historical background of the divided monarchy until the postexilic era. From the perspective of secular history, the period includes Neo-Assyrian, Neo-Babylonian, Persian, Hellenistic, and early Roman rules.[1] We detected a positive impact of Israel on Ishmael during the "Light" period. Would the "Darkness" of the nation characterized by syncretism and idolatry influence the Arab Ishmaelites as well? The following survey of Arabs during the first millennium B.C. may reveal, among other things, the answer to this question. For this purpose, we first identify individual Ishmaelite tribes. Subsequently, we present a historical sketch of the Ishmaelites and their relationships with neighboring political powers.

Cuneiform texts, including Neo-Assyrian and Neo-Babylonian chronicles, supply the primary extrabiblical source of information for the ninth to the sixth centuries B.C.[2] Starting from the sixth century, ancient north Arabian inscriptions supplement the information.[3] Classical historians such as Herodotus and Xenophon form the main source for the Persian period. Though a large number of Nabataean inscriptions were discovered up to this time, they are mostly graffiti,[4] and thus the reconstruction of Nabataean history relies primarily on classical sources, whether Greek, Latin, or Jewish.[5] Biblical information about the Ishmaelites during this period is gleaned primarily from the prophetic books, though the other biblical material written against a divided monarchy background will be considered.

The Twelve Princes of Ishmael

Of the twelve sons of Ishmael as they appear in Genesis 25:12–18,[6] only six are explicitly mentioned in cuneiform inscriptions (Nebayot, Qedar, Adbeel, Dumah, Massā', and Taymā').[7] The following section is a general overview of the extant historical information that pertains to the individual tribes descending from Ishmael.

Nebayot: Ishmael's Privileged Son

Nebayot is the firstborn of Ishmael (Gen. 25:13). Along with Qedar, the tribe of Nebayot was renowned for sheep raising (Isa. 60:7). These two names are often mentioned together in Assyrian records.[8] However, while Qedar often clashed with the Assyrians, Nebayot seemed to be less accessible to them.[9] Cuneiform texts suggest the Nebayot tribe was located somewhere south of the depression of *Sirḥān* to the east of Edom.[10] Two graffiti inscriptions found by Winnett and Reed on Jabal Ghunayem near Taymā' mentioning the name *Nabayāt* suggest a presence of Nebayot somewhere north of that oasis, but the exact location of this tribe is not known.[11] Some scholars have identified Nebayot with the Nabataean Arabs.[12] However, since Nabataean is spelled with an emphatic *ṭet* instead of a simple *taw* as in Nebayot, and the *yod* has been completely dropped, this correlation based on philological ground has been dismissed by many contemporary Orientalists.[13]

Dumah: Hong Kong of North Arabia

Dumah is generally identified with Assyrian *Adummatu*.[14] Esarhaddon relates how, in his attempt to subdue the Arabs, his father Sennacherib struck against their headquarters *Adummatu*, which he called "the stronghold of the Arabs," where he captured their king Haza'el, whom he calls "king of the Arabs."[15] Haza'el is also referred to in one inscription of Ashurbanipal as "king of the Qedarites."[16] From a geographical standpoint, Assyrian *Adummatu* is associated with medieval

Arabic Dûmat el-Jandal,[17] which was in ancient times a very important and strategic junction on the major trade route that linked Syria and Babylonia to Najd and the Hejaz area.[18] Dûmat el-Jandal lies at the southeastern end of al-Jawf, which means "the basin," and "denotes the whole lower region of Wādî-as-Sirḥān,"[19] the famous depression situated halfway between Syria and Mesopotamia. This depression with its plentiful water supply constituted a vital station for caravan traders coming from Taymāʾ before they proceeded to Syria or to Babylonia.[20]

This strategic location made Dumah the gate of north Arabia.[21] This oasis was the center of rule for many north Arabian queens and kings, as appears from Assyrian records.[22] Thus it was the religious and political center of the Ishmaelites in the north,[23] and hence an important target for the Assyrian kings and other invaders.

Qedar: Master of the Desert

Though Dumah was a great political, economic, and religious center in the north, it is Qedar that was the dominant military power of the Ishmaelites there.[24] Isaiah speaks of the great might of Qedar, its glory, and its gifted "archers" (Isa. 21:16–17). In his prophecy against Israel, Jeremiah refers to Kittim (RSV, Cyprus) and Qedar to denote "west" and "east" (Jer. 2:10). In a different setting, Jeremiah uses Qedar as a synonym for the children of the east (Jer. 49:28), and Ezekiel 27:21 associates "Arabia" with "all the princes of Qedar," suggesting a confederation of tribes under its leadership.[25] Thus it appears that in the prophetic era (800–450 B.C.) Qedar was the controlling Ishmaelite power in north Arabia west of the Euphrates.

This biblical profile of Ishmael's second son is further attested in cuneiform texts. In these inscriptions, Qedar appears to have occupied the Syrian Desert between Dumah and Tadmor (Palmyra), dominating a major part of the Syro-Arabian Desert.[26] As such, the Qedarites were in constant conflict with the Assyrians. Assyria, as well as the Neo-Babylonians, the Persians, and later the Romans, realized the importance of taking control of the commercial routes in north Arabia that were practically under the dominion of the Qedarites and their allies, and later the Nabataeans.[27] Onomastic studies have detected an infiltration of north Arabians, Qedarites in particular, into Babylonia and Assyria as early as the eighth century B.C.[28]

North Arabian inscriptions recovered in lower Egypt and Dedan have been the basis for identifying Nehemiah's opponent "Geshem the Arabian" as one of the kings of Qedar in mid-fifth century B.C.[29] The bowl inscription of Tell el-Maskḫuta may suggest a Qedarite presence in the Delta region of Egypt in the fifth century B.C.[30] It seems that after the middle of the fourth century the Qedarites disappeared from the records of history under this name.[31] However, arguing from historical continuity, Knauf thinks that "most probably the Nabataeans emerged from the tribe of Qedar."[32]

Assyrian inscriptions speak of Sennacherib's capturing of Arabian deities found in Dumah.[33] The chief deity was Atarsamain, "the morning star of heaven,"[34] the counterpart of Mesopotamian Ishtar.[35] In fact, the tribal league led by Qedar in the north was called by the Assyrians "the confederation of the god Atarsamain," whose cult was led by a series of queen-priestesses in Dumah.[36] The rest of the pantheon consists of the gods Dai, Nuhai (Nuhay), Ruldai (Ruḍa), Abirillu, and Atarquruma. While nothing is known about Dai, Abirillu, and Atarquruma, Thamudic graffiti later revealed that the deities Ruḍa, "the evening star," and Nuhay, "the sun-god," continued to be worshiped in addition to the chief deity, Atarsamain.[37] Herodotus in the fifth century identified two deities worshiped among the Arabs he met, a fertility god called Orotalt,[38] and a sky goddess Alilat, to be equated with Han-Ilat *(Allāt)* of the Tell el-Maskhûṭa bowl.[39]

Adbe'el: Sinai's Gatekeeper

Adbe'el (Gen. 25:13; 1 Chron. 1:29) is most likely to be identified with Idibi'ilu "of the land of Arubu"[40] who became a vassal of Tiglath Pileser III (744–727 B.C.) and was assigned the duty of being the Assyrian king's agent on the borders of Egypt.[41] His tribe was said to have dwelt far away "towards the west."[42] This fits the description of the western part of the Sinai area.[43]

Massā': The Wisdom Seeker

Massā' is the seventh of the children of Ishmael (Gen. 25:14; 1 Chron. 1:30). Tiglath Pileser III again refers to tribes from north Arabia that paid him tribute, including "the inhabitants of Mas'a [and] of Tema."[44] On the summit of Jabal Ghunayem, located about 14 kilometers south of Taymāʾ, Winnett and Reed discovered some graffiti texts mentioning the tribe Massā' in connection with Dedan and Nebayot.[45] These texts refer to the "war against Dedan," the "war against Nabayat," and the "war against Massā.'"[46] Thus these three tribes are put close to each other. Musil locates Massā' somewhere "in close proximity to the southern border of the Damascan territory and the western bound of the Aribi."[47] However, Musil's decision is influenced by the identification of Nabataeans as Nebayot, which is not very sure.[48] Thus Ephʿal's conclusion that the evidence point to "North Arabia, but to no specific territory within it" is still safer.[49] Finally, the tribe of Massā' is possibly connected with *masanoi* of north Arabia mentioned by Ptolemy,[50] and is the tribe where Lemuel, his mother, and Agur son of Yaqeh, the sages of Proverbs 30 and 31, originated.

Taymāʾ: The Chief Caravan City

Taymāʾ, the ninth of the children of Ishmael (Gen. 25:15; 1 Chron. 1:30), is normally associated with the ancient oasis of Taymāʾ, located northeast of the Hejaz district on the trade route between Yathrib (Medina) and Dumah.[51] Between Taymāʾ and Dumah "stands the most horrifying of north Arabian deserts, the Nafûd."[52] This desert is essentially composed of a series of sand dunes extending over 400 kilometers from north to south, which justifiably caused it to be called "the China Wall of Arabia" since it protected the peninsula from significant attacks from the north.[53] It is generally recognized that the present city of Taymāʾ, lying at the southwestern end of the Nafûd, is built on the remains of the ancient oasis by the same name.[54]

The earliest extrabiblical reference to Taymāʾ is found in the Assyrian inscriptions of Tiglath Pileser III. This Assyrian king claims to have received tributes from Taymā᾽ as well as from other Arabian oases.[55] Taymā᾽ was also one of the Arabian regions against which Jeremiah prophesied (Jer. 25:23).

The desert setting of Taymā᾽ and its involvement in trade is also affirmed by Job 6:19, which refers to caravans from this city needing water. Isaiah 21:14 invites the people of Taymā᾽ to provide water and food for their fugitive countrymen, in an apparent allusion to Tiglath Pileser's invasion of north Arabia in 738 B.C.[56] Assyrian records mention how this king defeated a coalition headed by Samsi, queen of the Arabs, and including Massā', the city of Taymā᾽, and the tribes of Saba', Hajappa, Badana, Hatti, and Idiba'il,[57] whose countries are far "towards the west."[58] Subsequently these tribes had to send tributes of gold, silver, camels, and spices of all kinds.[59] It should be noted that Sennacherib named one of his gates at Nineveh "the Desert Gate" and recognized the highly strategic position of Taymā᾽ as the door of the desert with the explanation, "The Gifts of the Sumu'anite and the Temeite Enter through it."[60]

Around 552 B.C. the Babylonian king Nabonidus (555–539 B.C.), the father of biblical Belshazzar (Dan. 5:1–31; 7:1), made the city of Taymā᾽ his residence and spent ten out of the sixteen years of his reign there.[61] Again, the inscriptions found 14 kilometers from the city of Taymā᾽ at the summit of Jabal Ghunayem refer to wars made against different north Arabian tribes (Massā', Nabayat, and Dedan).[62] Winnett and Reed see it unlikely for an oasis dependent on trade and peace like Taymā᾽ to involve itself in wars against its neighbors.[63] This is why they prefer to link the war mentioned against Massā' and Nabayat with Nabonidus' settlement in Taymā᾽ and suggest the possibility that the inhabitants of Taymā᾽ participated in these wars.[64] The Harran inscriptions do not explicitly mention attacks against Nabayat or Massā' by Nabonidus; however, one passage refers to the conflict with the "people of the land of the Arabs."[65]

The city of Taymā᾽ continued to prosper during the fifth century, and many of its inhabitants infiltrated Babylonia during that period.[66] In the Achaemenid period, the city probably became the seat of one of the Persian emperors.[67] By the first century B.C., the Nabataeans dominated Taymāʾ as part of their strategy to control the principal north Arabian trade stations.[68]

The Remaining Ishmaelite Tribes

Not a whole lot is known about the rest of Ishmael's sons. Montgomery suggests that "Yetur, Naphish, and Kedemah form a group together," Kedemah being another designation of the land of *benê qedem* (cf. earlier discussion).[69] Yetur, Naphish, and the Hagarenes are located by 1 Chronicles 5:19 in the Transjordan.[70] Yetur may be at the origin of the Itureans, mentioned in Luke 3:1, who were established in the Biqāᶜ Valley and the southern Anti-Lebanon district.[71] Finally, Ḥadad, Mibsam, and Mishmaᶜ cannot be identified further because of the lack of references concerning them. However, Montgomery notes that Hadad may be parallel to Hadoram, which appears among the descendants of Joktan (Gen. 10:26–30).[72] Musil proposes a better solution, which consists in emending Hadad into Harar, and identifies this tribe with the Ḥurarina people that lived by the mountain range northwest of Palmyra, which he calls the northern boundaries of the Ishmaelites.[73] Mibsam and Mishmaᶜ have been detected earlier as merging under the Simeonites (1 Chron. 4:24–27), and this is likely why they do not appear separately later in history.[74]

9

ARABS HAUNTED BY WORLD POWERS

HAVING IDENTIFIED IN THE PREVIOUS chapter the individual tribes of Ishmael in attested history, a chronological survey within the time frame of the first millennium B.C. follows. For this purpose, scriptural passages referring to Ishmaelites in nonprophetic material will be considered first. Subsequently, a survey of extrabiblical material will unfold Ishmael's relationship with foreign powers during this period. Prophetic references concerning Ishmaelites will be integrated in this historical survey since most of these prophecies were made against an Assyrian or Babylonian background.

Though Israel's neighboring foes were subdued during David's rule and peace reigned during Solomon's era, with the division of Israel's kingdom (931 B.C.) problems with these foes started once again as predicted by God (2 Sam. 7:14).[1] Psalm 83 seems to belong to this troublesome period in Israel's history. This psalm lists Ishmaelites and Hagarites as part of a coalition of Israel's foes (v. 6). The psalm is notoriously difficult to date since it does not refer to any specific historical event. Nevertheless, commentators have assumed all the possibilities from Samuel's time to the days of the Maccabees, yet with no definite conclusions.[2] However, the psalm lists the Assyrians as joining the coalition of Israel's enemies (v. 8). Thus it should be dated during the period of Assyrian threat against Israel. On the other hand, since Tyre is mentioned as one of the foes also (v. 7), the date cannot be prior to Amos's period because Tyre had kept a friendly relationship with Israel until that time (750 B.C.).[3] Therefore, the setting should be a preexilic one, or possibly, as Dumbrell suggests, within the timeframe of 750–722 B.C.[4] Still, historical reconstruction is impossible, since the text does not describe an actual attack, but an aggressive heart attitude of foes. Thus the best solution is that offered by Kraus, where "the prophetic singer is viewing an 'assault of nations' and authenticates the same with an array of specific names."[5]

Other than the previous passage there is practically no significant mention of Ishmaelites in nonprophetic material. Thus consideration of extrabiblical texts and prophetic references becomes necessary at this point.

EARLY FIRST MILLENNIUM B.C.

Apart from a brief reference, the first two centuries of the first millennium B.C. yield no information about Arabians in extrabiblical manuscripts. Macdonald notes that no pottery found in the Arabian Peninsula is "securely dated to the period between the eleventh and the sixth centuries."[6] This has led to suggestions that either the oases were not yet populated, or that Arabians lived totally a nomadic life before the sixth century B.C.[7] This last option seems more acceptable[8] and in agreement with biblical data gleaned so far. Winnett and Reed think that "the presence at Taymāʾ of the great well called al-Haddāj makes it highly probable that human occupation of the oasis dates back to a very remote period."[9] However, in view of the relative neglect that has characterized the archaeological work in Arabia in comparison with other areas of the ancient Near East, only further digs and findings may uncover the whole scenario of ancient Arabian civilization. Della Vida's old comments are still to the point despite the increasing interest[10] in that domain:

> Unfortunately, our knowledge of ancient Arabia is scanty and incomplete. What we know about it is just enough to let us understand how much we don't know. . . . Our most valuable help in the attempt to attain an understanding of pre-Islamic Arabia is epigraphical evidence, but by its very nature it is one-sided and obscure. Archaeological evidence is missing entirely, since regular excavations have never taken place in any part of Arabia.[11]

As pointed out at the outset of this study, the first text that refers to an Arab in secular history is found in the context of a battle that Shalmaneser III was involved in at Qarqar on the Orontes in Syria, in 853 B.C. There Shalmaneser III faced a coalition of forces that included Ahab of Israel, and a certain chief, named Gindibu' (Ar. *Jundub* = grasshopper or locust), who supplied the opponents of Assyria with a thousand camels.[12] Nothing else is mentioned about this man, and no other reference in the ninth century provides any information on north Arabian tribes.

Subdued by Tiglath Pileser III (745–727 B.C.)

The Assyrian records do not refer to Arabs between 853 B.C. and 738 B.C.[13] Beginning with the seventh year of the reign of Tiglath Pileser III (745–727), references to Arabians increase in the Assyrian chronicles[14] because of the recurrent attacks against Syria and Palestine.[15] It has been conjectured that north Arabian nomads were not directly endangered by the Assyrians, but their main concern was to keep the Assyrian military activities from jeopardizing their trade business.[16] Nevertheless, these Arabs proved to be "a constant thorn in the side of Assyria."[17] Starting with Tiglath Pileser III, the Assyrian records reveal peculiar information about a series of north Arabian queens. What the exact function of these queens was, the chronicles do not clarify. Still, their political and religious authority is made evident by the texts.[18] Thus, having occupied Gaza, installed Idi-bi'ili (Adbe'el) as his agent on the Egyptian border,[19] and cut the "incense road,"[20] Tiglath Pileser III received much tribute consisting of gold, silver, cattle, and other precious goods from many rulers, including "Menahem of Samaria" and Zabibi, "the queen of Arabia."[21]

Shortly after, Queen Samsi (Ar. *Shams,* meaning "sun"),[22] also called "queen of Arabia," rebelled against Tiglath Pileser, allying herself with the Damascus-Israel-Tyre coalition, but the coalition was totally defeated and the queen fled to the land of Bazu.[23] Later, she returned and was permitted to stay in power,[24] "probably because the Assyrians knew there was no substitute for the cooperation of the Arabs in the maintenance of the north-south trade."[25] However, Samsi was forced to bring tribute to the Assyrians and her defeat prompted seven other kingdoms involved in Arabian trade to bring tribute in order to secure the safety of their incense trade.[26] These were, Massāʾ, Taymāʾ, Sabaʾ, Haiappa (ʿEphah), Badana, Hattia, and Idibiʾlu,[27] and their tribute was comprised of "gold, silver, male and female camels and all kinds of spices."[28] Consequently, Tiglath-Pileser III was the first foreign ruler "to fasten the yoke on Arabian necks."[29]

Crushed by Sargon II (722–705 B.C.)

No matter how powerful the Assyrian subjection of Arab kingdoms along the "incense road" appeared to be, it seems that it was only temporary and incomplete.[30] In fact, Sargon II (722–705 B.C.) claimed to have crushed during his reign the tribes of Tamud, Ibadidi, Marsimanu, and Haiapa, "the Arabs who live, far away in the desert (and) who know neither overseers nor official(s) and who had not (yet) brought their tribute to any king."[31] Sargon II went on to say that he deported their survivors and "settled them in Samaria."[32] Yet Sargon's exaggeration in stating his success against the Arabs[33] is evident, for Thamud turns out to be a very prominent north Arabian tribe in postbiblical pre-Islamic times.[34]

Later Sargon II received gifts from the pharaoh of Egypt, from "the queen of the Arabs," Samsi, and It'amra, king of Saba.[35] The significance of Queen Samsi and the Arabs to Assyria is acknowledged by her mention alongside Pharaoh and the king of Saba,[36] which clarifies why "despite her repeated rebellions they did not depose her."[37] In a sense, there was no way for the Assyrians to render the existence of these nomads meaningless. Their bedouin lifestyle and ability to flee to remote parts of the inner desert made the military attempts to conquer them not only temporary and costly, but jeopardized the benefits of an uninterrupted incense trade.[38] Thus the Assyrians preferred to secure the collaboration of these Arabians and incorporate them somehow within the administrative structure of their kingdom.[39] During the remaining years of his reign, Sargon II did not have any more recorded troubles with the Arab nomads.

RULED BY SENNACHERIB V (704–681 B.C.)

During the reign of Sennacherib (704–681 B.C.) Arabs appear to have supported a rebellion in Babylon against Assyria. Some of them worked as mercenaries in service of the Chaldaean rebel, Merodach-baladan II in Babylon.[40] Eventually Sennacherib subdued the desert nomads led by Hazaʾel, king of Qedar, and the queen priestess Te'elhunu, who assisted Hazaʾel and those who rebelled in Babylonia against Assyrian suzerainty.[41] Both Hazaʾel and Te'elhunu took refuge in Adummatu (Dumah), "the fortress of the Arabs," where Sennacherib followed them. The besieged city eventually fell into his hands and Te'elhunu was captured and taken to Assyria, together with much spoil and the divine images of the Arabs.[42]

In the midst of all these military activities in north Arabia, it seems that the Arabian incense trade did not suffer a setback as a result,[43] and because of Sennacherib's "considerable prestige among the Arabs,"[44] Herodotus even makes him "king of Arabians and Assyrians."[45]

HARASSED BY ESARHADDON (680–669 B.C.)

Despite the Assyrian dominance over north Arabians under Sennacherib V, Hazaʾel managed somehow to stay in power. However, he soon realized that he could not unite all his men behind him, having suffered the loss of his religious emblems.[46] So he went to Nineveh with "heavy gifts" and begged Esarhaddon, Sennacherib's son and successor (680–669 B.C.), to return the images of Atarsamain, Dai, Nuhai, Ruldaiu, Abirillu, and Atarquruma,[47] which the Assyrian king returned after writing on them "an inscription (proclaiming) the (superior) might of Ashur," his "lord."[48] Esarhaddon obtained from Hazaʾel at that point an additional amount of tribute and sent with him a certain girl named Ta(r)bûʿa, of Arab descent, who was raised in the palace of his father Sennacherib who appointed her as a queen over the Arabs.[49]

Soon after that Hazaʾel died, and Iataʾ (Yauthaʿ, Uaiteʿ), his son, was set as his successor, having committed himself to boosting the tribute due to Esarhaddon.[50] However, it seems that the increase in tribute weighed heavily on the people; thus between 676 and 673 B.C. a certain Wahb "induced all the Arabs to revolt against Iataʾ (Yauthaʿ)."[51] The Assyrian army that came to assist Iataʾ crushed the rebellion and took Wahb and his men captives to Assyria, where Esarhaddon "put collars on them and bound them to the posts of [his] gate."[52]

A little later, between 673 and 669 B.C.,[53] Iataʾ himself tried to free his neck from the yoke of Esarhaddon.[54] However, he was defeated and "to save his life, forsook his camp, and, fleeing alone, escaped to distant (parts)."[55] As a result of this defeat, the images of north Arabian gods were captured once again and sent to Nineveh, to be restored later under Ashurbanipal, only after Iataʾ pledged allegiance to Assyria.[56]

While these Arabs were constantly causing troubles to Assyria west of the Euphrates, Esarhaddon, as well as all subsequent kings, had no other alternative than to cooperate with them. For their mastery of the desert roads and the great caravans of camels they possessed were a vital provisional need for any attempt to extend Assyrian dominion through Sinai into Egypt.[57]

Devastated by Ashurbanipal (668–627 B.C.)

Though peaceful at first, Ashurbanipal's reign became characterized by an internal conflict between him and his "evil brother"

Shamash-shum-ukin, who was then king of Babylon.[58] Though he initially pledged allegiance to Ashurbanipal, Iataʾ, king of Arabia, joined Babylonia in revolting against Ashurbanipal. He lent his forces to a certain Abiateʾ and his brother Aamu, sons of Teʾri, in order to assist Shamash-shum-ukin in his revolt in Babylon against Assyria.[59] This Arab-Babylonian coalition prompted Ashurbanipal to launch a fierce attack against the renegades, and ended up crushing them and setting fire to Arab tents, thus removing the continuous threat of Babylonia to Assyrian power.[60] Abiateʾ escaped boldly to Nineveh and beseeched Ashurbanipal to have mercy on him. The Assyrian king honored that demand, and appointed Abiateʾ "king of Arabia" instead of Iataʾ, the son of Hazaʾel. At the same time, the defeated Iataʾ fled to King Natnu of the Nabaiati (Nebayot), who somehow (possibly betrayal)[61] sent him back to Nineveh, where Ashurbanipal severely punished him.[62]

In the meantime in the western regions, Ammuladi, who followed Iataʾ as king of Qedar (Assyr. *Qi-id-ri*) with a possible endorsement from Iataʾs wife, Adia, rebelled against Assyria and attacked some of its vassal states in the west.[63] However, the Qedarites were defeated by the king of Moab,[64] and Ammuladi and the wife of Iataʾ (Uateʾ), the son of Hazaʾel, were taken to Nineveh.[65]

As confusing as it seems, a second Uate', son of Birdada, also designated as the nephew of Iataʾ (Uateʾ), the son of Hazaʾel, appeared on the scene. Uate' II declared himself the leader of the tribal confederacy in north Arabia.[66] He also allied himself with Abiateʾ, who forsook his allegiance to Ashurbanipal, having managed to receive military support from Natnu, king of Nebayot. The Arab forces camped somewhere in the neighborhood of Damascus.[67]

Having finished dealing with the Babylonian resistance to his rule, Ashurbanipal was left to face these Arab leaders, who "called up their forces for a dangerous attack against [his] territory."[68] Thus, in view of the urgency of the situation, the Assyrian army crossed the Tigris and the Euphrates at "their highest flood."[69] Ashurbanipal occupied the local wells, vital for these nomads and their cattle's sustenance, and managed to inflict severe damage on his enemies in the Ḥauran area south of Damascus.[70] The Assyrians captured Abiateʾ, and later Uate', and punished them harshly. The only one who escaped was the king of Nebayot, Natnu. However, even Natnu was deposed later by the Assyrians, and his son, Nuhuru, was set on his throne instead.[71] After this decisive battle, the Qedarites, who led the Arab confederation in the north, are not mentioned anymore in the Assyrian records.[72] However, their might was only partially curbed by Assyria, since "they are clearly there in strength at the beginning of the Babylonian period."[73] As Knauf put it, "one has the impression that the Assyrians coped so little with their relationships in the Arabian Desert, as the Byzantines or the Ottomans did later on, and that they expected from their Arab vassal kings a loyalty, which these could never impose on their subjects."[74]

The prophecy of Isaiah 21:13–17[75] addressing north Arabian tribes should be considered at this point.[76] In fact, if this doom is treated as a unit in terms of its historical framework, then it should be taken against an Assyrian background, since Qedar's fading glory is predicted as coming shortly (v. 16). The caravans of the Dedanites have to leave the main trade routes and flee to the thickets of the wilderness because the invading army is using the "incense road" (v. 13). Furthermore, the inhabitants of Taymāʾ are called to meet the wandering Dedanites with water and food, since they are fleeing from the sword and bended bows (vv. 14–15).[77] The reason for this devastation is given in verses 16–17. The Lord has decreed that the glory of Qedar will be reduced shortly. This prophecy seems to stretch Qedarite dominion to the region of Dedan and Taymāʾ.

The doom against the Arabs (Isa. 21:13–17) was likely fulfilled in Sargon's conquest of north Arabia. The description of this conquest refers to his deportation of north Arabian tribes from the vicinity of Taymāʾ and Dedan.[78] These bedouin communities were closely dependent on each other because of their common interest in incense trade. Since the cuneiform texts identify Qedar as the major military power among north Arabian nomadic groups, it is not strange to include trade communities existing within its sphere of impact in a prophecy describing an imminent judgment of this Ishmaelite power at the hand of Assyrians.[79]

DISCIPLINED BY THE CHALDAEANS

As the Neo-Assyrian Empire declined and the Neo-Babylonians rose to dominance, the Ishmaelite confederation in the Arabian Desert had some time to restore its might, despite what seemed to be a deadly blow at the hands of Ashurbanipal between 641and 638 B.C.[80] With Nebuchadnezzar in power, Syria and Palestine came under a new military threat. Having failed a military attempt against Egypt in 601 B.C., Nebuchadnezzar retreated to his land and focused on rebuilding his power and consolidating his forces.[81] However, in view of his intentions to check the kingdom of Judah in the near future, he deemed it strategic to attack the nomadic groups in north Arabia first.[82] This attack would achieve two goals. First, it would be "an easy way of boosting the army's morale and of obtaining large amounts of booty."[83] Second, it would be a necessary step to secure his "western lines of communication" endangered by the Qedarite power in the eastern desert.[84]

Nebuchadnezzar's attack on the Qedarites is described in two sources. First, it appears in the Chaldaean chronicles.[85] Second, it is described in Jeremiah's prophecies against the nations (49:28–33).[86] The Chaldaean chronicles note:

> (9) In the sixth year in the month of Kislev the king of Akkad mustered his army and marched to the Ḥatti-land.[87] From the Ḥatti-land he sent out his companies, (10) and scouring the desert they took much plunder from the Arabs, their possessions, animals and gods. In the month of Adar the king returned to his own land.[88]

The attack against the Arabs described in these inscriptions occurred in December 599 B.C.[89] The importance of this military operation for the Chaldaeans is highlighted by the fact that Nebuchadnezzar himself led the battle.[90] Though this war seems to have been totally uncalled for,[91] it was heaven's decree as a discipline on the circumcised (Gen. 17:22–25; Jer. 9:25–26)[92] children of the east because of their deep slide into idolatry (Jer. 2:10–11). If God used the "rod of men" (2 Sam. 7:14) to discipline apostate Judah, "beginning to bring disaster on the city that is called by [his] name," how can the Qedarites escape his righteous judgment (Jer. 25:29)? Jeremiah 49:28–33 describes vividly the predicted fate of north Arabian nomads under Nebuchadnezzar.

> Concerning Qedar and the kingdoms of Ḥazor,[93] which Nebuchadnezzar the king of Babylon smote. Thus said the LORD. Rise, come up against Qedar, destroy the sons of the east. Their tents and their flocks shall be taken. Their (tent) curtains and all their goods and their camels shall be borne away from them. They shall proclaim unto them, "Terror on every side." Flee, wander far away, dwell in the depth (of caves) O inhabitants of Hazor declares the LORD, for Nebuchadnezzar king of Babylon has plotted against you. He has devised a purpose against you. Rise up, advance against a nation at ease that dwells securely, declares the LORD, that has no gates, that has no bars, that dwells alone. Their camels shall become plunder, their herds of cattle, a spoil. I will scatter to the wind those who crop their hair, and I will bring their disaster from every side. Hazor will become a haunt of jackals, a desolate place forever. No one will live there, no man will sojourn there.

The Arab nomads under the leadership of Qedar are described here as a wealthy, separated, and secure nation, having recovered quite well from the Assyrian blows against them. However, they were sinking in deep spiritual darkness.[94] The above prediction put Nebuchadnezzar's military action against Qedar and the Arab nomads "who crop their hair" in divine perspective.[95] For these circumcised children of Abraham to become labeled as "the ones with shaven temples" may be an indication of a deep spiritual fall from their patriarchal age spiritual condition (see Job). In fact, it is Yahweh who tells him, "rise, come up against Qedar, destroy the sons of the east." Al-Ṭabarî, though the tradition he relates displays historical incongruities, notes that the reason for God's rage against the Arabs is that "they do not believe in Me, that they have taken other deities, and that they deny My prophets and messengers."[96] This spiritual darkness of Arabs parallels Israel's apostasy during the same historical period we labeled as the "Darkness of Israel." The same ripple effect principle that we observed during the "light" period is effected during the "darkness" time also.

The disastrous Babylonian attack on the Arabs is also predicted in Jeremiah's oracle of "the cup of God's wrath" (Jer. 25:15–38). In this oracle, the prophet lists the nations that are going to fall under God's judgment (vv. 15–26). Though there is no direct reference in the immediate context to the foreign power that will execute that judgment, there is a wide agreement that the Babylonians are in the background.[97] The cup of wrath is given first to Judah, and then extended to the surrounding nations. The list includes "all the kings of the land of Uz, . . . Dedan, Tema, Buz, and all who have shaven temples; all the kings of Arabia and all the kings of the mixed peoples that live in the desert"[98] (vv. 20, 23–24). This listing of Arab peoples is very exhaustive. Though Nebuchadnezzar had created havoc among the confederation of Qedar, the Babylonian march against Arabia clearly continued with his son Nabonidus.

Before considering Nabonidus's involvement with the Arabs, it is appropriate to refer briefly to a significant prophecy that should follow chronologically. Ezekiel 25:1–11 seems to imply that God's judgment on the Arabian nomadic tribes was for the sake of discipline rather than complete neutralization. The prophecy decrees the devastation of the lands of Ammon and Moab, and the settling of the children of the east in their land (25:1–14). Most likely, the military strike against Moab and Ammon happened in 582 B.C.[99] Having militarily annihilated both Ammon and Moab, and possibly deported their inhabitants according to the Chaldaean policy,[100] Nebuchadnezzar left the door wide open for the infiltration of the children of the east, clearly associated with Qedarites (Jer. 49:28), to appropriate that land and fulfill Ezekiel's prophecy.[101]

Around 552 B.C., under obscure circumstances, Nabonidus (555–539 B.C.) marched toward the city of Taymāʾ to settle in it.[102] His move is thought to be linked to his desire to rebuild the famous temple of the moon-god Sin in Harran. The Babylonian priests led his subjects in opposing his desire.[103] The opposition eventually forced the Babylonian king to withdraw to the Hejaz area, after appointing his son Belshazzar as vice-regent in Babylonia.[104] However, Nabonidus's pursuit of his goal was very costly for north Arabians. For in the process of his conquest, the Babylonian leader killed Taymāʾs king and destroyed the city, slaughtering all the flocks, starving the inhabitants, and killing many of them mercilessly.[105] The northern Qedarite capital, Dumah, may have been affected in the course of the Babylonian war to control Arabia.[106] Subsequently, according to the Harran inscriptions, Nabonidus rebuilt the city, repopulated it, built for himself a palace, and established Taymāʾ as his royal residence.[107]

Seemingly, Nabonidus established colonies in the major trade stations located on the incense road in the district of the Hejaz. In fact, one of his inscriptions reads, "I hied myself afar from my city Babylon (on) the road to Tema', Dadanu [Dedan], Padakku [Fadak], Ḥibrâ [Khaybar], Iadiḥu [Yadi'?], and as far as Iatribu [Yathrib, Medina]; ten years I went about amongst them, (and) to my city of Babylon I went not in."[108] By establishing firm control over the important stations on the internal and peripheral trade routes, Nabonidus controlled the "oil trade" of the ancient Near East.

The internal trade route was built along oases running from the south to the north. This route started with Sheba in the south running north through Mecca and Yathrib (Medina) proceeding farther to Taymāʾ after passing by Khaybar, Yadî', and Fadak. From Taymāʾ it went north to Dumah, where it split into two main sections: one road proceeded east to Babylon and the other northwest to where it met the Desert and Kings Highway, which connected with Palestine in the west and Damascus in the north. The peripheral road went from Yathrib to Maʿān passing by Dedan, Ḥegra, and Tabûk. In Maʿān it split into three: one proceeded north to Damascus, the second went northwest to Gaza (Mediterranean outlet) and then to Egypt, and the third proceeded southeast to the ʿAqaba.[109]

No wonder the Babylonians coveted the control of this intricate trade highway, a major money maker in the desert. As a result of this control, major producers and consumers sought Nabonidus's favor. Thus "the land (?) of Egypt, the city of the Medes, the land of the Arabs, and all the kings (who were) hostile" sent messengers "for peace and good relationships . . . before me."[110] Macdonald comments on this new situation, saying: "Nabonidus's ability to cut off or divert their [Egypt, the Medes, and the Arabs] profits from the incense trade must quickly have made them realize that their true interests lay in cooperation with him."[111]

Eventually, and for unknown reasons,[112] Nabonidus left Taymāʾ in the thirteenth year of his reign (542 B.C.).[113] Babylon fell to the Persian leader Cyrus in the year 539 B.C. and the Neo-Babylonian rule was replaced by the Medo-Persian Empire.

At Peace with the Persians

The earliest information about Arabs during the Achaemenid Persian rule comes from the Greek historian Herodotus and dates to the middle of the fifth century B.C. The Arabians, whose western boundary, according to Herodotus, was the Nile River, appear to have been on good terms with the Persian Empire.[114] Herodotus tells how Cambyses, while on his way to invade Egypt (525 B.C.), approached a king of the Arabs asking him for safe conduct and water supply.[115] These Arabs are the ones that inhabited the area "from Cadytis [Gaza] . . . to the city of Ienysus [al-ʿArish]."[116] In response to Cambyses's request, the Arabian king "filled camel-skins with water and loaded all his live camels with these; which done, he drove them into the waterless land and there awaited Cambyses' army."[117] It seems that this Arabian gesture was instrumental in making the Persian king pledge amicable relationship with these Arabs.[118]

As a result of this privileged situation, the Arabs were listed among the very few people on whom tribute was not laid.[119] Instead, they rendered gifts as a pledge of loyalty to the Persian king. The yearly gift brought by the Arabs to Persia amounted to "a thousand talents' [close to 30 tons] weight of Frankincense."[120] There is some evidence that the Arabians of Herodotus are to be associated with the Qedarites, whose realm of influence seems to have been extended during the Achaemenid period.[121]

The Aramaic inscriptions on a silver bowl discovered at Tell el-Maskhûṭa in Egypt and dated to the end of the fifth century B.C. refers to Qaynu son of Gashmu, king of Qedar, as making an offering to the deity Han'-Ilat.[122] Dumbrell identified Gashmu father of Qaynu with the biblical Geshem who opposed Nehemiah's rebuilding work (Neh. 2:19; 4:7).[123] Albright identified Nehemiah's opponent as the Gashm ben Shahr of the Liḥyanite inscription JS 349 found in Dedan.[124] In view of the fact that the name *gshm* was common in Arabia, some scholars are still hesitant in identifying "Geshem the Arab" (Neh. 2:19; 6:1–2) with any one of the above.[125] Those who identify Gashm ben Shahr as the biblical Geshem normally equate him with the father of Qaynu of Tell el-Maskhûṭa and end up implying that the Qedarite influence during the Achaemenid period stretched from north Arabia to south Palestine, Sinai, and northeast of Egypt.[126] On the other hand, those who do not equate the biblical Geshem with any of the two would see much less influence of Qedar.[127] Only further findings can clear up the matter.

What seems beyond doubt, though, is that north Arabian Ishmaelites seem to have prospered under the Achaemenid Persian rule, and the blows they suffered at the hands of the Assyrians and Chaldaeans did not prevent these nomads from continuing to play a significant role in ancient Near East history. The various records highlighting the considerable stature of the Ishmaelite nomads testify to the making of a great nation out of Hagar's offspring (Gen. 21:13). The consistent survival of these nomads in the desert is another witness to the faithfulness of divine oracles about Ishmael (Gen. 16:12). The rise and expansion of the Nabataean kingdom in the fourth century B.C. is another indication of this biblical and historical truth.

10

THE NABATAEANS: ISHMAEL FINALLY SETTLED

In 1812, when John Burckhardt disguised himself as an Arab Muslim sheikh vowing to offer a goat at Aaron's Tomb south of Jordan, he was setting the stage for a great archaeological discovery.[1] As a matter of fact, Burckhardt opened the doors of the vicinity of Petra to the scrutiny of the modern world. From then on, whoever travels to Jordan has to visit the famous city of Petra, capital of the Nabataean people. There is almost nothing like it in the world—a whole city carved in the rock. Magnificent tombs, sanctuaries, a treasury, and royal lounges are all artistically built in the rose-colored sand stone, bestowing on Petra the label of the "Rose-Red City." Contrary to the norm of many peoples in world history, the community that occupied that city and the regions associated with its kingdom did not leave any record of their history and origin. What we know about them has been gleaned from what others have said concerning them. Yet the people associated with Petra controlled the Syro-Arabian Desert and major parts of the Arabian Peninsula for centuries before and after Christ. Thus their history, particularly their origin, becomes crucial to our present study.

The Origin of the Nabataeans

After Xenophon (ca. 400 B.C.), there is no mention of north Arabians in recorded history until the year 312 B.C., when Diodorus makes the first known reference to Nabataean Arabs as a distinct people.[2] From then on, the Nabataeans managed to become representative of the north Arabian stock in classical sources. Who were these Nabataeans, where did they come from, and what happened to the prominent tribes of Qedar and Nebayot so that they were no longer mentioned individually by historians? These questions have puzzled scholars and archaeologists for centuries, and it is presumptuous to attempt to resolve these issues in the present study. Nevertheless, the evidence available so far, though not sufficient to offer very specific answers to these questions, can help establish the larger framework of the history of this peculiar people.

It is widely admitted among Nabataean scholars today that the Nabataean people are not from Aramaic stock.[3] Most modern scholars have abandoned the Aramaic origin view,[4] initially advocated by Quatremère in the nineteenth century.[5] Instead, it is generally agreed upon that the Nabataeans were a north Arabian tribe heavily influenced by Aramaic culture.[6] The evidence for this identification is linguistic, historical, religious, and cultural.

The Linguistic Argument

On the linguistic level, the Nabataean inscriptions, discovered mostly by Jaussen and Savignac,[7] revealed that Aramaic was the language used by the Nabataeans only for commercial and official purposes.[8] Dussaud noted the tendency of Near Eastern people to speak more than one language, asserting that the Nabataeans must have spoken an Arabic dialect also,[9] which Graf calls Aramaic-Arabic.[10] In fact, J. Cantineau established beyond doubt the prominence of Arabic influence on the Nabataean onomasticon.[11] Having done a philological study of 40 Nabataean names (representing 170 persons), Cantineau concluded that 21 of these names (representing at least 127 persons) are definitely Arabic. Moreover, of the remaining 19, only 2 present a possibility of being from Aramaic origin, 7 have doubtful readings, and 10 have a high likelihood of being Arabic also.[12] This invited Cantineau even to doubt that Aramaic had ever been a daily spoken language among the Nabataeans.[13]

The Historical Argument

On the historical level, early references to the Nabataeans also seem to tie them to north Arabian stock. Diodorus states in this regard:

> Consequently the Arabs who inhabit this country [Nabataea], being difficult to overcome in war, remain always unenslaved; furthermore, they never at any time accept a man of another country as their over-lord and continue to maintain their liberty unimpaired. Consequently neither the Assyrians of old, nor the kings of the Medes and Persians, nor yet those of the Macedonians have been able to enslave them, and although they led many great forces against them, they never brought their attempts to a successful conclusion.[14]

Diodorus is described by A. Negev as not only "the most reliable source as far as details relating to this region which he describes . . . . but also as a source concerning solely the early, formative stage in the history of the Nabataeans, free from any possible anachronistic contaminations."[15] The above reference makes it clear that Diodorus, relying on the eyewitness account of Hieronymus of Cardia,[16] associates the Nabataeans with the Ishmaelite north Arabian tribes that were not subdued by the Assyrians or by the Medo-Persians, or even the Macedonians. Furthermore, the inclusion of Medo-Persia in this statement implies that the Arabs mentioned by Herodotus as Persia's friends included the Nabataeans.[17] Milik put it emphatically: "I firmly maintain that whenever the father of European historiography speaks of 'Arabs' in a definite sense, he is referring almost always to the Nabataeans."[18]

If, in fact, Herodotus is including the Nabataeans in his references to the Arabs, then historical continuity is maintained between Assyro-Babylonian Arabians and Nabataean Arabs, though at this point this does not necessarily imply an equation between Nabataeans and the Nabayāt of the Assyrian Chronicles.[19]

The Religious Argument

On the religious level, the Nabataean pantheon presents also common ground with north and central Arabian deities. The principal gods worshiped by the Nabataeans were *Dushara*, *ʾAllât*, *Manôt*, *el-ʿUzzâ*, and *Hobal*, all of which are north Arabian deities.[20] The only exception is the god *Baʿl šamin* "lord of heavens," who is an Aramaic god normally associated with the temple *Sîʿ* north of *Jabal ed-Drûz* in southern Syria.[21]

The Social Life Argument

The final evidence relates to the lifestyle of these Nabataeans. Speaking of them, Diodorus says:

> It is their custom *neither to plant grain, set out any fruit-bearing tree, use wine, nor construct any house; and if anyone is found acting contrary to this, death is his penalty.* They follow this custom because they believe that those who possess these things are, in order to retain the use of them, easily compelled by the powerful to do their bidding. While there are many Arabian tribes who use the desert as pasture, the Nabataeans far surpass the others in wealth although they are not much more than ten thousand in number; for not a few of them are accustomed to bring down to the sea frankincense and myrrh and the most valuable kinds of spices, which they procure from those who convey them from what is called Arabia Eudaemon. (emphasis added)[22]

This passage makes it clear that in their early appearance the Nabataeans were a nomadic group perfectly adapted to the life of the desert, like all north Arabian tribes. The portrayal of the Nabataeans by Diodorus as a nomadic people in their early history does not contradict the fact that they settled down soon after that and became a sedentary community with a sophisticated societal and architectural civilization, as archaeological remains reveal.[23] The above description of these nomads resembles to a large extent what Jeremiah relates about the Rechabites (Jer. 35:6–10), though it does not imply that the two groups are to be equated.

Furthermore, these Arab nomads, despite the apparent polytheism evident in their pantheon, most likely had the custom of prohibiting graven images among them as J. Patrich suggested.[24] This sets them religiously apart from urban polytheistic societies, and may be an indication of a dormant monotheism lying in the background of their polytheistic rituals.[25] This bedouin lifestyle provides another piece of the argument for identifying these Nabataeans with the north Arabians who were portrayed in cuneiform texts as a purely nomadic people. Though the Aramaeans were originally nomadic, they nonetheless "settled in great urban centres like Damascus at an early stage."[26]

To recapitulate, the evidence reveals that the Nabataeans originated from north Arabia, speaking an Aramaeo-Arabic language, had a nomadic lifestyle, and were heavily involved, like the rest of Arabian tribes, in the traffic of frankincense and myrrh and other precious items transported from Arabia Felix (south Arabia). However, does the evidence provide a clue as to their specific bloodline? Can their identity as Ishmaelites receive further support? Can they be identified further with the tribe of Nebayot? Though the answer to the first question may be an easy one, the second proves to be not as simple.

With regard to the first question, the second-century B.C. book of Jubilees (20:11–13) mentions the following concerning the non-Israelite children of Abraham who dwelt in north Arabia:

> And he [Abraham] gave to Ishmael and to his sons, and to the sons of Keturah, gifts, and sent them away from Isaac his son,

> and he gave everything to Isaac his son. And Ishmael and his sons, the sons of Keturah and their sons, went together and dwelt from Paran to the entering of Babylon in all the land which is towards the East facing the desert. And these mingled with each other, and their name was called Arabs, and Ishmaelites.[27]

This tradition seems to establish the fact that the terms *Ishmaelites* and *Arabians* became synonymous. Furthermore, intermarriages among the different tribes that roamed all over north Arabia somewhat tied the descendants of Hagar and those of Keturah together ethnically. Those who were not Ishmaelite by blood became labeled "Ishmaelites" by geographical and cultural associations. This was most likely the reason that prompted Josephus, having listed the names of different Ishmaelite tribes, to conclude "these inhabited all the country from Euphrates to the Red Sea, and called it Nabatene. They are an Arabian nation and name their tribes from these, because of their own virtue and because of the dignity of Abraham their father."[28] This statement of Josephus was most likely not made in a cultural vacuum. There must have been a cultural context that associated the Nabataeans, as a north Arabian people, with the children of Ishmael, as the book of Jubilees relates. The Ishmaelite element in north Arabia was so prominent that it became with time representative of north Arabians in general. This historical fact makes the Nabataeans relevant to any study of the descendants of Abraham's firstborn.

The Nebayot Factor

Can the identification be pushed further? Can the Nabataeans be equated with a specific north Arabian tribe? Many efforts have been made to identify them with the Ishmaelite tribe of Nebayot based on the etymology of the two names (Gen. 25:12–18). Prominent scholars in the field have held to this equation.[29] However, an increasing number of scholars nowadays reject this identification based on philological considerations.[30] Starcky identified the philological difficulty at stake. He pointed out that the root from which the term *Nabataean* stems is *nbṭ*, spelled with an emphatic *ṭ*, while *nbyt* is spelled with a simple *taw*. Furthermore, the absence of the *yod* in *Nabataean (nbtw)* makes it more difficult to reconcile both.[31] Recently, Broome attempted to solve the problem by arguing that the ending *-ati* in *na-ba-a-a-ti* is not used in Assyrian as a plural suffix in proper names. Therefore, the root is not *nby*, but *nbt* with a simple *taw*, and the name was probably pronounced *nabātu* in Assyrian. "With the shift in stress and the shortening of the second syllable" the name would be pronounced *nabaṭû* with an emphatic *tet*, accounting for the name "Nabataeans."[32] Broome solves the problem raised by the recent discovery of the structure *nbyt* in the texts of Jabal Ghunayem near Taymāʾ[33] by relying on the Assyrian as the best authority for the original version of the name.[34]

However, Broome's solution to the difficulty did not rally wide support for the equation and the problem is still beyond any definite solution.[35] At present there seems to be enough evidence to identify the Nabataeans with north Arabians, who rallied mostly under the Ishmaelite umbrella. The sweeping presence of the Nabataeans in north Arabia by the end of the first millennium made them representative of the children of Ishmael, whether or not future evidence may equate them with Nebayot, or with Qedar,[36] the most powerful and prominent of Ishmael's children (Isa. 60:7).

A Brief Historical Sketch

Though Herodotus referred to the Nabataeans as early as the fifth century B.C., the first time they appear on the pages of recorded history as a distinct people is when they successfully defended themselves against the Greek leader Antigonus the One-Eyed, one of the commanders of Alexander the Great. Diodorus reports how Antigonus launched two attacks against the Nabataeans in 312 B.C., and both campaigns failed to subdue these nomads.[37] With Edom significantly shrunk as a nation because of its assistance to Nebuchadnezzar in the sacking of Jerusalem (Jer. 49:7–22; Ezek. 25:12–15; Obad. 1–9; Mal. 1:2–4),[38] the Nabataeans gradually moved to Mount Seir, benefiting from a power vacuum in Edom. They seem to have extended their presence quickly, for the Zenon papyri makes them part of the Hauran and north Transjordan by 259 B.C.[39] They gradually settled down and established themselves in the Negev and the Transjordan as a mighty political, cultural, and commercial power throughout the Hellenistic period with Petra as a capital.[40] The first Nabataean king named in the historical record is Aretas I (170–160 B.C.), who assisted the Maccabeans in their revolt against Antiochus Epiphanes (1 Macc. 5:24–28; 15:22; 2 Macc. 12:10–12). After Aretas I, a series of kings sat on the Nabataean throne, ending with Rabbel II (A.D. 70–106). The Nabataean golden age occurred during the reign of Aretas IV (9 B.C.–A.D. 40) when New Testament events took place. The Nabataeans had intense social and economical relationships with the Jewish nation, though the political relations fluctuated between friendship and conflict.[41] Finally, the Nabataean kingdom was politically annexed to Rome in A.D. 106 by the governor of Syria, Cornelius Palma.[42] The Romans, Bowersock notes, "took over what they called Arabia from another people who had developed the region with astonishing skill. These were the descendants of nomadic Arabs,"[43] who left a great legacy and were, according to Glueck, "one of the most gifted peoples of history."[44]

Summary of Part 3 Findings

The survey of Ishmael's history during the first millennium B.C. reveals several facts about these descendants of Abraham. First, these nomadic groups multiplied beyond numbering according to divine blessings (Gen. 17:20). They filled the Syro-Arabian Desert and populated major oases in it. They controlled the north Arabian incense roads and trade, and accumulated in the process huge wealth.

Second, the Ishmaelites in the north under the leadership of Qedar became a very powerful nomadic force that neither the Assyrians, the Chaldaeans, the Medo-Persians, nor the Macedonians were able to neutralize or subdue permanently (Gen. 16:12b). In that regard, Hitti rightly notes,

> Many references are made in the Assyrian annals to Arabian chiefs "kissing the feet" of the kings of Nineveh and offering them among other presents gold, precious stones, eyebrow dyes (kohl, antimony), frankincense, camels and donkeys. . . . The Assyrians, though rightly called the Romans of the ancient world, could not have brought under even a nominal rule more than the oases and a few tribes in North Arabia.[45]

Third, these nomads displayed religious idolatry, and their Abrahamic monotheism was moved to the background. According to Starcky's analysis, having started with the worship of *El,* soon after they personified the major stars, primarily the Moon and Venus, which were very important to the nomads, and associated with their personal God some object-deities.[46]

Arabs flooding into Israel to hear its king's wisdom is not witnessed in the period studied in this part of the book. Israel struggled with idolatry, too. Instead, there was some evidence of rising antagonism. Contribution from the wisdom of the East to the Hebrew legacy is not reflected on the pages of Scriptures as during the time of the united monarchy. The period of "Darkness of Israel" yielded a deeper darkness of Arabs, and discipline involved both concurrently (Jer. 25). Ishmael was to live "in the presence of all his brethren" (Gen. 16:12c). This oracle did not only involve geographical proximity. Religious dependence was embedded in that statement, too. Abraham's "Light" upheld in Israel stimulated light among Arabs. Israel's "Darkness" yielded greater darkness among Arabs. However, by the end of the first millennium a new era is about to begin with the dawning of Messiah's light. The expectations are greater, to the Jews first, to the rest of Abraham's children next, then to the Gentiles.

PART 4

ARABS IN THE LIGHT OF CHRIST

11

Arab Messianic Expectations

The coming of the Messiah, King of the Jews and the promised Seed of Abraham (Gen. 12:1–3), inaugurated a new era of blessing for Israel and the whole world. If the nations were blessed by Solomon's testimony and came from all around to listen to him and admire his godly wisdom, how much more would their blessings be when the Lord of Solomon incarnates and the Provider of his wisdom emerges in history. The prophetic books predicted judgments that were implemented on Israel and the nations around it because of spiritual apostasy. Yet the same books also predict the restoration and blessing of the elect remnant coming from both.

We already witnessed a ripple effect with regard to God's blessing (in the "Light" period) and discipline (in the "Darkness" period), starting with Israel and extending to its kin and the nations around it. Would a similar effect be legitimate in terms of the blessings of restoration? Between Jews and Gentiles, does the dawning of the messianic age involve the non-Israelite children of Abraham in a special way? The answer to these questions requires a quick survey of restoration oracles involving them and a description of the Arab-Jewish relationship that prevailed at the ushering in of the messianic age.

The chapters of part 4 will examine the New Testament to explore the condition of "Arabs in the Light of Christ."

God's Restoration Plan for Arabs

The restoration oracles that explicitly mention the Arab tribes descending from Abraham are mostly found in the comfort section of the book of Isaiah (chaps. 40–66). Psalm 72:10, 15 and Isaiah 11:14 are relevant as well. Though it is not our aim here to give full exegetical considerations to these passages, citing them in entirety is helpful for clarity and comparison. First, Isaiah 42:6–7, 10–11 (NRSV) says:

> (6) I am the LORD, I have called you in righteousness, I have taken you by the hand and kept you; I have given you as a covenant to the people, *a light to the nations,* (7) to open the eyes that are blind, to bring out the prisoners from the dungeon, from the prison those who sit in darkness. . . . (10) Sing to the LORD a new song, his praises from the end of the earth. Let the sea roar and all that fills it, the coastlands and their inhabitants. (11) Let *the desert* and *its towns* lift up their voice, the *villages that Qedar inhabits;*[1] let *the inhabitants of Sela*[2] sing for joy, let them shout *from the tops of the mountains.* (emphasis added)

Isaiah 60:1–7 (NRSV) says:

> (1) Arise, shine; for *your light has come,* and the glory of the LORD has risen upon you. (2) For darkness shall cover the earth, and thick darkness the peoples; but the LORD will arise upon you, and his glory will appear over you. (3) *Nations shall come to your light,* and *kings to the brightness of your dawn.* (4) Lift up your eyes and look around; they all gather together, they come to you; your sons shall come from far away, and your daughters shall be carried on their nurses' arms. (5) Then you shall see and be radiant; your heart shall thrill and rejoice,

> because the abundance of the sea shall be brought to you, *the wealth of the nations* shall come to you. (6) A *multitude of camels* shall cover you, the young camels of *Midian* and *Ephah;* all those from *Sheba* shall come. *They shall bring gold and frankincense,* and shall proclaim the praise the LORD. (7) All the flocks of *Qedar* shall be gathered; the rams of *Nebayot* shall minister to you; they shall be acceptable on my altar, and I will glorify my glorious house. (emphasis added)[3]

Psalm 72:10, 15 (NRSV) states:

> (10) May the kings of Tarshish and of the isles render him tribute, may *the kings of Sheba and Seba bring gifts. . . .* (15) Long may he live. May *the gold of Sheba* be given to him. May prayer be made for him continually, and blessings invoked for him all day long. (emphasis added)[4]

Isaiah 11:12, 14 says:

> He will raise a signal for the nations, and will assemble the outcasts of Israel, and gather the dispersed of Judah from the corners of the earth . . . *they shall plunder the people of the east.* (emphasis added)

An initial look at these messianic texts yields several observations about Arabian tribes in God's restoration program. First, the texts of Isaiah 42 and 60 together with Isaiah 49:6 seem to develop a common theme related to Messiah's eschatological light to the Gentiles, which was initially predicted in Isaiah 9:1–2. Setting aside the intricate discussion of the use of the Old Testament in the New,[5] and the problem of identification of Yahweh's servant,[6] it is generally agreed upon that these texts have messianic implications (Matt. 4:15–16; Luke 2:32; Acts 13:47), and predict among other things the future salvation brought about fully by Yahweh's anointed One.[7]

Second, though the salvific light of the Messiah is said to be extended to the Gentiles (Isa. 42:6; 49:6), the circumcised descendants of Abraham seem to be given preeminence in this Gentile salvation. In fact, these "light" prophecies explicitly highlight the names of Arabian tribes (Qedar, Nebayot, Midian, Ephah, and Sheba), though reference is made to God's visitation of the nations. This appears to be in harmony with a principle that guided Paul's outreach ministry. Greater privileges imply greater responsibilities and therefore logical and theological priority in God's visitation (Jer. 12:14–17; Rom. 1:16–17; 2:9–10). As circumcised children of Abraham, the Arabian tribes mentioned in Scripture passages quoted above come first among the Gentiles in God's plan of salvation of the nations. Their privilege as physical descendants of Abraham necessitates a theological priority in judgment and visitation. It seems that Paul caught this sequential priority of Arabs in God's plan for restoration of the Gentiles and went first to Arabia in response to his calling to preach among the nations (Gal. 1:15–17).[8]

Third, the messianic age will witness a detour of the wealth of Arabians to Jerusalem, most particularly to Israel's Messiah-King (Isa. 60:5–7). The preceding chapters revealed among many things the huge amount of wealth collected by different Arab tribes from incense and cattle trade (Ezek. 27:20–22). The Bible seems to divide the wealth of Arabia between flock and incense, assigning incense to the children of Keturah (whose name means "incense") and wealth in flock to the Ishmaelites. However, the previous historical survey revealed how the Ishmaelites had a great share in the privileged incense trade and ended up controlling it almost completely by the time of Christ. It looks as though in the messianic age, this coveted wealth of Arabia will be spoiled by the remnant of Israel (Isa. 11:14). However, Psalm 72:10, 15 and Isaiah 60:6–7 seem to imply that this spoiling of Arabian wealth will be peaceful and carried out as a voluntary response to the salvific light of Israel's Messiah.

ARAB-JEWISH CONTACTS

The previous chapters have established the fact that there was much common ground culturally and ethnically between the Arabian and

Israelite tribes. The survey of restoration prophecy revealed the inclusion of Arabs in Messiah's redemptive program. In attempting to highlight some of the contacts between these two peoples during the centuries relevant to the coming of Christ, this chapter sets a needed historical background for the story of the magi, which will be developed in the following chapters.

Jewish Presence in Arabia

The presence of massive Jewish communities in the Hejaz district (northwest Arabia) just prior to the rise of Islam has led to many unsuccessful attempts to account for this kind of Hebrew settlement in the oases along the famous incense road.[9] Professor Gadd notes that neither the exodus with Moses, the visit of the queen of Sheba to Solomon, Nebuchadnezzar's deportation of Judah, the return from the exile, nor any other event in Israel's history has presented in the opinion of recent writers any objective evidence "to show how the powerful Jewish communities in the north and (later) in the south of the peninsula came to be established there."[10]

With the publishing of the Harran inscriptions around the middle of the twentieth century, Gadd offered what seems to be the most plausible answer to this question.[11] Two phrases in these inscriptions related to Nabonidus's conquest of Taymāʾ and his settling in that city stand out as central to his proposition. The first inscription reads, "I [Nabonidus] hied myself from my city of Babylon (on) the road to Tema', Dadanu, Padakku, Khibrâ, Idakhu, and as far as Iatribu; ten years I went about amongst them (and) to my city of Babylon I went not in."[12] The second reads, "in plenty and wealth and abundance my people in the distant tracts *I spread abroad,* and in prosperity I took the road to my own land" (emphasis added).[13]

It is interesting that the cities mentioned in Nabonidus's statement coincide to a great extent with selected oases of northwest Arabia that reflected a massive Jewish presence by Muhammad's time. Thus the two statements made by Nabonidus who dwelt in Taymāʾ between 552 and 542 B.C. invited Gadd to conclude that the Neo-Babylonian king

> . . . planted colonies [*I spread abroad*] of his subjects in these six oases, round which he himself travelled for sojourn and for protection of the settlements. One of his strongholds, Dedan was to have a continuing history of the same process, for that place came to be under Minaean rule for some centuries, and was afterwards occupied by the Nabataeans. . . . The evidence given by H 2 combined with the known situation in later centuries may lead us to infer, with some confidence, that *Jews, whether from among the captives in Babylonia or from those remaining in their homeland, were strongly represented among these soldiers and settlers in Arabia.* (emphasis added)[14]

This kind of Jewish settlement in Arabia is not unparalleled, for the Jewish military community established at Elephantine, Egypt, in the fifth century B.C. is a witness to these Jewish movements in different areas of the ancient Near East.[15]

Moreover, an Aramaic fragment discovered at Qumran offers some support to Gadd's proposal. The document relates a tradition attributed to the presence of Nabonidus in Taymāʾ and published by J. T. Milik under the name "Prière de Nabonide."[16] The text tells how Nabonidus was struck with a severe illness for seven years while in Taymāʾ according to the decree of God the Most High, and how after much prayer, God sent a Jewish diviner who commanded him to give glory to God, and thus he was healed. The Jewish messenger told him that he had been sick for seven years because he addressed his prayers to idols of gold and silver, stone and wood.[17]

Gadd's theory was welcomed by I. Ben-Zvi, who published an important article detailing the issue of Jewish settlements in Arabia.[18] Ben-Zvi favored the idea that Jewish deportees were most likely among the soldiers and settlers of Nabonidus, since it is difficult to conclude that his army would be formed of Babylonian soldiers only.[19] After a detailed study of the evidence pointing to a Jewish presence in Arabia, he concluded:

> It must be admitted that the process of the spreading of Judaism among the Arab tribes was a typical phenomenon, not

> only with regard to the Nabataean tribes, but also with regard to the communities of Midian and other parts of Arabia that the Israelite tribes reached during the period of the first and second temple.[20]

Ben-Zvi underlined one more piece of evidence confirming the significant Jewish influence on Arabs by New Testament times. His analysis of theophoric (Yahwist) names from south Arabia proved that there were during the Hellenistic and the Roman eras large communities of Jews containing natives and proselytes. The evidence even suggests that many rulers from Ḥimyar, Sabâ, Raydân, Maʾîn, and Qatabân were Jews or, more likely, converts to Judaism.[21] Thus it becomes clear that Judaism and Jewish settlements in the Arabian Peninsula were most likely very significant in the postexilic period.

Arab-Jews Commonalities

Geographical proximity played a big role in the social exchange between Arabs and Jews (Gen. 16:12c). In addition, the common Abrahamic background also furthered this exchange. The extent of Arab-Jewish contacts prior to the coming of Christ is particularly illustrated by a series of historical and social data that we are going to survey in the rest of this chapter.

Political Interests

As the tribes of the Nabataeans settled in Edom and the immediate Transjordan, Arabs moved closer to Israel and the relationships of Nabataeans and Jews intensified on many levels. These relationships were often of a friendly nature.[22] Several incidents can be cited as examples of this kind of relationship between the two peoples. During the Maccabean revolt against Antiochus IV, Judas and Johnathan Maccabeus fled to the Transjordan, journeying three days through the wilderness until "they encountered the Nabataeans who met them peaceably," and helped them throughout their revolt against Antiochus

Epiphanes (1 Macc. 5:24–28).[23] In fact, 1 Maccabees 9:35 says it plainly: "And Jonathan sent his brother as leader of the multitude and begged the Nabataeans, *who were his friends,* for permission to store with them the great amount of baggage which they had" (emphasis added).

Josephus relates how after Caesar's victory over Antony in the battle of Actium, Herod feared for his life from the vengeance of the Roman emperor since he had sided with Antony. His aim was to get rid of Hyrcanus, the only one available from the royal family who could assume the rule after him. But Alexandra, the daughter of Hyrcanus, convinced her father to ask for help and protection from the king of the Arabs, Malichus, who was at the head of the Nabataean Empire at that time.[24]

According to Josephus, Antipater, father of Herod the Great, enjoyed great and intimate relationships with the Nabataeans, having married a relative of the king of Arabia. Thus the Nabataean king sent troops at several occasions to assist him in military conflicts and supported him in various other ways.[25] Moreover, Antipas, son of Herod the Great, married the daughter of the Nabataean king, Aretas IV (9 B.C.–A.D. 40). However, after Herod Antipas divorced his wife for the sake of marrying Herodias the wife of his brother Philip, Aretas IV launched a devastating attack against him, which was deemed by the people as a sign of God's disciplining hand on Herod for his killing of John the Baptist (Mark 6:17–29).[26]

Religious and Social Matters

Herod the Great, who ruled over Israel from 37 B.C. until 4 B.C., was half-Nabataean. His mother Cypros was of Arab-Nabataean descent, from a prominent family among the Arabs.[27] Herod's father, Antipater, was an Idumean whose ancestors converted to Judaism three generations earlier.[28] Thus Herod the Great was half-Nabataean and half-Idumean, but also a Jew through conversion of his ancestors on Antipater's side as Kasher ably argues.[29]

An "Arabian bodyguard" was found at Herod's court. He was taken into custody later with two Arab friends, suspected of involvement in a plot against Herod.[30] "One of the other two was a friend of Syllaeus, the steward of the Nabataean king Aretas IV; the other was sheikh of an Arabian tribe."[31] Herod was famous for his suspicions of treason. He killed his wife Mariamne I and her two sons for the same reason.[32]

On the commercial level, Jeremias notes that the Jewish trade with Arabia had "always been very brisk."[33] The writer of the letter of Aristeas mentioned that "a great quantity of spices, precious stones and gold is brought into the country by the Arabs."[34] The Arabian Desert provided the largest part of the incense used in the temple.[35] Furthermore, lions and various animals Herod the Great needed for his sport activities in Jerusalem were brought from Arabia.[36] Arabia was the source of the "fat stock" in Israel as early as the second century B.C.[37] Ben-Zvi also affirms that the Jews who started intermixing with Arabians as shepherds in the beginning joined them later on as merchants, accompanying Nabataean caravans from north Arabia to south Arabia.[38]

Religiously speaking, the Idumaeans converted to Judaism under John Hyrcanus I around 126 B.C.[39] and integrated fully in Jewish life.[40] Furthermore, a section of Iturea (from Yetur, son of Ishmael) joined the Jewish faith under Aristobulus about 103 B.C.[41] Later, Ptolemy, son of Mennaeus, king of Chalcis, capital of Iturea, received the children of Aristobulus II when they took refuge in his land. Social and religious contacts increased between the peoples.[42]

In view of the intensity of relationships between Arabs and Jews on various levels, it seems very normal to find Arabian Jews (Jewish diaspora) and Jewish Arabs (proselytes) among those present in Jerusalem on the day of Pentecost (Acts 2:10–11). The apostle Paul, compelled by the Lord to preach the gospel among the Gentiles, did not confer with flesh and blood but "went away at once into Arabia" (Gal. 1:15–17). Theologically, the priority of Arabians in God's restoration program for the Gentiles was most likely a major factor why Paul chose to head that way directly upon receiving his call. It is true that Arabia was a place of refuge and revelation for many of God's called servants. However, it is unthinkable that Paul, who started preaching from day one in Damascus after conversion (Acts 9:20) would just meditate silently in Arabia, which was then the Nabataean realm.[43] Hengel and Schwemer developed a strong argument for the theological and geographical reasons behind Paul's missionary visit to Arabia.[44] The attempt of the governor of Damascus to catch Paul was most likely a direct result of the apostle's controversial preaching among Arabs in the Nabataean realm that lasted around two years (2 Cor. 11:32).[45]

All of the above show close Arab-Jewish relationships and the exchange of cultural, social, and religious heritage[46] between the groups.[47] The spread of the Jewish faith in various districts of the Nabataean kingdom is an indication that Arabians had access to Jewish Scriptures. The archive of the Jewess Babatha found in Hegra showed that Jewish families led a peaceful life under the Nabataeans in a neighborhood of Arabs.[48] Arabs' common Abrahamic heritage with the Hebrew people makes it more likely that at least a remnant among them would also share their Jewish messianic expectations. According to Margoliouth, A Liḥyānî inscription may convey the presence of what is called "the sect of the Law," outside Israel, thus revealing the presence of Jewish monotheism in north Arabia.[49] In the same tomb inscription, "the father of the sculptor was named Marilah, ʿman of God,' which a monotheist may have borne."[50]

With all the preceding evidence, we would expect to find a remnant among the Arabs seeking God and awaiting the appearance of an eschatological figure among their theological kin the Jews. This is not strange, especially because Ishmael was called to dwell "in the presence of all his brethren" (Gen. 16:12c). Wise men seeking God are likely to be found in Arabia, expecting the advent of the Messiah-King of the Jews. Could the magi who came to visit Christ and worship him have come from Arabia, from among the Arabian children of Abraham (Matt. 2:1–12)? After all, they were meant to be called first among the Gentiles in God's restoration plan for the nations as shown earlier in this chapter. The next two chapters explore the evidence for such a claim and attempt to establish this proposal.

12

THE MAGI-ARAB WORSHIPERS OF CHRIST (PART 1)

THE STORY OF THE MAGI AS NARRATED by the apostle Matthew is a mysterious event that has attracted the interest of many readers of the New Testament. When faced with the episode of their visit to Jerusalem, mentioned only in the first Gospel (Matt. 2:1–12), the reader is challenged to answer several questions. Where did these magi come from, and what was their ethnic origin? What was the nature of the star that appeared to them in the east? Why would these Gentiles be interested in the King of the Jews? What is the significance of the gifts they offered to Christ? What role does their story play in the argument of Matthew's infancy narrative? All these questions are important and deserve serious consideration in order to establish the relevance of this story to biblical theology and to the theme developed in this book.

Since Matthew does not offer any explanation of this episode while attempting to prove the kingship of Jesus, the interpreter may infer that the evangelist assumed his readers' familiarity with many elements within the story.[1] Because of the mystery behind it, some have gone all the way to disclaim the historicity of the magi visit.[2] Yet others, while admitting the historicity of their visit, have proposed various answers to the questions mentioned earlier.

The previous chapter established the extensive sociopolitical and religious contacts between the Jews and their neighboring Arabs. This, added to the Arabian Abrahamic heritage, makes it highly possible that the wise men of Matthew's Gospel actually came from Arabia. However, at the outset of our examination of their story, it is appropriate to present a brief survey of the different traditions related to the magi. Later we will assess the validity of the view advocating the Arabian origin for the magi.

The Magi and Various Traditions

Evangelical scholars today commonly hold that the magi of Matthew's infancy narrative were Zoroastrian priests and astrologers from Persia[3] or Chaldaean astrologers from Mesopotamia.[4] These views have much going for them. The technicality of the word "magi," the bearing of astronomy on the story, and the testimony of a relatively large number of church fathers make these views very popular among commentators.

In fact the term *magi* (Gr. *mágos,* pl. *mágoi*) referred initially to members of a Median tribe that became responsible for the priestly function under the Persians (sixth–fourth centuries B.C.).[5] Their role in conducting sacred rituals at the offering of sacrifices was essential.[6] The magi were gifted with an ability to interpret special signs and dreams,[7] and may have adopted some form of Zoroastrianism (the teachings of Zarathustra)[8] by the time of Herodotus (450 B.C.).[9] Pliny and Tacitus associated them with magic and sorcery,[10] and the term *magician* derived from *mágos,* and was applied in the New Testament to sorcerers such as Simon of Samaria (Acts 8:11) and Elymas of Paphos (13:6, 8).

According to Yamauchi, beginning in the fourth century B.C. the magi became "increasingly associated" with Chaldaean astrology, which in turn was associated with Zoroaster. This led to the circulation of "a mass of astrological matter" attributed to Zoroaster.[11] Consequently, a patristic belief spread in Christian circles that Zoroaster predicted the coming of the Son of God,[12] and the coming of the magi to Jerusalem was attributed by some to "the Zoroastrian doctrine of the Savior."[13]

Church fathers holding that the magi came from Persia include Clement of Alexandria (*Stromata* 1.15), Origen (*Contra Celsum* 1.58–60), Chrysostom, Cyril of Jerusalem, and Cosmas Indicopleustes.[14] On the other hand, Celsus, Jerome, and Augustine were among those identifying the magi as Chaldaean astrologers who came from Babylon.[15]

As far as tradition is concerned, various sources claim different names and numbers for these magi. The sixth-century Syriac work "Cave of Treasures" claims that those who bore the gifts to the King were kings and sons of kings named Hôrmîzdah (king of Persia), Yazdegerd (king of Sabha), and Perôzâdh (king of Sheba, which "lies in the east").[16] The Syrian writer of *The Book of Adam and Eve* identified the magi as Hor (king of Persia), Basantor (king of Saba), and Karsudas (king of the East),[17] while the Armenian infancy gospel is the source of a familiar tradition that prevailed in the West identifying the magi as Balthasar king of Arabia, Gaspar king of India, and Melchior king of Persia.[18] Metzger also cites other sources, including the Syriac *Book of the Bee*, the Nestorian lexicographer Abû-l-Ḥasan bar Bahlûl, and the Armenian codex "S. Lazzaro no. 1649," which list no less than thirty different names from several ethnic groups, including Parthians, Assyrians, Medians, Barbarians, and Tharsis and the Isles.[19]

With respect to relics, a tradition associated with Marco Polo relates how when he traveled to Persia, he was led to visit the tombs of the magi about "fifty miles southwest of Tehran."[20] Another tradition holds that in A.D. 490, the emperor Zeno transported the tombs of the magi from Hadramaut (south Arabia) to Constantinople, and thence to Milan.[21]

The above survey of the most common traditions and views related to the origin and function of the magi reinforces the conviction that the strongest reliable interpretation is that which accounts best for the exegetical considerations. An Arabian origin of the magi best accounts for the biblical data.[22] The alternative views rely substantially on Zoroastrian predictions and astrology, which is a science abhorred in the Old Testament. On the contrary, an Arabian origin of the magi can be argued exegetically from the text of Matthew and from Old Testament expectations that play a major role in Matthew's introduction of the Messiah-King. The rest of this chapter and the next will develop the arguments supporting this view.

The Arabian Origin of the Magi

Evidence from the Term *Magi*

As noted above, the term *magi* was mostly used in reference to Persian priests and Babylonian astrologers. It largely had a negative sense, referring to fortunetellers, sorcerers, magicians, and those involved in occult practices and astrology.[23] However, as Delling puts it, the word *magos* consistently has been used in four ways.[24] While three of these meanings have negative connotations, a fourth refers, in a neutral sense, to a "possessor and user of supernatural knowledge and ability."[25] For example, Nebuchadnezzar called his Chaldaeans, his magi, and the prophets and asked them to interpret the dream that annoyed him. Whereas the magi and their companions failed to interpret his dream, Daniel succeeded, and therefore was appointed by Nebuchadnezzar as chief of the magi (Dan. 4:9).[26] In that sense also Pliny considers Moses a magos in Pharaoh's palace.[27] Josephus refers to another Jew, named Simon (Atomos), called *magos,* who was a friend of Felix the procurator of Judea, and was sent by him to convince Drusilla to marry him.[28]

While expressing his familiarity with the negative work of the magi,[29] Philo was only ready to accept *mageia* when it is a "science of discernment . . . a dignified and desirable branch of knowledge."[30] He calls Balaam a *magos* and refers to the spirit of prophecy as coming upon him in order to replace the "artificial system of divination."[31] Jewish tradition makes Balaam a prophet for the Gentiles (see *Sifre* on Deut. 34:10) and the father of Jannes and Jambres,[32] which invited Eusebius to consider the magi as his successors coming to watch the fulfillment of the prophecy of the star coming out of Jacob (Num. 24:17).[33]

The New Testament uses the word *magos* both in a negative sense and in a neutral sense. While it is clear that Simon the *magos* was doing feats of magic (Acts 8:9, 11), magic is not obvious in the case of Elymas (Acts 13:6, 8). Interestingly, the name "Elymas" is not known elsewhere in Greek, Hebrew, or Aramaic literature.[34] However, in Arabic it is *ʿAlîm*,[35] meaning "the knowledgeable one."[36] Bruce correctly notes that "Elymas" is not the translation of his name *Bar-Jesus*, but rather an interpretation of his function as a *magos*.[37] Most likely Elymas was a Jew with some Arabic connections who served as a counselor to the proconsul Sergios Paulus.[38] However, his ways were wicked and his oracles were false (Acts 13:6, 8), though his name was Bar-Jesus (meaning "son of Jesus") and he had unusual insight as a *magos*.

Thus it seems that the word can be used to refer to persons other than Persians or Chaldaeans, and it was applied to Jews and to Aramaic easterners (Balaam). In Matthew 2:1, 7, 16, it is most probably used in the neutral sense, referring to seekers of science, wisdom, and knowledge. True, the term was generally used in a negative way that involved spiritism. However, in Matthew's infancy narrative it probably has the sense of "possessor and user of supernatural knowledge and ability." In the sense of unusual insight, there were plenty of magi among the Arabian children of the east (1 Kings 4:30), among "the sons of Hagar who seek for wisdom upon the earth" (Baruch 3:23).

Evidence from the Early Church Fathers

Early church fathers are important in biblical interpretation because of their closeness in time and space to the apostolic interpretive tradition. Around A.D. 155 Justin Martyr wrote about a debate that took place twenty years earlier between him and a certain Jew named Trypho.[39] Relating the story of the magi in his *Dialogue with Trypho* Justin says the following:

> For, at the time of His birth, the Magi came *from Arabia* and

> worshipped Him, after they had met Herod, then the king of your country, whom Scripture calls king of Assyria because of his wicked ungodliness. . . . At the time when the Magi *from Arabia* came to King Herod and said. . . . Now, these Magi *from Arabia* came to Bethlehem, worshipped the child, and presented to Him gifts of gold, frankincense and myrrh. . . . There the *Arabian Magi* found Him. . . . Now when the *Arabian Magi* failed to return to Herod, etc. [40]

Nine times in his testimony, cited partially above, Justin Martyr claims that the magi came from Arabia.[41] Justin may very well reflect the apostolic tradition, for he was born A.D. 100–110 and raised in Neapolis (today's Nâblus), Samaria. He may also have been a Samaritan himself since he called the Samaritans his people.[42] Accordingly, he was in touch with early Palestinian traditions.[43] Justin's confidence concerning the Arabian origin of the magi in his apologetic dialogue against Judaism may reflect a wider belief as to their origin.[44] It is most likely not erroneously based on the gifts,[45] since he only makes one passing reference to them.

Around A.D. 208, in Carthage (North Africa), the famous Christian apologist Tertullian advocated the tradition that the magi were "kings" that came from Arabia.[46] He wrote:

> For apart from the fact, known to everybody, that the strength of the East, that is, its force and power, is customarily potent in gold and spices, it is certainly possible for the Creator to constitute gold the strength of the other nations besides: as (he says) by Zechariah, *And Judah shall encamp before Jerusalem and gather together all the valiance of the peoples round about, gold and silver.* But of that gift of gold David also says, *And there shall be given to him of the gold of Arabia;* and again, *The kings of the Arabs and of Saba shall offer him gifts.* For the Orient for the most part held the Magi for kings. (emphasis original)[47]

Tertullian's statements yield several observations. First, he identifies the East, where the magi came from, as Arabia, saying that "the strength of the East" is constituted of spices and gold. Second, he sees the nature of the gifts that the magi presented to the newborn King as strong evidence for an Arabian origin.[48] Third, he is the first known teacher to write that the magi were kings, that is, tribal chiefs. Fourth, he argues that the Messiah, King of Israel would take up, at his coming, the coveted wealth of Arabia "without fighting or armament."[49]

The claim that Tertullian followed Justin Martyr in the Arabian view is not certain,[50] for Tertullian asserted that he drew on an earlier tradition, widely spread in the Orient, about their kingship. If he was misled by Justin Martyr concerning the Arabian origin, then his failure to deal with an alternative view would look strange. Moreover, referring to Isaiah 8:4, Tertullian asserts that the power of Arabia that will be spoiled by the Messiah is "potent in gold and spices." However, Justin Martyr, using the same Old Testament passage, asserted that reference there is made to the power of the magi magic.[51] This proves that Justin Martyr struggled with the term *magi*, which Matthew used to refer to these visitors from the East.

About A.D. 96, when writing to the Corinthians concerning the resurrection of Christ, Clement of Rome mentioned the following:

> Let us observe the remarkable sign which is seen in the *regions of the east,* that is, the vicinity of *Arabia.* There is a bird which is named the phoenix. . . . When the time of its dissolution and death arrives, it makes for itself a coffinlike nest of *frankincense and myrrh* and the other spices. . . . But as the flesh decays, a certain worm is born, which is nourished by the juices of the dead bird and eventually grows wings. Then, when it has grown strong . . . it makes way *from the country of Arabia* to Egypt, to the city called Heliopolis.[52]

In this statement, Clement also identified the regions of the East of his time as being "the vicinity of Arabia," which he specified later as "the country of Arabia." From the story of the phoenix it can easily be concluded that the land of Arabia was associated with frankincense and myrrh.[53] Thus an Arabian origin of the magi seems very likely what Clement of Rome would have held on this issue.

Finally, Epiphanius (fourth century A.D.), bishop of Salamis in Cyprus, also believed that the magi were from the descendants of Keturah who were dismissed by Abraham and "settled in Magodia in Arabia."[54] He believed that these children of Keturah settled in Arabia Felix.[55] By putting the magi in Arabia Felix, Epiphanius must not have depended on Justin Martyr either, for the latter associated them with the vicinity of Damascus. Thus, the best way to account for the similarities and differences among these church fathers is to see that Justin, Tertullian, and Epiphanius were all depending on an earlier eastern tradition that referred to Arabia, without further specification, as the origin of these wise men.

Evidence from the Star of Bethlehem

Many attempts have been made to determine the nature of the star that drew the magi to Jerusalem and thence to Bethlehem.[56] Because of the extent of its brightness, the star has been identified as a supernova, which, according to Brown's estimation, can be "a hundred million times more luminous than our sun."[57] Kepler is the first known to have identified this star with a supernova.[58] Others have suggested Halley's Comet,[59] a conjunction of planets,[60] the brilliant Jupiter,[61] Saturn,[62] or Uranus.[63]

The Magi and Astronomy

Because of the centrality of the star in the trip of the magi, it has been assumed that these visitors would have had special interest in astronomy. As such, they were assumed to have been associated with Babylonians, famous for their astronomy, or with Persian magi who were astrologers associated later with the Chaldaens.[64] However, the Bible clearly condemns astrology, divination, and the worship of the stars (Deut. 4:19; Isa. 47:13; Jer. 8:2; 10:2; Amos 5:26).[65] Furthermore, the pseudepigraphic writings (200 B.C.–A.D. 200) seem to give a negative picture of these practices.[66] The claim of some church fathers that the magi were drawn by astrology to Christ so that magic art would vanish by the advent of the gospel and the worship of the Messiah[67] seems to be unwarranted by the Matthean text,[68] and driven by a contemporary contention against astrology.[69]

If interest in stars is a factor, Arabs were most famous for their fascination with the galaxy. Four of their tribes were named after stars.[70] Transjordanian archaeology revealed the astral basis for the Nabataean belief. Describing the zodiac-centered religious and social life of these Arabians, Glueck notes:

> The zodiac, with its counterclockwise and clockwise halves . . . dramatize *the great importance attached by the Nabataeans to the heavenly firmament.* They beheld in its orbs the reflections of their gods whose powers *governed the mysteries of nature and the conditions of mankind during life on earth* and its continuation in the hereafter. . . . These [astral] deities governed the seasons of the year, the zodiacal sequence of its changes, the moods of nature, the vagaries of fortune, the exigencies of life, the unexplorable unknown of the world beyond death, whose concealing curtain could not be penetrated by mortal gaze.[71]

This is definite evidence of the prominence of the zodiac in the life of Nabataean Arabs who controlled north Arabia by the time of Christ. Needless to say that bedouins have always displayed great interest in stars.[72] Hitti believes that the astral beliefs of the bedouin "centered upon the moon, in whose light he grazed his flocks."[73] Most important is Starcky's observation that nomads, by personifying the major stars that were very important to them, were associating with their personal God some object-deities.[74] This underlying monotheism, the interest in God's firmament, together with wisdom of the children of the east may have drawn these magi to ask for the King of the Jews. A better ground still is God's direct revelation to an elect remnant among the other descendants of Abraham (Isa. 60:6–7).

The Magi and God's Revelation

After a thorough study of Babylonian astronomy in relationship to the visit of the magi, Ferrari-D'Occhieppo, former chair of the Department of Theoretical Astronomy at the University of Vienna, asserted, "Even on the basis of the alleged relevance of the constellation and of the planets involved, the astrological evidence alone could not be sufficient to explain the pilgrimage of the Magi from their distant homeland to Jerusalem, nor their precise question about a newborn King of the Jews (Matt. 2:2)."[75]

If the star observed by the magi in the east could have been interpreted naturally, it would not have motivated those daily stargazers to leave their land and go to Jerusalem. Furthermore, no natural star, conjunction of stars, or even a supernova is able to lead people from Jerusalem to Bethlehem, which is a trip of 5 miles south. In addition, a natural astral appearance in heaven, no matter how brilliant it might be, could not have indicated the minute details in the town of Bethlehem. As a matter of fact, no star in heaven could come and stand just above the house where the child Jesus was (Matt. 2:10). It seems strange that a heavenly star "a hundred million times more luminous than the sun," as Brown put it, went unnoticed by the Jewish community in Jerusalem and its suburbs, and most important, by Herod, who meticulously inquired about the star (2:3, 8).

In a well-written article, Allison offered an answer to the above questions by suggesting that the star was a guiding angel.[76] Moved by similar concerns, Pentecost argued, "this star is better explained as a manifestation of the shining glory of God that He reveals [only] to those who are recipients of revelation."[77] Pentecost sees the shining of the star as parallel to the appearance of the "God of glory" to Abraham while in Ur of the Chaldees (Acts 7:2).[78] Seeing the star as the manifestation of God's glory solves the interpretive difficulty related to the star and fits better with the expectations of Old Testament predictions. However, the magi should be linked to Abraham rather than to Mesopotamia, the land of Abraham's origin. Abraham's Arabian children were singled out in the desert and became the recipients of a special revelation from God about the birth of the Messiah. These worshipers were led in a dream to go back to their land following a different route (Matt. 2:12). It is our conviction that they also may have been led to come to Jerusalem through a dream or a special revelation from heaven. This can explain why it took these magi a while before they arrived in Jerusalem. After Herod inquired from the magi about the time of the appearance of the heavenly sign of Christ, he killed all the children of age two and under. Thus it appears that the magi were reluctant to leave, though intrigued by the shining, until they received a confirmation from God similar to the appearance of the angel to the shepherds in the fields (Luke 2:1–12).

The Magi and the Prophetic Light

Since in his infancy narrative (chaps. 1–2) Matthew was building his argument on the motif of Scriptures' fulfillment, the story of the magi would be apparently fulfilling the messianic expectations of Isaiah 60:1–7. As a matter of fact, Isaiah 60:1–7 starts with the rising of the shining glory of the Lord over Jerusalem in the midst of surrounding darkness (vv. 1–2). It goes on to picture the nations and kings as being moved by that light (v. 3). Then it extends an invitation for Jerusalem to lift up its eyes and rejoice because the wealth of the nations shall be converted to it (vv. 4–5). The prophecy gives next an explicit description of Arabian caravans bringing their wealth of frankincense, gold, and animal stock and rejoicing in worshiping the Lord (vv. 6–7). In view of the opposition of Jerusalem's leadership to the Messiah, the rise of the glory of the Lord was restricted to a few elect Gentiles (Matt. 2:1–12) and a few elect Jews (17:1–8; Luke 2:1–12) who are recipients of God's revelation.[79] The bright shining was only perceived by the magi because it was only revealed to them as a precursor of the revelation of God's glory in the coming kingdom.[80]

Assuming that these magi were chiefs of tribes or "kings" as Tertullian related, one can easily see the connection between Isaiah's statement and the journey of the magi, drawn by the brilliance of the Star of Bethlehem, to Jerusalem. In summary, Isaiah 60:1–3 predicts the rising of Christ's brilliance above Jerusalem, a brilliance that will be seen by kings who will walk by its shining. The magi equated the brilliance with the star itself and came to Jerusalem attracted by it, bringing a token of loyalty and dedication of their wealth (Isa. 60:4–5) to the King of the Jews. Thus the whole of Isaiah 60:1–7 is likely behind Matthew 2:1–12, and those who were drawn by the shining glory of the Lord in Isaiah 60:1–3 were likely the Arabians offering him their gifts of spices and gold mentioned in Isaiah 60:6.

13

THE MAGI-ARAB WORSHIPERS OF CHRIST (PART 2)

THE PREVIOUS CHAPTER UNCOVERED THE diversity of traditions related to the origin of the magi. Traditions can be misleading and conflicting, however. Only a consideration of the text in its context can offer a reliable ground for sound conclusions. The biblical text itself strongly favors the Arabian origin of the magi. In-depth study confirms the validity of this theory and its complete harmony with Scriptures and biblical teaching. We already saw that the term *magi* does not rule out an Arabian origin, and that the earliest church fathers advocated this ethnicity with regard to these visitors. Furthermore, we noted that astronomy is most likely irrelevant to the story. God's direct revelation was probably behind the mysterious shining in heaven and the prompting of the magi to visit Jerusalem. Even if astronomy was at stake, Arabs were most famous for their interest in the constellations. In the following, we will consider further evidence related to geography, the gifts, and typological fulfillment of Scriptures.

Evidence from Geography

The magi were identified by Matthew as "from the east." Papias, the second-century bishop of Hierapolis in Asia Minor (died A.D. 130), claimed that Matthew initially wrote a first draft of his gospel in Hebrew.[1] If this is indisputable and if a copy of that draft survived until today, then a lot of ink would have been unnecessary in trying to determine where these magi came from. For Matthew would have been specific enough using the term *east* in Hebrew *(qedem)* to point out to his Jewish audience the origin of these famous visitors. In fact, "east" for a Hebrew audience was a clear designation of north Arabia and this is backed by the following argumentation.

First, the present study has already established that the children of the east *(benê qedem)* of the Old Testament are the Arab nomadic tribes formed mostly of the children that Abraham dismissed to the Syro-Arabian Desert east of Palestine (Gen. 25:1–6, 12–18). This fact is attested by the biblical use of the term that makes the Ishmaelites a prominent section among them (Judg. 6:3; 7:12; 8:10; Jer. 49:23; Ezek. 25:4, 10).[2] Thus the land of the east *(qedem)* was used as a geographical reference to Syro-Arabia in Old Testament times, as well as in New Testament times. In addition to the testimony of Clement of Rome, Justin Martyr, Tertullian, and Epiphanius of Salamis, Eusebius also referred to the "land of the east" as designating the dwelling place of the descendants of Abraham through Keturah.[3] Musil refers even to the recent bedouin use of the denominative verb *sharraq* stemming from the noun *sharq,* meaning in Arabic, east. This verb was used by bedouins whenever they wanted to move to the inner parts of the desert, regardless of the direction they were following with regard to the sun.[4] Thus the term *east* for a Hebrew audience was always linked with the Arabian Desert lying in the Transjordan.

Second, for twenty-first-century readers, especially those who live in areas remote from the Middle East and have wider geographical perspectives, the "east" may suggest Babylon, Persia, or even India and China. But for those who lived in Palestine in biblical times, going to these countries started by proceeding north. Moreover, most visitors from these countries avoided crossing the Arabian Desert because of its dangers and hazardous environment. Therefore, as Charbel observes, anyone who came from east of the Euphrates river had to enter Palestine from the north; consequently these countries were considered the land of the north.[5] Scriptural evidence for this geographical concept seems to back this claim. Several Old Testament passages referred to the Assyrians and the Babylonians as being the people of the north (Isa. 14:31; Jer. 1:13–15; 3:18; 4:6; 6:22; 16:15; 31:8; 46:10; Zeph. 2:13; Zech. 2:6; 6:6).[6]

Persia is also referred to as the land of the north in Isaiah 41:25a. The three references to Cyrus coming from the east (41:2, 25b; 46:11) may be advanced against this identification. However, there are two reasons why "east" is not normative there, and is not to be considered as a geographical designation for that land. First of all, the Hebrew term used to refer to the coming of Cyrus from the east is not *qedem* but *mizrakh*. While *qedem* means "in front of" and designates for the Israelite the area east of the Jordan,[7] *mizrakh* simply means "the rising (of the sun)." *Qedem* is geographical, while *mizrakh* is astronomical. Thus *qedem* as a geographical location is never used in reference to Persia or Babylon, and using *mizrakh* instead to refer to the east from a divine perspective establishes further the fact that the "east" direction *(qedem)* is for the Palestinian Jew a technical term referring to the Syro-Arabian Desert. Furthermore, this conclusion is also asserted by the designation of the land of Persia in the same verse as being "the north" (41:25a). Thus, as far as the Palestinian Jew is concerned, armies and kings coming from Persia or Babylon to the Holy Land were never mentioned with the connotation of "coming from the east."[8]

Not only did the narrator refer to these magi as being "from the east" (Matt. 2:1), but also they referred to their land as being the "east" (2:2, 9), thus using *the east* as the technical term applied in biblical times to the Arabian Desert, where they saw the star.[9] Montgomery notes, "this name, Kedem, i.e., East, can only be explained from a Palestinian point of view, and the region must have lain east of Palestine. And it lay in the so-called desert, the Roman Arabia Deserta."[10] Though the term *qedem,* the underlying Semitic concept behind the Greek *tē anatolē* was explicit enough for Matthew and his initial readers, it takes the twenty-first-century audience much effort to bridge the cultural gap to settle with Arabia. It is there that the magi should be placed and not in the lands of Assyria, Babylon, or Persia, biblically recognized as the land of the north.[11]

Evidence from the Gifts of the Magi

Having developed the geographical argument in favor of Arabia as the land of the magi, it is appropriate to consider the significance of the gifts of gold, frankincense, and myrrh to the theory of the Arabian origin.

Incense, the Ancient Oil of Arabia

From ancient times the Arabian Peninsula was known for its supremacy in the spice trade. As early as the fifth century B.C. Arabia specialized in the production of frankincense and myrrh.[12] In this regard, the historian Herodotus (fifth century B.C.) wrote, "Arabia is the most distant to the south of all inhabited countries: and this is the *only country that yields frankincense and myrrh* and casia and cinnamon and gum-mastich. All these but myrrh are difficult for the Arabians to get." [13]

In addition to Herodotus's testimony, the Roman naturalist Pliny the Elder (first century A.D.) makes very significant statements regarding the monopoly of Arabia in the production of frankincense and myrrh.

> The *chief products of Arabia* then are *frankincense and myrrh;* the latter it shares also with Cave-dwellers' country, but *no country besides Arabia produces frankincense* and not even the whole of Arabia. About in the middle of that country are the Astramitae [likely Hadramaut], a district of the Sabaei, the capital of their realm being Sabota, situated on a lofty mountain; and eight days' journey from Sabota is a frankincense-producing district belonging to the Sabaei called

> Sariba. . . . Adjacent to the Astramitae is another district, the Minaei, through whose territory *the transit for the export of the frankincense* is along one narrow track. It was *these people who originated the trade and who chiefly practise it, and from them the perfume takes the name "Minaean,"* none of the Arabs beside these have ever seen an incense-tree, and not even all of these, and it is said that there are not more than 3,000 families who retain the right of trading in it as a hereditary property, and that consequently the members of these families are called sacred.[14]

The Sabaeans mentioned by Pliny here come from Saba', which should be associated with biblical Sheba, and are the "most distinguished branch of the South Arabian family."[15] The Sabaeans dominated the incense trade for centuries and probably for millennia before Christ.[16] However, toward the end of the first millennium B.C. the power of incense marketing shifted northward to the Nabataean kingdom.[17]

Strabo, the first-century A.D. geographer, divides the country of Arabia into five divisions, two of which are myrrh-producing sections and frankincense-producing sections. He identifies Cataban as the frankincense-producing area and Hadramawt as the myrrh-producing land, both of which are located in south Arabia.[18]

Thus it was an established fact in the ancient world that all of Arabia spread a very delicious fragrance,[19] and that south Arabia in particular was the aromatic country[20] par excellence. Therefore, two of the three gift items that the magi presented to Christ formed a primary source for the economic power and wealth of the country of Arabia over a very lengthy period of time. Due to these important natural resources, the kingdom of Sheba became, according to Diodorus, the wealthiest kingdom in the ancient world.[21]

The Precious Gold of Arabia

The fame of the gold of Arabia is well confirmed in biblical references (1 Kings 10:10; Ps. 72:15; Isa. 60:6; Ezek. 27:22; 38:13) and classic writers as well. Diodorus Siculus (first century B.C.) again testifies to the fact that gold was a great source of strength for ancient Arabia.

> *There is also mined in Arabia the gold called "fireless," which is not smelted from ores, as is done among all other peoples,* but is dug out directly from the earth; it is found in nuggets about the size of chestnuts, and is so fiery-red in color that when it is used by artisans as a setting for the most precious gems it makes the fairest of adornments.[22]

> *The land which comes next is inhabited by Alilaei and Gasandi, Arab peoples, and is not fiery hot, like the neighboring territories. . . . The Land produces everything and is exceptionally fertile. . . . Gold they discover* in underground galleries which have been formed by nature and *gather in abundance*—not that which has been fused into a mass out of gold—dust, but the virgin gold which is called, from its condition when found, *"unfired" gold.* And as for size the smallest nugget found is about as large as the stone of fruit, and the largest not much smaller than a royal nut. This gold they wear about both their wrists and necks, perforating it and alternating with transparent stones. And since *this precious metal abounds in their land,* . . . they exchange it with merchants for equal parts of the latter wares.[23]

Psalm 72 as related in the Septuagint clearly predicts that the Messiah of Israel, Son of David, will be given of the "gold of Arabia." This confirms that the gold of that land was very famous and much sought after.

Classical sources and Scripture references mentioned earlier make it clear that gold was also a much sought after trade item in Arabia because of its abundance and the degree of purity it was famous for.[24]

The Nabataean Control of Arabian Trade

The Nabataean Arabs, Israel's Ishmaelite neighbors, who occupied the major oases on the incense road in north Arabia, started monopolizing the traffic of Arabian spices as early as the fourth century B.C.[25] Diodorus relates how the Syrians in their first surprise attack on Petra seized much frankincense and myrrh and about 500 talents of silver,[26] and how these Nabataeans were heavily involved in the trade of precious goods from Arabia northward, thus accumulating a lot of wealth from the trade business.[27]

However, incense traffic between Arabia, Syria, and Egypt dates much earlier than the time of the Nabataeans, and the account of the journey of the queen of Sheba to Jerusalem portraying her apparently successful visit to King Solomon is an indication of this fact (1 Kings 10). The discovery of eighth-century B.C. south Arabic pottery with Minaean inscriptions at Tell el-Kheleifeh (Eṣion-geber; modern ʿElāt) "furnished proof of early trade between Israel and Arabia."[28]

As Pliny explained, the journey along the principal overland route from the south to the north was made in sixty-five stages.[29] This route, at its northern end, was split into several branches leading to various destinations. One branch went through Aelana (modern ʾElāt),[30] another route went through Leuce Come, then Petra, and Rhinocolura (modern Al-ʿArish).[31] Another branch must have followed the Kings Highway through Transjordan (which the magi may have followed, taking off at a branch going westward to Jerusalem), while a different branch split off at Teima' going to Dumah and thence to Mesopotamia.[32]

Until its demise in around 100 B.C., merchants of the Minaean kingdom in the south were "the main transporters of aromatics to the Mediterranean," according to Graf.[33] Thereafter, the Nabataean Arabs distinguished themselves as "the primary conveyors of frankincense and myrrh from South Arabia, no longer just middlemen."[34] Graf explains that "in the process they developed numerous settlements along the caravan routes between the Hejaz and Damascus, and between Petra and Gaza."[35] Powerful Nabataean influence spread across Arabia.

Since Isaiah 60:6 is most likely in the background of the magi story, the gifts presented to Christ should constitute the strength of the nations offering them (60:5). This is why an Arabian origin for these magi fits perfectly the picture in view of the significance of the gift items to the prestige of their kingdom. With this perspective in mind, the magi should have come to Jerusalem accompanied by a caravan of camels,[36] carrying not small boxes of gifts as it is often pictured on Christmas cards, but a great share of their honor and power residing in frankincense, myrrh, and gold.

Arab Magi Fulfill Biblical Typology

An Arabian origin of the magi fits the expectation of typological narrative in the Old Testament. Hengel and Merkel divided chapter 2 of Matthew into five sections, each hinging on a specific geographical location predicted in prophecy.[37] Four of these are Bethlehem (Mic. 5:1, 2; Matt. 2:6), Egypt (Hos. 11:1; Matt. 2:15), Ramah (Jer. 31:25; Matt. 2:17–18), and Nazareth (Isa. 11:1; 53:3; Matt. 2:23). Matthew 2:11, with Isaiah 60:6 in the background, is associated with the "east."

Though Hengel and Merkel see Isaiah 60:6 behind the worship of the magi, they stop short of clearly identifying the visitors as Arabians,[38] which is what the prophecy explicitly teaches. Nevertheless, it seems that Hengel in a more recent publication favors this proposal.[39] Still, many other commentators, though seeing the same allusion to Isaiah, also stop short of asserting that these worshipers were Arabian.[40] They just see in the gifts a reference to Gentile tributes to the Lord. This uncertainty may be caused by the confusing use of the term *magi* and the general reference to the east. The following scenario is an attempt to offer additional exegetical evidence in favor of the Arabian origin of the magi.

Preliminary Considerations

That typology is an acceptable hermeneutical method is an established fact among commentators despite the differences regarding its latitude.[41] Von Rad sees that "our knowledge of Christ is incomplete without the witness of the Old Testament. . . . But the Old Testament must first of all be heard in its witness to the *creative Word of God in history;* and in these *dealings of God in history,* in his acts of judgment as well as his acts of redemption, we may everywhere *discern what is already a Christ-event*" (emphasis added).[42] For R. T. France, "typology is not confined to a rigid list of recognized 'types.' It springs from the conviction that there is a *consistency in God's dealings with men*, and it expresses itself in an interpretation of the Old Testament which traces the constant principles of God's working in history" (emphasis added).[43] This consistency in God's redemptive dealings displays "a *recurring rhythm* in past history which is taken up *more fully and perfectly* in the Gospel events" (emphasis added).[44]

With this in mind, it would be legitimate then to look for a pattern in God's design of Israel's redemptive history reflecting divine principles in dealing with his elect. This pattern, when present, is brought to full glory in the events of Jesus' life.[45] That Matthew is developing among other things in his infancy narrative a typological fulfillment of an Old Testament pattern is established beyond doubt by his use of Hosea's quote (Matt. 2:15). Realizing that the words of Hosea 11:1, which initially relate God's calling of Israel out of Egypt,[46] are spoken as a "historical record of the past," rather than "as a prophetical announcement of the future," Fairbairn sees that their fulfillment is possible "only because the event it recorded was typical."[47] Hosea 11:1 recalls God's calling of the nation to a role of testimony and a salvific work as a light to the Gentiles (cf. Exod. 19:6; Isa. 42:6).

Likewise, at the outset of his Gospel, Matthew presents Jesus, the "son of Abraham" (1:1), as "Light to the Gentiles" (1:3, 5, 6; 2:1, 2, 10, 22–23; 4:16). Consequently, he draws the nations to him (Isa. 60:1–7; Matt. 2:1–12), attracting those who are far off (Isa. 9:1–2; 42:6, 10–11; 49:6; 60:1–7). Having established him as Son of David, King of the Jews, by citing his genealogy (Matt. 1:1–17) and his birth fulfilling Isaiah 7:14 (Matt. 1:18–23), Matthew moves on to develop Isaiah's next messianic "light" prophecy (9:1–2), which determines the nature of the Messiah's ministry (2:1–4:16).

This section develops Christ's universal ministry as an Abrahamic Son of God who represents Israel as the King of the Jews and who will succeed where Israel stumbled (Isa. 42:18–22). Thus the magi story highlights *the east* (Matt. 2:1–12), the flight story focuses on *Egypt*

(2:13–18), and the return episode points to *Galilee* (2:19–23). Matthew 3:1–12 emphasizes that the true relationship to Abraham is through repentance and faith, while 3:6–4:11 highlights the object of faith, that is the true Son of God, and 4:12–16 culminates with the fulfillment of his light to the Gentiles prophecy (Isa. 9:1–2).[48]

Christ's identification with the nation Israel as the true Son of God (Hos. 11:1; Matt. 2:15) shows how events that accompanied Israel's calling to a life of victory and salvation among the nations set a pattern fulfilled in Christ's early life.[49]

Accordingly Jesus comes out of Egypt as Israel did (Matt. 13–23), passes through the water of baptism (3:13–17) as the people passed through the Red Sea (Exod. 13–14), goes into the wilderness of testing (Matt. 4:1–11) as Israel also did (Deut. 6–8), and establishes the charter of his kingdom (Matt. 5–7) as Israel received the Law at Mount Horeb (Exod. 19–24). Yet all of God's previous redemptive dealings following a similar pattern merge in Christ. Thus the typological "rhythm" reproduced in Christ's life is not restricted to Israel but extends to the life of its "redeemers" in the nation's early history, as the following argument shows.

The Typological Pattern

In his speech to the Sanhedrin (Acts 7) Stephen highlighted two Old Testament types that carried out a redemptive work in Israel's history, but, as in Christ's case, were rejected at first until the time appointed by God for their ministry. These were Joseph and Moses, who both stood as federal heads of the nation with its fate hinging to a large extent on the outcome of their salvific work. The pattern that seems to recur in the early life of Joseph, Moses, and Israel seems to contain three elements.

Community Threat—Internal Rejection

The first element is a threat on the life of God's anointed one by the covenant community during the initial revelation of his appointment from God. This is seen in the plotting of Joseph's brothers to kill him because of his dreams (Gen. 37:18–24; Acts 7:9–10). The same element recurs twice in the life of Moses: first his life was threatened at his birth by Pharaoh, and he was rejected by the Israelites upon his first attempt to deliver them (Exod. 2:13–14; Acts 7:23–28). The nation Israel as a whole was threatened by Canaanite syncretism that endangered its viability as an elect nation set apart to carry God's redemptive program among the nations (Gen. 38).

Egypt's Might—God's Protection

The second element in the typological pattern is the irony seen in the involvement of the land of Egypt in the survival of God's anointed one. Egypt is presented as a mighty fortress sovereignly moved by God to protect his called one. The universality of God's redemptive work in the Old Testament is expressed by the involvement of the Gentiles in protecting and providing for the redeemer. This protection is provided by the Gentiles during the initial phase of the life of God's anointed after the threat on his life.[50] Thus Joseph was protected in Egypt and promoted to become second in command after Pharaoh (Gen. 37:36; 39–42). Moses was sovereignly rescued by the daughter of Pharaoh and reared in Pharaoh's palace for forty years and reached a position similar to that of Joseph, being reckoned as the son of Pharaoh's daughter (Exod. 2). The Israelites were sent down to Egypt where they spent a period of 400 years in a period of incubation until the appointed time when they were called to assume their redemptive ministry among the nations (Exod. 19:6; Isa. 42:6).

Arabia's Wealth—God's Provision

A third element in the pattern is the involvement of Arabia in the survival of these typical characters. Arabia is often presented in Old Testament narratives as a land blessed by God with a coveted wealth of incense and aromatics (see above) and a land of divine revelation (Exod. 2:1–4; 19–24; Deut. 33:1–2; Hab. 3:3, 7; Gal. 4:25). As such it is sovereignly used by God to provide for his anointed one. Egypt protects and Arabia provides, and all is under his sovereignty and design of history and geography. In Joseph's case, the Arabian element is exemplified by the Ishmaelite/Midianite caravan traders who bought Joseph from his brothers with incense money while on their way to sell spices and aromatic goods in Egypt (Gen. 37:25–30; Acts 7:9). In Moses' case, Arabia appears in his flight to the incense trading land of Midian, where God sovereignly provided for him through Arabian Midianites and prepared him spiritually, when Pharaoh wanted to kill him as he was rejected by his own (Exod. 2:15–22; Acts 7:29). Thus God sovereignly used both Arabia and Egypt during the preparation of his anointed One for his work of redemption. In a similar fashion, Israel also spent forty years in Arabia preparing for its missionary role among the Gentiles (Exod. 19–24; Hab. 3:3, 7; Deut. 33:2; Num. 1–26). The wilderness of Arabia was the place where God supernaturally provided for Israel's survival and spiritual equipment before entering Canaan (Deut. 6–8).

Christ's Infancy—Typology Fulfillment

Matthew retrieves the element of threat in the typological pattern by vividly describing the disturbance of Herod and Jerusalem at the visit of the magi and deliberately recounting Herod's killing of the children of Bethlehem and its surrounding villages (Matt. 2:3, 16–18). As in the case of Moses, Joseph, and Israel, Jesus was sent to Egypt in order to protect him from Herod's plot against his life. He stayed there until Herod died (Matt. 2:13–15). The third element in the pattern is the involvement of Arabia in the preparatory phase of God's anointed. In Christ's case, this is seen in the magi coming from the east, with their expensive gifts of frankincense, myrrh, and gold, providing the poor family of Joseph (Luke 2:24) with the means to be able to pay for the expenses of the flight to Egypt and the sojourning there. Thus as in Joseph's story in Genesis (chap. 37), Arabian incense money was the human means that carried God's anointed one to Egypt for protection.

Hence, in Matthew's narrative, a Persian or Babylonian origin for the magi introduces a foreign element to the typological pattern established in Old Testament narratives. This pattern most likely sets the infrastructure of Matthew's development of the infancy narrative. True, it is acceptable to see the visit of the magi as a representation of Gentile salvation. However, we have already established the sequential priority of the Arabian children of Abraham in God's plan for Gentiles' restoration. Thus an Arabian origin of the magi not only fulfills prophetic expectations but also seems essential for the reproduction of the typological pattern forecast in prophecy (Isa. 60:6).

SUMMARY OF PART 4 FINDINGS

Part 4 has shown that Arabs were part of Old Testament restoration prophecies (Isa. 42:1–10; 60:1–7, etc.). Belonging to the Abrahamic stock and displaying the sign of God's covenant in their flesh, they were more accountable to God's revelation. Thus they came first in God's program of visitation of the nations; the more the privilege, the greater the responsibility. This was a primary reason why Paul visited Arabia first in his missionary activities as apostle to the Gentiles (Gal. 1:15–17). The Jewish presence in Arabia prior to the coming of Christ was very impressive. Mass conversions to Judaism among Arabs were witnessed during that time and testified by historical records. The presence of Jews from Arabia, natives, and proselytes in the days of Pentecost was a further attestation of this fact (Acts 2:11). Thus the gospel message traveled to Arabia as early as the days of Pentecost through those who heard it preached to them by the apostles (Acts 2:11).

On the other hand, the ethnic origin of the magi in Matthew's Gospel could not be determined only by the conventional use of the term *magos* or by their mere interest in the stars. If these were the only clues available, one would have ended up placing them either in Persia or in Babylonia, areas conventionally associated with astrological activities of magi. Since the term *magos* had wider applications, eastern traditions reflected among earliest church fathers associating the magi with Arabia become significant. Later eastern traditions testified strongly to the Arabian origin as well.[51]

Still the Arabian view was proven to rely on stronger exegetical considerations. In that regard, the preceding study has shown that the geographical designation "east" pointed exclusively in biblical times to the Transjordan, and more broadly to all of the north Arabian Desert. The gifts presented to the King of the Jews by the magi represented Arabian sources of wealth *par excellence.* Arabs were the chief producers and conveyors of incense and gold for centuries before Christ. They presented thirty tons of frankincense to the Persian king every year as a token of loyalty.[52] The prophecy of Isaiah 60:1–7 predicted the conversion of the wealth of the nations, primarily of Arabians, to the Messiah in Jerusalem at the dawning of the messianic light upon the nation of Israel. Thus it becomes natural to see Arab magi pledging their allegiance to the King of kings.

Additionally, the typological pattern developed in Old Testament narratives revealed the involvement of Arabia and Egypt repeatedly in the preparatory stage of the anointed one called by God to a work of redemption. Matthew presented the Messiah as the Light to the Gentiles in general (Matt. 1:3–6), while the Old Testament places the circumcised descendants of Abraham first in God's program of restoring the nations (Isa. 42:6, 11; 60:5–7; cf. Gal. 1:17). Having been dismissed to the land of the east for the sake of Abraham's seed (Gen. 25:5–6), it seems that Arabs (the magi) were called from the east back home to worship Christ, the long-awaited Seed. On the other hand, does prophetical history warrant us in expecting a double fulfillment of Arab visitation at Messiah's second coming (Isa. 60:1–7)? In many ways, kingdom related prophecies fulfilled partially at Messiah's first coming will be brought to consummation at his second. This is what the present study is proposing.

CONCLUSION

ARABS IN THE SHADOW OF ISRAEL

Arabs and God's Oracles

The fulfillment of the promise given by God to Abraham concerning a seed was humanly impossible in view of Sarah's chronic barrenness. Thus, after a long period of waiting, the couple felt compelled to opt for cultural means of appropriating an heir. Hagar's pregnancy from Abraham's union with her triggered a series of events that led the slave to the wilderness in an attempt to escape the unfortunate circumstances that transpired in Abraham's home after her pregnancy (Gen. 16:1–6). There, Hagar became the recipient of a special divine attention. The Lord covenanted to bless the maid and gave her promises concerning her son, whom he called Ishmael, as a confirmation that Yahweh listened to her affliction under slavery.

Thus a correct understanding of the oracles concerning Ishmael considers them in the context of God's comfort and active listening to the slave woman. As opposed to Hagar's subjection, helplessness, and fleeing uncompensated from the presence of her mistress, Ishmael was predicted to be a lover of freedom as a nomad, constantly fighting against those who would attempt to subdue him (16:12a–b).

Furthermore, he would live in the Arabian Desert in the presence of his kin the Israelites, as opposed to his mother's run-away condition (16:12c). He would have his compensation and inheritance directly from the Lord. Being close by would keep him near the unfolding of God's redemptive work through the elect nation. He would also be a continuous reminder to Israel that the Abrahamic blessings are to be appropriated by faith alone. In the process of Ishmael's dismissal from Abraham's home (21:9–21), he became the recipient of further divine promises that pledged to bless him and make him a great nation (17:20; 21:18).

Biblical and secular history revealed that Arab Ishmaelites multiplied exceedingly in the desert (16:10) and became a great nation and a mighty nomadic power, fulfilling God's promise foretold to Hagar. Though they did not leave many physical remains as nomads, they appeared in Assyrian and Babylonian chronicles as formidable foes and a much coveted economical power. Assyria and Babylonia chose to fight them, yet those perished and Arab Ishmaelites survived and flourished. Later, the Persians preferred to secure their friendship and benefit from their mastery of the desert for tactical purposes. In return, huge amounts of Arabian incense were channeled as gifts to these Persians. Ancient Arabs reached their political and economical climax with the Nabataean kingdom. The magnificence of this kingdom is still the object of admiration of many archaeologists and historians all over the world.

All of the divine oracles concerning Ishmael were literally fulfilled in biblical times and pre-Islamic history. While empires crumbled and powers vanished, they continued to increase in number and might as nomads in the desert and proved that God has heard Hagar as he had promised and had watched over her descendants for a purpose in history.

Arabs and the Abrahamic Legacy

A common misconception among Christians today is to infer that nonelection for the administration of God's redemptive purposes in history means spiritual alienation. The evidence presented in this study shows that this is not true in regard to Ishmael. God's election of Abraham's seed Isaac to perpetuate the program set for the Abrahamic covenant in history did not automatically alienate Ishmael from his share in the blessing of that covenant. Ishmael was put under the Abrahamic blessing through obedience to the rite of circumcision. God blessed him spiritually, as the book of Job with its Arabian setting clearly revealed. After the calling of Israel to the land of Canaan for a ministry of "light to the Gentiles" (Exod. 19:6; Isa. 42:6; 49:6), Ishmael and his descendants were among the first people to benefit spiritually from Israel's testimony. Despite a couple of conflicts over grazing land, the period called "the Light of Israel" evidenced an integration of Ishmaelites into Israel's social and theological life that culminated with the era of Solomon. The children of Ishmael were part of God's people and the royal family and kingdom administration.

However, during the period called "the Darkness of Israel," idolatry dominated the Ishmaelite tribes, as their monotheism moved into the background. As such, God's rod of discipline on Israel affected them heavily, also. Nonetheless, much like Israel, God's hand of judgment did not crush them completely. Many of the Jews most likely settled in Arabia during the postexilic period. Consequently, because of intense social and religious exchange between Jews and Arabs during the intertestamental period, Ishmael's line likely shared the messianic expectations common among the Jews.

The prophetic restoration oracles, especially in Isaiah (42:1–10; 60:1–7), reflect a theological priority for the Arabians in God's program of visitation to the Gentiles. Thus an elect handful among them was drawn by the shining light of the Messiah rising over Jerusalem. The Arabian magi responded in faith and came to offer their pledge of loyalty to the King of the Jews. Their story brings full circle the drama of the dismissal of Ishmael and Keturah's children to the east (Gen. 25:6). These were kept away for Isaac's sake, so that the unfolding of the Abrahamic covenant in history would not be affected by their sharing in their father's estate. Yet when the Seed of Abraham, Christ, was revealed in history, he made them the recipients of a special revelation in the east. He invited them to be first among the Gentiles to participate in his salvation. Paul's commission to preach the gospel to the Gentiles highlighted Arabia first in his outreach program (Gal. 1:15–18) as an additional application of Arab sequential priority in the redemptive program of the nations (Isa. 42:1–10; 60:1–7, etc.).

Arabs in the Future of Israel

The previous historical and theological survey identified the intimate link between Israel's religious condition and that of the Arabs throughout biblical history. Blessings and discipline were mutually transferable between Isaac's and Ishmael's lines. The fact that both groups stem out of the same Abrahamic root makes this unavoidable. God's decree that Ishmael would dwell "in the presence of all his brethren" (Gen. 16:12c) put a divine sanction on this reality, too. Thus in view of the partial reception of the Messiah by Israel at his first coming, the Arabs did not display mass conversions to Christ in history, either. The failure of Israel as a nation to submit to the Lordship of Jesus largely affected its closest theological kin, the Arabs. Nevertheless, as in Israel, Arabia witnessed many individual conversions to Christ. Organized churches sprouted in several areas of the Peninsula before Islam appeared.

On the other hand, the restoration oracles that were only partially exhausted at the first advent of Christ are still awaiting their full implementation at his second. Prophecy seems to predict the future restoration of a faithful remnant among the Jews through the purging of the Tribulation (Dan. 12:1; Matt. 24:21–22; Rom. 11:25–32). However, one more time also prophecy appears to forecast a crucial role to Arabs in the survival of the remnant of Israel.

Is it possible that the typological pattern witnessed in the preparation of God's anointed ones in the Old Testament would be partially reproduced during the Tribulation period, also? Does Revelation 12 teach that Arabia will be a place of shelter for the Jewish believers persecuted by the false Messiah and the Beast during the Tribulation (Rev. 12:6, 14)? Does this passage teach that Arabians will extend their provision to the faithful among their theological cousins while they are rejected by their own? If that is the case, then the protection of the believing remnant by Arabs in the Tribulation implies a mass conversion among the Arabs too. Scriptures make this the natural implication of hosting the elect (Matt. 10:40–42; 25:41–46). A future mass conversion to the Messiah from among Arabs would be consistent with the cause-effect theological link between Israel and its Ishmaelite kin witnessed in earlier biblical history. Whether end-time details described above are accurate or not, what seems undeniable is the intimacy between the religious fate of biblical Israel as a nation and that of the Arabs. If the Bible offers ground for a coming visitation among the Jews, it does the same for the Arabs as restoration prophecy foretells.

The present conflict in the Middle East over Abrahamic material blessings does not reflect a stereotype sustained in biblical history and prophecy. It does not even reflect the pattern of Arab-Jewish relationships in postbiblical history. On the contrary, it reveals a crisis in interpretation of history and theology. When the Lord called Abraham, whom both sides claim to be their physical ancestor, to go to the Promised Land, the patriarch sojourned in the land of Palestine as a foreigner, becoming a blessing to his neighbors, because his heart was set on the heavenly city engineered by God (Heb. 11:8–10). Since the Abrahamic promises are appropriated by faith in Christ only (Gal. 3:6–9; Eph. 3:6), this should create among Christians a desperate burden to refrain from political agendas and invest in the spiritual awakening predicted among both the Arabs and Jews. The same God who predicted a shining of Messiah's glory over a faithful remnant of the Jews (Isa. 60:1–3) foreordained the drawing of the Arab faithful remnant to the glory of salvation light (60:5–7). God's visitation of Jerusalem in messianic times cannot be separated from his visitation of his people among the Arabian tribes of Midian and Sheba (60:6) or the Christian worship of Ishmael's children (60:7). Removing unwarranted biases against Arabs, which neither the Bible nor history sustains, would play a healing role in the Middle East conflict. It would also create a better attitude for dialogue between the antagonists.

Meanwhile, prioritizing the redemptive mandate over the political agenda harmonizes well with the heartbeat of Christ in the Middle East equation (Acts 1:7–8). Eventually, only the impartation of the gospel can bring lasting peace among these Abrahamic cousins and in this privileged geographical area of the world.

ENDNOTES

INTRODUCTION: ARABS YESTERDAY AND TODAY

1. Susannah Tarbush, ed., *The Arab Image in the West: Conversazione [Forum] Held at Oxford 7–9 June 1998* (Amman, Jordan: Royal Institute for Inter-faith Studies and Centre for Lebanese Studies, 1998), 8.
2. Ibid., 17.
3. Ibid.
4. See, for example, Alois Musil, *Arabia Deserta: A Topographical Itinerary*, Oriental Explorations and Studies, no. 2 (New York: American Geographical Society, 1927); James Montgomery, *Arabia and the Bible* (Philadelphia: University of Pennsylvania Press, 1934), 37; Philip K. Hitti, *History of the Arabs from the Earliest Times to the Present* (London: Macmillan, 1970), 41; Robert Houston Smith, "Arabia," in *ABD,* 1:327.
5. Fred V. Winnett, "The Arabian Genealogies in the Book of Genesis," in *Translating and Understanding the Old Testament: Essays in Honor of Herbert Gordon May,* ed. Harry Thomas Frank and William L. Reed (Nashville: Abingdon, 1970), 171–96.
6. Josephus, *Jewish Antiquities* 1.12.4; see also the pseudepigraphal book of Jubilees, in J. H. Charlesworth, ed., *The Old Testament Pseudepigrapha* (New York: Doubleday, 1985), 2:94.

7. Unless otherwise specified, the information on Arab postbiblical history is gleaned from the following sources: P. K. Hitti, *History of the Arabs from the Earliest Times to the Present* (London: MacMillan Education, 1970); idem, *The Arabs: A Short History*, rev. ed. (South Bend, Ind.: Regnery/Gateway, 1970); Bernard Lewis, *The Arabs in History*, new ed. (Oxford: Oxford University Press, 1993); idem, *The Middle East: A Brief History of the Last 2,000 Years* (New York: Touchstone, 1997); al-Tabarî, *Tārîkh al-Umam wal-Mulûk [History of Nations and Kings]* (Beirut: Dār al-Fikr, 1987); John A. Garraty and Peter Gay, eds., *The Columbia History of the World* (New York: Harper & Row, 1972); J. M. Roberts, *The Penguin History of the World* (London: Penguin Books, 1976).
8. Hitti, *History of the Arabs,* 87–108.
9. Ibid.
10. *Diodorus* 3.47.5–8.
11. Hitti, *History of the Arabs,* 49–66.
12. Lewis, *The Arabs in History,* 19.
13. *Diodorus* 19.94–100.
14. Cf. Lewis, *The Middle East*, 39–41.
15. Cf. Hitti, *History of the Arabs*, 59–60.
16. Ibid.; Lewis, *The Arabs in History,* 15–31.
17. J. Starcky, "Pétra et la Nabatène," in *Dictionnaire de la Bible,* supplement VII (Paris: Letouzey & Ané, Éditeurs, 1966), cols. 919–20.
18. John Lewis Burckhardt, *Travels in Syria and the Holy Land* (London: J. Murray, 1822), 418–34.
19. Hitti, *History of the Arabs,* 74–78; Lewis, *The Arabs in History,* 21–22.
20. Hitti, *History of the Arabs,* 74–78.
21. Ibid.; Lewis, *The Arabs in History,* 21–22.
22. For an elaborate defense of the Christianity of "Philip the Arab," see Irfan Shahîd, *Rome and the Arabs: A Prolegomenon to the Study of Byzantium and the Arabs* (Washington, D.C.: Dumbarton Oaks, 1984), 65–93.

23. Monophysitism is "a movement that emphasized the divine nature of Christ in the Christological dispute of the fifth century." Everett Ferguson et al., eds., "Monophysitism," in *The Encyclopedia of Early Christianity* (New York: Garland, 1990), 620.
24. Nestorian belief emphasized the two separate natures of Christ. "For Nestorius himself, salvation required that both the human and divine natures of Christ be complete, to guarantee the integrity of the incarnation and to protect the divine Logos from the blasphemous assertion that God could suffer pain or weakness." Ferguson et al., eds., "Nestorius," in *The Encyclopedia of Early Christianity*, 648.
25. Lewis, *The Arabs in History*, 27–28; also Hitti, *History of the Arabs*, 78–84.
26. Hitti, *The Arabs: A Short History*, 25.
27. Cf. al-Sayyed Abd el-Aziz Salem, *Tārîkh al-Dawlah al-ʿArabiyyah* [*History of the Arab Nation*] (Beirut: Dar al-Nahdhah al-ʿArabiyyah, 1986), 309–40.
28. Garraty and Gay, *The Columbia History of the World*, 259.
29. Ibid.; Roberts, *The Penguin History of the World*, 316–20; Hitti, *The Arabs: A Short History*, 31.
30. al-Tabarî, *Tārîkh al-Umam wal-Mulûk*, 2:383–465.
31. *Allah* is the Arabic translation of the term *God* (Gr. *Theos;* Heb. *Elohim*) all throughout the Arabic Bible. The difference is in the nature of God, not his identity among Jews, Christians, and Muslims. For more on this, see Imad Shehadeh, "A Comparison and a Contrast Between the Prologue of John's Gospel and Qur'ānic Sûrah 5" (Th.D. diss., Dallas Theological Seminary, 1990), 77–85. See also the recent book of Timothy George, *Is the Father of Jesus the God of Muhammad? Understanding the Differences Between Christianity and Islam* (Grand Rapids: Zondervan, 2002).
32. Cf. Hitti, *The Arabs: A Short History*, 32.
33. al-Tabarî, *Tārîkh al-Umam wal-Mulûk*, 2:383–465.
34. See Barbara Ann Kipfer, ed., *Encyclopedia of Archaeology* (New York: Kluwer Academic/Plenum, 2000), 342–43.

35. C. J. Gadd, "The Harran Inscriptions of Nabonidus," *Anatolian Studies* 8 (1958): 35–92. For more on the different ethnic groups that populated Arabia on the eve of Islam, see F. E. Peters, ed., *The Arabs and Arabia on the Eve of Islam,* The Formation of the Classical Islamic World, vol. 3, ed. Lawrence I. Conrad (Brookfield, Vt.: Ashgate, 1999); also Michael Lecker, *Jews and Arabs in Pre- and Early Islamic Arabia,* Variorum Collected Studies Series, CS639 (Brookfield, Vt.: Ashgate, 1998).
36. See also Garraty and Gay, *The Columbia History of the World,* 260.
37. Abd el-Aziz Salem, *Tarîkh al-Dawlah al-ʿArabiyyah,* 228–38.
38. al-Tabarî, *Tārîkh al-Umam wal-Mulûk,* 3:1ff.; Hitti, *The Arabs: A Short History,* 35–36.
39. Ibid., 3:31–84.
40. Ibid., 3:192–336.
41. Ibid., 4:3–37.
42. Lewis, *The Arabs in History,* 45.
43. al-Tabarî, *Tārîkh al-Umam wal-Mulûk,* 4:37–47.
44. Ibid., vols. 4–5.
45. Hitti, *The Arabs: A Short History,* 56–70; see also Lewis, *The Middle East,* 54–79.
46. al-Tabarî, *Tārîkh al-Umam wal-Mulûk,* 6:5–76.
47. Ibid., 7:334–69.
48. For more details on this period, see Hitti, *The Arabs: A Short History,* 80–93; Garraty and Gay, *The Columbia History of the World,* 265–71.
49. al-Tabarî, *Tārîkh al-Umam wal-Mulûk,* 8:573ff.
50. For further details on this period, see Lewis, *The Middle East,* 75–97.
51. Cf. Garratay and Gay, *The Columbia History of the World,* 269.
52. Ibid.
53. Events and dates in this paragraph are mostly gleaned from Garraty and Gay, *The Columbia History of the World,* 269; Lewis, *The Middle East,* 102–29, 399–405.
54. Nahum M. Sarna, *The JPS Torah Commentary: Genesis* בראשית (Jerusalem: Jewish Publication Society, 1989), 122.

55. Erwin Rosenthal, *Judaism and Islam* (London: Thomas Yoseloff, 1961), 130.
56. Ian J. Bickerton and Carla L. Klausner, *A Concise History of the Arab-Israeli Conflict* (Englewood Cliffs, N.J.: Prentice Hall, 1991), 18.
57. Translated in Bernard Lewis, "An Apocalyptic Vision of Islamic History," *Bulletin of the School of Oriental and African Studies* 13, no. 2 (1950): 321; cited in Lewis, *The Arabs in History,* 57–58.
58. Bickerton and Klausner, *A Concise History of the Arab-Israeli Conflict,* 18.
59. Ibid.
60. A. Wessels, *Arab and Christian? Christians in the Middle East* (Kampen: Kok, 1995), 22.
61. Paul Johnson, *History of the Jews* (New York: Harper & Row, 1987), 176.
62. Ibid.
63. Ibid.
64. Ibid., 177–78.
65. Wessels, *Arab and Christian?* 22.
66. S. D. Goitein, *Arabs and Jews: Their Contact Through the Ages* (New York: Schocken, 1974), 130.
67. Cf. Ritchie Ovendale, *The Origins of the Arab-Israeli Wars* (London: Longman, 1992), 3. See also, David Vital, *The Origins of Zionism* (Oxford: Clarendon, 1975), 222–23.
68. Bickerton and Klausner, *A Concise History of the Arab-Israeli Conflict,* 22–23.
69. Ibid.
70. Ibid.
71. Walter Laqueur, ed., *The Israel-Arab Reader: A Documentary History of the Middle East Conflict,* updated and expanded ed. (New York: Bantam, 1970), 6–11.
72. Ovendale, *The Origins of the Arab-Israeli Wars,* 8.
73. Laqueur, *The Israel-Arab Reader,* 11–12.
74. Bickerton and Klausner, *A Concise History of the Arab-Israeli Conflict,* 25.

75. Ibid. See also Vital, *The Origins of Zionism*, 187–200.
76. Ovendale, *The Origins of the Arab-Israeli Wars,* 12.
77. Ibid., 9.
78. Cf. George Antonius, *The Arab Awakening* (New York, Capricorn, 1965), 35–60.
79. Ibid., 43.
80. Ibid., 79–125. See also Ovendale, *The Origins of the Arab-Israeli Wars,* 9–12.
81. Ovendale, *The Origins of the Arab-Israeli Wars,* 6.
82. T. G. Fraser, "The Arab-Israeli Conflict," in *Studies in Contemporary History,* ed. T. G. Fraser and J. O. Springhall (New York: St. Martin's, 1995), 8; see also Charles L. Geddes, ed., *A Documentary History of the Arab-Israeli Conflict* (New York: Praeger, 1991), 35–38.
83. Laqueur, "The Israel-Arab Reader," 15–17.
84. Ibid., 12–15.
85. Ann M. Lesch and Dan Tschirgi, *Origins and Development of the Arab-Israeli Conflict* (Westport, Conn.: Greenwood, 1998), 8.
86. Ibid.
87. Fraser, "The Arab-Israeli Conflict," 9–14.
88. Cf. Geddes, *A Documentary History of the Arab-Israeli Conflict,* xiv.
89. Lesch and Tschirgi, *Origins and Development of the Arab-Israeli Conflict,* 9.
90. Fraser, *The Arab-Israeli Conflict,* 14–18. For a discussion of the exploitation of Jewish sufferings by Zionist leaders, see Norman G. Finkelstein, *The Holocaust Industry: Reflections on the Exploitation of Jewish Suffering* (London: Verso, 2000).
91. Cf. Lesch and Tschirgi, *Origins and Development of the Arab-Israeli Conflict,* 14.
92. One Israeli soldier expressed this mind-set by commenting on his participation in immediate reprisal attacks against Palestinians: "I didn't think in terms of 'showing the Arabs.' . . . My thinking and my motives had their starting point in the destruction

of the Jews in Europe. To 'show' the Gentiles afar, and not those close at hand." Cited in Lesch and Tschirgi, *Origins and Development of the Arab-Israeli Conflict,* 14.

93. Ibid., 10.
94. Geddes, *A Documentary History of the Arab-Israeli Conflict,* 285–90.
95. Ibid., 303.
96. Ibid.
97. David K Shipler, *Arab and Jew: Wounded Spirits in a Promised Land* (New York: Times Books, 1986), 10.
98. Yossi Beilin, "More War Is Not the Route to Israel's Security," *New York Times,* 30 March 2002.

Chapter 1: The Unfortunate Beginning (Gen. 16:1–6)

1. Cf. W. Atallah, "Al-Kalbî," in *The Encyclopedia of Islam,* ed. H. A. R. Gibb et al., new ed. (Leiden: E. J. Brill, 1978), 4:494–96.
2. These traditions are recorded in his book, *Djamharat al-Nasab,* translated into German by W. Caskel. Werner Caskel, *Ghamharat an-Nasab ["The Abundance of Kinship"]: Das genealogische Werk des Hišām Ibn Muhammad al-Kalbî* (Leiden: E. J. Brill, 1966). See also Atallah, "Al-Kalbî," 4:494–96. Al-Kalbî was criticized for not being reliable because he relied on oral tradition. For restoring the balance in the scholarly criticism of al-Kalbî and giving al-Kalbî his true worth, see Theodore Nöldeke, *Geschichte der Perser und Araber zur Zeit der Sasaniden, aus der arabischen Chronik des Tabarî* (Leiden: E. J. Brill, 1879).
3. See, for example, the doctoral dissertation of René Dagorn, *la geste d'ismael dans l'onomastique et la tradition arabe* (Paris: Champion, 1982).
4. *Diodorus* 2.48.4–5.
5. J. H. Charlesworth, ed., *The Old Testament Pseudepigrapha* (New York: Doubleday, 1985), 2:94.
6. Josephus, *Jewish Antiquities* 1.12.4; 2.3.3.
7. Millar seems to imply that no one before Josephus equated

Ishmael with the Nabataean Arabs. Fergus Millar, "Hagar, Ishmael, Josephus and the Origin of Islam," *JJS* 44 (1993): 36. However, the references in Jubilees and Diodorus mentioned earlier seem to make the same connection earlier than Josephus.

8. See also Philip K. Hitti, *History of the Arabs from the Earliest Times to the Present* (London: Macmillan, 1970), 30–32; James Montgomery, *Arabia and the Bible* (Philadelphia: University of Pennsylvania Press, 1934), 27.
9. Montgomery, *Arabia and the Bible,* 38; Hitti, *History of the Arabs,* 31–32.
10. Hitti, *History of the Arabs,* 32; al-Tabari, *Taʾrîkh el-Umam wal-Mulûk [History of Nations and Kings]* (Beirut: Dar al-Fikr, 1987), 2:327–62; see also W. Caskel, *Ghamharat an-Nasab ["The Abundance of Kinship"]: Das genealogische Werk des Hišām Ibn Muhammad al-Kalbi).*
11. Robert Houston Smith, "Arabia," in *ABD,* 1:324; Israel Ephʿal, *The Ancient Arabs: Nomads on the Borders of the Fertile Crescent 9th–5th Centuries b.c.* (Leiden: E. J. Brill, 1982), 8–9.
12. Ephʿal, *The Ancient Arabs,* 8.
13. Like the people of Tema', Sheba, Massa', *Ba-da-na-a-a Ha-at-ti-a-a,* the Me'unites, the people of Nebaioth and *Te-e-me* (ibid.).
14. Ibid. However, the northern view has to account for the fact that Herodotus, as early as the fifth century B.C., refers to the *Arabians* of the south dealing with frankincense and myrrh. *Herodotus* 3.107–8.
15. A. Grohmann, "Al ʿArab," in *The Encyclopedia of Islam,* ed. H. A. R. Gibb et al., new ed. (Leiden: E. J. Brill, 1960), 1:524–27.
16. I am indebted to the following sources for this synopsis on Ishmael in the Qurʾan and Muslim tradition. *ʾAl Qurʾān ʾAl Karîm* (Kingdom of Saudi Arabia: Majmaʿ ʾal Malik Fahd litibāʿat ʿal Mishaffʾal Sharîf, n.d.); Rudi Paret, "Ismāʿîl," in *The Encyclopedia of Islam,* new ed. (Leiden: E. J. Brill, 1978), 4:184–85; A. J. Wensinck, "Ismāʿîl," in *FEI,* 3:543–44; Reuven Firestone, *Journeys in Holy Lands: The Evolution of the Abraham-Ishmael Legends in Islamic Exegesis* (Albany: State University of New York

Press, 1990); al-Tabarî, *Ta'rîkh al-Rusul wal-Mulûk*, ed. M. J. DeGoeje as *Annales* (Leiden: E. J. Brill, 1964); H. Schmid, "Ismael im Alten Testament und im Qur'an," *Judaica* 32 (1976): 76–81, 119–29.

17. See also al-Tabari, *Qisas al-Anbiya'* (Beirut: Dar al-Fikr, 1989).
18. Several Arab countries today govern lands that were the scene of prominent civilizations in the past, such as the Pharaonic, the Assyrian, the Babylonian, and the Canaanite, etc. Many people in these Arab countries are aware of the rich history behind them, and they boast in it. Some of these may actually belong to bloodlines stemming out of these ancestors. Yet, since a big majority of these people belong to Islam, they still consider themselves children of Abraham (through Ishmael) by faith. Finally, some Arab Christians, who do not belong to Ishmael's bloodline, cannot avoid the geo-cultural association with that biblical figure, also.
19. For a fuller discussion of this corporate sin of the nations and its backgrounds, see Allen P. Ross, *Creation and Blessings* (Grand Rapids: Baker, 1988), 238–48; Derek Kidner, *Genesis: An Introduction and Commentary*, Tyndale Old Testament Commentaries, ed. D. J. Wiseman (Downers Grove, Ill.: InterVarsity, 1967), 109–11; Umberto Cassuto, *From Noah to Abraham, Genesis VI:9–XI:32*, vol. 2 of *A Commentary on the Book of Genesis*, trans. Israel Abrahams (Jerusalem: Magnes, 1961–64), 225–49.
20. Cassuto suggests that this spreading of the blessing had even started at Haran, where Abraham dwelt until his father died. The souls that he took with him from Haran upon proceeding to Canaan were, according to Cassuto, proselytes that he "won" to the Lord; see Cassuto, *From Noah to Abraham, Genesis VI:9–XI:32*, 320–21.
21. With regard to this stop at Haran, Genesis 11:31 says וַיֵּשְׁבוּ שָׁם, suggesting a not so short period of stay (cf. Acts 7:4). Furthermore, Abraham stayed in Haran until his father Terah died and left the city when he was seventy-five years old (Gen. 11:32; 12:4–5; Acts 7:4).

22. The first verse of Genesis 16 "reverses the usual Hebrew word order," putting the subject *Sarah* before the verb construction, *did not bear,* for the sake of emphasis. J. Gerald Janzen, "Hagar in Paul's Eyes and in the Eyes of Yahweh (Genesis 16)," *Horizons in Biblical Theology* 13 (June 1991): 4; Phyllis Trible, "The Other Woman: A Literary and Theological Study of the Hagar Story," in *Understanding the Word: Essays in Honor of Bernhard W. Anderson,* ed. James T. Butler et al., JSOT supplement, no. 37, ed. David J. A. Clines and Philip R. Davies (Sheffield, England: JSOT Press, 1985), 222.
23. Janzen, "Hagar in Paul's Eyes and in the Eyes of Yahweh (Genesis 16)," 4.
24. H. Freedman, trans., *Midrash Rabbah, Genesis* (New York: Soncino, 1983), 1:380.
25. So also Gordon J. Wenham, *Genesis 16–50,* in WBC, 2:6.
26. Claus Westermann, *Genesis 12–36: A Commentary,* trans. John J. Scullion (Minneapolis: Augsburg, 1981), 238; see also Wenham, *Genesis 16–50,* 2:62. Gese equates Hagar in Galatians with the city of *El-Hegra* north of Dedan (al-ʿUla). Hartmut Gese, "Τὸ δὲ Ἁγὰρ Σινὰ ὄρος ἐν τῇ Ἀραβίᾳ (Gal. 4:25)," in *Das Ferne und Nahe Wort,* ed. Fritz Maass, BZAW 105, ed. Georg Fohrer (Berlin: Alfred Töpelmann, 1967), 81–94. Subsequently, Gese puts the Mount of Sinai in Dedan (northwest Arabia). For a rebuttal of this view, see G. I. Davis, "Hagar, El-Hegra and the Location of Mount Sinai," *VT* 22 (1972): 152–63.
27. The Hebrew verb Sarah used, עֲצָרַנִי, is in the qal stem, meaning "to restrain" or "to retain"; see *BDB,* 783. The Arabic cognate of the same root is *ʿasara* and has the nuance of pressing something by squeezing it within the palm of the hand. In that sense, Sarah acknowledges the direct intervention of God's hand in her barrenness. Ernest Klein notes that the meaning of "squeeze" is also present in the Hebrew עָצַר, and that it has possibly developed from the previous one, that is, "to restrain" (see Ernest Klein, *A Comprehensive Etymological Dictionary of the Hebrew Language for Readers of English* [New York: Macmillan, 1987],

481). Van Dyke translates the verb עֲצָרַנִי into Arabic *Amsakani ʿan,* meaning "held me back from," with the possibility of hand involvement (Cornelius Van Dyke, trans., *al-Kitāb al-Muqaddas* [Beirut: Dar al-Kitāb al-Muqaddas, n.d.], Genesis 16:2); see also Rohi Baalbaki, *Al-Mawrid: A Modern Arabic-English Dictionary* (Beirut: Dar El-ʿilm Lilmalaayin, 1992), 170. For a fuller study of the usage of the Hebrew verb עָצַר in Old Testament literature, see E. Kutsch, "Die Wurzel עָצַר, im Hebräischen," *VT* 2 (1952): 57–69.

28. Thus Trible, "The Other Woman," 222–23; Katheryn Pfisterer Darr, *Far More Precious Than Jewels: Perspectives on Biblical Women* (Louisville: Westminster/John Knox, 1991), 134.

29. For a similar conclusion, see Westermann, *Genesis 12–36,* 238; also Victor P. Hamilton, *The Book of Genesis: Chapters 1–17,* NICOT, ed. R. K. Harrison (Grand Rapids: Eerdmans, 1990), 445. While Westermann is inclined to see the author of Genesis as approving of Sarah's action, Zimmerli and von Rad (who admit that Sarah's action was perfectly in harmony with social customs and expectations) both see the author of the narrative as disapproving of her action (see Walther Zimmerli, *1. Moses 12–25: Abraham,* Zürcher Bibelkommentare [Zürich: Theologischer Verlag Zürich, 1976], 61–62; Gerhard von Rad, *Genesis: A Commentary,* rev. ed., trans. John H. Marks [Philadelphia: Westminster, 1972], 191); Wenham agrees with them on the displeasure of the narrator with Sarah's action, seeing in 16:2–3 an allusion to Genesis 3 (Wenham, *Genesis 16–50,* 2:7). Sailhamer goes even further to draw the details of the parallel structure intended by the narrator between Genesis 3 and Genesis 16:2–3 (John H. Sailhamer, *The Pentateuch as Narrative* [Grand Rapids: Zondervan, 1992], 153).

It seems that the narrator does not try to imply his approval or disapproval of the action of Sarah. Rather, his vivid description of the resulting complications aims at contrasting human efforts with divine intervention. Later, four of the twelve elect tribes of Israel (Dan, Naphtali, Gad, and Asher) were born through maidservants, even though Leah was not barren. At one point in the Jacob narrative, the narrator tells how Rachel believed that God vindicated her through her maid (Gen. 30:6). He also tells how Leah believed that God blessed her because she gave her maid to her husband and opened her womb in return. Hence she named the son she delivered Issachar (Gen. 30:17–18).

30. God allowed polygamy in marriage subsequent to the fall of man. Initially, his perfect will for marriage was monogamy, as displayed in Genesis 2:15–25. Polygamy started after the fall with Lamech, one of the descendants of Cain (Gen. 4:19–20). It was witnessed throughout the history of Israel and its legality acknowledged in the Law of Moses (Exod. 21:10; Deut. 21:15–17), though not widely practiced for economical and social reasons. However, imperfect human ways are always short of perfect divine plans. Thus, though allowed by God, these practices were almost always accompanied by complications, as in the story under consideration. In Christ, the fall and its consequences were actually and eschatologically reversed; hence the higher moral standard for Christian believers (Matt. 5–7). For a good discussion on marriage customs in Israel in ancient Near Eastern context, see Roland de Vaux, *Ancient Israel: Its Life and Institutions,* trans. John McHugh (New York: McGraw-Hill, 1961), 24–40.
31. *ANET*, 172; seignior is a reference to a free man, and hierodule to a priestess; see *ANET,* 166. Approximate dates of the quoted texts are adopted from John H. Walton, *Ancient Israelite Literature in Its Cultural Context* (Grand Rapids: Zondervan, 1989).
32. C. H. Gordon, "Biblical Customs and the Nuzu Tablets," *BA* 3 (1940): 3; see also E. A. Speiser, "New Kirkuk Documents Relating to Family Laws," *AASOR* 10 (1928–29): 1–73.
33. Julius Lewy, "On Some Institutions of the Old Assyrian Empire," *Hebrew Union College Annual* 27 (1956): 9–10. By *qadishtum* it is meant a "woman of lower social and legal standing" (ibid., 9).

34. A. K. Grayson and J. Van Seters, "The Childless Wife in Assyria and the Stories of Genesis," *Or* 44 (1975): 485–86. See also J. Van Seters, "The Problem of Childlessness in Near Eastern Law and the Patriarchs of Israel," *JBL* 87 (1968): 401–8.
35. Hamilton, *The Book of Genesis: Chapters 1–17,* 445. The inscriptions of Ur-Nammu (twenty-first century B.C.) yield also partial information on marriage customs that are similar to those presented above; see *ANET,* 523–25; J. J. Finkelstein, "The Laws of Ur-Nammu," *JCS* 22 (1968): 66–82; For evidence of this widespread practice in the whole ancient Near East, see also Thomas L. Thompson, *The Historicity of the Patriarchal Narratives: The Quest for the Historical Abraham,* BZAW 133, ed. Georg Fohrer (Berlin: Walter de Gruyter, 1974), 252–69; Van Seters, "The Problem of Childlessness," 401–8.
36. Van Seters, "The Problem of Childlessness," 401–8. At times, God's judgment on people was expressed by closing women's wombs, as in the case of the house of Abimelech (Gen. 20:1–17).
37. Thus Hamilton, *The Book of Genesis: Chapters 1–17,* 445; Westermann, *Genesis 12–36,* 238.
38. Hebrew: בֹּא־נָא אֶל־שִׁפְחָתִי אוּלַי אִבָּנֶה מִמֶּנָּה
39. Wenham, *Genesis 16–50,* 2:7. Cf. also Franz Delitzsch, *A New Commentary on Genesis,* trans. Sophia Taylor (Minneapolis: Klock & Klock, 1978), 2:16.
40. The verb אִבָּנֶה is in the reflexive niphal stem, which is derived from the Hebrew root בָּנָה (Ar. cognate *banā*), meaning "to build."
41. C. F. Keil and F. Delitzsch, *The Pentateuch,* vol. 1 of Biblical Commentary on the Old Testament, trans. James Martin (Grand Rapids: Eerdmans, 1956), 219; Delitzsch, *A New Commentary on Genesis,* 2:16. In this regard Delitzsch cites an older Arabic saying, *banā ʿalayhā,* meaning "to build on her," where "the family is represented as a house, procreation as building, and becoming a mother as being built up" (see ibid.). Delitzsch notes that in Assyrian, he who begets is called *bâni,* "my father," *abû bânija;* she who begets is called *bânitu;* and that which is begotten

binûtu or *nabnîtu* [emphasis original] (see ibid.). See also Nahum M. Sarna, *The JPS Torah Commentary: Genesis* בראשית (Jerusalem: Jewish Publication Society, 1989), 119; I. Blythin, "A Note on Isaiah XLIX 16–17," *VT* 16 (1966): 229–30. For Arabic parallels, see Lothar Kopf, "Arabische Etymologien und Parallelen zum Bibelwörterbuch," *VT* 8 (1958): 161–215.

42. That is, ten years plus the long stay in Haran until his father's death in addition to the time spent in traveling to and from Haran (Gen. 11:26; 30–32; 12:1–6; Acts 7:4).
43. Menahem M. Kasher, "Genesis," in *Encyclopedia of Biblical Interpretation,* ed. Harry Freedman (New York: American Biblical Encyclopedia Society, 1955), 2:216; Freedman, *Midrash Rabba: Genesis,* 1:381.
44. P. Cruveilhier, "Le Droit de la femme dans la Genèse et dans le receuil de Lois Assyriennes," *RB* 36 (1927): 365. See also de Vaux, *Ancient Israel,* 24–25.
45. Hamilton, *The Book of Genesis: Chapters 1–17,* 445.
46. Ibid., 445–46.
47. Ibid., 446.
48. Trible, "The Other Woman," 223.
49. Sarna, *The JPS Torah Commentary, Genesis* בראשית, 119; Wenham, *Genesis 16–50,* 2:8; the Laws of Ur-Nammu 22–23 and Law of Hammurabi 146 (*ANET,* 172).
50. Westermann, *Genesis 12–36,* 240.
51. Thus the NRSV. See *The Complete Parallel Bible, Containing the Old and New Testaments with the Apocryphal/Deuterocanonical Books, NRSV, REB, NAB, NJB* (New York: Oxford University Press, 1993).
52. See the NIV and the KJV.
53. Sadly, the NIV Study Bible generalizes this misinterpretation further in its comments on Genesis 16:12c, making the following unwarranted statement: "The hostility between Sarah and Hagar (see vv. 4–6) was passed on to their descendants (see 25:18)." See *The NIV Study Bible, New International Version,* ed. Kenneth Barker (Grand Rapids: Zondervan, 1985), 30. The NIV translation of 16:12c will be discussed in the following chapter.

54. Janzen, "Hagar in Paul's Eyes and in the Eyes of Yahweh (Genesis 16)," 6; George W. Coats, "The Curse in God's Blessing: Gen. 12:1–4a in the Structure and Theology of the Yahwist," in *Die Botschaft und die Boten: Festschrift für Hans Walter Wolff zum 70. Geburtstag,* ed. Jörg Jeremias and Lothar Perlitt (Neukirchen-Vluyn: Neukirchener Verlag, 1981), 31–41.
55. Wenham, *Genesis 16–50,* 2:8.
56. Shehadeh argues persuasively, saying, "First, the form of קָלַל used in Genesis 12:3 differs than the form in Genesis 16:4. In the former, it is the piel participle, while in the latter the qal preterite, each yielding different emphasis. Second, the curse spoken of in Genesis 12:3 hardly applies to Hagar, the mother of Abraham's firstborn. On the contrary, Ishmael was promised much blessings (Gen. 16, 21). Third, the example of Lot cannot be applied as Coats does because the word קָלַל is not used to describe the actions of Lot's men against Abraham's men. Furthermore, Lot remained in the land. Fourth, it may be too strong to say that Hagar's looking at Sarah in contempt [alternative translation is suggested earlier] resulted in her ultimate expulsion of the land. The narrative probably describes a response on Hagar's part which is inevitable. It is a response motivated by maternal pride. In using the word קָלַל to describe her attitude the narrative reveals how much of a problem this is now going to be to the fulfillment of the blessing. Hagar and Ishmael end up outside the land not because it was the curse of God, but because it was according to the plan and purpose of God." Imad Nicola Shehadeh, "Ishmael in Relation to the Promises to Abraham" (Th.M. thesis, Dallas Theological Seminary, 1986), 68–69.
57. From the Hebrew root *qalal,* Arabic cognate *qalla.*
58. Writing in Hebrew script, al-Fāsi renders the verb תֵּקַל into Arabic האנת *(hānat),* which means "to become easy or light." David ben Abraham Alfasi, *Kitāb Jāmi, al-Alfāz,* 2 vols., ed. Solomon L. Skoss (New Haven: Yale University Press, 1936-45). Koehler and Baumgartner agree with this translation, rendering it "to

be small, insignificant." *KB*, 1103. Klein notes, "the original meaning of the base קלל is 'to belittle,' 'to slight.' The meaning 'to curse' is secondary." He later confines that last meaning to the piel stem rather than to the qal. Klein, *Etymological Dictionary of the Hebrew Language*, 580. *BDB* (886) renders the verb in Genesis 16:4 "to be of little account."

59. Targum Neofiti correctly translates the verse, "the honor of her mistress was of little value in her sight." Martin McNamara, *Targum Neofiti 1: Genesis*, in *The Aramaic Bible: The Targums*, ed. Martin McNamara et al. (Collegeville, Minn.: Liturgical, 1992), 1A:98. See also Janzen, "Hagar in Paul's Eyes and in the Eyes of Yahweh (Genesis 16)," 5; Jo Ann Hackett, "Rehabilitating Hagar: Fragments from an Epic Pattern," in *Gender and Difference in Ancient Israel*, ed. Peggy L. Day (Minneapolis: Fortress, 1989), 12.
60. Matitiahu Tsevat, *The Meaning of the Book of Job and Other Biblical Studies: Essays on the Literature and Religion of the Hebrew Bible* (New York: KTAV, 1980), 55.
61. *BDB*, 329. For a discussion of Arabic nuances, see al-Fāsî, *Kitāb Jāmiʾ Al-Alfāz*, 1:559–60. Westermann (*Genesis 12–36*, 240) remarks, "Sarah's complaint that Hagar's conduct was חמס is but the subjective reaction of the one offended." Haag notes that חמס is rarely used with reference to a woman's action; it is normally done by a man. Though ancient Israel, according to Haag, used the term איש חמס, they never used the term אישת חמס. H. Haag, "חמס," in *TDOT*, 4:481.
62. Hamilton, *The Book of Genesis: Chapters 1–17*, 447.
63. Wenham, *Genesis 16–50*, 2:8.
64. It is doubtful that the patriarch was legally justified in his action. The Law of Hammurabi 146 indicates that in case the surrogate wife claims equality with her mistress, she is to be lowered back to her slave status. However, Hagar's pride in her pregnancy causing a devaluation of her mistress in her eyes cannot be counted as such. But the patriarch preferred to stay neutral, handing Hagar back to Sarah. Kidner, *Genesis: An Introduction and Commentary*, 126.

65. The original says, "Abraham aber spielt zwischen diesen beiden starkknochigen Frauen eine etwas unglücknicht Rolle." Hermann Gunkel, *Genesis* (Göttingen: Vandenhoeck & Ruprecht, 1910), 192.
66. Von Rad, *Genesis,* 191.
67. It is the piel stem.
68. *BDB,* 776. So Janzen, "Hagar in Paul's Eyes and in the Eyes of Yahweh (Genesis 16)," 7; Hamilton, *The Book of Genesis: Chapters 1–17,* 448; Trible, "The Other Woman," 225; Wenham, *Genesis 16–50,* 2:9.
69. Sarna, *The JPS Torah Commentary: Genesis* בראשית, 112.
70. Kasher, "Genesis," 2:218.
71. The difference would be that the roles are inverted. In Egypt, the Israelites are oppressed; here Sarah is the one who is afflicting the Egyptian woman. Hamilton, *The Book of Genesis: Chapters 1–17,* 448; Janzen, "Hagar in Paul's Eyes and in the Eyes of Yahweh (Genesis 16)," 7; Trible, "The Other Woman," 225; Wenham, *Genesis 16–50,* 2:9.
72. Janzen, "Hagar in Paul's Eyes and in the Eyes of Yahweh (Genesis 16)," 7.
73. Wenham, *Genesis 16–50,* 2:9.

Chapter 2: Hagar's Songs in the Night (Gen. 16:7–16)

1. Nahum M. Sarna, *The JPS Torah Commentary: Genesis* בראשית (Jerusalem: Jewish Publication Society, 1989), 120.
2. Hamilton, *The Book of Genesis: Chapters 1–17,* 451.
3. S. E. McEvenue, "A Comparison of Narrative Styles in the Hagar Stories," 69. Parallelism also includes the reference to the wilderness. Thus the expression מצא במדבר is used in a parallel situation with reference to God's calling and election of Israel (Hos. 9:10; 12:5; 13:5; Deut. 32:10; Jer. 2:2; 31:2; Ps. 89:21). See Wagner, "מצא," in *TDOT,* 8:478–79; also, Shemaryahu Talmon, "מדבר," in *TDOT,* 8:87–118.
4. Menahem M. Kasher, "Genesis," in *Encyclopedia of Biblical*

Interpretation, ed. Harry Freedman (New York: American Biblical Encyclopedia Society, 1955), 2:219.

5. For a fuller discussion of the motif of the well in the Bible, see Michael Fishbane, "The Well of Living Water: A Biblical Motif and its Ancient Transformations," in *"Shaʾarei Talmon": Studies in the Bible, Qumran, and the Ancient Near East Presented to Shemaryahu Talmon,* ed. Michael Fishbane and Emmanuel Tov (Winona Lake, Ind.: Eisenbrauns, 1992), 3–16.
6. Hamilton, *The Book of Genesis: Chapters 1–17,* 450–51; Skinner, *A Critical and Exegetical Commentary on Genesis,* 286–87; Delitzsch, *A New Commentary on Genesis,* 2:18–21. For a fuller discussion of the options, see the excursus of Westermann, *Genesis 12–36,* 242–44; also M. J. Lagrange, "L'ange de Iahvé," *RB* 12 (1903): 217; Gerhard von Rad, *Old Testament Theology,* vol. 1, trans. D. M. G. Stalker (New York: Harper, 1963), 285–89. Irvin makes a very helpful and thorough comparison of the appearances of the Angel of the Lord with similar motifs in ancient Near Eastern religious myths. Dorothy Irvin, *Mytharion: The Comparison of Tales from the Old Testament and the Ancient Near East,* AOAT, ed. Kurt Bergerhof et al. (Neukirchen-Vluyn: Neukirchener, 1978), 60.
7. Hebrew, שׁוּר, Arabic, *Sûr.*
8. See also *BDB,* 1004.
9. The Hebrew word translated "mistress" is גְּבִרְתִּי, which derives from the root verb גבר, meaning "to be strong." The derivative noun גְּבוּרָה (Ar. *jabarût*) meaning "strength" or "power"; see also *BDB,* 150.
10. This is the hithpa'el stem; *BDB,* 776.
11. Jacob, *The First Book of the Bible, Genesis,* 107.
12. See also Tsevat's comments on verse 9 in *The Meaning of the Book of Job and Other Biblical Studies,* 60.
13. R. W. Neff suggested that verses 11 and 12 are later additions to the text. Robert Wilbur Neff, "Annunciation in the Birth Narrative of Ishmael," *BR* 17 (1972): 59–60. For a defense of the unity of the narrative from a critical scholarship perspective, see

T. Desmond Alexander, "The Hagar Traditions in Genesis xvi and xxi," *Studies in the Pentateuch,* VT supplements, no. 41, ed. J. A. Emerton et al. (Leiden: E. J. Brill, 1990), 139.

14. Trible, "The Other Woman," 228.
15. *KB,* 2:447; *BDB,* 1035.
16. Kasher, "Genesis," 2:221.
17. Martin Luther, *Luther's Commentary on Genesis,* vol. 1, trans. J. Theodore Mueller (Grand Rapids: Zondervan, 1958), 284.
18. Raymond Brown, *The Birth of the Messiah: A Commentary on the Infancy Narratives in the Gospels of Matthew and Luke* (New York: Doubleday, 1993), 155–59.
19. פֶּרֶא אָדָם and יָדוֹ בַכֹּל וְיַד כֹּל בּוֹ.
20. A clause where the relative pronoun is omitted. For examples of this kind of relative clause, see W. Gesenius, *Gesenius' Hebrew Grammar*, ed. E. Kautzsch, trans. A. E. Cowley (Oxford: Clarendon Press, 1910), 485–89.
21. Hebrew MT, יָדוֹ בַכֹּל וְיַד כֹּל בּוֹ.
22. Hebrew MT, פֶּרֶא אָדָם.
23. The pronominal suffix (3ms) of the noun יָדוֹ in יָדוֹ בַכֹּל וְיַד כֹּל בּוֹ goes back to the closest antecedent, which is אָדָם in the predicate clause פֶּרֶא אָדָם. Thus this writer suggests a translation that will reflect the omitted relative pronoun אשר that links the two sentences together. Thus a possible translation of the verse is, "and he will be a wild donkey of a man *whose* hand is upon everyone and everyone's hand upon him." Emphasis added.
24. The athnach also points to a secondary divider in poetry. Gesenius, *Hebrew Grammar,* 59, 61.
25. Verse 12 starts with a conjunctive ו linking it logically to the previous verse. The lack of an athnach inserted by the Masoretes at the end of verse 11 supports the coordinate nature of this conjunctive ו and the continuation of the comfort motif by logical implication. The second ו in וְעַל־פְּנֵי should most likely play the role of the first one, making the third prediction connected to the wider context rather than being an implication of the second trait of Ishmael.

26. Whether the verb "dwell" denotes an attitude of Ishmael or a geographical reference should be determined in the clearer parallel usage of it in Genesis 25:18. This would be one application of the hermeneutical principle requiring that the interpretation of obscure passages be governed by that of less problematic ones dealing with the same subject. Bernard Ramm, *Protestant Biblical Interpretation* (Grand Rapids: Baker, 1970), 104–6.
27. See earlier discussion. For the explanatory aspect of the *wāw copulativum,* see Gesenius, *Hebrew Grammar,* 484–85.
28. It is acceptable to expect an easing in Sarah's dealing with Hagar after her return to Abraham's house and sharing of Yahweh's revelation to her.
29. For a similar conclusion, see Westermann, *Genesis 12–36,* 247.
30. Thus, Kasher, "Genesis," 2:221; Sarna, *The JPS Torah Commentary: Genesis* בראשית, 121; Keil and Delitzsch, *The Pentateuch,* 1:220; Hamilton, *The Book of Genesis: Chapters 1–17,* 454; Wenham, *Genesis 16–50,* 2:11; Trible, "The Other Woman," 228; Skinner, *A Critical and Exegetical Commentary on Genesis,* 287, etc.
31. John H. Sailhamer, "Genesis," in NIV *Bible Commentary,* vol. 1: Old Testament, ed. Kenneth L. Barker and John Kohlenberger III (Grand Rapids: Zondervan, 1994), 16.
32. Allen Ross, "Genesis," in *The Bible Knowledge Commentary,* ed. John F. Walvoord and Roy B. Zuck (Wheaton, Ill.: Victor, 1985), 57.
33. Morris S. Seale, *The Desert Bible: Nomadic Culture and Old Testament Interpretation* (New York: St. Martins, 1974), 89. E. A. Speiser, "Genesis" in *The Anchor Bible,* vol. 1 (New York: Doubleday, 1964), 363.
34. Shehadeh, "Ishmael in Relation to the Promises to Abraham," 79.
35. Francis I. Andersen, *Job: An Introduction and Commentary,* Tyndale Old Testament Commentaries, ed. D. J. Wiseman (Downers Grove, Ill.: InterVarsity, 1976), 281.
36. Shimon Bar-Efrat, *Narrative Art in the Bible,* JSOT supplement,

no. 70, ed. David J. A. Clines and Philip R. Davies, Bible and Literature series , no. 17, ed. David M. Gunn (Sheffield: Almond, 1989), 207.

37. Skinner, *A Critical and Exegetical Commentary on Genesis,* 287.
38. Ibid. For a valuable treatise on the bedouin culture and life, see Clinton Bailey, *Bedouin Poetry from Sinai and the Negev: Mirror of a Culture* (Oxford: Clarendon, 1991); Francesco Gabrieli, ed., *L'Antica Societa Beduina* (Roma: Centro Di Studi Semitici, Istituto Di Studi Orientali-Universita, 1959).
39. Wenham, *Genesis 16–50,* 2:11.
40. Seale, *The Desert Bible,* 88–89. Seale cites a line of poetry from the ninth-century anthology, the *Hamāsa,* compiled by Abu Tammam (845), saying: "If a wild donkey dies—The tribe has always another" *(In dhahaba ʿayrun fa-ghayrun fiʾlrahti).* Seale, *The Desert Bible,* 89.
41. Seale, *The Desert Bible,* 88.
42. *BDB,* 89, renders the expression "against." Van Dyke in the Arabic translation of the Bible renders it "upon," (Ar. *ʿala*), yielding the same end result. Cornelius Van Dyke, trans., *al-Kitāb al-Muqaddas* (Beirut: Dar al-Kitāb al-Muqaddas, n.d.), Genesis 16:12.
43. LXX: αἱ χεῖρες αὐτοῦ ἐπὶ πάντας, καὶ αἱ χεῖρες πάντων ἐπ' αὐτόν (Sir Lancelot C. L. Brenton, *The Septuagint with Apocrypha, Greek, and English* [Grand Rapids: Zondervan, 1982], 18).
44. Sarna, *The JPS Torah Commentary: Genesis* בראשית, 121.
45. de Vaux, *Ancient Israel,* 10–13.
46. Willem H. Gispen, *Commentaar op het Oude Testament: Genesis* (Kampen: Kok, 1972), 2:128. Translation adopted from Wenham, *Genesis 16–50,* 2:11.
47. D. S. Margoliouth, *The Relations Between Arabs and Israelites Prior to the Rise of Islam* (London: Oxford University Press, 1924), 1.
48. *The Holy Bible,* NASB (Nashville: Nelson, 1971).
49. *The Holy Bible,* KJV (Nashville: Nelson, 1978).
50. *Life Application Bible,* NIV (Wheaton, Ill.: Tyndale, 1991).
51. *The Holy Bible,* NRSV (Nashville: Nelson, 1989).

52. Michael Maher, trans., *Targum Pseudo-Jonathan: Genesis,* in *The Aramaic Bible—The Targums,* ed. Martin McNamara (Collegeville, Minn.: Liturgical, 1992). The underlying Aramaic text of Genesis 16:12 in Pseudo-Jonathan reads, וישרי ועל אנפי כל אחוי יתערבב; and for Genesis 25:18 it reads, אחוי שרא באחסנתיה על אנפי כל; see M. Ginsburger, *Pseudo-Jonathan, Thargum Jonathan ben Usiël zum Penthateuch* (Berlin: S. Calvary, 1903).
53. Bernard Grossfeld, trans., *The Targum Onkelos to Genesis,* in *The Aramaic Bible, The Targums,* ed. Martin McNamara (Wilmington, Del.: Michael Glazier, 1988). The underlying Aramaic text of Onkelos reads, ועל אפי כל אחוהי ישרי; and for Genesis 25:18, שרא על אפי כל אחוהי; see Alexander Sperber, ed., *The Pentateuch According to Targum Onkelos,* vol. 1, in *The Bible in Aramaic Based on Old Manuscripts and Printed Texts* (Leiden: E. J. Brill, 1959).
54. *The Torah* תורה, *The Five Books of Moses: A New Translation of the Holy Scriptures According to the Masoretic Text* (Philadelphia: Jewish Publication Society, 1962). In 25:9, the text locates the cave of Machpelah as עַל־פְּנֵי Mamre (Ar. ʾ*amām*, i.e., "in front of Mamre"); and in 25:18 it locates Shur as נָפָל Egypt. Interestingly, the NIV renders this term in 25:9 "near," and in 25:18a, "near the border of," while it renders it in 25:18b, "in hostility with." Therefore, it is clear that whoever is giving the expression a sense of hostility is not doing so on mere philological ground but on theological and historical preunderstanding.
55. *BDB,* 818–19.
56. The exact location of Shur is not certain yet. For further discussion on its location, see John E. Hartley, "Havilah," in *ISBE,* 2:634.
57. The verb *nafâl,* used in this fulfillment statement has an idiomatic nuance, meaning "to settle." *BDB,* 657.
58. The NRSV translator, likely realizing the importance of the geographic context in 25:18, renders the fulfillment statement, "he settled down alongside of all his people," while he translated the prediction in 16:12, "he shall live at odds with all his kin." In

that regard, the NRSV is not as consistent as the NIV in connecting the prediction with the fulfillment in the sense of hostility.

59. This daughter is given different names in Genesis 28:9 and 36:3. She is called Mahalath in 28:9 and Basma in 36:3. Most likely the reference is to the same person. Furthermore, there is a discrepancy between the text in Genesis 26:34, where Basma is referred to as one of the Hittite women that Esau married, and the text in Genesis 36, which makes her definitely the daughter of Ishmael, sister of Nebayot. The weight of evidence in 36:4, 10, 13, 17 seems to be in favor of this last conclusion. Cf. *BDB*, 142.
60. There is an interchange between Ishmaelites (Gen. 37:25, 27, 28b) and Midianites (Gen. 37:28a, 36) in the Joseph narrative. The likely explanation is that the two groups were associated with each other by virtue of their nomadic lifestyle in the north Arabian Desert. This lifestyle also facilitated their intermarriage, especially at the early stage of their existence (Gen. 25:1–6, 12–18), when it was likely for tribe members to seek marriage from outside their own tribe. For other solutions to this difficulty and further consideration of this problem, see the next note; see also Sarna, *The JPS Torah Commentary: Genesis* בראשית, 260; Hamilton, *The Book of Genesis: Chapters 18–50*, 421–24. In any case, they were north Arabian nomads related somehow to Ishmael.
61. It is noted that the term *Ishmaelites* in the Joseph narrative is used interchangeably with the term *Midianites* (cf. Gen. 37:27–28 with Gen. 37:28, 36). The synonymous use of the two terms in that context may be due to one of three factors. First, it may indicate that *Ishmaelites* was a technical term designating individuals with a bedouin lifestyle, as it is used in a parallel situation in Judges 8:24. While the caravan was identified ethnically as Midianite, it was Ishmaelite in terms of lifestyle. Second, it may be that intermarriages between these two ethnic entities early in their existence occurred to such an extent that the designation of the one became appropriate for the other (Jubilees

20:11–13). Third, critical scholars in general have attributed this interchange of terms to the difference in sources used by the editor of the Genesis narrative (J and E). This argument is not preferred, especially when Judges 8:24 makes it unnecessary. For a more detailed discussion of this subject and further elaboration on the proposed solutions, see Hamilton, *The Book of Genesis: Chapters 18–50,* 422–23; Wenham, *Genesis 16–50,* 2:353–54; Sarna, *The JPS Torah Commentary: Genesis* בראשית, 260. The typological use of the Arabian caravan in the survival of Joseph will be discussed in further details in the last section of this book.

62. Tsevat, *The Meaning of the Book of Job and Other Biblical Studies,* 62; Hamilton, *The Book of Genesis: Chapters 1–17,* 454–55. They refer to parallels in Exodus 20:3, Isaiah 65:3, and Deuteronomy 21:16.

63. Thus Hamilton says, "Ishmael will both give and receive some crushing blows [his hand upon everyone and everyone's hand upon him]. For this reason the first part of the last line of the announcement—*weʾal-penê*—should not be translated 'before,' or 'east of,' or 'in the vicinity of,' but as 'in defiance of, against.'" Hamilton, *The Book of Genesis: Chapters 1–17,* 454–55. However, in view of the logical independence of the third prediction from the second one, as defended earlier, Keil and Delitzsch (*The Pentateuch,* 1:220–21) are correct in concluding, "עַל-פְּנֵי denotes, it is true, to the east of (cf. chp. xxv. 18), and this meaning is to be retained here; but the geographical notice of the dwelling-place of the Ishmaelites hardly exhausts the force of the expression, which also indicated that Ishmael would maintain an independent standing before (in the presence of) all the descendants of Abraham." For a good discussion of the use of the term עַל-פְּנֵי in the Old Testament, see Joel F. Drinkard Jr. ("ʿAL PÉNÊ as 'East of,'" *JBL* 98 [1978]: 285–86), who translates עַל-פְּנֵי in Genesis 16:12c "in the vicinity of," yielding the same nuance as "in the presence of." For translating עַל-פְּנֵי in Genesis 16:12c "away from" or "apart from," see de Vaux, *Ancient Israel,* 14; Wenham, *Genesis 16–50,* 2:11.

64. In the first six verses, there are five different references to Hagar as "the slave" (Heb. שִׁפְחָה).
65. Tsevat, *The Meaning of the Book of Job and Other Biblical Studies,* 65.
66. Thus also Sarna, *The JPS Torah Commentary: Genesis* בראשית, 121. The LXX (Brenton, *The Septuagint with Apocrypha, Greek, and English,* 18) reads the Hebrew noun ראי as a qal active participle with 1cs suffix רֹאִי, meaning "who sees me," as in 13b. The Vulgate renders it the same way, too. This makes the term more consistent with the later part of verse 13. While Westermann (*Genesis 12–36,* 247) prefers the LXX reading here, still "there are no inherent problems" with the MT רֳאִי. Hamilton, *The Book of Genesis: Chapters 1–17,* 455.
67. Hamilton, *The Book of Genesis: Chapters 1–17,* 455.
68. Westermann, *Genesis 12–36,* 247.
69. This is a much-debated text and commentators have not been able to form any consensus on how to translate it. It is beyond the scope of this work to discuss textual problems not central to the present study. However, this writer feels that it is not necessary to emend the MT reading in order to make more sense out of the expression אַחֲרֵי רֹאִי. This expression can be taken to mean: (1) "the back of Him Who sees me," taking אַחֲרֵי as a substantive noun (cf. Exod. 33:23), (2) "upon the One Who sees me," taking אַחֲרֵי as a preposition, (3) as Booij suggests, "would I have gone here indeed looking for him that looks after me?" Thijs Booij, "Hagar's Words in Genesis 16:13b," *VT* 30 (January 1980): 1–7. For possible emendations of the text and further elaboration on the subject, see H. Seebass, "Zum Text von Gen. xvi 13b," *VT* 21 (1971): 254–56.
70. Booij, "Hagar's Words in Genesis 16:13b," 1–7.
71. As in Exodus 33:23.
72. The location of Bered has not been discovered yet. Possible location is northeast of Sinai. For more details about possible identifications of the site, see Gary A. Herion, "Bered," in *ABD,* 1:676.

Chapter 3: The Pursuit of Destiny (Gen. 17; 21:1–21)

1. Thus Sarah is seen laughing (18:12), as well as Lot's sons-in-law (19:14), those who heard of Isaac's birth (21:6), Ishmael (21:9), and Isaac with Rebecca (26:8). John H. Sailhamer, *The Pentateuch as Narrative* (Grand Rapids: Zondervan, 1992), 159.
2. See the NKJV, NASB, CEV, LB, NCB, RSV, and NRSV.
3. See the NAV.
4. Sailhamer, *The Pentateuch as Narrative,* 159. See also Victor P. Hamilton, *The Book of Genesis: Chapters 1–17,* NICOT, ed. R. K. Harrison (Grand Rapids: Eerdmans, 1990), 479.
5. There is a general tendency among evangelicals to parallel the election of Isaac (17:19, 21) with that of Jacob (25:23; 27:18–40) and conclude that the spiritual fate of Ishmael as one of the nonelect is comparable to the spiritual fate of Esau as one of the nonelect. As an example of this tendency, Ross's comments on Esau's marriage to the daughter of Ishmael in Genesis 28:9 is significant. "Ironically, the unchosen son of *Isaac* married into the unchosen line of *Ishmael.* . . . Esau had no understanding of the Abrahamic Covenant and its purity. He was still living on the human level [emphasis original]" (Allen Ross, "Genesis," in *The Bible Knowledge Commentary,* ed. John F. Walvoord and Roy B. Zuck [Wheaton, Ill.: Victor, 1985], 74). This inference is consistent with the NIV text, which portrays Ishmael and the Ishmaelites as living in hostility with the Israelites. In fact, commenting on Genesis 16:12 from the NIV, Ross says, "God promised that Hagar would be a matriarch—her son would become the father of a great tribe of *wild, hostile people* (cf. 25:18), living in the Arabian desert" (ibid., 57, emphasis added). The same author comments on Genesis 25:18 saying, "The Ishmaelites *lived in hostility toward all their brothers,* a fulfillment of God's word to Hagar [emphasis original]" (ibid., 68). At that early stage of Israel's history, there was barely any contact between the Ishmaelites and the Israelites as peoples to sustain any alleged hostility. If Mosaic authorship is assumed, then the only period

where the two came in touch with each other is the time preceding the descent of Jacob and his children to Egypt (Gen. 46), and Genesis portrays a peaceful relationship between the two peoples during that period (25:9; 28:9; 37:25–28).

6. "And my covenant will be in your [pl.] flesh, an everlasting covenant," וְהָיְתָה בְרִיתִי בִּבְשַׂרְכֶם לִבְרִית עוֹלָם (Gen. 17:13).
7. Derek Kidner, *Genesis: An Introduction and Commentary,* TOTC, ed. D. J. Wiseman (Downers Grove, Ill.: InterVarsity, 1967), 131.
8. Hamilton, *The Book of Genesis: Chapters 1–17,* 480.
9. For a good survey of circumcision among early Semites, see George A. Barton, "Circumcision (Semitic)," in *Encyclopedia of Religion and Ethics,* ed. James Hastings (New York: Charles Scribner's Sons, n.d.), 3:679–80.
10. Flavius Josephus, *Jewish Antiquities,* trans. H. St. J. Thackeray, Loeb Classical Library (Cambridge, Mass.: Harvard University Press, 1987), 1.12.2; Karl Mras, ed., *Eusebius Werke: Die Praeparatio Evangelica* (Berlin: Akademie Verlag, 1982), 6.11.
11. For a fuller discussion of circumcision in Islam, see A. J. Wensinck, "Khitān, circumcision," in *First Encylopedia of Islam,* ed. M. Th. Houtsma et al. (Leiden: E. J. Brill, 1987), 5:20–22; Fergus Millar, "Hagar, Ishmael, Josephus and the Origin of Islam," *JJS* 44 (1993): 34–45; D. S. Margoliouth, "Circumcision (Mohammadan)," in *Encyclopaedia of Religion and Ethics,* ed. James Hastings (New York: Charles Scribner's Sons, n.d.), 3:677–79. For circumcision in Scriptures, see Roland de Vaux, *Ancient Israel: Its Life and Institutions,* trans. John McHugh (New York: McGraw-Hill, 1961), 46–48; John Skinner, *A Critical and Exegetical Commentary on Genesis* (Edinburgh: T & T Clark, 1930), 296–98; Gordon J. Wenham, *Genesis 16–50,* in WBC, 2:23–24.
12. For legal rights of inheritance with regard to a maid's children, see the Hammurabi Code in *ANET,* 173, and the law of Lipit Ishtar, *ANET,* 159–61.
13. J. Preuss, *Biblical and Talmudic Medicine,* trans. F. Rosen (New York: Sanhedrin, 1978), 404–6; *ANET,* 420. Thus also Nahum Sarna, *The JPS Torah Commentary: Genesis* בראשית (Jerusalem:

Jewish Publication Society, 1989), 146; Victor P. Hamilton, *The Book of Genesis: Chapters 18–50,* NICOT, ed. R. K. Harrison and Robert L. Hubbard Jr. (Grand Rapids: Eerdmans, 1995), 77.

14. מְצַחֵק is the piel masculine singular participle of the root צחק ("to laugh"). The narrator may be using a wordplay to tie the pieces of the narrative together under a laughter motif. Thus also, E. A. Speiser, *Genesis,* in *ABD,* 1:155; Claus Westermann, *Genesis 12–36: A Commentary,* trans. John J. Scullion (Minneapolis: Augsburg, 1981), 339.
15. Ishmael is portrayed there as "sporting with an idol and bowing down to it." Michael Maher, trans., *Targum Pseudo-Jonathan: Genesis,* in *The Aramaic Bible: The Targums,* ed. Martin McNamara et al. (Collegeville, Minn.: Liturgical, 1992), 1B:75. In his treatment of Ishmael and Esau in the Pseudo-Jonathan and the book of Jubilees, Syrén concludes, "the ethnogeographical factor may long have determined the attitude taken towards Ishmael and Esau." Roger Syrén, "Ishmael and Esau in the Book of *Jubilees* and Targum Pseudo-Jonathan," in *The Aramaic Bible: Targums in their Historical Context,* ed. D. R. G. Beattie and M. J. MaNamara, JSOT supplement, no. 166, ed. David J. A. Clines and Philip R. Davies (Sheffield: Sheffield Academic , 1994), 310–15.
16. It sees Ishmael "doing improper actions, <such as jesting in a foreign cult> *[sic].*" Martin McNamara, "Targum Neofiti 1: Genesis," in *The Aramaic Bible: The Targums,* ed. Martin McNamara et al. (Collegeville, Minn.: Liturgical 1992), 1A:113.
17. H. Freedman, and Maurice Simon, eds., *Midrash Rabbah: Genesis,* trans. H. Freedman (New York: Soncino, 1983), 1:469–70.
18. Sarna, *The JPS Torah Commentary: Genesis* בראשית, 122.
19. Wenham, *Genesis 16–50,* 2:82.
20. Skinner, *A Critical and Exegetical Commentary on Genesis,* 322.
21. Sarna, *The JPS Torah Commentary: Genesis* בראשית, 146.
22. Through the statement, "saw the son of Hagar the Egyptian."
23. Gerhard von Rad, *Genesis: A Commentary,* rev. ed., trans. John H. Marks (Philadelphia: Westminster, 1972), 232.

24. Speiser, *Genesis,* 1:155.
25. Ibid.
26. Westermann, *Genesis 12–36,* 339.
27. François Lenormant, *La Genèse: Traduction d'après l'Hébreu* (Paris: Maisonneuve et Cie, 1883), 37.
28. Wenham, *Genesis 16–50,* 2:82.
29. Hamilton, *The Book of Genesis: Chapters 18–50,* 78–79.
30. George W. Coats, *Genesis,* FOTL (Grand Rapids: Eerdmans, 1983), 1:153.
31. Wenham, *Genesis 16–50,* 82.
32. Ibid.
33. Ibid.
34. Hamilton, *The Book of Genesis: Chapters 18–50,* 78–79.
35. Coats, *Genesis,* 1:153.
36. Freedman and Simon, *Midrash Rabbah: Genesis,* 1:469–70.
37. Sir Lancelot C. L. Brenton, *The Septuagint with Apocrypha, Greek, and English* (Grand Rapids: Zondervan, 1982), 24. The Greek text reads, "παίζοντα μετὰ Ἰσαακ τοῦ υἱοῦ αὐτῆς." The verb παίζω, when used with the preposition μετὰ, normally means, "playing, amusing oneself or dancing." BAGD, 604. This addition of "with Isaac her son" in the Septuagint has prompted Speiser to conclude that perhaps it reflected the oldest Hebrew reading (Speiser, *Genesis,* 155).
38. James H. Charlesworth, *The Old Testament Pseudepigrapha* (New York: Doubleday, 1985), 2:90.
39. Speiser, *Genesis,* 155; Westermann, *Genesis 12–36,* 339.
40. That is, the years before Isaac was born. Ishmael was thirteen years old when he was circumcised on the day that God announced the future birth of Isaac (Gen. 17:23–27).
41. Von Rad, *Genesis: A Commentary,* 232.
42. Cornelius Van Dyke translates 21:10 into Arabic thus: wara'at sārah ʾibna hāgar almisriyya alladhi waladathu l'ibrahîm yamzaḥ (that is, "joking"). See Cornelius Van Dyke, trans., *al-Kitāb al-Muqaddas* (Beirut: Dar al-Kitāb al-Muqaddas, n.d.), Genesis 21:9.

43. This is most likely why Hannah released Samuel to temple service after his weaning (1 Sam. 1:29). For further discussion of the subject of weaning, see the treatment of this subject by Glenn L. Thompson, "Ishmael and Judah: Two Notes on Genesis" (paper presented at the ETS Annual Meeting, Washington, D.C., 1993).
44. Westermann (*Genesis 12–36,* 339) describes Sarah's demand as "an uncompromising and relentless intervention on behalf of her son and his future."
45. B. Jacob, *The First Book of the Bible, Genesis,* trans. and ed. Ernest I. Jacob and Walter Jacob (New York: KTAV, 1974), 137.
46. Westermann, *Genesis 12–36,* 339.
47. Wenham, *Genesis 16–50,* 2:82.
48. Ibid.
49. Wenham (*Genesis 16–50,* 2:82) notes that the qal participle of the verb "cast out" (piel form of, גרשׁ) is often used with reference to divorce (e.g., Lev. 21:7, 14; 22:13), and "clearly that is implied here too."
50. Phyllis Trible, "The Other Woman: A Literary and Theological Study of the Hagar Story," in *Understanding the Word: Essays in Honor of Bernhard W. Anderson,* ed. James T. Butler et al., JSOT supplement, no. 37, ed. David J. A. Clines and Philip R. Davies (Sheffield, England: Journal for the Study of the Old Testament Press, 1985), 231–32.
51. Ibid.
52. Sarna, *The JPS Torah Commentary: Genesis* בראשׁית, 147, emphasis added. For further light on the contemporary legal aspects of Sarah's demand, see F. Charles Fensham, "The Son of the Handmaid in Northwest Semitic," *VT* 19 (1969): 317–21; Thomas L. Thompson, *The Historicity of the Patriarchal Narratives: The Quest for the Historical Abraham,* BZAW 133, ed. Georg Fohrer (Berlin: Walter de Gruyter, 1974), 263–67. For the respective paragraphs of Hammurabi's code, see *ANET,* 173; for the Lipit Ishtar code, see *ANET,* 159–61.
53. Westermann, *Genesis 12–36,* 339.

54. Ibid.
55. See Sarna, *The JPS Torah Commentary: Genesis* בראשית, 146.
56. Thus also Wenham, *Genesis 16–50,* 2:83.
57. Sarna, *The JPS Torah Commentary: Genesis* בראשית, 147. Sarna also notes that "there is a delicate shift here from Sarah's motivation to God's. Her sole interest is to safeguard her son's inheritance. God is concerned with the question of posterity and his ultimate purposes" (ibid.).
58. The expression כִּי בְיִצְחָק יִקָּרֵא לְךָ זָרַע in verse 12c is ambiguous. However the majority of commentators settle with the meaning reflected above. Westermann (*Genesis 12–36,* 340) says, "the promise means the people of Israel, that Abraham's seed (Isa. 41:8) comes only through Isaac;" likewise, Wenham (*Genesis 16–50,* 2:83) points out that "the elect line of Abraham's descendants will run through Isaac." However, God reminded the patriarch that Ishmael would also be blessed because he is his seed (כִּי זַרְעֲךָ הוּא). While there are many who can claim physical descent from Abraham (זרעו), only those who are born after Isaac's pattern, that is, by faith, will be called true children of Abraham (Gal. 3:7; 4:28).
59. Sarna, *The JPS Torah Commentary: Genesis* בראשית, 147.
60. The LXX has, καὶ ἐπέθηκεν ἐπὶ τὸν ὦμον αὐτῆς τὸ παιδίον, suggesting that Abraham put the child, who was still a baby, on Hagar's shoulder (Brenton, *The Septuagint with Apocrypha, Greek, and English,* 24). However, since Ishmael by then was at least fifteen years old, Speiser is correct in suggesting that the translation of verse fourteen should be, "Early next morning Abraham got some bread and a skin of water to give to Hagar. He placed them on her back and sent her away with the child" (Speiser, *Genesis,* 154–55). Skinner and Dillman assume the validity of the LXX reading and use it to support the view of a doublet in the Hagar/Ishmael narrative (Skinner, *A Critical and Exegetical Commentary on Genesis,* 322–23; August Dillman, *Die Genesis* [Leipzig: S. Hirzel, 1892], 286). In order to solve this problem, Alexander attributes this verse to the late Priestly source

together with the redactional notes in 16:16; 17:24–5; and 21:5. Thus, after excluding it from the original text, he says, "there no longer remains any reason why the two accounts could not have originally formed part of the same document"; see T. Desmond Alexander, "The Hagar Traditions in Genesis xvi and xxi," *Studies in the Pentateuch,* VT supplements, no. 41, ed. J. A. Emerton et al. (Leiden: E. J. Brill, 1990),w 146.

However, the problem can be solved by merely resorting to grammatical considerations. The MT reading of verse 14b is: וַיִּתֵּן אֶל־הָגָר שָׂם עַל־שִׁכְמָהּ וְאֶת־הַיֶּלֶד וַיְשַׁלְּחֶהָ. The literal translation of the text is as follows: "and he [i.e., Abraham] gave [i.e., the bread and the skin of water] to Hagar setting them upon her shoulder, and the child and sent her away." Thus, the direct object אֶת־הַיֶּלֶד is not necessarily modified by שָׂם. Rather, the ו in front of this direct object may be taken as a conjunctive linking "the child" to the verb וַיִּתֵּן directly as a direct object having the prefix אֶת, rather than to the participle שׂם. This conclusion agrees more with the chronology of the narrative (16:16; 17:24–25; 21:5) and is strengthened further by the angel's instruction to Hagar later to take Ishmael by his hand (v. 18). Thus also Wenham, *Genesis 16–50,* 2:84; Sarna, *The JPS Torah Commentary: Genesis* בראשית, 147; C. F. Keil and F. Delitzsch, *The Pentateuch,* vol. 1 of Biblical Commentary on the Old Testament, trans. James Martin (Grand Rapids: Eerdmans, 1956), 244–45.

61. A rabbinical tradition notes: "This, however, teaches that Sarah cast an evil eye on him, whereupon he was seized with feverish pains." Freedman and Simon, *Midrash Rabbah: Genesis,* 1:472.
62. See also Jacob, *The First Book of the Bible, Genesis,* 138. The piel of שלח used here means "sent her off." Hamilton, *The Book of Genesis: Chapters 18–50,* 82.
63. Westermann, *Genesis 12–36,* 341.
64. Beer-Sheba is at the southern border of the land of Israel as indicated in the formula "from Dan to Beersheba" (Judg. 20:1; 1 Sam. 3:20, etc.). H. Cazelles sees that the location of this biblical site is probably that of the wells of "Wadi Bir Seba," rather

than at Tell Beer-Shebah at Tell Saba (Henri Cazelles, "Abraham au Negeb," in *Die Väter Israels: Beiträge zur Theologie der Patriarchenüberlieferungen im Alten Testament*, ed. Manfred Görg [Stuttgart: Verlag Katholisches Bibelwerk GmbH, 1989], 25). For a detailed consideration of this geographical location, see the thorough article by Dale W. Manor, "Beer-Sheba," in *ABD*, 1:641–45; Mervyn D. Fowler, "The Excavations of Tell Beer-Shebah and the Biblical Record," *PEQ* 114 (1982): 7–11.

65. Westermann, *Genesis 12–36*, 341.
66. Trible, "The Other Woman," 234.
67. Hamilton (*The Book of Genesis: Chapters 18–50*, 83) sees that Hagar in a sense "utters one of the first prayers in the Bible." The cohortative אַל־אֶרְאֶה ("do not let me see") is the one used to express a wish. Where the wish is negative he adds, "the speaker is in some kind of distress."
68. Jacob, *The First Book of the Bible, Genesis*, 138.
69. The same way Mary Magdalene, who because of tears filling her eyes, could not recognize the risen Lord standing in front of her (Matt. 20:13–16).
70. Ishmael is referred to here as "the lad" (Heb. נער). This implies relative maturity and moral responsibility (cf. Gen. 37:2; 18:7; 19:4). So Wenham, *Genesis 16–50*, 2:83.
71. Hamilton, *The Book of Genesis: Chapters 18–50*, 85.
72. Freedman and Simon, *Midrash Rabbah: Genesis*, 1:474.

Chapter 4: The Jewish Ishmael (Gal. 4:21–31)

1. It is of significance here that the term *flesh* in "according to the flesh," which describes Ishmael's birth, is not used in the sense of sinful desire. It is rather used in the sense of human natural effort as distinct from the supernatural ways of God. In that sense it differs from its use in Galatians 5:19–21, where the apostle lists the sinful works of the flesh.
2. The writer assumes that the epistle was written to the churches of south Galatia, which were established by Paul during his first

missionary journey (Acts 13–14). The date for the writing of this epistle is around A.D. 49. For a defense of these assumptions, see Donald Guthrie, *New Testament Introduction* (Downers Grove, Ill.: InterVarsity, 1990), 465–81.

3. The majority of commentators identify the disruptive teaching among Galatian believers as being caused by Judaizers, who were Jewish Christians adopting a separatistic attitude toward Gentile Christians by asking them to obey circumcision and observe the law for salvation or for perfecting their Christian faith. Proponents of this view on the identity of the agitators include Hans Dieter Betz, *Galatians: A Commentary on Paul's Letter to the Churches in Galatia* (Philadelphia: Fortress, 1979), 7; F. F. Bruce, *The Epistle to the Galatians: A Commentary on the Greek Text* (Grand Rapids: Eerdmans, 1982), 25–27, 31–32; J. B. Lightfoot, *Saint Paul's Epistle to the Galatians* (London: Macmillan, 1884), 27, 52–53; Donald Guthrie, *Galatians,* New Century Bible Commentary, ed. Ronald E. Clements and Matthew Black (Grand Rapids: Eerdmans, 1973), 10–11; Richard N. Longenecker, *Galatians,* in WBC, 41:lxxxix–c; Herman N. Ridderbos, *The Epistle of Paul to the Churches of Galatia* (Grand Rapids: Eerdmans, 1953), 15–16. For a survey of different options and a defense of the view of Judaizers, see Ronald Y. K. Fung, *The Epistle to the Galatians* (Grand Rapids: Eerdmans, 1988), 3–9; Longenecker, *Galatians,* 41:lxxxix–c.
4. Charles Kingsley Barrett, "The Allegory of Abraham, Sarah and Hagar in the Argument of Galatians," in *Rechtfertigung: Festschrift für Ernest Käsemann zum 70. Geburtstag,* ed. Johannes Friedrich et al. (Göttingen: Vandenhoeck & Ruprecht, 1976), 10.
5. For a survey of criticism concerning this part of the epistle, see ibid., 1–16.
6. James Montgomery Boice, *Galatians,* in The Expositor's Bible Commentary, ed. Frank E. Gaebelein (Grand Rapids: Zondervan, 1976), 10:482.
7. For a good study on the use of typology and the Old Testa-

ment in New Testament writings, see A. T. Hanson, *Studies in Paul's Technique and Theology* (London: SPCK, 1974); R. N. Longenecker, *Biblical Exegesis in the Apostolic Period* (Grand Rapids: Eerdmans, 1975).

8. Guthrie, *Galatians,* 126.
9. Longenecker, *Galatians,* 217.
10. Bruce, *The Epistle to the Galatians,* 223.
11. Ibid, 224.
12. For a full discussion of the Hagar/Sarah story in Jewish writings as compared to Paul's, see Longenecker's excursus on the subject in *Galatians,* 200–206.
13. Among the proponents of this view, see Longenecker, *Galatians,* 217; Guthrie, *Galatians,* 126; Timothy George, *Galatians,* The New American Commentary, ed. E. Ray Clendenen (Nashville: Broadman & Holman, 1994), 30:346; John Eadie, *Commentary on the Epistle of Paul to the Galatians* (Minneapolis: Klock & Klock, 1977), 372; Betz, *Galatians,* 249–50; G. Walter Hansen, *Galatians,* The IVP New Testament Commentary series, ed. Grant R. Osborne (Downers Grove, Ill.: InterVarsity, 1994), 148; R. A. Cole, *The Epistle of Paul to the Galatians* (Grand Rapids: Eerdmans, 1989), 135; Lightfoot, *Saint Paul's Epistle to the Galatians,* 184.
14. See the earlier notes on the midrashic traditions.
15. Bruce, *The Epistle to the Galatians,* 224. Thus also Fung, *The Epistle to the Galatians,* 213.
16. Bruce, *The Epistle to the Galatians,* 225.
17. Thus the literal translation of the Greek phrase would become, "as then, the one born according to the flesh persecuted the one according to the Spirit, so even now" (4:29).
18. *The English Hexapla: Exhibiting the Six Important English Translations of the New Testament Scriptures* (London: Samuel Bagster and Sons, 1841), Galatians 4:29.
19. That is, the social inclusion of Gentile believers in the Abrahamic community based on faith alone.
20. Ridderbos, *The Epistle of Paul to the Churches of Galatia,* 181.

21. Kenneth J. Thomas, "Covenant in Relation to Hagar and Ishmael in Galatians," *Bible Translator* 37 (1986): 446.
22. Trible, "The Other Woman," 238.
23. *The Holy Bible,* NASB (Nashville: Nelson, 1971).

CHAPTER 5: SUNRISE OF ABRAHAM'S CHILDREN

1. It was mentioned earlier that the book of Judges records a moral lapse in the history of Israel. However, it only served to consolidate Israel's various tribes and seal the need for a king to rule as God's vice-regent.
2. For assumed dates of biblical books, see Gleason L. Archer Jr., *A Survey of the Old Testament Introduction* (Chicago: Moody, 1974).
3. These are Nebayoth (נבית); Qedar (קידר), Adbeel (אדבאל), Mibsam (מבשם), Mishma (משמע), Dumah (דומה), Massa (משא), Ḥadad (הדד), Tema (תימא), Yetur (יתור), Naphish (נפיש), and Kedemah (קדמה; cf. Gen. 25:12–18). "Hagar," "the sons of Hagar," or "the Hagarenes" are also used in reference to Ishmaelite groups.
4. Eph'al gives an exhaustive listing of variations of the term *Arab,* which are associated with Ishmaelite tribes in particular and bedouin tribes in general that lived in the Syro-Arabian Desert. These occur in biblical and cuneiform references; Israel Eph'al, *The Ancient Arabs: Nomads on the Borders of the Fertile Crescent 9th–5th Centuries b.c.* (Leiden: E. J. Brill, 1982), 6–7.
5. The Greco-Roman counterpart of this designation is the term *Saracens* (Gr. *sarakênoi*) that appears in classical literature. The expression stems most likely from Arabic *sharqiyyûn*, meaning "easterners." That this refers mostly to Ishmaelites is established by Fergus Millar, "Hagar, Ishmael, Josephus and the Origin of Islam," *JJS* 44 (1993): 41–43. See also G. W. Bowersock, "Mavia, Queen of the Saracens," in *Studien zur antiken Sozialgeschichte: Festschrift Friedrich Vittinghoff,* Kölner historische Abhandlungen, no. 28, ed. Werner Eck, Hartmut Galsterer, and Hartmut Wolff, (Köln, Wien: Böhlau, 1980), 477–95; and

David F. Graf, *Rome and the Arabian Frontier: From the Nabataeans to the Saracens*, Variorum Collected Studies Series: CS594 (Brookfield, Vt.: Ashgate, 1997).

6. See the Monolith-Inscription of Shalmaneser III in Daniel David Luckenbill, *Ancient Records of Assyria and Babylonia* (Chicago: University of Chicago Press, 1926), I § 610; and *ANET*, 278–79.
7. Meaning "grasshopper." Thus also Rohi Baalbaki, *Al-Mawrid: A Modern Arabic-English Dictionary* (Beirut: Dar el-Ilm Lilmalayin, 1992), 434.
8. These are the words of Shalmaneser: "Karkar, his royal city, I destroyed, I devastated, I burned with fire. 1,200 chariots, 1,200 cavalry, 20,000 soldiers of Hadad-ezer, of Aram (? Damascus) *[sic]*; . . . 1,000 camels of Gindibu', the Arabian" (Luckenbill, *ARAB*, I § 611).
9. Philip K. Hitti, *History of the Arabs from the Earliest Times to the Present* (London: Macmillan, 1970), 37. For a detailed study of the bedouin social life, see the essay in Joseph Henninger, ed., *Arabica Varia: Aufsatze zur Kulturegeschichte Arabiens und seiner Randgebiete, contributions à l'histoire culturelle de l'Arabie et de ses régions limitrophes*, OBO (Göttingen: Universitätsverlag Freiburg Schweiz Vandenhoeck & Ruprecht, 1981), 90:13–48; Francesco Gabrieli, ed., *L'Antica Societa Beduina* (Roma: Centro Di Studi Semitici, Istituto Di Studi Orientali-Universita, 1959); Pierre Briant, *Etat et pasteurs au Moyen-Orient ancien* (Paris: Éditions de la Maison des sciences de l'homme, 1982).
10. For a thorough study of the camel in ancient history, see Hilde Gauthier-Pilters and Anne I. Dagg, *The Camel: Its Evolution, Ecology, Behavior, and Relationship to Man* (Chicago: University of Chicago Press, 1981).
11. For a complete listing of the references to Arabians in Assyrian and Babylonian inscriptions, see Trude Weiss Rosmarin, "Aribi und Arabien in den Babylonisch-Assyrischen Quellen," *JSOR* 16 (1932): 1–37. For a detailed discussion of the history of usage of the term *Arab*, see Eph^cal, *The Ancient Arabs*, 5–12, 62–64, 237–40. See also Smith, "Arabia," in *ABD*, 1:325.

12. An inscription from the seventh year of Sargon says, "Upon a trust (inspiring oracle given) by my Lord Ashur, I crushed the tribes of Tamud, Ibadidi, Marsimanu, and Haiapa, the Arabs who live far away, in the desert (and) who know neither overseers nor official(s) and who had not yet brought their tribute to any king. I deported their survivors and settled (them) in Samaria." Luckenbill, *ARAB,* II, § 17–18; *ANET,* 286. The biblical account in 2 Kings 17:24 speaks about Assyrians' implanting people from Mesopotamia in Samaria. This does not necessarily contradict Sargon's claim. Most of the time, the conquered people were moved by Assyrians to various places before their ultimate destination.
13. For reservations concerning Sargon's exaggerated claim, see Ephᶜal, *The Ancient Arabs,* 105–8. For finding traces of Arabian presence in Samaria, see George Andrew Reisner, Clarence Stanley Fisher, and David Gordon Lyon, *Harvard Excavations at Samaria* (Cambridge, Mass.: Harvard University Press, 1924), 1:247.
14. Hitti, *History of the Arabs,* 41; Ephᶜal, *The Ancient Arabs,* 6–10; James Montgomery, *Arabia and the Bible* (Philadelphia: University of Pennsylvania Press, 1934), 27–36; René Dussaud, *Les arabes en Syrie avant l'Islam* (Paris: Ernest Leroux, 1907), 2. See also Ran Zadok, *On West Semites in Babylonia During the Chaldean and Achaemenian Periods: An Onomastic Study* (Jerusalem: H. J. & Z. Wanaarta and Tel Aviv University, 1977), 192.
15. For further considerations of this subject, see Roland de Vaux, *Ancient Israel: Its Life and Institutions,* trans. John McHugh (New York: McGraw-Hill, 1961), 1–14.
16. Ephᶜal, *The Ancient Arabs,* 6–10.
17. A. Grohmann, "Al ᶜArab," in *The Encyclopedia of Islam,* ed. H. A. R. Gibb et al., new ed. (Leiden: E. J. Brill, 1960), 1:524. This suggestion is supported by the fact that Arabian tribes that dwelt in the *qedem* (north Arabia) descended from the Arabian patriarch Abraham (through Ishmael and Keturah). Abraham himself was called Aramaean (Gen. 25:1–6; 13–18; Deut. 26:5).

18. The original German text reads as follows: "Für die ältesten Zeiten ist eine genaue Unterscheidung zwischen Arabern und Aramäern nicht möglich, da beide Volksgruppen Beduinen waren. Auch die assyrischen Könige machten keinen scharfen Unterschied zwischen Arabern und Aramäern." Rosmarin, "Aribi und Arabien in den Babylonisch-Assyrischen Quellen," 1.
19. It may be argued that the expression "משׂא בערב" used in Isaiah 21:13 can be an earlier reference to the collective use of the term under consideration (translation, "oracles concerning the Arabs"). However, the clearer reference is in Jeremiah 25:24, as pointed out above.
20. Hitti, *History of the Arabs,* 41.
21. Second Chronicles 21:16 is offered by Hitti as support for this fact since it mentions "the Arabians that are near the Cushites." The same author suggests that this is most likely a reference to "the Arabians of the southwest," that is, "the Sabaeans." Hitti, *History of the Arabs,* 41.

    Though Herodotus referred to the dwellers of south Arabia as Arabians, and considered also all the land east of the Nile as Arabia (*Herodotus,* trans. A. D. Godly, Loeb Classical Library [Cambridge, Mass.: Harvard University Press & London: William Heinemann, 1963], 2.8, 12, 15, 19; 3.107), it seems that the Arabians of 2 Chronicles 21:16 (likely the same as those of 2 Chron. 17:10–11) are better identified with the nomadic tribes of northwest Arabia in the Hejaz area. The equation, or at least the proximity implied by Habakkuk between Cushan and Midian (Hab. 3:7), makes that a better option. In addition, the Arabians of the Midian area are more likely to have threatened Jehoshaphat than the ones in the south closer to Yemen. The reader is also referred to the Septuagint rendering of Psalm 72:10, 11, 15. See Lancelot C. L. Brenton, *The Septuagint Version: Greek and English* (reprint, Grand Rapids: Zondervan, 1988). The MT reads *Sheba* in verse 10, which has been rendered *Arabians* in the LXX. This also backs Hitti's claim that the tribes dwelling in the southwest kingdom of the Sabaeans should be designated as "Arabians," against the hesitation shown by Smith ("Arabia," 325) and Ephʿal (*The Ancient Arabs,* 62–64).

22. For the general agreement on this fact, see Montgomery, *Arabia and the Bible,* 41; see also Hitti, *History of the Arabs,* 43; Ephʿal, *The Ancient Arabs,* 9–10; D. S. Margoliouth, "Children of the East," in *Hasting's Dictionary of the Bible,* ed. James Hasting (New York: Charles Scribner's Sons, 1902), 635; Raymond Philip Dougherty, *The Sealand of Ancient Arabia,* in *Yale Oriental Series Researches* (New Haven, Conn.: Yale University Press, 1932), 19:172; Alois Musil, *Arabia Deserta: A Topographical Itinerary,* Oriental Explorations and Studies, no. 2 (New York: American Geographical Society, 1927), 494–97. However, it should be noted that *benê qedem* included at times the descendants of Esau who intermarried with the Ishmaelites (Gen. 28:9), and whose genealogical lists display names that are, in the main, Arabic (Gen. 36:10–14; 1 Chron. 1:35–37). Thus also Hitti, *History of the Arabs,* 40.
23. Arabic *Sharqiyyun,* whence the word *Saracens.* See also Musil, *Arabia Deserta,* 494.
24. Ibid.
25. For further references, see Genesis 29:1; Numbers 23:7; and Isaiah 11:14; the discussion of Hitti, *History of the Arabs,* 42–43; and the thorough treatment of the subject by Musil, *Arabia Deserta,* 494–97.
26. Ephʿal, *The Ancient Arabs,* 63.
27. Genesis 25:17–18; Jubilee 20:11–13. The geographical designations of respective Ishmaelite tribes will be defined further in the following chapter as the Assyrian records are considered.
28. Genesis 37:25–28; Jubilee 20:11–13.
29. Cuneiform texts mention Arabs in reference to military attacks made against different Ishmaelite tribes starting from the ninth century B.C. (see the next section). Moreover, it is highly debated whether there are pottery or any other artifacts representing these Arabians before the sixth century B.C. For a discussion of this issue, see Peter J. Parr, "Aspects of the Archaeology of North-West Arabia in the First Millennium B.C.," in

L'Arabie préislamique et son environment historique et culturel: Actes du colloque de Strasbourg 24–27 juin 1987, Université des sciences humaines de Strasbourg: Travaux du Centre de Recherche sur the Proche-Orient et la Grèce Antiques 10, ed. T. Fahd (Leiden: E. J. Brill, 1989), 39–66; P. J. Parr, G. L. Harding, and J. E. Dayton, "Preliminary Survey in N.W. Arabia, 1968," *Bulletin of the Institute of Archaeology* 10 (1971): 193–242.

30. See the discussion on Job's date in the following chapter. Montgomery correctly notes that the "antique elements of the Job story are entirely true to the facts of the second millennium." Montgomery, *Arabia and the Bible,* 56.
31. René Dussaud, *La pénétration des arabes en Syrie avant l'Islam* (Paris: Librairie Orientaliste Paul Geuthner, 1955), 175; Musil, *Arabia Deserta,* 479; Nahum Sarna, *The JPS Torah Commentary: Genesis* בראשית (Jerusalem: Jewish Publication Society, 1989), 122; Eph[c]al, *The Ancient Arabs,* 238–39.
32. While all other Ishmaelite tribes appear in some form in Assyrian and Babylonian chronicles, and the later biblical record, as it will be related in chapter 5, only Hadar, Mibsam, and Mishma are not included. Montgomery, *Arabia and the Bible,* 46.
33. de Vaux, *Ancient Israel,* 5–6.
34. For further discussion of the subject, see de Vaux, *Ancient Israel,* 6; R. R. Wilson, *Genealogy and History in the Biblical World,* Yale Near Eastern Researches, no. 7 (New Haven, Conn.: Yale University Press, 1977); Robert D. Culver, "Peculiarities and Problems of Genealogical Method and of Text in the Book of Chronicles," *Bulletin of the Evangelical Theological Society* 5 (1962): 35–41.
35. For the geographical details of the conflict between the two groups, see Alois Musil, *The Northern Hegaz: A Topographical Itinerary,* Oriental Explorations and Studies, no. 1 (New York: American Geographical Society, 1926), 283–85.
36. Cf. William J. Dumbrell, "The Midianites and Their Transjordanian Successors" (Th.D. diss., Harvard University, 1970), 1–183.

37. For the development of the political history of the Midianites as head of a tribal league, see William J. Dumbrell, "The Midianites and Their Transjordanian Successors," 1–183; idem, "Midian: A Land or a League?" *VT* 25 (1975): 323–37. See also Ernst Axel Knauf, *Midian: Untersuchungen zur Geschichte Palestinas und Nordarabiens am Ende 2. Jahrtausends v. Chr.*, Abhandlungen Des Deutschen Palestinavereins, ed. Siegfried Mittmann and Manfred Weippert (Wiesbaden: Otto Harrassowitz, 1988).
38. Dumbrell, "The Midianites and Their Transjordanian Successors," 163–64.
39. Possibly as Dumbrell notes, the two accounts (1 Chron. 5:10; 5:19–22) are two separate events that occurred within the same time frame. Ibid., 189.
40. A similar situation occurred between Abraham's men and Lot's, but the patriarch prevented further aggravations through separation (Gen. 13:5–18).
41. Besides their involvement in livestock trade with other nations (Ezek. 27:21), the Ishmaelites were facilitators of incense trade by virtue of their ability to protect trade caravans against attacks, since they controlled most of the Syro-Arabian Desert. Moreover, two major oases of theirs, Taymāʾ and Dumah, were strategically located on trade routes securing trade items from south and central Arabia, northeast and northwest. For further information on this subject, see Parr, Harding, and Dayton, "Preliminary Survey in N.W. Arabia, 1968," 193–242; ʾAbd el-Rahmān al-Tayyib al-Ansarî, "Baʿdh Mudun el-Qawāfel al-Qadîmah fi l-Mamlakah lʿArabiyyah ʾSsuʿûdiyyah [Some Ancient Caravan Cities in the Kingdom of Saudi Arabia]," in *Petra and the Caravan Cities: Proceedings of the Symposium Organised at Petra in September 1985 by the Department of Jewish Antiquities of Jordan*, ed. Fawzi Zayadine (Amman: Department of Antiquities, 1990), 15–26; Mikhail Ivanovitch Rostovzeff, *Caravan Cities*, trans. D. and T. Talbot Rice (Oxford: Clarendon, 1932); Kjeld Nielsen, *Incense in Ancient Israel*, VT supplement, no. 38, ed. J. A. Emerton et al. (Leiden: E. J. Brill, 1986).

42. Sarna, *The JPS Torah Commentary: Genesis* בראשית, 122.
43. The text in 2 Samuel 17:25 reads "Jether the Israelite" instead of "Jether the Ishmaelite" as it is clearly outlined in 1 Chronicles 2:17. This may be a case of corruption in the transmission of the text due to graphic confusion between the terms הַיִּשְׁמְעֵאלִי and הַיִּשְׂרְאֵלִי. There is no point of mentioning the origin of Jether if he was an Israelite, since the text does not do that with any other Israelite individual. In addition, the name Jether is a short Hebraized form of Jethro (Ar. *Yathrun*), which is the Midianite (Arabian) name of Moses' father-in-law (meaning "abundance"); see Montgomery, *Arabia and the Bible,* 30.
44. Sarna, *The JPS Torah Commentary: Genesis* בראשית, 122.
45. *Herodotus* 3.97.
46. Ephᶜal, *The Ancient Arabs,* 88.
47. Several arguments have been advanced suggesting that the queen of Sheba most likely came from a north or central Arabian trade garrison post instead of coming from the south Arabian kingdom of Sheba. The main arguments are as follows: (1) The Sabaeans were referred to as present in north Arabia as early as the writing of the book of Job (Job 1:15). (2) South Arabian manuscripts fail to show any evidence of kingship rule in present Yemen prior to the eighth century B.C. (3) Extrabiblical manuscripts do not reveal the presence of queens in south Arabia or in Ethiopia at all. (4) According to cuneiform texts, plenty of queens are shown among the tribes in northern and central Arabia. Proponents of this view include Hitti, *History of the Arabs,* 42; Nigel Groom, *Frankincense and Myrrh: A Study of the Arabian Incense Trade* (London and Beirut: Longman Group Ltd. and Librairie du Liban, 1981), 38–54; Ephᶜal, *The Ancient Arabs,* 227–29; Édouard Dhorme, *A Commentary on the Book of Job,* trans. Harold Knight (Nashville: Nelson, 1984), xxv. There is a historical tradition that linked the queen of Sheba with Ethiopia, and attributed the coming of the Ethiopian eunuch in Acts 8 to the validity of that tradition. However, many Orientalists today place Sheba in Arabia (mostly south) rather

than Ethiopia; cf. G. Lloyd Carr, *The Song of Solomon,* The Tyndale Old Testament Commentaries (Downers Grove, Ill.: InterVarsity, 1984), 19; Ephᶜal, *The Ancient Arabs,* 88.

48. Nelson Glueck (*Rivers in the Desert: A History of the Negev* [New York: Farrar, Straus and Cudahy, 1959], 162–63) develops the argument that besides her aim of hearing Solomon's wisdom, this queen came to arrange an agreement with Solomon to get freedom to use the trade routes that the king of Israel controlled at that time in northwest Arabia.

49. The writer came to this conclusion independently. For a similar conclusion, see James A. Montgomery, "Arabic Names in I. and II. Kings," *The Moslem World* 31 (1941): 267; Bernhard Moritz, "Edomitische Genealogien. I," *ZAW* 44 (1926): 86.

50. There is a discrepancy between the text in Genesis 26:34, where Basma is referred to as one of the Hittite women that Esau married, and the text in Genesis 36 that makes her definitely the daughter of Ishmael, sister of Nebayot. Reconciliation between both accounts seems beyond reach at this point (cf. Gordon J. Wenham, *Genesis 16–50,* in WBC, 2:336–37; Claus Westermann, *Genesis 12–36: A Commentary,* trans. John J. Scullion (Minneapolis: Augsburg, 1981), 562). It seems that Moses used two different records about the early life of Esau. Chapters 26–28 reflected an Israelite tradition, while chapter 36 gave the Edomite tradition. However, as Delitzsch held, one of these traditions (possibly the Israelite one, since the Edomite one gives a more thorough genealogical account) may have used by-names for the same persons which was and is still a common custom among nomadic tribes. C. F. Keil and F. Delitzsch, *The Pentateuch,* vol. 1 of Biblical Commentary on the Old Testament, trans. James Martin (Grand Rapids: Eerdmans, 1956), 320–21; *BDB,* 142.

51. For a discussion of the possible dates of writing of the book of Job and of Proverbs, see Archer, *A Survey of the Old Testament Introduction,* 454–74.

CHAPTER 6: JOB, SON OF THE ARABIAN DESERT

1. In his introductory considerations on the study of Proverbs, W. McKane devotes close to 160 pages to the survey of international wisdom literature. William McKane, *Proverbs: A New Approach* (Philadelphia: Westminster, 1970), 51–208.
2. For a discussion of Egyptian wisdom literature in relation to the Bible, see Nili Shupak, "Egyptian 'Prophetic' Writings and Biblical Wisdom Literature," *BN* 54 (1990): 81–102; also idem, *Where Can Wisdom Be Found? The Sage's Language in the Bible and in Ancient Egyptian Literature,* OBO 130 (Göttingen: Vandenhoeck & Ruprecht, 1993); John D. Ray, "Egyptian Wisdom Literature," in *Wisdom in Ancient Israel: Essays in Honour of J. A. Emerton,* ed. John Day et al. (Cambridge: Cambridge University Press, 1995), 17–29; Ernst Würthwein, "Egyptian Wisdom and the Old Testament," in *Studies in Ancient Israelite Wisdom,* ed. James L. Crenshaw, the Library of Biblical Studies, ed. Harry M. Orlinsky (New York: KTAV, 1976), 113–33; Ronald J. Williams, "The Sage in Egyptian Literature," in *The Sage in Israel and the Ancient Near East,* ed. John G. Gammie and Leo G. Perdue (Winona Lake, Ind.: Eisenbrauns, 1990), 19–30. For putting the biblical wisdom literature in ancient literary contexts, though not exclusively Egyptian, see Bruce Waltke, "The Book of Proverbs and Ancient Wisdom Literature," *Bib Sac* (1979): 221–38; K. A. Kitchen, "Proverbs and Wisdom Books of the Ancient Near East: The Factual History of a Literary Form," *TB* 28 (1977): 69–114; W. F. Albright, "Some Canaanite-Phoenician Sources of Hebrew Wisdom," in *Wisdom in Israel and in the Ancient Near East, Presented to Professor Harold Henry Rowley,* ed. M. Noth and D. Winton Thomas, VT supplement, ed. G. W. Anderson et al. (Leiden: E. J. Brill, 1969), 3:1–15.
3. *ANET,* 486, no. 256.
4. Édouard Dhorme, *A Commentary on the Book of Job,* trans. Harold Knight (Nashville: Nelson, 1984), xvi.
5. Samuel Rolles Driver and George Buchanan Gray, *A Critical and*

Exegetical Commentary on the Book of Job, Together with a New Translation (Edinburgh: T & T Clark, 1977), xxix.

6. Gleason L. Archer Jr., *A Survey of the Old Testament Introduction* (Chicago: Moody, 1974), 454; see also the discussion of Driver and Gray, *A Critical and Exegetical Commentary on the Book of Job,* xxix. The first mention of the epithet *ʾawwāb* in reference to Job is found in Sura 38:44. In fact, the Qurʾan refers to Job in four different places (4:163; 6:84; 21:83, 84; 38:41–44). The first two occurrences mention him in a listing of saintly people who were the object of God's inspiration. Sura 21 refers very briefly to his suffering and God's subsequent restoration. Sura 38:41–44 speaks a little more of Satan's affliction of Job, and relates the tradition that Job was told to strike the ground with his foot to get a refreshing drink and wash himself (38:42). Verse 43 refers again to his restoration by *ʾAllah.* Meanwhile, the last verse (44) relates another tradition, in which Job is told to strike with a bundle of thin grass. Though the object he is supposed to strike is unstated, Muslim tradition identifies it as his wife. The verse ends with this statement: *ʾInnâ wajadnâhu ṣâbiran niʿma-l ʿabdu ʾinnahu ʾawwâbun,* meaning, "We have found him patient, how excellent a slave. Verily, he is returning (in repentance)." Muḥammad T. Al-Hilâlî and Muḥammad M. Khân, trans. and eds., *Interpretation of the Meanings of the Noble Qurʾân in the English Language, A Summarized Version of Aṭ-Ṭabarî, Al-Qurṭubî and Ibn kathîr, with comments from Ṣaḥîḥ Al-Bukharî* (Riyadh: Maktaba Dar-us-Salam, 1993).
7. Dhorme, *A Commentary on the Book of Job,* 2.
8. This tradition will be developed later. See Sir Lancelot C. L. Brenton, *The Septuagint with Apocrypha, Greek, and English* (London: Samuel Bagster & Sons, 1851), 698.
9. One Jewish tradition holds that Job was not a historic figure, but just a parable drawn for theological truth rather than a historical reality. *The Babylonian Talmud, Baba Bathra,* 15a; *Bereshith Rabba,* § 57; also Dhorme, *A Commentary on the Book of Job*, xv.

10. This may be the reason why the writer did not give his genealogy or that of his friends (see Dhorme, *A Commentary on the Book of Job*, xv). Only the direct ancestry of Elihu is given (Job 32:1).
11. Genesis 29:1 may only mean that Jacob went through the land of the children of the east and thence to the city of Nahor as Musil argues. Alois Musil, *Arabia Deserta: A Topographical Itinerary*, Oriental Explorations and Studies, no. 2 (New York: American Geographical Society, 1927), 494. Furthermore, Aram Nahraïm may not be equated with Mesopotamia, but may point to a place in the vicinity of Damascus. For a development of this argument, see Tony Maalouf, "Ishmael in Biblical History" (Ph.D. diss., Dallas Theological Seminary, 1998), 120, n. 45. See also Beke's treatment, in letters to the *Athenaeum*, November 23, 1861; February 1, 15; March 1, 29; and May 24, 1862. Beke is cited by Arthur P. Stanley, *Lectures on the History of the Jewish Church* (London: John Murray, 1893), 1:425–28.
12. Robert H. Pfeiffer, "Edomitic Wisdom," *ZAW* 12 (1926): 19.
13. *ANET*, 18–22.
14. That is, an Aramaic text. See Brenton, *The Septuagint with Apocrypha, Greek, and English*, 698.
15. See Dhorme's hasty dismissal of this tradition (*A Commentary on the Book of Job*, xviii). A tradition is not supposed to stand on four legs. Some items in it may be accurate, others may not. This applies to the Syriac tradition found in the LXX.
16. Ibid., xx–xxi.
17. Roy B. Zuck, "Job," in *The Bible Knowledge Commentary*, ed. John F. Walvoord and Roy B. Zuck (Wheaton, Ill.: Victor, 1985), 717.
18. Teiman is to be identified, not as a city, but as a region in the southern part of Edom. Roland de Vaux, "Téman, Ville ou Région d'Edom?" *RB* 76 (1969): 379–85. Musil believes that because of Jeremiah 49:7, "we must locate the people of Têman in the eastern part of northern Edom, whence led and still lead the main routes connecting north and south, avoiding the deep

gorges and ravines in the western part of northern Edom." Alois Musil, *The Northern Hegaz: A Topographical Itinerary,* Oriental Explorations and Studies, no. 1 (New York: American Geographical Society, 1926), 250.

19. Cf. the same construction, בארץ עוץ, in Job 1:1.
20. G. Frederick Owen, "The Land of Uz," in *Sitting with Job: Selected Studies on the Book of Job,* ed. Roy B. Zuck (Grand Rapids: Baker, 1992), 246.
21. See also James Montgomery, *Arabia and the Bible* (Philadelphia: University of Pennsylvania Press, 1934), 47; Bernhard Moritz, "Edomitische Genealogien. I," *ZAW* 44 (1926): 81–93.
22. Brenton, *The Septuagint with Apocrypha, Greek, and English,* 698.
23. Marvin Pope, *Job: Introduction, Translation, and Notes. The Anchor Bible,* ed. William Foxwell Albright and David Noel Freedman (Garden City, N.Y.: Doubleday, 1965), 15:3–4; Dhorme, *A Commentary on the Book of Job,* xxiv; N. H. Tur-Sinai, *The Book of Job: A New Commentary* (Jerusalem: Kiryath Sepher, 1967), 3; Jean Lévêque, *Job et son Dieu. Tome I: Essai d'exégèse et de théologie biblique* (Paris: Librairie Lecoffre. J. Gabalda et Cie Éditeurs, 1970), 87–89. Rabbi Saadia cites a tradition that puts the land of Uz in "al-Ghûtah," a fertile and well-watered plain in the vicinity of Damascus. Saadiah Ben Joseph al-Fayyûmî, *The Book of Theodicy: Translation and Commentary on the Book of Job,* Yale Judaica series, no. 25, ed. Leon Nemoy, trans. L. E. Goodman (New Haven, Conn.: Yale University Press, 1988), 151.
24. Josephus, *Jewish Antiquities* 1.6.4
25. Thus Pope, *Job: Introduction, Translation, and Notes,* 3.
26. Cf. Dhorme, *A Commentary on the Book of Job,* xxiv; Pope, *Job: Introduction, Translation, and Notes,* 3. For Arabic traditions, see Guy Le Strange, *Palestine Under the Moslems. A Description of Syria and the Holy Land from a.d. 650 to 1500. Translated from the Works of Medieval Arab Geographers* (London: Alexander P. Watt, 1890), 515–16; Abulfeda, *Mukhtasar tārîkh al-bashar,* trans. Heinrich L. Fleischer as *Abulfedā historia anteislamica, Arabice* (London: Lipsiae, 1831 and Darf, 1986). Yākût believes that "the

tomb of Sam (Shem) ibn Nûh is here [at Nawâ]." Le Strange, *Palestine Under the Moslems,* 516.

27. Pope, *Job: Introduction, Translation, and Notes,* 3; Édouard Dhorme, "Le Pays de Job," *RB* 20 (1911): 102–7. Again, Yāqût relates that the place of the well is "where Job dwelt, and where ʾAllah tried him. There is here a spring, where (at ʾAllah's command-see Qur'ān xxxviii. 41) he struck with his feet the rock that was over it (and the water gushed out). Job's tomb also is here." Le Strange, *Palestine Under the Moslems,* 427.
28. Le Strange, *Palestine Under the Moslems,* 220–23. Dhorme also mentions the presence of a Deir-Ayûb and Bîr-Ayûb in Palestine near the vicinity of ʿAmwâs, as well as other springs of Job to the north of Beit-ʿUr and to the northeast of *ḥalḥul,* on the Hebron road. Dhorme, *A Commentary on the Book of Job,* xxiv.
29. Tur-Sinai, *The Book of Job,* lliv–lxvi.
30. Pope, *Job: Introduction, Translation, and Notes,* 4.
31. Dhorme, *A Commentary on the Book of Job,* xxiv–xxv. See also Lévêque, *Job et son Dieu,* 87–89; Robert L. Alden, *Job,* New American Commentary, ed. E. Ray Clendenen (Nashville: Broadman & Holman, 1993), 11:29; David J. A. Clines, *Job 1–20,* in WBC, 17:9–11.
32. Pope renders the phrase, "a son of the land of *Uṣṣa.*" Pope, *Job: Introduction, Translation, and Notes,* 4.
33. Luckenbill, *ARAB,* I § 585, p. 208.
34. Alois Musil, *Arabia Petraea,* vol. 2, Kaiserliche Akademie der Wissenschaften (Wien: A. Hölder, 1907), pt. 1, 337, 339.
35. Owen, "The Land of Uz," 246. For further description of al-Jawf area, see Frank Hugh Foster, "Is the Book of Job a Translation from an Arabic Original?" *AJSL* 49 (1932): 23.
36. For further discussion of Dumah and the depression of Wādî Sirhān, see *ARNA*, 71–73; Israel Ephʿal, *The Ancient Arabs: Nomads on the Borders of the Fertile Crescent 9th–5th Centuries b.c.* (Leiden: E. J. Brill, 1982), 120–21.
37. Owen, "The Land of Uz," 246.
38. Before Owen, Foster has settled for the al-Jawf area as Job's

homeland. Foster, "Is the Book of Job a Translation from an Arabic Original?" 23.

39. Speaking of Arab "sheikhs," de Vaux says, "the Arabs set great store by personality and character, and expect their sheikh to be prudent, courageous, noble-hearted . . . and rich." Roland de Vaux, *Ancient Israel: Its Life and Institutions,* trans. John McHugh (New York: McGraw-Hill, 1961), 8. All of the above qualifications and much more were true of Job.
40. The reference to owning cows (Job 1:3) means that Job undertook agricultural activity, beside the bedouin lifestyle reflected by his ownership of 3,000 camels and 7,000 sheep (1:3). This half-settled lifestyle is further indicated by reference to the homes of his children (1:4, 19).
41. Clines, *Job 1–20,* 10.
42. For a survey of textual difficulties in Job, see G. R. Driver, "Problems in the Hebrew Text of Job," in *Wisdom in Israel and in the Ancient Near East, Presented to Professor Harold Henry Rowley,* ed. M. Noth and D. Winton Thomas, VT supplement, ed. G. W. Anderson et al. (Leiden: E. J. Brill, 1969), 3:72–93. Saadiah, in the tenth century, isolated in the book of Job ninety rare and unique words in the Old Testament, and explained them on the basis of cognates. Saadiah Ben Joseph al-Fayyûmî, *The Book of Theodicy: Translation and Commentary on the Book of Job,* Yale Judaica series, no. 25, ed. Leon Nemoy, trans. L. E. Goodman (New Haven, Conn.: Yale University Press, 1988).
43. See the comments on 2:11 by Abraham Ben Meir Ibn Ezra in *Biblia Rabbinica,* ed. Jacob Ben Hayim Ibn Adoniya (Jerusalem: Makor, 1972), 4:197. Ibn Ezra says:
   . . . כי משה כתב ספר איוב והקרוב אלי כי הוא ספר מתורגם על כן הוא קשה בפירוש כדרך כל ספר מתורגם.
   Ibn Ezra believes "that Moses wrote the book of Job, and it seems to me [him] that it is a translated book, therefore it is difficult to interpret like every translated book."
44. Tur-Sinai, *The Book of Job,* xxx–xl.
45. W. F. Albright, "The Name of Bildad the Shuhite," *AJSL* 42 (1942): 34.

46. See, for example, A. Guillaume ("The Arabic Background of the Book of Job," in *Promise and Fulfillment: Essays Presented to Professor S. H. Hooke,* ed. F. F. Bruce [Edinburgh: T & T Clark, 1963], 109), who believes that Aramaisms in Job "are very rare indeed, and that the Elihu and Wisdom chapters contain words and forms familiar in Arabic but unknown in Biblical Hebrew." Similarly, N. Sarna concluded in his detailed discussion of the language of Job that the number of so-called Aramaisms is "greatly reduced by reference to the Canaanite dialects, Accadian and Arabic . . . . the very presence of Aramaic words—if, indeed, they be exclusively Aramaic would tend to argue against an Aramaic original, for several occur in conjunction with a Hebrew synonym." Nahum Sarna, "Studies in the Language of Job" (Ph.D. diss., The Dropsie College for Hebrew and Cognate Learning, 1955), 144.
47. D. S. Margoliouth, *The Relations Between Arabs and Israelites Prior to the Rise of Islam* (London: Oxford University Press, 1924), 41.
48. Albert Schultens, *Liber Jobi* (Lugduni Batavorum: Apud Johannem Luzac, 1737).
49. Foster, "Is the Book of Job a Translation from an Arabic Original?" 21–45.
50. The whole Sura 29 in the Qurʾan is called "the spider," which may rule out the idea of mutual dependence.
51. Foster, "Is the Book of Job a Translation an Arabic Original?" The writer is aware of this proverbial saying, which is still widely used in Arab culture today.
52. Ibid., 22–23.
53. Guillaume, "The Arabic Background of the Book of Job," 106–27.
54. For full consideration of the stay of Nabonidus in Taymāʾ, see C. J. Gadd, "The Harran Inscriptions of Nabonidus," *Anatolian Studies* 8 (1958): 35–92. Guillaume ("The Arabic Background of the Book of Job," 107) believes that "the raids which the *Chaldaeans* made on Job's camels and servants (i. 12 f.) may

well have occurred during Nabonidus's wars and skirmishes with the local Arabs."

55. Guillaume, "The Arabic Background of the Book of Job," 108–9.
56. Ibid.
57. It should be admitted at once that this is an argument from silence.
58. Curt Kuhl, "Neuere Literarkritik des Buches Hiob," *Theologische Rundschau* 21 (1953): 304; Lévêque, *Job et son Dieu,* 87. However, if Moses, or even an Ishmaelite or Kenite scribe (1 Chron. 2:55) in Solomon's time is the author of the book, this would account for this familiarity.
59. Dhorme, *A Commentary on the Book of Job,* cxx–cli.
60. The original French text is: "l'hypothèse d'une traduction de Job sur un original arabe devrait, pour pouvoir être retenue, présenter d'autres lettres de créances." Lévêque, *Job et son Dieu,* 87.
61. Cf. Montgomery, *Arabia and the Bible,* 172–73.
62. Dhorme, *A Commentary on the Book of Job,* xx–xxi; see also Albright's onomastic discussion in which he concludes, "it is undeniable that the personal names [in Job] belong to the second millennium B.C." ("The Name of Bildad the Shuhite," 35).
63. So Margoliouth, *The Relations Between Arabs and Israelites,* 39.
64. For the sake of clarity, this term does not mean that the language of the tradition is classical Arabic, but means a Syro-Arabian Desert origin.
65. This is a logical inference unless one believes in the dictation theory, which does not seem to be what happened. See Luke 1:1–4, which confirms the use of many sources, oral and written, by biblical writers.
66. In addition to the previously highlighted evidence for this likelihood, ancient Arab traditions assert that Job was one of Isaac's descendants. Al-Ṭabarî writes, "Ibn Ḥumayd-Salamah-Ibn Isḥâq—someone who is not to be doubted—Wahb b. Munabbih: Job was a man of the Byzantines [i.e., connected with Edom in

the context], and his full name was Job b. Mawṣ b. Râziḥ b. Esau b. Isaac b. Abraham. On the other hand, someone other than Ibn Isḥāq says that he was Job b. Mawṣ b. Raghwîl b. Esau b. Isaac, and someone also said that he was Job b. Mawaṣ b. Raghwîl." It appears clearly that this tradition associates Job with the descendants of Esau and Basma, Ishmael's daughter. See Abu Jaᶜfar Muhammad b. Jarîr al-Tabarî, "Prophets and Patriarchs," in *The History of al-Ṭabarî (Taʾrîkh al-rusul wal-mulûk)*, Bibliotheca Persica, ed. Eshan Yar-Shater, trans. William M. Brimmer (Albany: State University of New York Press, 1987), 2:140.

67. Albright notes, "The linguistic and cultural distinctions between Aram and Edom were just as hazy as the difference between the forms of the names in square Hebrew script. The essentially Aramaic character of the Edomite culture [Arabic implied here also] is well illustrated by the fact that the Arab Nabateans adopted the Aramaic language and culture when they settled in the land of Edom." Albright, "The Name of Bildad the Shuhite," 36.
68. Even Edom (Esau), who was an Aramaean since Jacob was called one (Deut. 26:5), may have adopted a dialect that reflects strong Arabism, because the descendants of Seir reveal an onomasticon full of Arabic names (Gen. 36:20–28).
69. Cf. Robert Gordis, *The Book of God and Man: A Study of Job* (Chicago: University of Chicago Press, 1965), 210. Gordis reacted, as highlighted above, against the following statement made by Thomas Carlyle in his lecture on Arabs and Islam: "One Jewish quality these Arabs manifest; the outcome of many or of all high qualities; what we may call religiosity. . . . They had many Prophets, these Arabs; Teachers each to his tribe, each according to the light he had. But indeed, have we not from of old the noblest proofs, still palpable to every one of us, of what devoutness and noblemindedness had dwelt in these rustic thoughtful peoples? Biblical critics seem agreed that our 'book of Job' was written in that region of the world. I call that, apart from all

theories about it, one of the grandest things ever written with pen. *One feels, indeed, as if it were not Hebrew;* such a noble universality, different from noble patriotism or sectarianism, reigns in it." Gordis believes that Carlyle combines "reverence for the Bible with prejudice against the people that produced it." See Robert Gordis, "The Language and Style of Job," in *Sitting with Job: Selected Studies on the Book of Job,* ed. Roy B. Zuck (Grand Rapids: Baker, 1992), 83 n. 16. Gordis is also unhappy with Renan for finding "nothing particularly Hebrew" in the essential ideas of the book, though Renan is definitely opposed to the theory of translation from an Arabic original. See E. Renan, *Le Livre de Job* (Paris, 1864), xvii.

70. See the note of Lévêque, *Job et son Dieu,* 176.
71. The location of the land of Uz and of Teiman has been pointed out earlier. If Eliphaz is from Teima' instead, his residence would be the well-known oasis of Taymāʾ that is located in the northeast of the Hejaz area. Bildad came from Shuah, which Albright locates along the Middle Euphrates ("The Name of Bildad the Shuhite," 36); better still, Musil put Shuah to the south in the vicinity of Midian because Shuah is associated with Midian and Dedan, the children of Keturah in Genesis 25:1–6 (Musil, *Northern Hegaz,* 251). Naʿama, the land of Zophar, is not identifiable. If it involves a case of graphical confusion and is to be read Raʿama instead, location would also be to the south associated with the Dedanites and the Minaeans (ibid.). Finally, Buz is to be located also somewhere in the depression of Wādi Sirhān because of its association with *ʿUṣ* (cf. Gen. 22:21; and ibid., 251).
72. J. Lévêque, *Job et son Dieu,* 148–77. For a discussion on the meaning of the name "Shadday," see Mathias Delcor, "Des inscriptions de Deir ʾAlla aux traditions bibliques, à propos des *šdyn*, des *šedim*, et de *šadday*," in *Die Väter Israels: Beiträge zur Theologie der Patriarchenüberlieferungen im alten Testament,* ed. Manfred Görg (Stuttgart: Verlag Katholisches Bibelwerk GmbH, 1989), 33–40.

73. Montgomery, *Arabia and the Bible,* 154. For a fuller treatment of the term and the concept of *Allâh* in the Arabic language, see Imad Nicola Shehadeh, "A Comparison and a Contrast Between the Prologue of John's Gospel and Qur'anic Surah 5" (Th.D. diss., Dallas Theological Seminary, 1990).
74. Montgomery, *Arabia and the Bible,* 174.
75. Ibid.
76. Cazelles highlights the distinctions between patriarchal *El* and Canaanite *El.* He says in this regard, "Le El ugaritico-phénicien avec ses problèmes de sexualité est différent du El qu'honorent les patriarches en arrivant sur le sol de Canaan;" meaning, "The Ugaritic-Phoenicien El with his problems of sexuality is different from El whom the patriarchs worshiped upon their arrival to the land of Canaan." H. Cazelles, "Yahwisme, ou Yahwé en son peuple," in *Etudes d'histoire religieuse et de philologie biblique,* Sources Bibliques, ed. H. Cazelles (Paris: J. Gabalda et Cie Éditeurs, 1996), 36. However, Cross believes that "when we read such a title as ʾēl ʾĕlōhê yiśrāʾēl, "ʾEl, the god of (the Patriarch Jacob) Israel,' it seems necessary to suppose that the older god of the Fathers, the tribal or clan deity or deities of the Patriarchal stock was early identified with the Canaanite ʾEl. The epithet '[ ] ʾēl ʾĕlōhê abîkā,' ʾEl, the god of your father, similarly seems to be a transparent reference to ʾEl. Does it not follow then that ʾēl ʿôlām, ʾēl šadday, etc., are variant cult forms of ʿEl?" Frank Moore Cross, Jr., "Yahweh and the God of the Patriarchs," *Harvard Theological Review* 55 (1955): 234–35.
77. Original: "l'épithète de *très haut* (t'ly, cf. *ʿelyôn* de la Bible) que lui donnent plusieurs inscriptions [from south Arabia] convient tout à fait à l'antique *El.*" J. Starcky, "Recension de *Le antiche divinità semitiche,*" *RB* 67 (1960): 275.
78. Starcky, "Recension de *Le antiche divinità semitiche,*" 276.
79. Hamilton A. R. Gibb, "Pre-Islamic Monotheism in Arabia," *Harvard Theological Review* 55 (1962): 271. See also the same thesis developed by W. Montgomery Watt, "Belief in a 'High God' in Pre-Islamic Mecca," in *Studies in the History of Religions*

31, Proceedings of the XII International Congress of the I.A.H.R., ed. C. Jouco Bleeker, Geo Widengren, and Eric J. Sharpe (Leiden: E. J. Brill, 1975), 228–34.

80. Montgomery, *Arabia and the Bible,* 174–75, 187.
81. Ibid., 40.
82. Ibid.
83. Ibid., 174–75, 187.
84. Though *El* was the most commonly used name for God, Yahweh may have been attested in extrabiblical texts under a shorter form. Cazelles terminates his discussion concerning the origin of Yahwism by concluding the following: (1) The primitive form of the divine name seems to be the short *Yah, Yô, Yaw(i/e/a?).* This form does not appear in the patriarchal onomasticon. It corresponds to the Akkadian pronoun "mine," which expresses the religion of the God of the fathers. However, this name does not appear in west Semitic. (2) Syrian toponyms from the land of *Sutu (Shasu)* bear the name of *Ya, Yah/ʾa, Yawa/e.* (3) A Hurrian group south of the area of Alalah bear this name in Edom-Seir with the ending *e* typical of the Hurrian. (4) It is under the name Yahweh that the God of the Fathers is recognized as a national God in an alliance established in the vicinity of Edom. (5) Under this form, this deity is known as a royal God, particularly in Ephraem, Bethlehem-Ephratah, and among the Levites. (6) By uniting the worship of *Yahweh* of Seir with that of *ʿehyw* of the Minaean district, the prophets have reinterpreted the vocalization considering the *e* as an ancient contracted *ay,* and subsequently attaching the noun to the root *hyy,* "to be." (7) The beginning of Yahwism started by worshiping Yahweh as the God of the Mosaic covenant having given his people the ten moral commandments (see Cazelles, "Yahwisme, ou Yahwé en son peuple," 46–47).
85. Ernst Axel Knauf, *Midian: Untersuchungen zur Geschichte Palestinas und Nordarabiens am Ende 2. Jahrtausends v. Chr.,* Abhandlungen Des Deutschen Palestinavereins, ed. Siegfried Mittmann and Manfred Weippert (Wiesbaden: Otto Harrassowitz, 1988), 50–53.

For the biblical writer who is describing the coming of the Lord from the south, God will advance from Sinai-Midian toward Seir, then proceed to Paran and Kadesh Barnea.

86. Larry Williams, *The Mount Sinai Myth: Formerly, The Mountain of Moses* (New York: Wynwood, 1990). Confirmation of these findings is awaiting future archaeological work. What is clear though, is that, biblically speaking, the Mountain of God, Horeb, is associated with the land of Midian, which is situated in northwest Arabia, thus suggesting the presence of Mount Sinai somewhere in Midian (Exod. 3:1–5; Gal. 4:25). See also the follow-up based on Williams's book by Howard Blum, *The Gold of Exodus: The Discovery of the True Mount Sinai* (New York: Simon & Schuster, 1998).
87. Emily Beke, ed., *The Late Dr. Charles Beke's Discoveries of Sinai in Arabia and of Midian* (London: Trübner & Co., 1878). Musil, *Northern Hegaz*, 286–98.
88. W. J. Phythian-Adams, "Israel in the Arabah," *PEQ* 65 (1933): 137–46.
89. Montgomery, *Arabia and the Bible*, 46–47.
90. Cazelles, "Yahwisme, ou Yahwé en son peuple," 46–47; Gösta W. Ahlström, *Who Were the Israelites?* (Winona Lake, Ind.: Eisenbrauns, 1986), 58–59; Knauf, *Midian*, 50–53.
91. Cf. Lars E. Axelsson, *The Lord Rose Up from Seir: Studies in the History and Tradition of the Negev and Southern Judah*, Coniectanea Biblica Old Testament Series, no. 25 (Stockholm: Almqvist and Wiksell, 1987). M. C. Astour, "Yahweh in Egyptian Topographic Lists," in *Festschrift Elmar Edel 12. Martz 1979*, Ägypten und Altes Testament 1, ed. M. Görg and E. Pusch (Wiesbaden: Bamberg, 1979), 17–33.
92. Ernst Axel Knauf, "Seir," in *ABD*, 5:1073. See also Knauf, *Midian*, 50–53. Against the identification of Egyptian *sʾrr* with Hebrew šēir, see M. C. Astour, "Yahweh in Egyptian Topographic Lists," 17–33.
93. Ahlström, *Who Were the Israelites?* 58. Ahlström believes that the mention of Asherah next to Yahweh "indicates his possession of a consort." Against the identification of Yahweh's Asherah as his

consort, see the article of A. Lemaire ("Who or What Was Yahweh's Asherah?" *BAR* 6 [December 1984]: 42–51) in which he argues for identifying "Asherah" with a sacred tree. The reasons advanced for this identification can be summarized as follows: (1) The drawing on the jar excavated at Kuntillet ʿAjrud in no way suggests that the word "Asherah . . . as used in the inscription means a goddess or a consort." (2) There is no mention of "Asherah" in the Phoenician texts that are close in time to the alleged inscriptions (i.e., early in the first millennium B.C.). (3) Scriptural examples including Judges 6:25–26, 30 and 1 Kings 16:33 reveal that the word "Asherah" is legitimately prefixed with the definite article *ha,* which rules out the possibility that the word is used there as a personal name. (4) Adding a pronominal suffix, such as *-y* meaning "my," to the word "Asherah" (as both inscriptions in *Khirbet el Kom* and *Kuntillet ʿAjrud* imply) is another support for the case that it is not used as a personal name. (5) The suggestion that "Asherah" is a reference to a "high place," "holy place," or "sanctuary" is not sufficient, since scriptural references (2 Kings 18:4; Deut. 16:21–22; Mic. 5:13) seem to distinguish between the *asherahs* and the "hill-shrines" *(bamot)* associated with the "sacred pillars" *(massebot).* (6) Micah 5:13; Exodus 34:13; and Deuteronomy 12:3 imply that *asherah* is a wooden object that can be pulled down, cut, and burned. It generally stands up (2 Kings 13:6). (7) Finally, interpreting asherah as a sacred tree or grove conforms very well with what we know generally about the cultic places of the ancient Near East (Egypt, Mesopotamia, and Syria-Palestine). Nevertheless, Lemaire admits that when associated with Baal, Asherah could be understood as being a goddess (ibid., 50).

Chapter 7: Agur and Lemuel, Wise Men from Arabia

1. For example, Whybray reflects the general consensus among many modern scholars asserting that Proverbs 22:17–24:22 is characterized by a "clear dependence on an Egyptian handbook." R. N. Whybray, "The Social World of the Wisdom Writers," in

The World of Ancient Israel, ed. R. E. Clements (Cambridge: Cambridge University Press, 1989), 230, 237. For a discussion of parallelism and influence of Amenemope's instructions on Proverbs 22:17–24:22, see Paul Overland, "Structure in the Wisdom of Amenemope and Proverbs," in *"Go to the Land I Will Show You,"* ed. Joseph E. Coleson and Victor H. Matthews (Winona Lake, Ind.: Eisenbrauns, 1996), 275–91; John Ruffle, "The Teaching of Amenemope and Its Connection with the Book of Proverbs," *Tyndale Bulletin* 28 (1977): 29–68. According to J. Walton, the once debated date of writing of the Instruction of Amenemope is now established based on new fragments found, and is to be set around 1200 B.C. during the Ramesside era. See John H. Walton, *Ancient Israelite Literature in Its Cultural Context* (Grand Rapids: Zondervan, 1989), 174.

2. John Day, "Foreign Semitic Influence on the Wisdom of Israel and Its Appropriation in the Book of Proverbs," in *Wisdom in Ancient Israel: Essays in Honour of J. A. Emerton,* ed. John Day et al. (Cambridge: Cambridge University Press, 1995), 62.
3. It is out of the focus of our study to deal with the intricate discussion over where to end Agur's words (at verse 4? 6? 14? or all the way to 33?) and Lemuel's sayings (at 31:9 or all the way until v. 31). Murphy relates the uncertainty over the limits of Agur's sayings in his survey with no clear conclusions. Roland E. Murphy, *The Tree of Life: An Exploration of Biblical Wisdom Literature,* 2d ed. (Grand Rapids: Eerdmans, 1990), 25. On the other hand, Gottlieb argues that chapter 31 is to be attributed as a whole to Lemuel's mother. It is true that 31:1–9 is a prose section, and 31:10–31 is an acrostic poem. However, she argues, the Bible is full of sections with mixed genres. For example, Job 1–2 and 42:7–17 are prose sections, while the dialogue of Job with his friends is poetic. Also, Gottlieb cites the prose section of Isaiah 38:1–8 followed by the poetic section ending in verse 20 only to be followed by two verses (21–22) that revert to prose. In Proverbs 31, the prose section (vv. 1–9) is connected with the acrostic poetic section (vv. 10–31) by the Hebrew term ḥayil

(vv. 3, 10). In verse 3 Lemuel is exhorted by his mother not to waste his ḥayil on ungodly women and worldly delight, while in the poetic section she introduces him to the woman of ḥayil that he should seek (v. 10). See Claire Gottlieb, "The Words of the Exceedingly Wise: Proverbs 30–31," in *The Biblical Canon in Comparative Perspective, Scripture in Context,* vol. 4, ed. K. Lawson Younger Jr. et al.; Ancient Near Eastern Texts and Studies, vol. 11 (Lewiston, N.Y.: Edwin Mellen, 1991), 278–79, 282–92. Since the text in both chapters does not clearly break the sayings by introducing any other sage or source of wisdom saying, the writer will assume for the sake of argument that chapter 30 belongs to Agur and chapter 31 to Lemuel.

4. The MT of 30:1 reads הַמַּשָּׂא at the end of the first colon, and as such it stands in apposition to "the words" (דברי). However, the apparatus grants several possible emendations; the first two are, הַמַּשָּׂאִי and מִמַּשָּׂא. In 31:1, the Masoretes put the disjunctive athnach under the word "king" (מֶלֶךְ), thus suggesting ending the first sentence with "a king," and beginning the next with "a burden."
5. The MT of 30:1a–b says, דִּבְרֵי אָגוּר בִּן־יָקֶה הַמַּשָּׂא נְאֻם הַגֶּבֶר לְאִיתִיאֵל.
6. *La Sainte Bible: Nouvelle Version Segond Révisée* (Villiers-le-bel, France: Alliance Biblique Universelle, 1993), 652.
7. Original text is "Paroles d'Agour, fils de Yaqé. Sentence de cet homme pour Ethiel." Ibid.
8. The Targum of Proverbs 30:1a: מלוי דאגור בר יקה דקבל נביותא; Merino translates it, "verba agur fili jache: qui succepit prophetiam," that is, "the words of Agur son of Jakeh, who received a prophecy." The Targum of Proverbs 31:1a, מילוהי דלמואל מלכא נביותא, is translated by Merino, "verba lamuel regis: Prophetia . . . ," that is, "the words of Lemuel the king: the Prophecy . . ." Luis Diez Merino, *Targum de Proverbios. Edición Príncipe del Ms. Villa-Amil n.o 5 de Alfonso de Zamora,* Bibliotheca Hispana Bibilica, (Madrid: Consejo Superior de Investigaciones Científicas Instituto "Francisco Suárea," 1984), 11:199–200, 237–39.

9. The MT of 31:1 says, מִילוֹהִי דלמואל מלכא נביותא.
10. The Greek reads: Οἱ ἐμοὶ λόγοι εἴρηνται ὑπὸ Θεοῦ, βασιλέως χρηματισμὸς, ὃν ἐπαίδευσεν ἡ μήτηρ αυτοῦ. See Sir Lancelot C. L. Brenton, *The Septuagint with Apocrypha, Greek, and English* (Grand Rapids: Zondervan, 1982), 813. Deist comments on the Septuagint translation, saying, "it is impossible to take the Hebrew *melek* as genitive of *massāʾ* as does the LXX." Ferdinand Deist, "Prov. 31:1: A Case of Constant Mistranslation," *JNSL* 6 (1978): 1–2.
11. Original is מִילוֹהִי דלמואל מלכא נביותא, translated by Merino, "verba lamuel regis: Prophetia . . ." Merino, *Targum de Proverbios. Edición Príncipe del Ms. Villa-Amil n.o 5 de Alfonso de Zamora,* 199–200, 237–39.
12. According to John Day, the majority of scholars today translate *massāʾ* as a proper name instead of "an oracle," as it will be reflected in the following argument. Day, "Foreign Semitic Influence on the Wisdom of Israel and Its Appropriation in the Book of Proverbs," 55–56.
13. The *Graecus Venetus* is a fourteenth-century Greek translation of selected Old Testament books directly from the MT done by a Jew who lived in Venice, Italy. It renders the MT of 30:1a into, λόγοι ἀγούρου υἱέως ἰακέως τοῦ μασάου. See Oscar von Gebhardt, ed., *Graecus Venetus* [microform] (Leipzig: F. A. Brockhaus, 1875).
14. The Arabic Van Dyke renders the MT this way: for 30:1a, *Kalām ʿAjûr bin muttaqiat massā;* for 31:1a *Kalām Lamûʾîl malik Massa.* Cornelius Van Dyke, trans., *al-Kitāb al-Muqaddas* (Beirut: Dar al-Kitāb al-Muqaddas, n.d.). The genitive construction, *muttaqiat massā,* means "the pious one (feminine gender) of Massa." It is based on reading the MT, יקהת מַשָּׂא, instead of הַמַּשָּׂא יָקֶה as the Masoretes put it. יקהת is the construct form of the feminine active participle of the verb יקה (Ar. *waqā*), meaning "to be pious" (*BDB,* 429).
15. These versions include the NASB, RSV, JB, and NEB.
16. See also the translation of Murphy, *The Tree of Life,* 25.

17. Delitzsch notes, "What author, whether poet or prophet, would give to his work the title of מַשָּׂא, which in itself means everything, and thus nothing." Franz Delitzsch, *Biblical Commentary on the Proverbs of Solomon,* trans. M. G. Easton (Grand Rapids: Eerdmans, 1952), 2:262.
18. For a fuller discussion see *BDB,* 670–72. McKane believes that the problem of having *massā'* as a prophetic oracle in Proverbs is alleviated by the presence of another prophetic term *ne'ûm,* and thus it should not be deemed inappropriate for the literary setting. William McKane, *Proverbs: A New Approach* (Philadelphia: Westminster, 1970), 644. However, *massā'* as highlighted above, when used with reference to an oracle, almost always involves a judgment context, while *ne'ûm* does not necessarily imply judgment, but a saying inspired by God, as in 2 Samuel 23:1 and here. Furthermore, Zöckler notes that *massā'* + *ne'ûm* both in the prophetic sense is "a combination unknown in the whole prophetical literature of the Old Testament." Otto Zöckler, "The Proverbs of Solomon," in *A Commentary on the Holy Scriptures: Critical, Doctrinal, and Homiletical by John Peter Lange,* ed. Philip Schaff, trans. Charles A. Aiken (New York: Charles Scribner, 1870), 10:247. Even McKane himself realizes later that the phrase *ne'ûm haggeber* looks "very odd, if *haggeber* is Agur." Therefore, he admits that "the best that can be done is to read *hammassā'î* and to suggest that the change of text has been brought about by the proximity of *hammassā'î* to *ne'ûm.*" McKane, *Proverbs,* 644.
19. Cf. Delitzsch, *Biblical Commentary on the Proverbs of Solomon,* 2:261. See also 2 Kings 9:25; 2 Chronicles 24:27; Isaiah 13:1; 14:28; 15:1; 17:1; 19:1; 21:1; Ezekiel 12:10, etc.
20. Since *hammassā'* is a noun determined with a prefix, and is used in apposition to the genitive structure *dibrey 'Agûr,* in good Semitic syntax it should be described further and cannot stand alone by itself without a qualifier and not look very odd. This is especially true, since "the oracle" is not introducing new facts about the term *dibrey* ("the words"), and cannot

function as predicate for "the words of Agur." In fact, the word "saying" in the next coli is also in apposition to "the words," and because it is starting a nominal sentence it is determined twice, once with the genitive, "of the man," and a second time with the prepositional phrase, "to Ithiel." Delitzsch makes a similar observation, "משׂא never occurs by itself in the sense of a divine, a solemn utterance, without having some more clearly defining addition." Delitzsch, *Biblical Commentary on the Proverbs of Solomon,* 2:262.

21. Toy affirms that if *hammassāʾ* is read "the oracle" this would relieve the question from the geographical discussion. "But, if it be adopted, it must probably be regarded as not original, since *sayings* is a sufficient description of what follows." Crawford H. Toy, *A Critical and Exegetical Commentary on the Book of Proverbs,* ICC, ed. S. R. Driver, Alfred Plummer, and Charles Augustus Briggs (Edinburgh: T & T Clark, 1970), 518.
22. For these possibilities, see *BDB,* 672, and the apparatus to the *BHS.*
23. Toy realized the parallelism of the Agur opening title with Balaam's. Therefore, he concluded that in order to maintain the parallelism the second qualifying statement should also be descriptive of the man, and the second colon should be translated "utterance of the man who has wearied himself." Toy, *A Critical and Exegetical Commentary on the Book of Proverbs,* 520.
24. K. A. Kitchen, "Proverbs and Wisdom Books of the Ancient Near East: The Factual History of a Literary Form," *TB* 28 (1977): 100–102.
25. Delitzsch, *Biblical Commentary on the Proverbs of Solomon,* 2:262.
26. Cf. Ferdinand Deist, "Proverbs 31:1: A Case of Constant Mistranslation," *JNSL* 6 (1978): 2. See also Toy, *A Critical and Exegetical Commentary on the Book of Proverbs,* 539. Deist proposes that the relative pronoun ʾšr should go back not to "words" but to Lemuel, and thus the translation would be, "the words of Lemuel, king of Massa, whose mother instructed him" (see Deist, "Proverbs 31:1: A Case of Constant Mistranslation," 2–3).

27. Rabbinic traditions identified Agur and Lemuel as by-names for Solomon and translated *massāʾ* as "prophecy." R. Ibn Ezra and R. Ralban identify Agur and Lemuel as *nom-de-plume* for Solomon. *Biblia Rabbinica,* ed. Jacob Ben Hayim Ibn Adoniya (Jerusalem: Makor, 1972), 4:187–91. However, R. Saadia before them believed that these were unidentifiable. Saadia ben Joseph al-Fayyoûmî, *Version arabe des Proverbes, surnommés livre de la recherche de la sagesse de r. Saadia ben Iosef al-Fayyoûmî, publiée pour la première fois et accompagnée de notes hébraïques avec une traduction française d'après l'arabe,* ed. and trans. Joseph Derenbourg and Mayer Lambert, Oeuvres complètes de r. Saadia ben Iosef al-Fayyoûmî, ed. J. Derenbourg (Paris: Ernest Leroux, 1894), 6:182. Modern Hebrew translators of the MT identify both Agur and Lemuel as belonging to the tribe of Massa. *The Writings,* כתובים*: A New Translation of the Holy Scriptures According to the Masoretic Text* (Philadelphia: Jewish Publication Society, 1982). The suggestion that Agur and Lemuel are *nom-de-plume* for Solomon is completely defenseless and not based on any palpable evidence. Toy, *A Critical and Exegetical Commentary on the Book of Proverbs,* 518; Marvin E. Tate, "Proverbs," in *The Broadman Bible Commentary,* ed. Clifton J. Allen (Nashville: Broadman, 1971), 5:93.
28. James L. Crenshaw, "A Mother's Instruction to Her Son (Proverbs 31:1–9)," *Perspectives in Religious Studies* 15 (1988): 15.
29. So also Delitzsch, *Biblical Commentary on the Proverbs of Solomon,* 2:262; Crenshaw, "A Mother's Instruction to Her Son (Proverbs 31:1–9)," 14; Ernst Axel Knauf, *Ismael: Untersuchungen zur Geschichte Palestinas und Nordarabiens im 1. Jahrtausend v. Chr.,* Abhandlungen des Deutschen Palestinavereins, ed. Siegfried Mittmann and Manfred Weipert (Wiesbaden: Harrassowitz, 1989), 72; Israel Ephʿal, *The Ancient Arabs: Nomads on the Borders of the Fertile Crescent 9th–5th Centuries b.c.* (Leiden: E. J. Brill, 1982), 218–19; Michael Fox, "Agur Son of Jakeh," in *Encyclopedia Judaica* (Jerusalem: Encyclopedia Judaica Jerusalem, 1971), 2:434; Michael Fox and Harold L. Ginsberg, "Lemuel," in

Encyclopedia Judaica (Jerusalem: Encyclopedia Judaica Jerusalem, 1971), 11: col. 12; Murphy, *The Tree of Life,* 25; and many others.

30. Day, "Foreign Semitic Influence on the Wisdom of Israel and its Appropriation in the Book of Proverbs," 55–70.
31. After exhausting all cases of alleged parallelism between "the sayings of the wise" (22:17–24:22) and the earlier instructions of Amenemope, Ruffle suggested "that this passage was contributed by an Egyptian scribe working at the court of Solomon based on his memories of a text that he had heard and, maybe, used in his tribal training." Ruffle, "The Teaching of Amenemope and Its Connection with the Book of Proverbs," 65.
32. Meaning in Hebrew, "the gathered," and since it is of foreign origin it may mean, based on Arabic *âjar,* "the compensated one." Delitzsch, *Biblical Commentary on the Proverbs of Solomon,* 2:261.
33. See the occurrence of the name *ʾgr* in A. Van den Branden, *Les inscriptions thamoudéennes* (Louvain, 1950), 495; and in G. Lankester Harding, *An Index and Concordance of Pre-Islamic Arabian Names and Inscriptions* (Toronto: University of Toronto Press, 1971), 22. See also the occurrence of the name *yqhmlk* in Sabaean and Qatabanean inscriptions in G. Ryckmans, *Les noms propres sud-sémitiques* (Louvain, 1934–35), 2:74; and in Harding, *Index and Concordance of Pre-Islamic Arabian Names and Inscriptions,* 681; see *wqh'l* in Ryckmans, *Les noms propres sud-sémitiques*, 54; and in Harding, *Index and Concordance of Pre-Islamic Arabian Names and Inscriptions,* 648; see *mlkwqh* and *ʿmwqh,* which stem from the same root, in Ryckmans, *Les noms propres sud-sémitiques,* 1:226; and in Harding, *Index and Concordance of Pre-Islamic Arabian Names and Inscriptions,* 442, 566. For a more detailed discussion of the issue, see Israel Ephʿal, "'Arabs' in Babylonia in the 8th Century B.C." *JAOS* 94 (1974): 108–15; Ran Zadok, "Arabians in Mesopotamia during the Late-Assyrian, Chaldaean, Achaemenian and Hellenistic Periods Chiefly According to Cuneiform Sources," *ZDMG* 131 (1981):

42–84. Eph^{c}al also points out the toponyms ^{uru}*Dûr* ^{m}*Ú-gur-ri* and ^{uru}*Dûr* ^{m}*Aq-qí-ia* in "the territory of bit Amukani" on the southwestern border of Babylonia, and he sees some possibility of associating them with Agur and Yakeh of Proverbs 30:1. Eph^{c}al, *The Ancient Arabs,* 219. See also D. S. Margoliouth, *The Relations Between Arabs and Israelites Prior to the Rise of Islam* (London: Oxford University Press, 1924), 30.

34. Anton Jirku, "Das n. pr. Lemu'el (Prov. 31:1) und der Gott Lim," *ZAW* 66 (1954): 151.
35. Thus Crenshaw, "A Mother's Instruction to Her Son (Proverbs 31:1–9)," 11.
36. Margoliouth, *The Relations Between Arabs and Israelites,* 30.
37. Ibid.
38. See *ANET,* 283; and the discussion of W. F. Albright, "The Biblical Tribe of Massa and Some Congeneres," in *Studi Orientalistici in Onore di Giorgio Levi Della Vida* (Roma: Istituto per L'Oriente, 1956), 1:1–14.
39. Ptolemy, *Geography* 5.18.2.
40. *ARNA,* 90, 101.
41. N. H. Tur-Sinai, *The Book of Job: A New Commentary* (Jerusalem: Kiryath Sepher, 1967), lxi, 522.
42. "In Arabia the word is still employed for troops of raiders, a sense to which close parallels can be found in the Qur'ān." Margoliouth, *The Relations Between Arabs and Israelites,* 31.
43. Alois Musil, *The Manners and Customs of the Rwala Bedouins,* Oriental Explorations and Studies, no. 6, ed. J. K. Wright (New York: American Geographical Society, 1928), 50.
44. Saadia, *Version arabe des Proverbes.*
45. Margoliouth, *The Relations Between Arabs and Israelites,* 31.
46. The original is: "les voyantes des rois." E. Lipinski, "Les 'Voyantes des Rois' en Prov. XXXI 3," *VT* 23 (1973): 246. That Aramaic was common (in addition to Arabic) among north Arabian Ishmaelite tribes is evident from the study of their onomasticon. Zadok, "Arabians in Mesopotamia During the Late-Assyrian, Chaldaean, Achaemenian and Hellenistic Periods Chiefly Ac-

cording to Cuneiform Sources," 42–84; Ephʿal, "'Arabs' in Babylonia in the 8th Century B.C.," 108–15. For a thorough study of cases of Arabisms in the sayings of Agur and Lemuel, see F. Mühlau, *De Proverbiorum quae dictuntur Aguri et Lemuelis origine atque indole* (Leipzig: Metzger & Wittig, 1869).

47. Based on familiarity with the Old Testament, it was suggested that Agur and Lemuel were native Israelites who lived in Arabia. This familiarity is especially true in Agur's sayings that have affinities with the book of Job, as highlighted earlier, and with some psalms. But there are no compelling reasons to believe that, since Lemuel was king of Massa. This view was proposed by Zöckler, "The Proverbs of Solomon," and F. Mühlau, *De Proverbiorum quae dictuntur Aguri et Lemuelis origine atque indole.*
48. Thus Delitzsch, *Biblical Commentary on the Proverbs of Solomon,* 2:266. See also the interesting remarks of Albright, "The Biblical Tribe of Massa and Some Congeneres," 10–11.
49. Cf. Philip K. Hitti, *History of the Arabs from the Earliest Times to the Present* (London: Macmillan, 1970), 42.
50. A major Ishmaelite tribe (Gen. 25:12–18). Knauf argues for translating "the curtains of Suleima" in 1:5, instead of "curtains of Solomon," as it is usually translated. Sulayma is an Ishmaelite tribe that is coupled with the Nabataeans in the Nabataean inscriptions. Knauf, *Ismael,* 92–111.
51. See the fascinating treatment of this issue under the section, "The Nomad in Love," in Morris S. Seale, *The Desert Bible: Nomadic Tribal Culture and Old Testament Interpretation* (New York: St. Martin's, 1974), 53–73.
52. The book of Songs presents affinities with other ancient Near Eastern love poetry. For a discussion of these affinities, see Michael Fox, *The Song of Songs and the Ancient Egyptian Love Songs* (Madison: University of Wisconsin Press, 1985); Peter Craigie, "The Poetry of Ugarit and Israel," *TB* 22 (1971): 11–15; G. Lloyd Carr, "The Love Poetry Genre in the Old Testament and the Ancient Near East: Another Look at Inspiration," *JETS*

(1982): 491–95; J. S. Cooper, "New Cuneiform Parallels to the Song of Songs," *JBL* 90 (1971): 157–60.

53. Seale, *The Desert Bible*, 53–73. See also Song 1:5, 14; 2:14; 3:4, 6; 4:3; 5:4. Seale gives interesting parallelism between the poetry of al-Mutanabbî and ᶜAnatara and Song 2:7; 3:6; 4:12; and 7:3. See ibid., 59–61 and 53–73 for many other similarities.
54. Assuming an early date for the Exodus (1446 B.C.), this historical survey would extend over a period close to a millennium.
55. Margoliouth, *The Relations Between Arabs and Israelites*, 39.

Chapter 8: What Became of Ishmael?

1. For the period extending from around 400 B.C. (which is the last period attested in Xenophon) until 312 B.C., when the Nabataeans were mentioned for the first time in history by Diodorus, there are practically no historical records concerning Arabians. For this period, speculations have to be made until there is further light from future archaeological discoveries.
2. Primary sources include Daniel David Luckenbill, *Ancient Records of Assyria and Babylonia*, 2 vols. (Chicago: University of Chicago Press, 1926). idem, *The Annals of Sennacherib* (Chicago: University of Chicago Press, 1924); *ANET;* and others. Important secondary sources include William J. Dumbrell, "The Midianites and Their Transjordanian Successors" (Th.D. diss., Harvard University, 1970); Philip K. Hitti, *History of the Arabs from the Earliest Times to the Present* (London: Macmillan, 1970); *The Cambridge Ancient History*, rev. ed. (Cambridge: Cambridge University Press, 1961–); Ran Zadok, "Arabians in Mesopotamia During the Late-Assyrian, Chaldean, Achaemenian and Hellenistic Periods Chiefly According to Cuneiform Sources," *ZDMG* 131 (1981): 42–84; Israel Ephᶜal, *The Ancient Arabs: Nomads on the Borders of the Fertile Crescent 9th–5th Centuries b.c.* (Leiden: E. J. Brill, 1982); Ernst Axel Knauf, *Ismael: Untersuchungen zur Geschichte Palestinas und Nordarabiens im 1. Jahrtausend v. Chr.*, Abhandlungen des Deutschen Palestinavereins, ed. Siegfried

Mittmann and Manfred Weipert (Wiesbaden: Harrassowitz, 1989); M. C. A. Macdonald, "North Arabia in the First Millennium B.C.E.," in *Civilizations of the Ancient Near East,* ed. Jack Sasson (New York: Charles Scribner's Sons, 1995), 2:1355–69; James A. Montgomery, *Arabia and the Bible* (Philadelphia: University of Pennsylvania Press, 1934); Giorgio Levi Della Vida, "Pre-Islamic Arabia," in *The Arab Heritage,* ed. Nabih Amin Faris (Princeton, N.J.: Princeton University Press, 1946), 25–57; and others.

3. The main collection of these texts is found in *ARNA*.
4. David F. Graf, "Nabateans," in *ABD,* 1:970.
5. See the essential works of J. Starcky, "Pétra et la Nabatène," in *Dictionnaire de la Bible,* supplement 7 (Paris: Letouzey & Ané, Éditeurs, 1966), 886–1017; G. W. Bowersock, *Roman Arabia* (Cambridge, Mass.: Harvard University Press, 1983).
6. "These [are] the names of the sons of Ishmael, by their names, according to their generations: the firstborn of Ishmael Nebayoth (נבית), Qedar (קדר), Adbeel (אדבאל), Mibsam (מבשׂם), Mishma (משמע), Dumah (דומה), Massa (משׂא), Ḥadar (חדר), Tema (תימא) Yetur (יטוּר), Naphish (נפישׁ), and Kedemah (קדמה). They dwelt from Havilah unto Shur, that [is] before Egypt, as you go toward Assyria. He settled in the presence of all his brethren" (Gen. 25:13–18).
7. Fred V. Winnett, "The Arabian Genealogies in the Book of Genesis," in *Translating and Understanding the Old Testament: Essays in Honor of Herbert Gordon May,* ed. Harry Thomas Frank and William L. Reed (Nashville: Abingdon, 1970), 194.
8. See the occurrences of *Nabaiati, Qi-id-ri,* and *Qi-da-ri* in *ANET,* 298–300.
9. Macdonald, "North Arabia in the First Millennium B.C.E.," 1360.
10. Alois Musil, *Arabia Deserta: A Topographical Itinerary,* Oriental Explorations and Studies, no. 2 (New York: American Geographical Society, 1927), 492. Calling Basma Nebayot's sister (Gen. 28:9), in reference to her marriage to Esau, may be a deliberate allusion by the narrator to the intermixing between the

Edomites and the clan of Nebayot. Therefore, a location of Nebayot in proximity to Edom may be warranted by the Genesis text.

11. Cf. Winnett, "The Arabian Genealogies in the Book of Genesis," 194; *ARNA,* 113–20. See also Macdonald, "North Arabia in the First Millennium B.C.E.," 1359.
12. Thus Musil, *Arabia Deserta,* 478, 492; René Dussaud, *La pénétration des arabes en Syrie avant l'Islam* (Paris: Librairie Orientaliste Paul Geuthner, 1955), 22; E. C. Broome, "Nabaiati, Nebaioth and the Nabataeans: The Linguistic Problem," *JSS* 18 (1973): 1–16; Gary Dean Baldwin, "Nabataean Cultural Influences upon Israel Until 106 A.D." (Th.D. diss., Southwestern Baptist Theological Seminary, 1982), 13–122.
13. This identification will be discussed further later in this survey. However, for a dismissal of that possibility, see A. S. Fulton, "Nebaioth," in *ISBE,* 2:503; Hitti, *History of the Arabs,* 67; Eph^cal, *The Ancient Arabs,* 222–23; Knauf, *Ismael,* 92–111.
14. Pierre Briant, *Etat et pasteurs au Moyen-Orient ancien* (Paris: Editions de la Maison des sciences de l'homme, 1982), 117; Knauf, *Ismael,* 69–71; Eph[c]al, *The Ancient Arabs,* 118–21.
15. *ARAB* II § 518a, 536; *ANET,* 291.
16. Cf. *ARAB* II § 869. For further details, see *ARNA,* 71; Eph[c]al, *The Ancient Arabs,* 118–19; Musil, *Arabia Deserta,* 531–33; Dumbrell, "The Midianites and Their Transjordanian Successors," 192–200.
17. Musil, *Arabia Deserta,* 531–53; Macdonald, "North Arabia in the First Millennium B.C.E.," 1360.
18. *ARAB* II § 358; Montgomery, *Arabia and the Bible,* 45; for a detailed discussion of the importance of Dumah, see *ARNA,* 71–73; Musil, *Arabia Deserta,* 531–35; Eph[c]al, *The Ancient Arabs,* 116–25. According to LaSor, the oracle against Dumah (Isa. 21:11–12) seems to fit the description of the suggested place better than Deyr ed-Dûmeh in the vicinity of Hebron mentioned in Joshua 15:52. W. S. LaSor, "Dumah," in *ISBE,* 1:995.
19. *ARNA,* 71.

20. Cf. Ephʿal, *The Ancient Arabs,* 120–21.
21. *ARNA,* 15–19, 71–72.
22. *ANET,* 291–92, 298–301.
23. Knauf, *Ismael,* 69.
24. Hitti, *History of the Arabs,* 42.
25. This confederation may have been patterned after the Kinda kingdom that existed in central Arabia on the eve of Islam. According to Moscati, this kingdom had "the form of a confederation, in which one tribe has a predominant position, and one family of that tribe holds the government." Moscati believes that the Kinda confederation pattern was "so often accomplished in the past." Sabatino Moscati, *The Semites in Ancient History: An Inquiry into the Settlement of the Beduin and Their Political Establishment* (Cardiff: University of Wales Press, 1959), 127. For a full discussion of the Kinda kingdom, see G. Olinder, *The Kings of Kinda of the Family of ʿĀkil al-Murār* (Lund, 1927).
26. Hitti, *History of the Arabs,* 42; Macdonald, "North Arabia in the First Millennium B.C.E.," 1359.
27. A. Grohmann, "Al ʿArab," in *The Encylopedia of Islam,* ed. H. A. R. Gibb et al., new ed. (Leiden: E. J. Brill, 1960), 1:525.
28. Zadok, "Arabians in Mesopotamia During the Late-Assyrian, Chaldean, Achaemenian and Hellenistic Periods Chiefly According to Cuneiform Sources," 42–84; Israel Ephʿal, "'Arabs' in Babylonia in the 8th Century B.C.," *JAOS* 94 (1974): 108–15.
29. These inscriptions will be discussed in further detail in the historical survey. However, for identifying biblical Geshem with the Geshem of Tell el-Maskḥuta's inscription (Egypt), see William J. Dumbrell, "The Tell el-Maskḥuta Bowls and the 'Kingdom' of Qedar in the Persian Period," *BASOR* 203 (1971): 33–44. For identification with Geshem b. Shahr of the Dedanite inscription, see W. F. Albright, "Dedan," in *Geschichte und Altes Testament, Festschrift A. Alt,* ed. W. F. Albright et al. (Tübingen: J. C. B. Mohr, 1953): 6.
30. Cf. A. S. Fulton, "Kedar," in *ISBE,* 3:5; Dumbrell, "The Tell el-Maskḥuta Bowl," 33–44.

31. Macdonald, "North Arabia in the First Millennium B.C.E.," 1359.
32. Knauf's original German: "aus den Qedar sind wahrscheinlich die Nabatäer hervorgegangen." Knauf, *Ismael,* 66, 92–111.
33. *ANET,* 291.
34. Macdonald, "North Arabia in the First Millennium B.C.E.," 1360.
35. *ARNA,* 72.
36. *ANET,* 299.
37. A. K. Irvine, "The Arabs and the Ethiopians," in *Peoples of the Old Testament Times,* ed. D. J. Wiseman (Oxford: Clarendon, 1973), 292.
38. Macdonald ("North Arabia in the First Millennium B.C.E.," 1360) identifies this fertility god as Ruḍa.
39. *Herodotus* 2.3.8.
40. Musil thinks that since Adbe'el was also identified as of "the land of Arubu," this would prove that "the Sinai Peninsula as well as the regions on the frontier of the Damascan settlements and the oasis of Adumu, was regarded as belonging to the Aribi." Musil, *Arabia Deserta,* 478.
41. *ANET,* 282–84; Alois Musil, *The Northern Hegaz: A Topographical Itinerary,* Oriental Explorations and Studies, no. 1 (New York: American Geographical Society, 1926), 291.
42. *ANET,* 283.
43. Ephᶜal sees Adbe'el's territory as on "the border of Egypt." Ephᶜal, *The Ancient Arabs,* 25.
44. *ANET,* 283.
45. *ARNA,* 89.
46. Ibid., 90, 101.
47. Cf. Musil, *Arabia Deserta,* 478.
48. See the discussion of this point in chapter 10.
49. Ephᶜal, *The Ancient Arabs,* 219.
50. Ptolemy, *Geography* 5.18.2; see also C. G. Rasmussen, "Massa," in *ISBE,* 3:277.
51. Macdonald, "North Arabia in the First Millennium B.C.E.," 1361; for further details on that oasis, see Jaussen et Savignac, *Mission archéologique en Arabie,* Publications de la Société des Fouilles

Archéologiques (Paris: Ernest Leroux, Éditeurs and Librairie Paul Geuthner, 1909–22), 2:144; Musil, *Arabia Deserta,* 516–17.

52. cf. Briant, *Etat et pasteurs au Moyen-Orient ancien*, 117–19.
53. Ibid.
54. Dussaud, *La pénétration des arabes en Syrie avant l'Islam,* 176. Musil, *Arabia Deserta,* 477; *ARNA,* 88. Winnett (ibid.) thinks that "the presence of the great well called al-Haddāj" in the present city of Taymāʾ "makes it highly probable that human occupation of the oasis dates back to a very remote period."
55. *ANET,* 283–84.
56. Cf. D. A. Dorsey, "Tema," in *ISBE,* 4:758.
57. Grohmann identifies three of these last tribes: *Hayappa* being *ʿEfa* the Midianite tribe that dwelt east of *Taymāʾ; Badan* being a tribe southeast of the oasis of *el-Ulaʾ-Dedan;* and *Idibaʾil* as being the biblical *Adebeʾel* of Genesis 25:13, who resided near Gaza. A. Grohmann, "Al 'Arab," in *The Encyclopedia of Islam,* ed. H. A. R. Gibb et al., new ed. (Leiden : E. J. Brill, 1960), 1:524–27. Saba' should be a northern colony of the southern kingdom of Sheba. Hitti, *History of the Arabs,* 42.
58. *ANET,* 283.
59. Ibid., 283–84; Musil, *Arabia Deserta,* 477; *ARNA,* 88; Hitti, *History of the Arabs, from the Earliest Times to the Present,* 37; D. A. Dorsey, "Tema," in *ISBE,* 4:758. For a good discussion on the nature of these different tribes mentioned above, see the discussion of Musil, *Arabia Deserta,* 288–91.
60. Daniel David Luckenbill, *The Annals of Sennacherib* (Chicago: University of Chicago Press, 1924), 113.
61. *ANET,* 313.
62. *ARNA,* 90. It should be noted that Dedan, one of the descendants of Keturah (Gen. 10:6), is an important city in the northern Hejaz (modern al-ʿUla). It has been suggested that this city was for some time the headquarters of the Sabaeans in the northern part of the peninsula. The Sabaeans at the height of their commercial power controlled the transport routes leading through Hejaz northward to the Mediterranean ports and

planted colonies along these routes (see Hitti, *History of the Arabs,* 42). This may explain the presence of the Sabaeans in the north as early as the events of the book of Job (1:15). For a detailed discussion on Dedan, see Ephᶜal, *The Ancient Arabs,* 180–84, 211–15; *ARNA,* 113–21.

63. *ARNA,* 90–91.
64. Ibid., 90; see also Gadd, "The Harran Inscriptions of Nabonidus," 78, 84.
65. Gadd, "The Harran Inscriptions of Nabonidus," 59.
66. Garth Bawden and Christopher Edens, "History of Taymāʾ and Hejazi Trade During the First Millennium B.C.," *Journal of the Economic and Social History of the Orient* 32 (1989): 48–103. See also A. Livingstone, "Arabians in Babylonia/Babylonians in Arabia: Some Reflections à propos New and Old Evidence," in *L'Arabie préislamique et son environment historique et culturel: Actes du colloque de Strasbourg 24–27 juin 1987,* ed. T. Fahd, Université des sciences humaines de Strasbourg: Travaux du Centre de Recherche sur the Proche-Orient et la Grèce Antiques 10 (Leiden: E. J. Brill, 1989), 97–105; Israel Ephᶜal, "'Arabs' in Babylonia in the 8th Century B.C.," *JAOS* 94 (1974): 108–15.
67. Knauf, "Tema," in *ABD,* 6:347.
68. Ibid.
69. Montgomery, *Arabia and the Bible,* 46.
70. See also Knauf, *Ismael,* 80.
71. Dussaud, *La pénétration des arabes en Syrie avant l'Islam,* 176–78; Knauf, *Ismael,* 80, 46; Montgomery suggests that this is "an interesting case of the permanence of an ancient stock and illustrative of the mobility of Arabian tribes" (*Arabia and the Bible,* 46).
72. Montgomery, *Arabia and the Bible,* 46.
73. Musil, *Arabia Deserta,* 493. Dussaud sees Musil's genius in this identification. Dussaud, *La pénétration des arabes en Syrie avant l'Islam,* 176.
74. Dussaud, *La pénétration des arabes en Syrie avant l'Islam,* 175; Musil, *Arabia Deserta,* 479; Ephᶜal, *The Ancient Arabs,* 238–39.

Chapter 9: Arabs Haunted by World Powers

1. See the historical narratives starting with 1 Kings 11:14.
2. For a survey of these different attempts, see Hans-Joachim Kraus, *Psalms 60–150: A Commentary,* trans. Hilton C. Oswald (Minneapolis: Augsburg/Fortress, 1989), 161–62. See also William J. Dumbrell's discussion in "The Midianites and Their Transjordanian Successors" (Th.D. diss., Harvard University, 1970), 189–90.
3. Dumbrell, "The Midianites and Their Transjordanian Successors," 190.
4. Ibid.
5. Kraus, *Psalms 60–150,* 161.
6. M. C. A. Macdonald, "North Arabia in the First Millennium B.C.E.," in *Civilizations of the Ancient Near East,* ed. Jack Sasson (New York: Charles Scribner's Sons, 1995), 1364.
7. See the discussion of Peter J. Parr, "Aspects of the Archaeology of North-West Arabia in the First Millennium B.C.," in *L'Arabie préislamique et son environment historique et culturel: Actes du colloque de Strasbourg 24–27 juin 1987,* Université des sciences humaines de Strasbourg: Travaux du Centre de Recherche sur the Proche-Orient et la Grèce Antiques 10, ed. T. Fahd (Leiden: E. J. Brill, 1989), 39–66, where he notes that there is no evidence of sedentary life "at any of the oasis centres of northern Arabia such as Adummatu (al-Jawf), Taymāʾ, or Dedan (al-ʿUla) in the first millennium prior to about the 6th century B.C.," which, he remarks, is in agreement with Assyrian texts that refer consistently to Arabs as nomads.
8. Thus also Macdonald, "North Arabia in the First Millennium B.C.E.," 1364.
9. *ARNA,* 88.
10. See, for example, the recent valuable work on pre-Islamic Arabia by Robert G. Hoyland, *Arabia and the Arabs: From the Bronze Age to the Coming of Islam* (London: Routledge, 2001).
11. Giorgio Levi Della Vida, "Pre-Islamic Arabia," in *The Arab*

Heritage, ed. Nabih Amin Faris (Princeton, N.J.: Princeton University Press, 1946), 26–27.

12. *ANET,* 279 (*ARAB,* I § 611).
13. Israel Eph^cal, *The Ancient Arabs: Nomads on the Borders of the Fertile Crescent 9th–5th Centuries b.c.* (Leiden: E. J. Brill, 1982), 81.
14. Trude Weiss Rosmarin, "Aribi und Arabien in den Babylonisch-Assyrischen Quellen," *JSOR* 16 (1932): 8.
15. A. K. Irvine, "The Arabs and the Ethiopians," in *Peoples of the Old Testament Times,* ed. D. J. Wiseman (Oxford: Clarendon, 1973), 290.
16. Macdonald, "North Arabia in the First Millennium B.C.E.," 1364.
17. Irvine, "The Arabs and the Ethiopians," 290.
18. For a detailed discussion on these queens, see N. Abbot, "Pre-Islamic Arab Queens," *AJSL* 58 (1941): 1–22.
19. *ANET,* 282.
20. Sabatino Moscati, *The Semites in Ancient History: An Inquiry into the Settlement of the Beduin and Their Political Establishment* (Cardiff: University of Wales Press, 1959), 123.
21. *ANET,* 283 (*ARAB,* I § 772).
22. Hitti mentions the possibility of her name being *Shamsiyah,* which means, in Arabic, "umbrella." Philip K. Hitti, *History of the Arabs from the Earliest Times to the Present* (London: Macmillan, 1970), 37.
23. *ANET,* 283–84. The land of Bazu is described as a waterless region, which is recognized by scholars as located somewhere in north Arabia. For further discussion, see Alois Musil, *Arabia Deserta: A Topographical Itinerary,* Oriental Explorations and Studies, no. 2 (New York: American Geographical Society, 1927), 482–85; Eph^cal, *The Ancient Arabs,* 130–37.
24. However, she functioned under the authority of an Assyrian overseer [lú]*qêpu.* Eph^cal, *The Ancient Arabs,* 86.
25. Macdonald, "North Arabia in the First Millennium B.C.E.," 1364.
26. Ibid.
27. *ANET,* 283. Three of the above tribes—Massā', Taymā', and

Adbe'el—are among the descendants of Ishmael (Gen. 25:12–18; 1 Chron. 1:29–30). They dwelt in north Arabia and Sinai. ᶜEphah is a Midianite tribe listed among the children of Keturah (Gen. 25:4) and was located in north Arabia east of Taymāʾ. While Ephᶜal admits having no clear data about Badana, Grohmann identifies it as located southeast of the oasis el-'Ula, which is biblical Dedan. Hattia is unidentifiable so far. Saba' is normally associated with the kingdom of Sheba in south Arabia. According to Ephᶜal, "recent research on South Arabia has removed all doubt about the existence of the kingdom of Sheba" in the south as early as the eighth century B.C. However, against the assertion of Macdonald ("North Arabia in the First Millennium B.C.E.," 1365), Ephᶜal is reluctant to admit that the southern kingdom of Sheba, which is 1,000 kilometers from Taymāʾ, brought tribute to Sargon II. Instead, he sees in the Assyrian text (using LÚ instead of URU) an impression of designating a nomadic group of the north here. Ephᶜal, *The Ancient Arabs,* 88; A. Grohmann, "Al ᶜArab," in *The Encyclopedia of Islam,* ed. H. A. R. Gibb et al., new ed. (Leiden: E. J. Brill, 1960), 525. The presence of Saba' in the north is evident from Job 1:15, and from the presence of Saba' among the descendants of Keturah (Gen. 25:1–6) who lived in the Hejaz area and were heavily involved in incense trade, possibly as agents to the Sabaeans of the southern kingdom of Sheba (Gen. 10:28). See the development of this subject in Nigel Groom, *Frankincense and Myrrh: A Study of the Arabian Incense Trade* (London: Longman Group Ltd.; Beirut: Librairie du Liban, 1981).

28. *ANET,* 283 (*ARAB,* I § 778).
29. Hitti, *History of the Arabs,* 37.
30. Grohmann, "al-ᶜArab," 525.
31. *ANET,* 286 (*ARAB,* II § 17).
32. *ANET,* 286. Though doubting the extent of the resettling of nomads in Samaria, Ephᶜal sees in the Assyrian implanting of these nomads in an agricultural land an attempt to enhance incense trade in that region and "divert to that area some of the

Arabian trade in which the nomads played an important role." He points out the recovering in Samaria of few texts, dated after the fall of the city, that contain Arabic names. Ephʿal, *The Ancient Arabs,* 108–9.

33. Irvine, "The Arabs and the Ethiopians," 290.
34. Thamud is a north Arabian tribe located in the upper Hejaz area. The Qurʾan assumes the prominence of Thamud before Muhammad's time. This tribe is portrayed in the Qurʾan as having been annihilated by God through a major earthquake or volcanic eruption because, having become extremely rich, it indulged in sinful living (Sura 7:76; 41:12, 16). The tribe of Thamud appears also in classical writers as inhabiting the eastern coast of the Red Sea (see *Diodorus* 3.44.6). For further details on Thamud as it is portrayed in inscriptions, classic literature, the Qurʾan, and ancient Arab writers, see A. Van den Branden, *Histoire de Thamoud* (Beyrouth, 1960); Musil, *Northern Hegaz,* 291–92; H. H. Bräu, "Thamûd," in *FEI,* 736. It is appropriate to mention here that the so-called Thamudic inscriptions are not named so because they belong to that tribe. Instead, contrary to the settled nature of that tribe, they were written mostly by nomads in a north Arabian dialect, apparently with a south Arabian alphabet, and are found all over the Arabian Peninsula. For a fuller discussion of the subject, see A Van den Branden, *Les inscriptions thamoudéennes* (Louvain, 1950); Jacques Ryckmans, "Aspects nouveaux du problème Thamoudéen," *Studia Islamica* 5 (1956): 5–17; Moscati, *The Semites in Ancient History,* 125–27.
35. *ANET,* 286 (*ARAB,* II § 18).
36. This king is generally acknowledged as being over the kingdom of Sheba in south Arabia, and one of the *Mukarribs,* which are south Arabian king-priests, mentioned in south Arabic inscriptions. Hitti, *History of the Arabs,* 38, 52; Ephʿal, *The Ancient Arabs,* 228–29.
37. Macdonald, "North Arabia in the First Millennium B.C.E.," 1365.
38. Ibid.

39. Ibid. See also Ephʿal, *The Ancient Arabs,* 108–9.
40. Rosmarin, "Aribi und Arabien in den Babylonisch-Assyrischen Quellen," 11. Macdonald notes that cuneiform texts show that Arab settlement in Babylonia, which may have started possibly as early as the eighth century B.C., increased gradually as time went by. Macdonald, "North Arabia in the First Millennium B.C.E.," 1365–66. For further consideration of this issue, see Zadok, "Arabians in Mesopotamia during the Late-Assyrian, Chaldean, Achaemenian and Hellenistic Periods Chiefly According to Cuneiform Sources," 42–84; Israel Ephʿal, "'Arabs' in Babylonia in the 8th Century B.C." *JAOS* 94 (1974): 108–15; A. Livingstone, "Arabians in Babylonia/Babylonians in Arabia: Some Reflections à propos New and Old Evidence," 97–105.
41. *ANET,* 291, 301; Hitti, *History of the Arabs,* 38; Ephʿal, *The Ancient Arabs,* 118–23; Knauf, *Ismael,* 4, 81f.
42. *ANET,* 291, 301.
43. Macdonald, "North Arabia in the First Millennium B.C.E.," 1366.
44. Dumbrell, "The Midianites and Their Transjordanian Successors,"195.
45. *Herodotus* 2.141. For a fuller discussion of the possible reasons behind this label, see Ephʿal, *The Ancient Arabs,* 141–42.
46. Macdonald, "North Arabia in the First Millennium B.C.E.," 1366.
47. For a discussion of ancient Arab deities, see G. Ryckmans, *Les religions arabes préislamiques,* Biliothèque du Muséon 26 (Louvain: Publications Universitaires, 1951).
48. *ANET,* 291.
49. Ibid., 291–92 (*ARAB,* II § 518a).
50. The increase was "10 minas of gold, 1000 choice gems, 50 camels and 1000 leather bags of spices." See the translation of Ephʿal, *The Ancient Arabs,* 128. See also, *ANET*, 292.
51. *ANET,* 292; Knauf, *Ismael,* 99.
52. *ANET*, 292.
53. For dating of events during Esarhaddon's reign, see Ephʿal, *The Ancient Arabs,* 125–26.
54. This rebellion of Iataʾ against Esarhaddon may be the same as

his later rebellion against Ashurbanipal. While Eph^cal (*The Ancient Arabs,* 125–30) is inclined to see two separate insurgencies, Knauf (*Ismael,* 98–100) sees only one described, which is the rebellion against Ashurbanipal.

55. *ARAB,* II § 946.
56. *ANET,* 297–300.
57. Eph[c]al, *The Ancient Arabs,* 137–42; Hitti, *History of the Arabs,* 38–39; Macdonald, "North Arabia in the First Millennium B.C.E.," 1366.
58. *ANET,* 298.
59. Ibid., 298–300 (*ARAB,* II § 817–831).
60. *ANET,* 299; Dumbrell, "The Midianites and Their Transjordanian Successors," 207–8.
61. Eph[c]al, *The Ancient Arabs,* 143.
62. *ANET,* 298.
63. Ibid.
64. Eph[c]al, *The Ancient Arabs,* 143; Dumbrell, "The Midianites and Their Transjordanian Successors," 206–7.
65. *ANET,* 298.
66. Dumbrell, "The Midianites and Their Transjordanian Successors," 207. See also *ANET,* 298–99.
67. Irvine, "The Arabs and the Ethiopians," 291.
68. *ANET,* 299.
69. Ibid.
70. Knauf, *Ismael,* 101–2.
71. *ANET,* 300–301.
72. cf. Dumbrell, "The Midianites and Their Transjordanian Successors," 213.
73. Ibid.
74. Original German: "man hat den Eindruck, daß die Assyrer mit den Verhältnissen in der arabischen Wüste so wenig zurechtkamen wie später die Byzantiner oder die Osmanen, und daß sie von ihren arabischen 'Vasallenkönigen' eine loyalität erwarteten, die diese ihren 'Untertanen' gegenüber niemals durchsetzen konnten." Knauf, *Ismael,* 101.

75. The oracle against Dumah (Isa. 21:11–12) has been called "the most enigmatic in the whole book of Isaiah, which is not without its obscurities." Otto Kaiser, *Isaiah 13–39: A Commentary* (Philadelphia: Westminster, 1974), 129. If Dumah is to be taken as referring to Edom because of its association with Seir in verse 11 (thus, Edward J. Young, *The Book of Isaiah,* NICOT, ed. R. K. Harrison [Grand Rapids: Eerdmans, 1969], 2:76–79; J. Ridderbos, *Isaiah,* Bible Student's Commentary, trans. John Vriend [Grand Rapids: Zondervan, 1985], 182–83), then it is not directly related to the Ishmaelites. If, on the contrary, it should be treated as Assyrian *Adummatu,* biblical Dumah (thus Hans Wilderberger, *Isaiah 13–27: A Continental Commentary,* trans. Thomas H. Trapp [Minneapolis: Fortress, 1997], 331–38), then it should be considered together with verses 13–17 that predict a judgment against north Arabian tribes. In any case, there is not enough information in the oracle to identify it with any specific historical incident. In case Ishmaelite Dumah is at stake, Sennacherib's conquest of *Adummatu,* in which he succeeded in catching the Qedarite king Haza'el and Te'elhunu, queen of the Arabs, as highlighted earlier in this study, may serve as a background for this oracle. Watts prefers to take Dumah as meaning "silence," thus avoiding the debated identification as a proper noun (John D. W. Watts, *Isaiah 1–33,* WBC [Waco, Tex.: Word, 1985], 24:275).
76. The writer assumes that Isaiah's ministry and writing are set against an Assyrian background (740–700 B.C.). For a discussion of this assumption, see Andrew E. Hill and John H. Walton, *A Survey of the Old Testament* (Grand Rapids: Zondervan, 1991), 319–25.
77. Dumbrell's view ("The Midianites and Their Transjordanian Successors," 260) that verses 14–15 are describing the Qedarite attack against Dedanite caravans is unlikely, since verses 16–17 are introduced with the expression כִּי (rendered "for" in most translations), making the logical cause-and-effect connection between both sections of the prophecy. Furthermore, it is

unlikely that the Qedarite power, concerned with the safety of incense trade and getting much benefit as a result, would attack the caravans that it is supposed to protect.

78. *ANET,* 286. Haiapa is usually identified as ʿEphah, which is a Midianite tribe (Gen. 25:4) and should have dwelt therefore in the Hejaz area, where Dedan and Taymāʾ are also located. Thus the caravans of Dedan would be affected by any military activity in that vicinity, whether Dedan is directly involved in the war or not. For further details on this view, see O. Procksch, *Isaiah: Chapters i–xxxix* (Leipzig, 1930), 271–75.
79. Dumbrell, who sees in 21:1–10 a description of the fall of Babylon under the Medo-Persians, believes that 21:11–17 should refer to the fall of the Qedarites under the same Persian sword in 539 B.C. Dumbrell, "The Midianites and Their Transjordanian Successors," 258–61. Though Dumbrell's argument is possible, the main difficulty it faces is that Qedar appears under the Persians as having stretched its impact to the Delta in Egypt, passing by south Palestine and the Sinai, as it will be shown later in this study and as Dumbrell himself points out in the same context (ibid., 261). Since Isaiah's ministry fits in with the Assyrian rule, it may be preferable to take the fall of Babylon as referring not to the eventual one under Cyrus (539 B.C.) but to one of the sackings of rebellious Babylon under the Assyrians. In 710 B.C., the city fell to Sargon II, and again it fell to Sennacherib in 703 B.C. "The close connection of chaps. 21 and 22 favors the latter occasion." Watts, *Isaiah 1–33,* 272.
80. For a good survey of the decline of Assyria and the rise of Babylonia as a major political power, see D. J. Wiseman, *Chronicles of Chaldaean Kings 626–556 b.c. in the British Museum* (London: Trustees of the British Museum, 1956), 5–42.
81. Ibid., 29–30.
82. For a full treatment of Arabs under the Chaldaeans, see Ephʿal, *The Ancient Arabs,* 170–191; Dumbrell, "The Midianites and Their Transjordanian Successors," 247–301.
83. Macdonald, "North Arabia in the First Millennium B.C.E.," 1367.

84. Dumbrell, "The Midianites and Their Transjordanian Successors," 247.
85. It appears in BM 21946 lines 9–10. Wiseman, *Chronicles of Chaldaean Kings,* 70–71.
86. The campaigns of Nebuchadnezzar are very scantily related in Josephus based on Berossus's account. See Josephus, *Against Apion* 1.19–21.
87. The Ḥatti-land in Neo-Babylonian inscriptions "encompasses all of Syro-Palestine." Ephʿal, *The Ancient Arabs,* 173.
88. Wiseman, *Chronicles of Chaldaean Kings,* 71.
89. Ibid., 31.
90. Ephʿal, *The Ancient Arabs,* 172.
91. Macdonald, "North Arabia in the First Millennium B.C.E.," 1367.
92. Jeremiah says: "The days are surely coming, says the LORD, when I will attend to all those who are circumcised only in the foreskin: Egypt, Judah, Edom, the Ammonites, Moab, and all those with shaven temples who live in the desert [a reference to north Arabians]. For all these nations are uncircumcised, and all the house of Israel is uncircumcised in heart" (9:25–26). The "shaving of temples" may refer to the prohibition of the children of Israel from doing that in Leviticus 19:27, possibly because of its connection with idol worship (see also the connection in *Herodotus* 3.8).
93. The Hebrew ולממלכות חצור translated "kingdoms of Ḥazor" is ambiguous. There is a general consensus that it cannot mean the city of Ḥazor northeast of Galilee, for the judgment is clearly describing the nomads of the Arabian Desert. Since the Septuagint has "the queen of the palace" (τη βασιλισση της αυλης = למלכת חצר), instead of "kingdom of Ḥazor," Dumbrell has preferred to translate the expression "kings of the encampments," taking חצור as a collective noun from the root חצר that has two clear nuances in Arabic (ḥaḍara = "to dwell" and ḥaṣara = "to confine"). Furthermore, he takes לממלכות as standing in apposition to "Qedar" since the conjunctive *waw* does not show in the LXX, and it may not be original. ממלכות

may be translated "prince" or "king—a possibility in the Phoenician. Dumbrell, "The Midianites and Their Transjordanian Successors," 272, 275. On the other hand, while Ephʿal admits the possibility of this translation, he prefers to take the term Hazor as a proper noun referring to a "region unfamiliar from any other sources," because verse 33 treats it as a feminine proper noun. Ephʿal, *The Ancient Arabs,* 175. The problem is beyond a definite solution at this point.

94. Wiseman notes: "Sargon, Sennacherib and Esarhaddon had all used their capture of the gods of the Arabs to bargain for more effective control over the desert tribesmen." Wiseman, *Chronicles of Chaldaean Kings,* 32.
95. Cf. the connection to idol worship in *Herodotus* 3.8.
96. Abu Jaʿfar Muhammad b. Jarîr al-Tabarî, "The Ancient Kingdoms," in *The History of al-Ṭabarî* (*Taʾrîkh al-rusul wal-mulûk*), trans. Moshe Perlmann Bibliotheca Persica, ed. Eshan Yar-Shater (Albany: State University of New York Press, 1987), 4:66. The tradition makes Berechiah b. Hananiah b. Zerubabel b. Shealtiel the messenger sent from God to incite Nebuchadnezzar to undertake the military chastisement. However, one can sense from this tradition that the Arabs expected their ancestors to believe in the prophets of Israel.
97. R. K. Harrison, *Jeremiah and Lamentations: An Introduction and Commentary,* The Tyndale Old Testament Commentaries, ed. D. J. Wiseman (Downers Grove, Ill.: InterVarsity, 1973), 124–27; Charles H. Dyer, "Jeremiah," in *The Bible Knowledge Commentary, Old Testament,* ed. John F. Walvoord and Roy B. Zuck (Wheaton, Ill.: Victor, 1985), 1160–62.
98. Cf. the NRSV.
99. According to Josephus, Nebuchadnezzar attacked both designated lands in the twenty-third year of his reign, which is 582 B.C. Josephus, *Jewish Antiquities* 10.9.7.
100. William J. Dumbrell, "The Tell el-Maskhûṭa Bowls and the 'Kingdom' of Qedar in the Persian Period," *BASOR* 203 (1971): 40.
101. Knauf comments about this Qedarite expansion, saying, "it was

this territorial and political extension of their realm, resulting in decreased contacts between the disparate tribes and clans, not military defeat by one of the empires, that brought the Ishmaelite confederacy to an end." Ernst Axel Knauf, "Ishmaelites," in *ABD,* 3:519.

102. *ANET,* 313; C. J. Gadd, "The Harran Inscriptions of Nabonidus," *Anatolian Studies* 8 (1958): 79–89; *ARNA,* 88; Hitti, *History of the Arabs,* 39; Raymond P. Dougherty, *The Sealand of Ancient Arabia,* Yale Oriental Series, Researches (New Haven, Conn.: Yale University Press, 1932), 19:161. Dussaud suggests a sojourn of Nabonidus in Taymāʾ that extended from 552–544 B.C. totaling twelve years instead of ten; cf. Dussaud, *La pénétration des arabes en Syrie avant l'Islam,* 176.
103. Gadd, "The Harran Inscriptions of Nabonidus," 88.
104. *ARNA,* 89; Hitti, *History of the Arabs,* 39; D. A. Dorsey, "Tema," in *ISBE,* 4:758.
105. *ANET,* 313.
106. Dumbrell argues that Nabonidus must have subdued Adummatu (Dumah) and kept it under control during his stay in Arabia in order to neutralize the Qedarites who, if they were free to act, may have been a major hindrance to his mobility in the northern part of the peninsula. Dumbrell, "The Tell el-Maskhûṭa Bowls," 40. However, though Dumah may have been checked at Nabonidus's initial entry into Arabia, there is no strong evidence to believe that it was subdued all the time during his stay in Taymāʾ. This becomes more likely if the Liḥyanite inscription found in Dedan mentioning Geshem ben Shahr indicates a Qedarite control over the oasis of Dedan by virtue of identifying this Geshem with the father of Qaynu of Tell el-Maskhûṭa. The Qedarite control, as Graf conjectures, would be understandable if Nabonidus appointed a Qedarite overseer in Dedan after he killed its king and the king of Taymāʾ. For a fuller development of this suggestion, see David F. Graf, "Arabia During Achaemenid Times," in *Achaemenid History IV: Centre and Periphery-Proceedings of the Groningen 1986 Achaemenid*

History Workshop, ed. Heleen Sancisi-Weerdenburg and Amélie Kuhrt (Leiden: Nederlands Instituut voor het Nabije Oosten, 1990), 131–48.

107. See also *ARNA,* 89; Dorsey, "Tema," 4:758. Winnett says that somewhere beneath the sands that now cover the site of Taymāʾ lies the palace of Nabonidus (*ARNA,* 89).

108. Gadd, "The Harran Inscriptions of Nabonidus," 59. Yathrib (modern Medina) was a major trade station in the south Hejaz. Khaybar, Yadi,' and Fadak are caravan stations on the incense road leading to Taymāʾ. Dedan was a major Minaean colony and center for south Arabian incense trade (Ezek. 27:15, 20–22). Ibid., 83–84.

109. For a fuller discussion, see Mikhail Ivanovitch Rostovzeff, *Caravan Cities,* trans. D. and T. Talbot Rice (Oxford: Clarendon, 1932); ʿAbd el-Rahmān al-Tayyib al-Ansarî, "Baʿdh Mudun el-Qawāfel al-Qadîmah fi l-Mamlakah lʿArabiyyah ʾSsu'ûdiyyah. [Some Ancient Caravan Cities in the Kingdom of Saudi Arabia]," in *Petra and the Caravan Cities: Proceedings of the Symposium Organised at Petra in September 1985 by the Department of Jewish Antiquities of Jordan,* ed. Fawzi Zayadine (Amman: Department of Antiquities, 1990), 15–26.

110. Gadd, "The Harran Inscriptions of Nabonidus," 59.

111. Macdonald, "North Arabia in the First Millennium B.C.E.," 1367. Most likely, the Arabs there are those of the Syro-Arabian Desert west of the Euphrates who constantly harassed the Assyrians (see the above discussion).

112. Possibly linked to the dangerous movements of Cyrus's army in the region.

113. Gadd, "The Harran Inscriptions of Nabonidus," 63.

114. *Herodotus* 2.8, 12, 15, 19; 3.4–9. For a development of the use of the terms *Arabs* and *Arabia*, in classic sources, see Pierre Briant, *Etat et pasteurs au Moyen-Orient ancien* (Paris: Éditions de la Maison des sciences de l'homme, 1982), 120–25.

115. *Herodotus* 3.4–9.

116. Ibid., 3.5. For the identification of the two cities as Gaza and al-

'Arish, see Graf, "Arabia During Achaemenid Times," 138; Macdonald, "North Arabia in the First Millennium B.C.E.," 1367.

117. *Herodotus* 3.9.
118. Ibid., 3.7.
119. Ibid., 3.91.
120. Ibid., 3.97. Some Achaemenid royal inscriptions refer to the subjection of a group of Arabs, possibly Hagarenes, other than the Qedarites that enjoyed a privileged status under Persia. For discussing alternative views in this regard, see Xenophon, *Cyrop.* 1.1.4; 2.1.5; 4.2.31; 7.4.16, and 5.14; Graf, "Arabia During Achaemenid Times," 143–46; Ephᶜal, *The Ancient Arabs,* 209; Briant, *Etat et pasteurs au Moyen-Orient ancien,* 122.
121. Because of the nomadic tribal character of the Qedarite realm, Dumbrell's remarks are to the point here. "A 'kingdom' of Qedar, means, we take it, a fluctuating sphere of influence. In the case of such a mobile society it would be imprecise to speak of boundaries." Dumbrell, "The Tell el-Maskhûṭa Bowls," 43, n. 41; see also André Lemaire, "Un nouveau roi arabe de Qédar dans l'inscription de l'autel à encens de Lakish," *RB* 81 (1974): 63–72. For a reservation against Dumbrell's assumptions, see John R. Bartlett, "From Edomites to Nabataeans: A Study in Continuity," *PEQ* 111 (1979): 53–66.
122. Dumbrell, "The Tell el-Maskhûṭa Bowls," 33–44; *ARNA,* 116. "Han" stands as the determinative prefix of ʾIlat, which is the feminine form of ʾIl, making Han-ʾIlat, Arabic, "Al-'Ilāhat," contracted into "Allāt," meaning, "the goddess." See the discussion of Joseph T. Milik, "Origine des Nabatéens," in *Studies in the History and Archaeology of Jordan,* ed. Adnan Hadidi (Amman, Hashemite Kingdom of Jordan: Department of Antiquities, 1982), 1:261–65.
123. Dumbrell, "The Tell el-Maskhûṭa Bowls," 33–44.
124. W. F. Albright, "Dedan," in *Geschichte und Altes Testament, Festschrift A. Alt,* ed. G. Ebling (Tübingen: J. C. B. Mohr, 1953), 6.
125. Thus Macdonald, "North Arabia in the First Millennium B.C.E.,"

1368; *ARNA,* 116–17; Briant, *Etat et pasteurs au Moyen-Orient ancien,* 172–73.

126. Recently Graf has presented a very persuasive argument in support of this identification. Graf, "Arabia During Achaemenid Times," 139–43.
127. Kaufmann notes that the Ammonites and the Arabs that opposed Nehemiah were small colonies located in the Transjordan, which had crossed over the Jordan and installed themselves in Samaria between the time of Zerubbabel and the return of Nehemiah Y. Kaufmann, *History of the Religion of Israel* (New York: Union of American Hebrew Congregations, 1970), 4:364–66; see also Briant, *Etat et pasteurs au Moyen-Orient ancien,* 173.

Chapter 10: The Nabataeans: Ishmael Finally Settled

1. John Lewis Burckhardt, *Travels in Syria and the Holy Land* (London: J. Murray, 1822), 418–34.
2. *Diodorus* 19.94.1–5.
3. J. Healy defined the Aramaeans as "a new population group which emerged in northern Syria after the fall of the old Hittite empire in c. 1200 B.C. These people came to rule the old Hittite-dominated kingdoms of the region. . . . The Aramaeans themselves had been nomadic originally but they were settled in great urban centers like Damascus at an early stage." John F. Healey, "Were the Nabataeans Arabs?" *Aram* 1 (1989): 39, 42.
4. See the survey in this regard done by Gary Dean Baldwin, "Nabataean Cultural Influences upon Israel Until 106 A.D." (Th.D. diss., Southwestern Baptist Theological Seminary, 1982), 52–63.
5. Etienne M. Quatremère, *Mémoires sur les Nabatéens* (Paris: Imprimerie Royale, 1835), 2:97–160.
6. For a recent survey and study of the issue, see David F. Graf, "The Origin of the Nabataeans," *Aram* 2 (1990): 45–75.
7. Pères Antonin Jaussen and Raphael Savignac, *Mission archéologique en Arabie,* 6 vols., Publications de la Société des

Fouilles Archéologiques (Paris: Ernest Leroux, Éditeurs and Librairie Paul Geuthner, 1909–22).

8. J. Starcky, "Pétra et la Nabatène," in *Dictionnaire de la Bible,* supplement 7 (Paris: Letouzey & Ané, Éditeurs, 1966), col. 924; P. Hammond, "Nabateans," in *ISBE,* 3:466–68; David F. Graf, "Nabataeans," in *ABD,* 3:970–73.
9. René Dussaud, *La pénétration des arabes en Syrie avant l'Islam* (Paris: Librairie Orientaliste Paul Geuthner, 1955), 22.
10. Graf, "The Origin of the Nabataeans," 67.
11. Jean Cantineau, "Nabatéen et Arabe," *Annales de l'Institut d'études orientales* 1 (1934–35): 77–97. The Nabataean onomasticon is the list of names gathered from Nabataean scripts found in various places.
12. Ibid., 91.
13. Ibid., 77.
14. *Diodorus* 2.48.4–5.
15. Avraham Negev, "The Early Beginnings of the Nabataean Realm," *PEQ* 108 (1976): 127.
16. *Diodorus* 19.100.1–2.
17. See the previous chapter related to Arabs under the Achaemenid rule.
18. Joseph T. Milik, "Origine des Nabatéens," in *Studies in the History and Archaeology of Jordan,* ed. Adnan Hadidi (Amman, Hashemite Kingdom of Jordan: Department of Antiquities, 1982), 1:262. Original French text: "je maintiens fermement que lorsque le père de l'historiographie européenne parle, au défini, des 'Arabes', il se refère presque toujours aux Nabatéens."
19. For a defense of this continuity, and a sympathy with the Nabataean-Nebayot equation, see John R. Bartlett, "From Edomites to Nabataeans: A Study in Continuity," *PEQ* 111 (1979): 53–66.
20. Cantineau, "Nabatéen et Arabe," 82. For a fuller discussion, see Starcky, "Pétra et la Nabatène," cols. 985–1016; G. Ryckmans, *Les religions arabes préislamiques,* Biliothèque du Muséon 26 (Louvain: Publications Universitaires, 1951), 7–24.

21. Cantineau, Nabatéen et Arabe," 82.
22. *Diodorus* 19.94.2–4.
23. For a discussion of the Nabataean sedentary culture, see Nelson Glueck, *Deities and Dolphins: The Story of the Nabataeans* (New York: Farrar, Straus and Giroux, 1965).
24. Joseph Patrich, "Prohibition of a Graven Image Among the Nabataeans: The Evidence and Its Significance," *Aram* 2 (1990): 185–96.
25. For a development of this theory, see Joseph Henninger, "La religion bédouine préislamique," in *L'Antica Societa Beduina,* ed. Francesco Gabrieli (Roma: Centro Di Studi Semitici, Istituto Di Studi Orientali-Universita, 1959), 115–40.
26. Healey, "Were the Nabataeans Arabs?" 42.
27. J. H. Charlesworth, ed., *The Old Testament Pseudepigrapha* (New York: Doubleday, 1985), 2:94.
28. Flavius Josephus, *The Works of Josephus, Complete and Unabridged,* trans., William Whiston, new updated ed. (Peabody, Mass.: Hendrickson, 1987), *Ant.* 1.12.4. For a critical discussion of Josephus's equation between Arabs and Ishmaelites, see Fergus Millar, "Hagar, Ishmael, Josephus and the Origin of Islam," *JJS* 44 (1993): 23–45.
29. Among those who argue for identity of the terms are Baldwin, "Nabataean Cultural Influences upon Israel until 106 A.D.," 19ff.; E. C. Broome, "Nabaiati, Nebaioth and the Nabataeans: The Linguistic Problem," *JSS* 18 (spring 1973): 1–16; Dussaud, *La pénétration des arabes en Syrie avant l'Islam,* 22; Kammerer, *Pétra et la Nabatène* (Paris, 1929), 28, 110, 112; Alois Musil, *Arabia Deserta: A Topographical Itinerary,* Oriental Explorations and Studies, no. 2 (New York: American Geographical Society, 1927), 478–92.
30. Among those who have dismissed the equality between the two terms are Glueck, *Deities and Dolphins,* 4; Philip K. Hitti, *History of the Arabs from the Earliest Times to the Present* (London: Macmillan, 1970); Graf, "Nabateans," 3:970–73; Starcky, "Pétra et la Nabatène," cols. 902–3; James Montgomery, *Arabia and the Bible* (Philadelphia: University of Pennsylvania Press, 1934), 31.

The majority of these scholars hold to an ethnic continuity between the Ishmaelites and the Nabataeans.

31. Starcky, "Pétra et la Nabatène,"902–3.
32. Broome, "Nabaiati, Nebaioth and the Nabataeans," 1–16.
33. *ARNA*, 99–101.
34. Broome, "Nabaiati, Nebaioth and the Nabataeans," 13.
35. As an example of recent challenges, see M. Abu Taleb, "Nabayati, Nebayot, Nabayat, and Nabatu: The Linguistic Problem Revisited," in *Dirasat* 11, no. 4 (Amman: University of Jordan, 1984), 3–11; see also Graf, "The Origin of the Nabataeans," 45–75.
36. Ernst Axel Knauf (*Ismael: Untersuchungen zur Geschichte Palestinas und Nordarabiens im 1. Jahrtausend v. Chr.*, Abhandlungen des Deutschen Palestinavereins, ed. Siegfried Mittmann and Manfred Weipert [Wiesbaden: Harrassowitz, 1989], 92–111) identifies the Nabataeans with the Qedarites based on historical continuity. His theory is challenged by Graf, "The Origin of the Nabataeans," 45–75.
37. *Diodorus* 19.94–100.
38. For more details on the Edomites, their decline, and the Nabataean control of their land, see Bartlett, "From Edomites to Nabataeans," 57–59; J. Lindsay, "The Babylonian Kings and Edom, 605–550 B.C.," *PEQ* 108 (1976): 23–39.
39. Starcky, "Pétra et la Nabatène," col. 904.
40. For a discussion on the history of the Nabataeans, see G. W. Bowersock, *Roman Arabia* (Cambridge, Mass.: Harvard University Press, 1983); Starcky, Pétra et la Nabatène, cols. 886–1017; Graf, "Nabateans," 970–73; Hammond, "Nabataeans," 466–68; Hitti, *History of the Arabs,* 67–86.
41. The Arab-Jewish relationships will be developed later in part 4.
42. Starcky, "Pétra et la Nabatène," cols. 919–20.
43. Bowersock, *Roman Arabia,* 11.
44. Glueck, *Deities and Dolphins,* 3.
45. Hitti, *History of the Arabs,* 39.
46. Starcky, "Recension de *Le antiche divinità semitiche,*" *RB* 67 (1960): 276.

Chapter 11: Arab Messianic Expectations

1. It is interesting to note that the Targum of Isaiah renders Qedar "the desert of the Arabians." Bruce D. Chilton, trans., "The Isaiah Targum," in *The Aramaic Bible,* ed. Martin McNamara et al. (Wilmington, Del.: Michael Glazier, 1987), 2:82.
2. The LXX renders Sela, πετρα, (rock). Allusion is most likely to the capital of the Nabataean kingdom, Petra (see Jer. 49:16; Obad. 3) whose inhabitants were probably associated by the translators of the LXX with Nebayot. The mention of Qedar in the immediate context, together with the parallel passage referring to Qedar and Nabayot in Isaiah 60:7, makes this also likely. For more information on Sela, see Wann M. Fanwar, "Sela," in *ABD,* 5:1073–74.
3. The Targum of Isaiah renders verses 6 and 7 thus: "The *caravans of the Arabians* shall cover you around, the dromedaries of *Midian* and *Ephah;* all those from *Sheba* will come. They shall be burdened with gold and frankincense, and those who come with them will be declaring the praises of the Lord. All the *sheep of the Arabians* shall be gathered into your midst, the rams of *Nebat* shall minister to you" (emphasis added). Chilton, "The Isaiah Targum," 116.
4. The Septuagint version of Psalm 72:10, 15 reads: "*The kings of Tharsis and the isles shall bring presents: the kings of the Arabians and Saba shall offer him gifts.* And all kings shall worship him; all the Gentiles shall serve him. . . . And he shall live and there *shall be given him of the gold of Arabia:* and men shall pray for him continually; and all the day shall they praise him" (emphasis added). Lancelot C. L. Brenton, *The Septuagint Version: Greek and English* (Grand Rapids: Zondervan, 1988).
5. It is beyond the aim of this section to address this issue. For a discussion of the use of the Old Testament in the New, see Krister Stendahl, *The School of St. Matthew and Its Use of the Old Testament* (Lund: G. W. K. Gleerup, 1954); John W. Drane, "Typology," *EvQ* 56 (1978): 195–210.
6. For a discussion of the identity of the Servant of the Lord, see

Otto Eissfeldt, *The Old Testament: An Introduction,* English trans. (New York: Harper and Row, 1965), 330–36; H. H. Rowley, *The Servant of the Lord* (London: Lutterworth, 1952).

7. J. Ridderbos, *Isaiah,* Bible Student's Commentary, trans. John Vriend (Grand Rapids: Zondervan, 1985), 99; Edward J. Young, *The Book of Isaiah,* NICOT, ed. R. K. Harrison (Grand Rapids: Eerdmans, 1972), 3:121–22, 274–79.
8. Recently Hengel and Schwemer published a very useful book on the unknown years of Paul's life and ministry between Damascus and Antioch. The fourth chapter is a strong defense of the geographical and theological priority of Arabia in Paul's outreach ministry. Martin Hengel and Anna Maria Schwemer, *Paul Between Damascus and Antioch: The Unknown Years,* trans. John Bowden (Louisville: Westminster/John Knox, 1997), 106–26. See also J. Spencer Trimingham, *Christianity Among the Arabs in Pre-Islamic Times* (London: Longman, 1979), 41–85.
9. H. Lammens, *L'Arabie occidentale à la veille de l'Hégire* (Beyrouth: Imprimerie Catholique, 1928), 51–99; *ARNA,* 91, n. 23; Josef Horovitz, "Judaeo-Arabic Relations in Pre-Islamic Times," *Islamic Culture* 3 (1929): 171.
10. C. J. Gadd, "The Harran Inscriptions of Nabonidus," *Anatolian Studies* 8 (1958): 87.
11. Ibid., 35–92.
12. Ibid., 80. Gadd identifies the cities thus: Dadanu stands for the oasis of Dedan; Padakku is Fadak; Khibrâ is the well-known oasis of Khaybar; Iadikhu, though the most obscure, is to be identified with the district of Yadi', which lies, according to Yaqût (4:1013), between Faddak and Khaybar and is still to be discovered; finally, Iatribu is the famous Yathrib, Medina.
13. Ibid.; Gadd concludes that "my people in the distant tracks" is a reference to "his subjects."
14. Ibid., 86.
15. See the discussion of R. K. Harrison, "Elephantine Papyri," in *ISBE,* 2:58–61; Gadd, "The Harran Inscriptions of Nabonidus," 86 n. 4.

16. J. T. Milik, "'Prière de Nabonide' et autres écrits du cycles de Daniel," *RB* (1956): 407–15.
17. Mathias Delcor, *Religion d'Israël et proche orient ancien: Des Phéniciens aux Esséniens* (Leiden: E. J. Brill, 1976). Margoliouth notes, "One Simeon of Taima is mentioned as an authority [*Zebachim,* 32b]; he was a contemporary of R. Akiba, and lived in Yabneh [*Sanhedrin,* 17a]. Taima is mentioned as a Jewish centre by the poet Shammam, who lived under the first three Caliphs: he compares the traces of a ruined dwelling with the Hebrew writing of a doctor (ḥabr) of Taima." D. S. Margoliouth, *The Relations Between Arabs and Israelites Prior to the Rise of Islam* (London: Oxford University Press, 1924), 58.
18. Izḥak Ben-Zvi, "Les origines de l'établissement des tribus d'Israël en Arabie," *Muséon* 74 (1961): 143–90.
19. Ibid., 148.
20. Original French text: "Il faut admettre que le processus de la propagation du judaïsm parmi les tribus arabes fut un phénomène typique non seulement en ce qui concerne les tribus nabatéennes, mais également à l'égard des peuplades de Midiân et des autres contrées d'Arabie, que les tribus d'Israël atteignirent à l'époque du premier et du deuxième Temple." Ben-Zvi, "Les origines de l'établissement des tribus d'Israël en Arabie," 155.
21. Ibid., 167.
22. David F. Graf, "Nabateans," in *ABD,* 1:972; G. W. Bowersock, *Roman Arabia* (Cambridge, Mass.: Harvard University Press, 1983), 12–27.
23. Bruce Metzger, ed., *The Apocrypha of the Old Testament* (New York: Oxford University Press, 1965), 232. See also 2 Maccabees 12:10–12.
24. Josephus, *Jewish Antiquities* 15.6.1–3.
25. Josephus, *The Jewish War* 1.6.2–4; 1.8.9.
26. Josephus cites how Herod Antipas eventually lost his tetrarchy and was banished with his wife by the Roman emperor Caius. *Jewish Antiquities* 18.252.
27. Josephus, *The Jewish War* 1.8.9.

28. Josephus, *Jewish Antiquities* 8.9.1.
29. For a defense of Herod's clear Jewishness and the likelihood of that of his mother, too, see the interesting discussion of Aryeh Kasher, *Jews, Idumeans, and Ancient Arabs* (Tübingen: Mohr, 1988), 126–27. With regard to Herod's relationships with his neighbors the Arabs, Kasher notes, "he [Herod] quickly abandoned his vain illusions and became the sworn enemy of the Nabataeans; it is therefore not surprising that Jewish-Nabataean confrontation reached its peak in his days" (ibid., 208). However, Graf ("Nabateans," 971–72) notes that "Nabataean relationships with Herod the Great appear to have been friendly as a result of Syllaeus, who even attempted to marry Herod's sister, until Herod made the arrangement dependent on his conversion to Judaism."
30. Josephus, *The Jewish War* 1.29.3; Joachim Jeremias, *Jerusalem in the Times of Jesus: An Investigation into Economic and Social Conditions During the New Testament Period* (Philadelphia: Fortress, 1969), 68–69.
31. Josephus, *The Jewish War* 1.29.3; Jeremias, *Jerusalem in the Times of Jesus*, 68–69.
32. Josephus, *The Jewish War* 1.27. 2–6.
33. Jeremias, *Jerusalem in the Times of Jesus,* 37.
34. *Pseudo-Aristeas* 114, in Henry Barclay Swete, *An Introduction to the Old Testament in Greek* (New York: KTAV, 1968), 571.
35. Josephus, *The Jewish War* 6.8.3; Jeremias, *Jerusalem in the Times of Jesus,* 37.
36. Josephus, *Jewish Antiquities* 15.8.1; also Jeremias, *Jerusalem in the Times of Jesus,* 37.
37. Jeremias, *Jerusalem in the Times of Jesus,* 37.
38. Ben-Zvi, "Les origines de l'établissement des tribus d'Israël en Arabie," 155–56.
39. Josephus, *Jewish Antiquities* 13. 9.1.
40. Kasher, *Jews, Idumaeans and Ancient Arabs,* 63.
41. Josephus, *Jewish Antiquities* 13.11.3.
42. Ben-Zvi, "Les origines de l'établissement des tribus d'Israël en Arabie," 152.

43. Cf. Robert G. Hoyland, *Arabia and the Arabs: From the Bronze Age to the Coming of Islam* (New York: Routledge, 2001), 64–78; Bowersock, *Roman Arabia.*
44. Hengel and Schwemer, *Paul Between Damascus and Antioch,* 106–26. This writer came to his conclusion regarding the logical priority of Arabia in God's redemptive program for the Gentiles independently from Hengel's similar argument.
45. Ibid. Historical and archaeological evidence, though scarce, confirm the presence of organized churches in north Arabia from the early centuries in the pre-Islamic Christian period. In 1998, S. Thomas Parker, professor of history at North Carolina State University, discovered in the vicinity of Aqaba in south Jordan what has been confirmed to be the oldest purpose-built Christian church in the world. This church building goes back to the end of the third century. Around that time also church historians Salaminius Sozomen (c 375–c 447), Socrates Scholasticus (380–450), and Theodoret of Cyrrhus (c 390–c 458) affirm the presence of such bishops in Arabia as Asterius (bishop of Petra), Beryllus (bishop of Bostra), and Moses, who was appointed by the Arab Christian queen Maria as bishop over the Saracens. According to Trimingham, another bishop over Arabs from Mesopotamia was present as an observer at the Council of Nicea in 325. The same historians confirm the presence of organized churches in north Arabia, whose roots go back even to apostolic time (cf. Socrates, *Ecclesiastical History* 1.8; 3.8; 3.25; 4.36; 5.10; Sozomen, *Ecclesiastical History* 1.13; 6:34; 6.38; 7.1; 7.19; Theodoret, *Ecclesiastical History* 2.6; 4.20; 4.23). For a fuller treatment of the rise of Christianity among the Arabs, see Trimingham, *Christianity Among the Arabs in Pre-Islamic Times,* 41–124; Trimingham, "Mawiyya: The First Christian Arab Queen," *Theological Review, Near East School of Theology* 1, no. 1 (1978): 3–10; and Kenneth Cragg, *The Arab Christian: A History in the Middle East* (London: Mowbray, 1992).
46. Margoliouth notes, "It does not surprise us to find Arabic words used for 'a she-camel with her bridle', 'a pack-saddle', 'a man

with an amputated foot'; for 'caravan' [שיירא = sayyārah, *Erubim*, I, § 8]; for 'mare' [רמך = ramkah, *Kelaim*, viii]; for 'bandit' [הרמי = ḥarāmî, *Nedarim*, iii, § 4]; but the reason in some other cases is more obscure, and though in the case of some of these expressions we know their date sufficiently well to be able to draw from their usage certain chronological inferences, in some others the possibility of coincidence cannot be disregarded. So far as these words are pre-Islamic it is likely that they were learned through association with members of the Nabataean state, whose relations with the Jews we have seen. The formula for a bill of divorce which gives two Aramaic and one Arabic synonym for this notion is reminiscent of the dialect of this community." Margoliouth, *The Relations Between Arabs and Israelites,* 58–59.

47. See also Nelson Glueck, *Rivers in the Desert: A History of the Negev* (New York: Farrar, Straus and Cudahy, 1959), 162–63.
48. Cf. Yigael Yadin, *Bar-Kokhba: The Rediscovery of the Legendary Hero of the Second Jewish Revolt against Rome* (New York: Random House, 1971), 222–53; Bowersock, *Roman Arabia,* 76–78; Graf, "Nabateans," 972.
49. Margoliouth, *The Relations Between Arabs and Israelites,* 40. On monotheism in Arabia in New Testament times, see also Hengel and Schwemer, *Paul Between Damascus and Antioch,* 120–126.
50. Margoliouth, *The Relations Between Arabs and Israelites,* 40.

Chapter 12: The Magi-Arab Worshipers of Christ (Part 1)

1. This study assumes that Matthew was writing to an audience of mostly Jewish background, familiar with Old Testament Scriptures and Palestinian Jewish customs and references, a view that was common among early church fathers. Merrill C. Tenney, *New Testament Survey* (Grand Rapids: Eerdmans, 1961), 141–52.
2. R. H. Gundry, *Matthew: A Commentary on His Literary and Theological Art* (Grand Rapids: Eerdmans, 1982), 26–27. Gundry claims that the story of the magi is a midrashic interpretation

of the shepherds' episode mentioned in Luke 2:8–20. Others have claimed that the story is a Midrash on the oracles of Balaam J. Daniélou, *Infancy Narratives* (New York: Herder and Herder, 1968), 84. However, if the historicity of the events is denied, the inspiration of the text may become questionable. Though Matthew as a Jew might have been influenced by the midrashic interpretive style, there are no compelling reasons to doubt the historicity of the event, especially since Matthew is arguing from fulfillment of prophecies (Matt. 2:6, 15, 18, 23). For a challenge of Gundry's approach to Matthew's Gospel, see Scott Cunningham and Darrell L. Bock, "Is Matthew a Midrash?" *Bib Sac* 144 (1987): 157–80. For a support of the historicity of the present narrative, see Xavier Léon-Dufour, *The Gospels and the Jesus of History,* trans. and ed. John McHugh (New York: Image, 1970), 233–36.

3. David Hughes, *The Star of Bethlehem* (New York: Walker, 1979), 193. Boa notes that the Septuagint of Daniel translates the Babylonian *ashaphim* (astrologers) as μάγος eight times. Kenneth D. Boa, "The Star of Bethlehem" (Th.M. thesis, Dallas Theological Seminary, 1972), 5.
4. Edwin M. Yamauchi, *Persia and the Bible* (Grand Rapids: Baker, 1990), 481; idem, "The Episode of the Magi," in *Chronos, Kairos, Christos,* ed. Jerry Vardaman and Edwin M. Yamauchi (Winona Lake, Ind.: Eisenbrauns, 1989), 15–39. For further support of either of the two alternatives (Persia or Babylonia), see Leon Morris, *The Gospel According to Matthew* (Grand Rapids: Eerdmans, 1992), 35–36; Donald A. Hagner, *Matthew 1–13,* WBC, ed. David A. Hubbard and Glenn W. Barker (Dallas: Word, 1993), 33A:26–27; R. T. France, *The Gospel According to Matthew* (Grand Rapids: Eerdmans, 1985), 81; W. D. Davies and Dale C. Allison Jr., *A Critical and Exegetical Commentary on the Gospel According to Saint Matthew,* ICC, ed. J. A. Emerton, C. E. B. Cranfield, and G. N. Stanton (Edinburgh: T & T Clark, 1988), 1:227–31; Konradin Ferrari-D'Occhieppo, "The Star of the Magi and Babylonian Astronomy," in *Chronos, Kairos,*

Christos, ed. Jerry Vardaman and Edwin M. Yamauchi (Winona Lake, Ind.: Eisenbrauns, 1989), 41–53.

5. *Herodotus* 1.101. Their priestly function included offering libations (cf. Strabo 15.3.14) and serving fire before altars (cf. *Strabo* 15.3.15; *Xenophon* 4.5.14).
6. *Herodotus* 1.132.
7. Ibid., 1.107, 120, 128.
8. Zoroastrianism is a religious concept that was taught by the Persian sage Zarathustra; it is also known as Mazdaism. It is believed that Zarathustra lived around the sixth century B.C., though this is a debated date now (see Yamauchi ["The Episode of the Magi," 25] who favors a date back to 1000 B.C.). Zarathustra taught the worship of the high god Ahura Mazda, who is the god of good works and ethical actions. Death and Darkness were represented by the arch demon Angra Mainyav. The whole universe is divided between these two cosmic forces. Therefore, dualism pervades Zoroastrian thinking. However, Yamauchi notes that the magi were in conflict with Zoroastrianism for two reasons: (1) they were polytheistic while Zoroastrianism is "either monotheistic or dualistic;" (2) the magi were from northwest Iran, while Zoroaster originated from the northeast (ibid.). For more on Zoroastrianism, see Mary Boyce, *Zoroastrians: Their Religious Beliefs and Practices* (London: Routledge & Kegan Paul, 1979); W. White, "Zoroastrianism," in *The Zondervan Pictorial Encyclopedia of the Bible,* ed. Merrill C. Tenney (Grand Rapids: Zondervan, 1975, 1976), 5:1016–17.
9. Thus the conclusion of Raymond Brown, *The Birth of the Messiah: A Commentary on the Infancy Narratives in the Gospels of Matthew and Luke,* updated ed. (New York: Doubleday, 1993), 167.
10. Tacitus, *Annals* 2.27; 12.22, 59; Pliny, *Natural History,* trans. H. Rackham, Loeb Classical Library (Cambridge, Mass.: Harvard University Press, 1968–69), 30.2.
11. Yamauchi, *Persia and the Bible,* 472, 474.
12. Clement of Alexandria, *Stromata* 1.15; *The Arabic Gospel of the*

Infancy, 7.1; see also Brown, *The Birth of the Messiah,* 168. For an analysis of this prophecy from three pieces of art heavily Christianized, see Jacqueline Lafontaine-Dosogne, "Le cycle des Mages dans l'Évangile arabe de l'Enfance du Christ à Florence," in *Mélanges d'Islamologie,* contrib. R. Anciaux et al., Correspondance d'Orient 13 (Bruxelles: Publications du Centre pour l'Étude des Problèmes du Monde Musulman Contemporain, 1976), 2:287–94.

13. G. Gnoli, "The Magi," in *The Encyclopedia of Religion,* ed. M. Eliade (New York: Macmillan, 1986), 9:81; Yamauchi, *Persia and the Bible,* 481.
14. See the survey of Davies and Allison, *A Critical and Exegetical Commentary on the Gospel According to Saint Matthew,* 228.
15. Ibid.
16. J. C. Marsh-Edwards, "The Magi in Tradition and Art," *The Irish Ecclesiastical Record* 85 (1956): 6–7; Bruce M. Metzger, "Names for the Nameless in the New Testament: A Study in the Growth of Christian Tradition," in *Kyriakon: Festschrift Johannes Quasten,* ed. Patrick Granfield and Josef A. Jungmann (Münster Westfalen: Aschendorff, 1970), 2:82.
17. Marsh-Edwards, "The Magi in Tradition and Art," 6–7.
18. Metzger, "Names for the Nameless in the New Testament," 80–82; Marsh-Edwards, "The Magi in Tradition and Art," 6–7.
19. Metzger, "Names for the Nameless in the New Testament," 83–85.
20. A. V. W. Jackson, "The Magi in Marco Polo and the Cities in Persia from Which They Came to Worship the Infant Christ," *JAOS* 26 (1905): 79–83; Manuel Komroff, ed., *The Travels of Marco Polo,* revised from Marsden's translation (New York: Boni & Liveright, 1926), 37–39; and Yamauchi, *Persia and the Bible,* 491.
21. Yamauchi, *Persia and the Bible,* 491.
22. This view was strongly advocated by Antonio Charbel in his eye-opening article on the Nabataean origin of the magi, though many arguments developed in the present section are original.

Antonio Charbel, "Mateo 2,1–12: Los Magos en el Abiente del Reino Nabateo," *Revista Biblica* 46 (1984): 147–58. Bishop also endorses the Arabian origin of the Magi. E. F. F. Bishop, "Arabia in the New Testament," *The Moslem World 34* (1944), 194; also, idem, "Some Reflections on Justin Martyr and the Nativity Narratives," *EvQ* 39 (1967), 30–39.

23. Brown, *The Birth of the Messiah,* 167.
24. G. Delling, "μάγος," in *TDNT,* 4:356–59.
25. Ibid.
26. Josephus, *Jewish Antiquities* 10.10.3–6.
27. Pliny, *Natural History,* 30.2.11.
28. Josephus, *Jewish Antiquities* 20.7.2
29. Philo, *De Vita Mosis* 1.92; 1.277; *De Specialibus Legibus* 3.93.
30. Philo, *De Specialibus Legibus* 3.100.
31. Philo, *De Vita Mosis* 1.276, 277.
32. Numenius of Apamea (second century A.D.) quoted in Eusebius, *Praeparatio Evangelica* 9.8; see also Targum Pseudo-Jonathan on Exodus 1:15 and Numbers 22:2.
33. Eusebius, *Demonstratio Evangelica* 9.1; see also Davies and Allison, *A Critical and Exegetical Commentary on the Gospel According to Saint Matthew,* 231. Balaam is an interesting case of the use of the term since he is associated with the *Qedem* (Num. 22:5; 23:7) that the previous study has identified with the Syro-Arabian Desert west of the Euphrates. He is also associated with the ambiguous location of Aram Naharaim.
34. E. F. F. Bishop, "Arabia in the New Testament," 194; F. F. Bruce, *Paul: Apostle of the Heart Set Free* (Grand Rapids: Eerdmans, 1977), 162 n. 11.
35. The ending "as" would be caused by the hellenization of the name.
36. Cornelius Van Dyke, trans., *al-Kitāb al-Muqaddas* (Beirut: Dar al-Kitāb al-Muqaddas, n.d.). ᶜAlîm is designed after the form *faᶜîl,* which is a form of exaggeration, implying that the person is not only *ᶜâlem,* that is, a person of knowledge, but *ᶜalîm,* that is, a person of unusual knowledge. Thus Bruce (*Paul,* 162) is

correct in noting that Elymas is not the translation of his name "Bar-Jesus" (which ironically means "son of God the Savior"), but rather an interpretation of his function as a *magos*. In that sense, he was like the wise men in Nebuchadnezzar's palace, but using his knowledge the wrong way, and in that sense he was a false prophet.

37. Bruce, *Paul,* 162.
38. For the existence of Jewish Arabs (proselytes) and Arab Jews (Hebrews), see Acts 2:11.
39. Cf. Ludwig Schopp, ed., *Writings of Saint Justin Martyr,* trans. Thomas B. Fall (New York: Christian Heritage, 1948), 9–10. See also Bishop, "Some Reflections on Justin Martyr and the Nativity Narratives," 30–39.
40. Schopp, ed., *Writings of Saint Justin Martyr,* 271–73. Emphasis added.
41. Cf. Justin Martyr, *Dialogue with Trypho* 77–78, 88, 102, 103, 106.
42. Ibid., 120.
43. Ibid.; see also Schopp, introduction to *Writings of Saint Justin Martyr,* 9–10. For a synopsis of Justin Martyr's biography and writings, see Canon H. Scott Holland, "Justinus Martyr," in *A Dictionary of Christian Biography,* ed. Henry Wace and William C. Piercy (Peabody, Mass.: Hendrickson, 1994), 617–35.
44. See also Antonio Charbel, "Mateo 2,1–12: Los Magos en el Abiente del Reino Nabateo," *Revista Biblica* 46 (1984): 149; Bishop, "Some Reflections on Justin Martyr and the Infancy Narratives," 32–39. Though Bishop was doubtful about some details in the infancy narrative of Justin Martyr, he fully endorses his theory about the Arabian origin of the magi.
45. Yamauchi may not be accurate in asserting that Justin's awareness that "these substance [magi's gifts] came from Arabia may have influenced [him] . . . to assert that the Magi came from Arabia." Yamauchi, *Persia and the Bible,* 485.
46. Tertullian, *Adversus Marcionem,* ed. and trans. Ernest Evans (London: Oxford University Press, 1972), 3.13.8; 1: 209.

47. Ibid., 3.13.8.
48. Ibid.
49. Ibid.
50. Yamauchi, *Persia and the Bible,* 485.
51. Cf. Martyr, *Dialogue with Trypho*, 77–78.
52. Michael W. Holmes, ed., *The Apostolic Fathers,* trans. J. B. Lightfoot and J. R. Harmer (Grand Rapids: Baker, 1989), 42–43. Emphasis added.
53. In view of his statements, the Arabian origin of the magi may look very plausible for Clement of Rome. See also Brown, *The Birth of the Messiah,* 169–70; Bishop, "Some Reflections on Justin Martyr and the Infancy Narratives," 33; David Hughes, *The Star of Bethlehem Mystery* (London: J. M. Dent & Sons, 1979), 38. However, Hughes seems to prefer the Persian view, though he fails to offer any reason to discredit the Arabian origin.
54. Frank Williams, trans., *The Panarion of Epiphanius of Salamis* (Leiden: E. J. Brill, 1994), *De Fide* 8.1.2. It is not clear here whether Epiphanius could have related the word "magi" to the place of their dwelling in Magodia. This place is at present beyond possible identification by the writer.
55. Philip R. Amidon, trans. and ed., *The Panarion of St. Epiphanius, Bishop of Salamis. Selected Passages* (Oxford: Oxford University Press, 1990), 4.1.6, p. 30.
56. For a comprehensive bibliography on the subject, see A. Strobel, "Weltenjahr, grosse Konjunktion und Mesiasstern," *ANRW* 2.20.2 (1987): 988–1187.
57. Brown, *The Birth of the Messiah,* 171.
58. Johannes Kepler, *De Stella Nova in Pede Serpentarii* (Prague: Pauli Sessi, 1606).
59. J. Vardaman, *The Year of the Nativity* (Mississippi State: Cobb Institute of Archaeology, 1983), cited in Yamauchi, *Persia and the Bible*, 482.
60. Hughes, *The Star of Bethlehem.*
61. Konradin Ferrari-d'Occhieppo, "The Star of Bethlehem," *Quarterly Journal of the Royal Astronomical Society* 19 (1978): 517.

62. Franz Zinniker, *Probleme der sogenannten Kindheitsgeschichte bei Mattäus* (Freiburg/Schweiz: Paulusverlag, 1972).
63. Joseph E. Ciotti, "The Magi's Star: Misconceptions and New Suggestions," *Griffith Observer* 42 (December 1978): 2–11. For a more detailed survey of the different views, see Brown, *The Birth of the Messiah*, 171–73.
64. For a discussion of Babylonian astrology, see Ferrari-d'Occhieppo, "The Star of the Magi and Babylonian Astronomy"; E. Yamauchi, "Chaldea, Chaldaens," in *The New International Dictionary of Biblical Archaeaology,* ed. E. M. Blaiklock and R. K. Harrison (Grand Rapids: Zondervan, 1983), 123–25.
65. D. A. Hagner, "ἀστήρ," in *NIDNTT,* ed. Colin Brown (Grand Rapids: Zondervan, 1986), 3:735.
66. *1 Enoch* 8:3; *Sibylline Oracles,* 3d bk., lines 229–36; *Jubilee* 12:17, in J. H. Charlesworth, ed., *The Old Testament Pseudepigrapha,* 2 vols. (New York: Doubleday, 1985).
67. Ignatius, *Ephesians* 19.3; Justin Martyr, *Dialogue with Trypho,* 78; Tertullian, *On Idolatry,* 9.
68. The text seems to present the magi as righteous people rejoicing greatly (2:10) at the seeing of the star, and not willing to cooperate with Herod, but rather obedient to the divine message (2:12).
69. See full discussion in Davies and Allison, *A Critical and Exegetical Commentary of the Gospel According to Saint Matthew,* 228–29.
70. Cited by Hughes, *The Star of Bethlehem Mystery,* 38.
71. Glueck, *Deities and Dolphins,* 453. Emphasis added. See also Ditlef Nielsen, *Die altarabische Mondreligion und die mosaische Überlieferung* (Strassburg: K. J. Trübner, 1904). Recently, there has been unfolding of astrological interests that existed among the Israelis or at least some Jewish sects. The reader is referred to Manfred R. Lehmann, "New Light on Astrology in Qumran and the Talmud," *Revue de Qumran* 8 (December 1975): 599–602; see James H. Charlesworth, "Jewish Astrology in the Talmud, Pseudepigrapha, The Dead Sea Scrolls, and Early

Palestinian Synagogues," *Harvard Theological Review* 70 (July–October 1977): 183–200.

72. Joseph Henninger, "La religion bédouine préislamique," in *L'Antica Societa Beduina,* ed. Francesco Gabrieli (Roma: Centro Di Studi Semitici, Istituto Di Studi Orientali-Universita, 1959), 132. See also idem, "Über Sternkunde und Sternkult in Nord und Zentralarabien," *Zeitschrift für Ethnologie* 79 (1954): 82–117, esp. 88–93, 110–15. The three pagan deities that prevailed in Mecca before Muhammad's religious reform were *ʾal-Lât, ʿal-ʿUzzâ,* and *Manât.* While the last one, *Manât,* has no astral character, *ʾal-Lât* and *ʿal-ʿUzzâ* represented most likely two phases of the planet Venus, that is, the star of the morning and the star of the evening. Henninger, "La religion bédouine préislamique," 133; Julius Wellhausen, *Reste arabischen Heidentums,* 2d ed. (Berlin, 1897), 217–24; C. Brockelmann, "Allah und Die Götzen, der Ursprung des islamischen Monotheismus," *Archiv für Religionswissenschaft* 21 (1922): 99–121. Yet this seeming devotion to astral manifestation did not rule out a monotheistic belief in *Allah* the creator of heaven and earth. H. A. R. Gibb, "Pre-Islamic Monotheism in Arabia," *Harvard Theological Review* 55 (1962): 269–80; H. Cazelles, "Yahwisme, ou Yahweh en son peuple," in *Etudes d'Histoire Religieuse et de Philologie Biblique,* Sources Bibliques, ed. H. Cazelles (Paris: J. Gabalda et Cie Éditeurs, 1996), 35–47.
73. Philip K. Hitti, *History of the Arabs from the Earliest Times to the Present* (London: Macmillan, 1970), 97.
74. This is the second phase in the degradation of Semitic religion from nomadic monotheism to sedentary polytheism. J. Starcky, "Recension de *Le antiche divinità semitiche,*" *RB* 67 (1960): 276.
75. Ferrari-d'Occhieppo, "The Star of the Magi and Babylonian Astronomy," 46.
76. Dale C. Allison Jr. "What Was the Star That Guided the Magi?" *Bible Review* 9 (1993): 20–24.
77. J. Dwight Pentecost, *The Words and Works of Jesus Christ: A Study of the Life of Christ* (Grand Rapids: Zondervan, 1981), 67.

78. Ibid.
79. Ibid.
80. This glory of the Lord may be linked to the glory of God that has left the temple during the time of Ezekiel since Israel lost its role as a testimony to the Gentiles. Interestingly, there is no reference to the glory of the Lord filling the temple in the days of Ezra, but rather a prediction by Haggai that the glory will come back in the messianic temple (Hagg. 2:6–9). Eugene H. Merrill, *An Exegetical Commentary: Haggai, Zechariah, Malachi* (Chicago: Moody, 1994), 38–42. Though the kingdom was only inaugurated at the first coming of Christ, still the temple of the Lord walked among the Jews in the person of the Messiah; therefore a display of his glory came to be manifested at his birth and close to his death (Matt. 2:1–12; 17:1–8), and was restricted to a handful of elect individuals in view of the opposition that accompanied both his birth and his death.

Chapter 13: The Magi-Arab Worshipers of Christ (Part 2)

1. Cited by Eusebius, *Ecclesiastical History* 3.39.16; see also Irenaeus, *Against Heresies* 3.1.1.
2. For a short synopsis, see D. S. Margoliouth, "Children of the East," in *Hasting's Dictionary of the Bible,* ed. James Hasting (New York: Charles Scribner's Sons, 1902), 635.
3. Karl Mras, ed., *Eusebius Werke: Die Praeparatio Evangelica* (Berlin: Akademie Verlag, 1982), 9.29.3.
4. Alois Musil, *Arabia Deserta: A Topographical Itinerary,* Oriental Explorations and Studies, no. 2 (New York: American Geographical Society, 1927), 494–97.
5. Antonio Charbel, "Mateo 2,1–12: Los Magos en el Abiente del Reino Nabateo," 153; H. J. Richards, "The Three Kings (Mt. ii.1–12)," *Scripture* 8 (1956): 23.
6. Charbel, "Mateo 2,1–12: Los Magos en el Abiente del Reino Nabateo,"153.
7. For the Jew living in Palestine, there was a simple way to deter-

mine the geographical directions. The person would stand with his face to the Arabian Desert beyond the Transjordan, and that would be his east, פָּ, meaning "in front of" (Heb. *qedem*). Then the south would be to his right hand, the north would be to his left, and the west behind his back. In Arabic, the right hand is called *yamîn,* which accounts for the name of the country of Yemen situated far in south Arabia. The left hand is called *shimāl,* and it is the same word used for the north. For further discussion, see Joel F. Drinkard Jr., "ʿAL PĔNÊ as 'East of,'" *JBL* 98 (1978): 285–86.

8. See also Charbel, "Mateo 2,1–12: Los Magos en el Abiente del Reino Nabateo,"153.
9. Some translators have rendered the expression ἐν τῇ ἀνατολῇ in 2:2, 9 "at its rising" instead of "in the east" because of a similar use in some classical sources. See NRSV; W. D. Davies and Dale C. Allison Jr., *A Critical and Exegetical Commentary on the Gospel According to Saint Matthew* (Edinburgh: T & T Clark, 1988), 1:236. However, the translation "in the east" is a much better one for the following reasons. First, though the rendering "at its rising" is a legitimate one, it necessitates an additional pronoun αὐτοῦ (its) which is lacking in Matthew's construction. The presence of αὐτοῦ immediately before τὸν ἀστέρα should not discourage its use after ἀνατολῇ as Davies and Allison suggest (ibid.), for in 2:9 the phrase clearly lacks the pronoun, which is not supplied by the context either. Second, Matthew's failure to use the definite article in 2:1 before ἀνατολῶν should not imply that 2:1 and 2:2 are to be translated differently. In fact, the first use may have an underlying general concept of rising of the sun (מזרח), while the second is a definite term since it is used as a technical term (קדם) referring to a geographical land. The Greek has ἀνατολή for both terms, and this accounts for the confusion. Third, by saying that they saw his star "in the east," the magi were using a technical term reckoned in that context as the Syro-Arabian Desert, and thus the hearers would understand them saying, "we saw his star in the (Arabian)

Desert" (see earlier references to Clement of Rome, and Tertullian and Eusebius). Failure to recognize this nuance of the term accounts for a confusing translation.

10. James Montgomery, *Arabia and the Bible* (Philadelphia: University of Pennsylvania Press, 1934), 56–57. Benson also felt compelled to opt for Arabia instead of Chaldea because of the designation of the "east." Joseph Benson, *The New Testament of Our Lord and Savior Jesus Christ: With Critical, Explanatory, and Practical Notes,* vol. 1, "Matthew to the Acts of the Apostles" (New York: Carlton & Phillips, 1854), 30. Benoit says: "L'«Orient» d'où ils viennent désigne sans doute ces régions de l'Arabie qui s'étendent à l'est du Jourdain et de la mer Morte." Translation: "The 'east' where they came from designates without doubt the regions of Arabia which stretch east of the Jordan river and the Dead Sea." R. P. P. Benoit, *La sainte Bible: L'évangile selon Saint Matthieu* (Paris: Les Éditions du Cerf, 1950), 43.
11. See the same recent conclusion also of P. André Feuillet, "Le Sauveur messianique et sa mère," *Divinitas* (1990): 36.
12. Incense had many uses in the ancient world. These included worship practices and ritualistic orders; it was also used as cosmetic and served in medicine, while it was part of the secret of Egyptian embalming and the like. For the various uses of frankincense and myrrh and other spices, see Kjeld Nielsen, *Incense in Ancient Israel,* VT supplement, no. 38, ed. J. A. Emerton et al. (Leiden: E. J. Brill, 1986), 11–13, 37–94; Gus W. Van Beek, "Frankincense and Myrrh," *BA* 23 (1960): 82–86.
13. *Herodotus* 3.107. Emphasis added. Herodotus obviously refers to south Arabia here.
14. Pliny, *Natural History,* trans. H. Rackham, Loeb Classical Library (Cambridge, Mass.: Harvard University Press, 1968–69), 12.30. Emphasis added. For a discussion of the geographical location of these places, see Israel Ephᶜal, *The Ancient Arabs: Nomads on the Borders of the Fertile Crescent 9th–5th Centuries b.c.* (Leiden: E. J. Brill, 1982), 86–88; Philip K. Hitti, *History of the Arabs from the Earliest Times to the Present* (London: Macmillan, 1970), 49–66.

15. Hitti, *History of the Arabs,* 52.
16. Nielsen, *Incense in Ancient Israel,* 22–24.
17. Kjeld Nielsen, "Incense," in *ABD,* 3:408.
18. *The Geography of Strabo,* trans. Horace Leonard Jones, Loeb Classical Library (Cambridge, Mass.: Harvard University Press, 1931), 16.4.4. Hadramawt is one of the children of Joktan, son of Eber, who settled in south Arabia (Gen. 10:26). See also Theophrastus, *Enquiry into Plants,* trans. Arthur Hort, Loeb Classical Library (Cambridge, Mass.: Harvard University Press; London: William Heinemann, 1968–69), 9.4.2.
19. *Herodotus* 3.113.
20. *The Geography of Strabo* 16.4.25.
21. *Diodorus* 3.47.5–8. Van Beek ("Frankincense and Myrrh," 87) establishes the conversion between the cost of the pound of frankincense then, and what it may cost now based on information from Pliny (*Natural History* 12.32.65). According to Pliny, the best frankincense cost 6 denarii for the pound, the second choice 5 denarii, and the third choice 3 denarii. The percentage rate of the cost of a pound of frankincense was 2.5–5 percent of the average annual income per pound.
22. *Diodorus* 2.50.1. Emphasis added.
23. Ibid., 3.45.6–8. Emphasis added.
24. Hitti (*History of the Arabs,* 48) notes that al-Maqdisî and al-Hamdāni (tenth century) devote a paragraph each for the minerals of Arabia, emphasizing particularly its gold.
25. Diodorus Siculus, who traveled throughout Egypt during 60–57 B.C. and lived in Rome for several years, described the Nabataeans in their early settlement in the Transjordan (312 B.C.) as nomads who already then trafficked in the exotic products of Arabia and Africa and India. *Diodorus* 19.94–97; also Nelson Glueck, *Deities and Dolphins: The Story of the Nabataeans* (New York: Farrar, Straus and Giroux, 1965), 4; Hitti, *History of the Arabs,* 67–68.
26. *Diodorus* 19.94.1–10; 95.1–7.
27. Glueck, *Deities and Dolphins,* 44. The Nabataeans were

nevertheless able to recover all the spoils when they pursued the invaders, overcame, and defeated them. *Diodorus* 19.96.1–4.

28. Glueck, *Deities and Dolphins,* 44.
29. Pliny, *Natural History* 12.32.63–64. This journey begins at Shabwa and included stops at Timna', Marib, Ma'in, Yathrib (Medina), Dedan (Al-ʿUla), and Gaza.
30. *The Geography of Strabo* 16.4.4.
31. Ibid., 16.4.24.
32. Van Beek, "Frankincense and Myrrh," 76. For a fuller study of incense trade routes, refer to the thesis of Mark Sloan Zieze, "Incense in the Period of the Hebrew Monarchy: A Geographical, Historical and Archaeological Investigation" (M.A. thesis, Cincinnati Christian Seminary, 1987), 61–70. The reader is also referred to the work of Nigel Groom, *Frankincense and Myrrh: A Study of the Arabian Incense Trade* (London: Longman; Beirut: Librairie du Liban, 1981).
33. *The Geography of Strabo* 16.4.18.
34. David F. Graf, "Nabateans," in *ABD,* 4:970.
35. Ibid.
36. Most likely, the magi came to offer allegiance to the king of the Jews with big convoys accompanied by military protection, as was the norm for trade caravans that crossed the desert then. This may explain why all Jerusalem noticed their visit and was troubled along with Herod when they came to worship the King of the Jews (Matt. 2:3). For more on caravans, see Zieze, "Incense in the Period of the Hebrew Monarchy," 103–10.
37. Martin Hengel and Helmut Merkel, "Die Magier aus dem Osten und die Flucht nach Agypten (Mt 2) in der Antiken Religionsgeschichte und der Theologie des Matthew," in *Orientierung an Jesus: Zur Theologie der Synoptiker, Festschrift für Josef Schmid,* ed. P. Hoffmann (Freiburg: Herder, 1973), 139–69. Hengel and Merkel note that the last three quotations are clearly stated as fulfillment of Scripture (2:15, 17–18, 23), while in the story of the magi, there is one explicit quotation used to confirm the place of birth (2:6), and one implicit fulfillment in

2:11 with the offering of frankincense, myrrh, and gold. Accordingly, they break the chapter, which forms a unit, into five sections: the initial appearance of the magi in Jerusalem (2:1–6) fulfills Micah 5:1–2 and 2 Samuel 5:2; the worship of the magi (2:7–12) fulfills Isaiah 60:6 and Psalm 72:10; the flight of the holy family to Egypt (2:13–15) fulfills Hosea 11:1; the killing of the children (2:16–18) fulfills Jeremiah 31:15; and the ascent of Jesus to Nazareth (2:19–23) fulfills the ambiguous prophecy of the Nazarene. Ibid., 141–42.

38. It was shown earlier that Midian, Ephah, and Sheba were Arabian tribes of the descendants of Keturah (Gen. 25:1–6), who intermarried heavily with Ishmaelites and became rallied later under Ishmael's umbrella.
39. Martin Hengel and Anna Maria Schwemer, *Paul Between Damascus and Antioch: The Unknown Years,* trans. John Bowden (Louisville: Westminster/John Knox, 1997), 106–26.
40. See, for example, R. H. Gundry, *The Use of the Old Testament in St. Matthew's Gospel with Special Reference to the Messianic Hope,* VT supplement, no. 18, ed. W. C. van Unnik et al. (Leiden: E. J. Brill, 1967), 206–11; Davies and Allison, *A Critical and Exegetical Commentary on the Gospel According to Saint Matthew,* 250–51.
41. For a discussion of Matthew's use of the Old Testament, see Krister Stendahl, *The School of St. Matthew and Its Use of the Old Testament* (Lund: G. W. K. Gleerup, 1954); John W. Drane, "Typology," *EvQ* 56 (1978): 195–210.
42. Gerhard von Rad, "Typological Interpretation of the Old Testament," in *Essays on Old Testament Hermeneutics,* ed. Claus Westermann, English ed. and trans. James Luther Mays (Richmond, Va.: John Knox, 1963), 39.
43. R. T. France, "'In All the Scriptures': A Study of Jesus' Typology," *TSF Bulletin* 56 (1970): 13.
44. G. W. H. Lampe and K. J. Woollcombe, *Essays on Typology* (Naperville, Ill.: Alec R. Allenson, 1957), 27.
45. See also France, "'In All the Scriptures': A Study of Jesus' Typology," 13–14.

46. Douglas Stuart, *Hoseah-Jonah,* WBC, ed. David A. Hubbard and Glenn V. Barker (Waco: Word, 1987), 31:176; G. I. Davis, *Hosea,* New Century Bible Commentary, ed. Ronald E. Clements and Matthew Black (Grand Rapids: Eerdmans, 1992), 254.
47. Patrick Fairbairn, *The Typology of Scripture* (Grand Rapids: Zondervan, 1960), 380–81.
48. Raymond Brown, *The Birth of the Messiah: A Commentary on the Infancy Narratives in the Gospels of Matthew and Luke,* updated ed. (New York: Doubleday, 1993), 215.
49. R. T. France, *The Gospel According to Matthew: An Introduction and a Commentary,* Tyndale New Testament Commentaries, ed. Leon Morris (Leicester, U.K.: Intervarsity, 1985), 86.
50. See, for example, F. Martin, "Naître entre juifs et païens," *Filologia Neotestamentaria* 1 (1988): 85.
51. The two Syriac books, *The Cave of Treasures* and *The Book of Adam and Eve,* present different names for the three kings believed to be the magi. However, both traditions picture two of these kings as Arabian kings. Bruce M. Metzger, "Names for the Nameless in the New Testament: A Study in the Growth of Christian Tradition," in *Kyriakon: Festschrift Johannes Quasten,* ed. Patrick Granfield and Josef A. Jungmann (Münster Westfalen: Aschendorff, 1970), 2:79–99.
52. *Herodotus* 3.97.

BIBLIOGRAPHY

Books and Essays

Albright, W. F. "The Biblical Tribe of Massa and Some Congeneres." Vol. 1 of *Studi Orientalistici in Onore di Giorgio Levi Della Vida.* Roma: Istituto per L'Oriente, 1956.

Alexander, T. Desmond. "The Hagar Traditions in Genesis xvi and xxi." *Studies in the Pentateuch.* VT supplements, no. 41. Edited by J. A. Emerton et al. Leiden: E. J. Brill, 1990.

al-Tabarî, Abu Ja^cfar Muhammad b. Jarîr. *Ta'rîkh al-rusul wal-mulûk.* Edited by M. J. DeGoeje as *Annales.* Leiden: E. J. Brill, 1964.

Andersen, Francis I. *Job: An Introduction and Commentary.* The Tyndale Old Testament Commentaries. Edited by D. J. Wiseman. Downers Grove, Ill.: InterVarsity, 1976.

Bar-Efrat, Shimon. *Narrative Art in the Bible. JSOT* supplement, no. 70. Edited by David J. A. Clines and Philip R. Davies. Bible and Literature Series, no. 17. Edited by David M. Gunn. Sheffield: Almond, 1989.

Barrett, Charles Kingsley. "The Allegory of Abraham, Sarah and Hagar in the Argument of Galatians." In *Rechtfertigung: Festschrift für Ernest Käsemann zum 70. Geburtstag,* edited by Johannes Friedrich et al., 1–16. Göttingen: Vandenhoeck & Ruprecht, 1976.

Bartlett, John R. *Edom and the Edomites. JSOT* supplement, no. 77. Edited by David J. A. Clines and Philip R. Davies. Sheffield: Sheffield Academic, 1989.

Betts, Robert Brenton. *Christians in the Arab East: A Political Study.* Atlanta: John Knox, 1978.

Betz, Hans Dieter. *Galatians: A Commentary on Paul's Letter to the Churches in Galatia.* Philadelphia: Fortress, 1979.

Biblia Rabbinica. Edited by Jacob Ben Hayim Ibn Adoniya. Jerusalem: Makor, 1972.

Bickerton, Ian J., and Carla L. Klausner. *A Concise History of the Arab-Israeli Conflict.* Englewood Cliffs, N.J.: Prentice Hall, 1991.

Bowersock, G. W. *Roman Arabia.* Cambridge, Mass.: Harvard University Press, 1983.

Briant, Pierre. *Etat et pasteurs au Moyen-Orient ancien.* Paris: Editions de la Maison des sciences de l'homme, 1982.

Brown, Raymond. *The Birth of the Messiah: A Commentary on the Infancy Narratives in the Gospels of Matthew and Luke.* New York: Doubleday, 1993.

Bruce, F. F. *The Epistle to the Galatians: A Commentary on the Greek Text.* Grand Rapids: Eerdmans, 1982.

Caskel, Werner, ed. and trans. *Ghamharat an-Nasab ("The Abundance of Kinship"): Das genealogische Werk des Hišam Ibn Muhammad al-Kalbî.* Leiden: E. J. Brill, 1966.

Cassutto, Umberto. *A Commentary on the Book of Genesis.* Vol. 2 of *From Noah to Abraham, Genesis VI:9–XI:32.* Translated by Israel Abrahams. Jerusalem: Magnes, 1961–64.

Cazelles, H. "Yahwisme, ou Yahwé en son peuple." In *Etudes d'Histoire Religieuse et de Philologie Biblique,* edited by H. Cazelles, 35–47. Sources Bibliques. Paris: J. Gabalda et Cie Éditeurs, 1996.

Clines, David J. A. *Job 1–20.* WBC. Edited by David A. Hubbard. Dallas: Word, 1989.

Coats, George W. *Genesis.* Vol. 1 of *Forms of the Old Testament Literature.* Grand Rapids: Eerdmans, 1983.

Cole, R. A. *The Epistle of Paul to the Galatians.* Grand Rapids: Eerdmans, 1989.

Cortese, Enzo. "Promises and Blessings for Jews and Arabs in the Pentateuch." In *Divine Promises to the Fathers in Three Monotheistic Religions: Proceedings of a Symposium Held in Jerusalem March 24–25, 1993,* edited by Alviero Niccacci, 28–46. Jerusalem: Franciscan, 1995.

Courbage, Youssef, and Philippe Fargues. *Christians and Jews Under Islam.* Translated by Judy Mabro. London: I. B. Tauris, 1997.

Cragg, Kenneth. *The Arab Christian: A History in the Middle East.* London: Mowbray, 1992.

Crenshaw, James L. "Clanging Symbols." In *Justice and the Holy: Essays in Honor of Walter Harrelson,* edited by Douglas A. Knight and Peter J. Paris, 51–64. Atlanta: Scholars, 1989.

Daniélou, J. *Infancy Narratives.* New York: Herder and Herder, 1968.

Davies, W. D., and Dale C. Allison Jr. *A Critical and Exegetical Commentary on the Gospel According to Saint Matthew.* 3 vols. ICC. Edited by J. A. Emerton, C. E. B. Cranfield, and G. N. Stanton. Edinburgh: T & T Clark, 1988.

Day, John. "Foreign Semitic Influence on the Wisdom of Israel and Its Appropriation in the Book of Proverbs." In *Wisdom in Ancient Israel: Essays in Honour of J. A. Emerton,* edited by John Day et al., 55–70. Cambridge: Cambridge University Press, 1995.

Day, John, et al., eds. *Wisdom in Ancient Israel: Essays in Honour of J. A. Emerton.* Cambridge: Cambridge University Press, 1995.

de Vaux, Roland. *Ancient Israel: Its Life and Institutions.* Translated by John McHugh. Grand Rapids: Eerdmans, 1997.

Delitzsch, Franz. *A New Commentary on Genesis.* Vol. 2. Translated by Sophia Taylor. Minneapolis: Klock & Klock, 1978.

———. *Biblical Commentary on the Proverbs of Solomon.* Vol. 2. Translated by M. G. Easton. Grand Rapids: Eerdmans, 1952.

Della Vida, Giorgio Levi. "Pre-Islamic Arabia." In *The Arab Heritage,* edited by Nabih Amin Faris, 25–57. Princeton, N.J.: Princeton University Press, 1946.

Dhorme, Édouard. *A Commentary on the Book of Job.* Translated by Harold Knight. Nashville: Nelson, 1984.

———. "The Language of the Book of Job." In *Sitting with Job: Selected*

Studies on the Book of Job. Edited by Roy B. Zuck. Grand Rapids: Baker, 1992.

Driver, Samuel Rolles, and George Buchanan Gray. *A Critical and Exegetical Commentary on the Book of Job, Together with a New Translation.* Edinburgh: T & T Clark, 1977.

Dussaud, René. *La pénétration des arabes en Syrie avant l'Islam.* Paris: Librairie Orientaliste Paul Geuthner, 1955.

———. *Les arabes en Syrie avant l'Islam.* Paris: Ernest Leroux, 1907.

Eadie, John. *Commentary on the Epistle of Paul to the Galatians.* Minneapolis: James and Klock Christian, 1977.

Eph^cal, Israel. *The Ancient Arabs: Nomads on the Borders of the Fertile Crescent 9th–5th Centuries b.c.* Leiden: E. J. Brill, 1982.

Ferrari-D'Occhieppo, Konradin. "The Star of the Magi and Babylonian Astronomy." In *Chronos, Kairos, Christos.* Edited by Jerry Vardaman and Edwin M. Yamauchi. Winona Lake, Ind.: Eisenbrauns, 1989.

Firestone, Reuven. *Journeys in Holy Lands: The Evolution of the Abraham-Ishmael Legends in Islamic Exegesis.* Albany: State University of New York Press, 1990.

Fox, Michael. "Agur Son of Jakeh." In *Encyclopedia Judaica,* 2: col. 434. Jerusalem: Encyclopedia Judaica Jerusalem, 1971.

Fox, Michael, and Harold L. Ginsberg. "Lemuel." In *Encyclopedia Judaica,* 11: col. 12. Jerusalem: Encyclopedia Judaica Jerusalem, 1971.

France, R. T. *The Gospel According to Matthew.* Grand Rapids: Eerdmans, 1985.

Fraser, T. G. *The Arab-Israeli Conflict.* In *Studies in Contemporary History.* Edited by T. G. Fraser and J. O. Springhall. New York: St. Martin's, 1995.

Freedman, H., and Maurice Simon, eds. *Midrash Rabbah: Genesis.* Vol. 1. Translated by H. Freedman. New York: Soncino, 1983.

Fung, Ronald Y. K. *The Epistle to the Galatians.* Grand Rapids: Eerdmans, 1988.

Gabrieli, Francesco, ed. *L'Antica Societa Beduina.* Roma: Centro Di Studi Semitici, Istituto Di Studi Orientali-Universita, 1959.

Gawlikowski, Michel. "Les Arabes de Syrie dans l'antiquité." In *Immigration and Emigration Within the Ancient Near East: Festschrift E.*

Lipinski. Edited by K. Van Lerberghe and A. Schoors. Leuven: Uitgeverij Peeters en Departement Oriëntalistiek, 1995.

Geddes, Charles L., ed. *A Documentary History of the Arab-Israeli Conflict.* New York: Praeger, 1991.

Glueck, Nelson. *Deities and Dolphins: The Story of the Nabataeans.* New York: Farrar, Straus and Giroux, 1965.

Goitein, S. D. *Jews and Arabs: Their Contacts Through the Ages.* New York: Schocken, 1955.

Gordis, Robert. "The Language and Style of Job." In *Sitting with Job: Selected Studies on the Book of Job.* Edited by Roy B. Zuck. Grand Rapids: Baker, 1992.

Gottlieb, Claire. "The Words of the Exceedingly Wise: Proverbs 30–31." In *The Biblical Canon in Comparative Perspective.* Edited by K. Lawson Younger Jr. et al., Ancient Near Eastern Texts and Studies, vol. 11. Lewiston, N.Y: Edwin Mellen, 1991.

Graf, David F. "Arabia During Achaemenid Times." In *Achaemenid History IV: Centre and Periphery-Proceedings of the Groningen 1986 Achaemenid History Workshop,* edited by Heleen Sancisi-Weerdenburg and Amélie Kuhrt, 131–48. Leiden: Nederlands Instituut voor het Nabije Oosten, 1990.

———. "Nabateans." In *The Anchor Bible Dictionary.* Edited by David Noel Freedman. New York: Doubleday, 1992.

Grohmann, A. "Al ᶜArab." In *The Encyclopedia of Islam,* edited by H. A. R. Gibb et al, 1:524–27. New ed. Leiden: E. J. Brill, 1960.

Groom, Nigel. *Frankincense and Myrrh: A Study of the Arabian Incense Trade.* London: Longman Group; Beirut: Librairie du Liban, 1981.

Guillaume, A. "The Arabic Background of the Book of Job." In *Promise and Fulfillment: Essays Presented to Professor S. H. Hooke.* Edited by F. F. Bruce. Edinburgh: T & T Clark, 1963.

Guthrie, Donald. *Galatians.* New Century Bible Commentary. Edited by Ronald E. Clements and Matthew Black. Grand Rapids: Eerdmans, 1973.

Hackett, Jo Ann. "Rehabilitating Hagar: Fragments from an Epic Pattern." In *Gender and Difference in Ancient Israel.* Edited by Peggy L. Day. Minneapolis: Fortress, 1989.

Hagner, Donald A. *Matthew 1–13.* WBC. Edited by David A. Hubbard and Glenn W. Barker. Dallas: Word, 1993.

Halevy, J. "Arabie." In *Dictionnaire de la Bible.* Edited by F. Vigouroux. Paris: Letouzey et Ané, 1903.

Hamilton, Victor P. *The Book of Genesis.* 2 vols. NICOT. Edited by R. K. Harrison. Grand Rapids: Eerdmans, 1990, 1995.

Harding, G. Lankester. *An Index and Concordance of Pre-Islamic Arabian Names and Inscriptions.* Toronto: University of Toronto Press, 1971.

Hartley, John E. *The Book of Job.* NICOT. Edited by R. K. Harrison. Grand Rapids: Eerdmans, 1988.

Hengel, Martin, and Helmut Merkel. "Die magier aus dem Osten und die Flucht nach Ägypten (Mt 2) in der Antiken Religionsgeschichte und der Theologie des Matthew." In *Orientierung an Jesus: Zur Theologie der Synoptiker, Festschrift für Josef Schmid.* Edited by P. Hoffmann. Freiburg: Herder, 1973.

Hengel, Martin, and Anna Maria Schwemer. *Paul Between Damascus and Antioch: The Unknown Years.* Translated by John Bowden. Louisville: Westminster/John Knox, 1997.

Henninger, Joseph. "La religion bédouine préislamique." In *L'Antica Societa Beduina.* Edited by Francesco Gabrieli. Roma: Centro Di Studi Semitici, Istituto Di Studi Orientali-Universita, 1959.

Henninger, Joseph, ed. *Arabica Sacra: Contributions à l'histoire Religieuse de l'Arabie et de ses régions limitrophes.* In Orbis biblicus et orientalis. Vol. 40. Göttingen: Universitätsverlag Freiburg Schweiz, Vandenhoeck & Ruprecht, 1981.

Hitti, Philip K. *History of the Arabs, from the Earliest Times to the Present.* London: Macmillan, 1970.

Holland, Canon H. Scott. "Justinus Martyr." In *A Dictionary of Christian Biography.* Edited by Henry Wace and William C. Piercy. Peabody, Mass.: Hendrickson, 1994.

Hughes, David. *The Star of Bethlehem.* New York: Walker, 1979.

Ibn Ezra, Abraham Ben Meir. *Ibn Ezra's Commentary on the Pentateuch: Genesis.* Translated by H. Norman Strickman and Arthur M. Silver. New York: Menorah, 1988.

Irvine, A. K. "The Arabs and the Ethiopians." In *Peoples of the Old Testament Times.* Edited by D. J. Wiseman. Oxford: Clarendon, 1973.

Jacob, B. *The First Book of the Bible: Genesis.* Translated and edited by Ernest I. Jacob and Walter Jacob. New York: KTAV, 1974.

Jaussen, Antonin. *Coutumes des Arabes au pays de Moab.* Paris: Librairie Victor Lecoffre, J. Gabalda, 1909.

Jaussen, Antonin, and Raphael Savignac, Pères. *Mission archéologique en Arabie.* 6 vols. Publications de la Société des Fouilles Archéologiques. Paris: Ernest Leroux, Éditeurs and Librairie Paul Geuthner, 1909–22.

Jeremias, Joachim. *Jerusalem in the Times of Jesus: An Investigation into Economic and Social Conditions During the New Testament Period.* Philadelphia: Fortress, 1969.

Kasher, Aryeh. *Jews, Idumeans, and Ancient Arabs: Relations of the Jews in Eretz-Israel with the Nations of the Frontiers and the Desert during the Hellenistic and Roman Era (332 bce–70 ce).* Texte und Studien zum antiken Judentum, 18. Tübingen: J. C. B. Mohr (Paul Siebeck), 1988.

Kasher, Menahem M. "Genesis." Vols. 2 and 3 of *Encyclopedia of Biblical Interpretation.* Edited by Harry Freedman. New York: American Biblical Encyclopedia Society, 1955.

Keil, C. F., and F. Delitzsch. *The Pentateuch.* Vol. 1 of Biblical Commentary on the Old Testament. Translated by James Martin. Grand Rapids: Eerdmans, 1956.

Kidner, Derek. *Genesis: An Introduction and Commentary.* Tyndale Old Testament Commentaries. Edited by D. J. Wiseman. Downers Grove, Ill.: InterVarsity, 1967.

Knauf, Ernst Axel. "Ishmaelites." In *The Anchor Bible Dictionary.* Edited by David Noel Freedman. New York: Doubleday, 1992.

———. "Massa." In *The Anchor Bible Dictionary.* Edited by David Noel Freedman. New York: Doubleday, 1992.

———. "Seir." In *The Anchor Bible Dictionary.* Edited by David Noel Freedman. New York: Doubleday, 1992.

———. *Ismael: Untersuchungen zur Geschichte Palestinas und Nordarabiens im 1. Jahrtausend v. Chr.* Abhandlungen des

Deutschen Palestinavereins. Edited by Siegfried Mittmann and Manfred Weipert. Wiesbaden: Otto Harrassowitz, 1989.

Lambdin, Thomas O. *Introduction to Biblical Hebrew.* New York: Scribner's, 1971.

Lammens, H. *L'Arabie occidentale à la veille de l'Hégire.* Beyrouth: Imprimerie Catholique, 1928.

Landes, G. M. "Ishmaelites." In *The Interpreter's Dictionary of the Bible.* Edited by George Arthur Buttrick. Nashville: Abingdon, 1986.

Lange, John Peter. *Commentary on the Holy Scriptures: Proverbs.* Translated by Philip Schaff. Grand Rapids: Zondervan, 1950.

Laqueur, Walter. *A History of Zionism.* New York: Shocken, 1989.

Léon-Dufour, Xavier. *The Gospels and the Jesus of History.* Translated and edited by John McHugh. New York: Image,1970.

Lévêque, Jean. *Job et son Dieu. Tome I: Essai d'exégèse et de théologie biblique.* Paris: Librairie Lecoffre. J. Gabalda et Cie Éditeurs, 1970.

Lewis, Bernard. *The Arabs in History.* New ed. Oxford: Oxford University Press, 1993.

Lightfoot, J. B. *Saint Paul's Epistle to the Galatians.* London: Macmillan, 1884.

Livingstone, A. "Arabians in Babylonia/Babylonians in Arabia: Some Reflections à propos New and Old Evidence." In *L'Arabie préislamique et son environment historique et culturel: Actes du colloque de Strasbourg 24–27 juin 1987,* edited by T. Fahd, 97–105. Université des sciences humaines de Strasbourg: Travaux du Centre de Recherche sur le Proche-Orient et la Grèce Antiques, no. 10. Leiden: E. J. Brill, 1989.

Longenecker, Richard N. *Galatians.* WBC. Edited by David A. Hubbard and Glenn W. Barker. Dallas: Word, 1990.

Lozachmeur, Hélène, ed. *Présence arabe dans le Croissant Fertile avant l'Hégire: Actes de la table ronde internationale (Paris, 13 Novembre 1993).* Paris: Éditions Recherche sur les Civilisations, 1995.

Luckenbill, Daniel David. *Ancient Records of Assyria and Babylonia.* 2 vols. Chicago: University of Chicago Press, 1926.

———. *The Annals of Sennacherib.* Chicago: University of Chicago Press, 1924.

Macdonald, M. C. A. "North Arabia in the First Millennium B.C.E." In *Civilizations of the Ancient Near East.* Edited by Jack Sasson. New York: Charles Scribner's Sons, 1995.

Maher, Michael, trans. *Targum Pseudo-Jonathan: Genesis,* vol. 1B of *The Aramaic Bible: The Targums.* Edited by Martin McNamara et al. Collegeville, Minn.: Liturgical, 1992.

Margoliouth, D. S. *The Relations Between Arabs and Israelites Prior to the Rise of Islam.* London: Oxford University Press, 1924.

McKane, William. *Proverbs: A New Approach.* Philadelphia: Westminster, 1970.

Metzger, Bruce M. "Names for the Nameless in the New Testament: A Study in the Growth of Christian Tradition." In *Kyriakon: Festschrift Johannes Quasten.* Edited by Patrick Granfield and Josef A. Jungmann. Münster Westfalen, Germany: Aschendorff, 1970.

Meyer, Eduard. *Die Israeliten und ihre Nachbarstämme.* Halle: Max Niemeyer, 1906.

Milik, Joseph T. "Origine des Nabatéens." In *Studies in the History and Archaeology of Jordan,* edited by Adnan Hadidi, 1:261–65. Amman, Hashemite Kingdom of Jordan: Department of Antiquities, 1982.

Millard, A. R., and D. J. Wiseman, eds. *Essays on the Patriarchal Narratives.* Leicester, U.K.: Intervarsity, 1980.

Millard, Fergus. *The Roman Near East: 31 b.c.–a.d. 337.* Cambridge, Mass.: Harvard University Press, 1993.

Montgomery, James. *Arabia and the Bible.* Philadelphia: University of Pennsylvania Press, 1934.

Morris, Leon. *The Gospel According to Matthew.* Grand Rapids: Eerdmans, 1992.

Moscati, Sabatino. *The Semites in Ancient History: An Inquiry into the Settlement of the Beduin and Their Political Establishment.* Cardiff: University of Wales Press, 1959.

Moscati, Sabatino, ed. *Le antiche divinità semitiche.* Studi Semitici I. Roma: Centro di Studi Semitici, Istituto di Studi Orientali-Università di Roma, 1958.

Mühlau, F. *De Proverbiorum quae dictuntur Aguri et Lemuelis origine atque indole.* Leipzig: Metzger & Wittig, 1869.

Müller, W. W. "Frankincense." In *The Anchor Bible Dictionary.* Edited by David Noel Freedman. New York: Doubleday, 1992.

Murphy, Roland E. *The Tree of Life: An Exploration of Biblical Wisdom Literature.* 2d ed. Grand Rapids: Eerdmans, 1990.

Musil, Alois. *Arabia Petraea.* 3 vols. Kaiserliche Akademie der Wissenschaften. Wien: Alfred Hölder, 1907–8.

———. *Arabia Deserta: A Topographical Itinerary.* Oriental Explorations and Studies, no. 2. New York: American Geographical Society, 1927.

———. *The Manners and Customs of the Rwala Bedouins.* Oriental Explorations and Studies, no. 6. Edited by J. K. Wright. New York: American Geographical Society, 1928.

———. *The Northern Ḥejâz. A Topographical Itinerary.* Oriental Explorations and Studies, no. 1. New York: American Geographical Society, 1926.

Negev, Avraham. *Nabatean Archaeology Today.* New York: New York University Press, 1986.

Nielsen, Ditlef. *Die altarabische Mondreligion und die mosaische Überlieferung.* Strassburg: K. J. Trübner, 1904.

Nielsen, Kjeld. *Incense in Ancient Israel.* VT supplement, no. 38. Edited J. A. Emerton et al. Leiden: E. J. Brill, 1986.

Nöldeke, Theodore. *Geschichte der Perser und Araber zur Zeit der Sasaniden, aus der arabischen Chronik des Tabarî.* Leiden: E. J. Brill, 1879.

———. *Über die Amalekiter und einige andere Nachbarvölker der Israeliten.* Göttingen, 1864.

Ovendale, Ritchie. *The Origins of the Arab-Israeli Wars.* London: Longman, 1992.

Owen, G. Frederick. "The Land of Uz." In *Sitting with Job: Selected Studies on the Book of Job.* Edited by Roy B. Zuck. Grand Rapids: Baker, 1992.

Paret, Rudi. "Ismā'īl." In *The Encyclopedia of Islam,* 4:184–85. Edited by E. van Donzel et al. New ed. Leiden: E. J. Brill, 1978.

Parr, Peter J. "Aspects of the Archaeology of North-West Arabia in the First Millennium B.C." In *L'Arabie préislamique et son environment historique et culturel: Actes du colloque de Strasbourg 24–27 juin 1987.* Edited by T. Fahd. Université des sciences humaines de Strasbourg: Travaux du Centre de Recherche sur le Proche-Orient et la Grèce Antiques 10. Leiden, E. J. Brill, 1989.

———. "Contacts between North West Arabia and Jordan in the Late Bronze and Iron Ages." In *Studies in the History and Archaeology of Jordan,* edited by Adnan Hadidi, 1:127–33. Amman: Department of Antiquities, 1982.

Patrich, Joseph. *The Formation of the Nabatean Art, Prohibition of a Graven Image Among the Nabateans.* Leiden: E. J. Brill, 1990.

Pope, Marvin. *Job: Introduction, Translation and Notes.* Vol. 15 of The Anchor Bible. Edited by William Foxwell Albright and David Noel Freedman. Garden City, N.Y.: Doubleday, 1965.

Porter, J. L. *Five Years in Damascus: Including an Account of the History, Topography, and Antiquities of That City.* 2 vols. London: John Murray, 1855.

Renan, Ernest. *The Book of Job: Translated from the Hebrew with a Study upon the Age and Character.* Translated by A. F. G. and W. M. T. London: W. M. Thomson, 1889.

Rey-Coquais, J. P. "L'Arabie dans les routes de commerce entre le Monde Méditerranéen et les côtes Indiennes." In *L'Arabie préislamique et son environment historique et culturel: Actes du colloque de Strasbourg 24–27 juin 1987,* edited by T. Fahd, 225–39. Université des sciences humaines de Strasbourg: Travaux du Centre de Recherche sur le Proche-Orient et la Grèce Antiques, no. 10. Leiden: E. J. Brill, 1989.

Ridderbos, Herman N. *The Epistle of Paul to the Churches of Galatia.* Grand Rapids: Eerdmans, 1953.

Ross, Allen P. "Genesis." In *The Bible Knowledge Commentary, Old Testament.* Edited by John F. Walvoord and Roy B. Zuck. Wheaton, Ill.: Victor, 1985.

Rostovzeff, Mikhail Ivanovitch. *Caravan Cities.* Translated by D. and T. Talbot Rice. Oxford: Clarendon, 1932.

Ryckmans, G. *Les religions arabes préislamiques.* Bibliothèque du Muséon, no. 26. Louvain: Publications Universitaires, 1951.

Ryckmans, Jacques. "Religion of South Arabia." In *The Anchor Bible Dictionary.* Edited by David Noel Freedman. New York: Doubleday, 1992.

Sailhamer, John H. *The Pentateuch as Narrative.* Grand Rapids: Zondervan, 1992.

Sarna, Nahum M. *The JPS Torah Commentary: Genesis.* Jerusalem: Jewish Publication Society, 1989.

Seale, Morris S. *The Desert Bible: Nomadic Tribal Culture and Old Testament Interpretation.* New York: St. Martin's, 1974.

Shahîd, Irfan. *Rome and the Arabs.* Washington, D.C.: Dumbarton Oaks Research Library and Collection, 1984.

Skinner, John. *A Critical and Exegetical Commentary on Genesis.* Edinburgh: T & T Clark, 1930.

Smith, Robert Houston. "Arabia." In *The Anchor Bible Dictionary.* Edited by David Noel Freedman. New York: Doubleday, 1992.

Smith, William Robertson. *Lectures on the Religions of the Semites: The Fundamental Institutions.* New York: KTAV, 1969.

Speiser, E. A. Genesis. *The Anchor Bible.* Garden City, N.Y.: Doubleday, 1964.

Starcky, J. "Pétra et la Nabatène." In *Dictionnaire de la Bible,* supplement VII:886–1017. Paris: Letouzey & Ané, Éditeurs, 1966.

Syrén, Roger. "Ishmael and Esau in the Book of *Jubilees* and Targum Pseudo-Jonathan." In *The Aramaic Bible: Targums in their Historical Context,* edited by D. R. G. Beattie and M. J. MaNamara, 310–15. *JSOT* supplement, no. 166. Edited by David J. A. Clines and Philip R. Davies. Sheffield: Sheffield Academic, 1994.

———. *The Forsaken First-Born: A Study of a Recurrent Motif in the Patriarchal Narratives. JSOT* supplement, no. 133. Edited by David J. A. Clines and Philip R. Davies. Sheffield: Sheffield Academic, 1993.

Tate, Marvin E. *Proverbs.* The Broadman Bible Commentary. Edited by Clifton J. Allen. Nashville: Broadman, 1971.

Toy, Crawford H. *A Critical and Exegetical Commentary on the Book of Proverbs.* ICC. Edited by S. R. Driver, Alfred Plummer, and Charles Augustus Briggs. Edinburgh: T & T Clark, 1970.

Trible, Phyllis. "The Other Woman: A Literary and Theological Study of the Hagar Story." In *Understanding the Word: Essays in Honor of Bernhard W. Anderson.* Edited by James T. Butler et al., 221–46. *JSOT* supplement, no. 37. Edited by David J. A. Clines and Philip R. Davies. Sheffield: Journal for the Study of the Old Testament Press, 1985.

Trimingham, J. Spencer. *Christianity among the Arabs in Pre-Islamic Times.* London: Longman, 1979.

Tsevat, Matitiahu. *The Meaning of the Book of Job and Other Biblical Studies: Essays on the Literature and Religion of the Hebrew Bible.* New York: KTAV, 1980.

Tur-Sinai, N. H. *The Book of Job: A New Commentary.* Jerusalem: Kiryath Sepher, 1967.

Upham, Francis W. *The Wise Men: Who They Were and How They Came to Jerusalem.* New York: Nelson & Phillips, 1873.

Van Beek, Gus W. "South Arabian History and Archaeology." In *The Bible and the Ancient Near East: Essays in Honor of William Foxwell Albright.* Edited by G. Ernest Wright. Garden City, N.Y.: Doubleday, 1961.

Van Seters, J. *Abraham in History and Tradition.* New Haven, Conn.: Yale University Press, 1975.

Walton, John H. *Ancient Israelite Literature in Its Cultural Context.* Grand Rapids: Zondervan, 1989.

Waters, John W. "Who Was Hagar?" In *Stony the Road We Trod: African American Biblical Interpretation.* Edited by Cain Hope Felder. Minneapolis: Augsburg/Fortress, 1991.

Watt, W. Montgomery. "Belief in a 'High God' in Pre-Islamic Mecca." In *Studies in the History of Religions 31, Proceedings of the XII International Congress of the I.A.H.R.* Edited by C. Jouco Bleeker, Geo Widengren, and Eric J. Sharpe. Leiden: E. J. Brill, 1975.

Wenham, Gordon J. *Genesis 16–50.* WBC. Vol. 2 Edited by David A. Hubbard and Glenn W. Barker. Dallas: Word, 1994.

Wensinck, A. J. "Ismâᶜîl." In *First Encyclopedia of Islam.* Edited by M. Th. Houtsma et al. Leiden: E. J. Brill, 1987.

———. "Khitān, circumcision." In *The Encyclopedia of Islam.* Edited by E. van Donzel et al. New ed. Leiden: E. J. Brill, 1978.

Westermann, Claus. *Genesis 12–36: A Commentary.* Translated by John J. Scullion. Minneapolis: Augsburg, 1981.

Whybray, R. N. *Introduction to the Pentateuch.* Grand Rapids: Eerdmans, 1995.

———. *The Book of Proverbs: A Survey of Modern Study.* Leiden: E. J. Brill, 1995.

Winnett, F. V., and W. L. Reed. *Ancient Records from North Arabia.* Toronto: University of Toronto Press, 1970.

Winnett, Fred V. "The Arabian Genealogies in the Book of Genesis." In *Translating and Understanding the Old Testament: Essays in Honor of Herbert Gordon May.* Edited by Harry Thomas Frank and William L. Reed. Nashville: Abingdon, 1970.

Yamauchi, Edwin M. "The Episode of the magi." In *Chronos, Kairos, Christos.* Edited by Jerry Vardaman and Edwin M. Yamauchi. Winona Lake, Ind.: Eisenbrauns, 1989.

———. *Persia and the Bible.* Grand Rapids: Baker, 1990.

Zayadine, Fawzi, ed. *Petra and the Caravan Cities: Proceedings of the Symposium Organised at Petra in September 1985 by the Department of Antiquities of Jordan.* Amman: Department of Antiquities, 1990.

Zöckler, Otto. "The Proverbs of Solomon." In *A Commentary on the Holy Scriptures: Critical, Doctrinal, and Homiletical by John Peter Lange.* Translated by Charles A. Aiken and edited by Philip Schaff. New York: Charles Scribner, 1870.

Zuck, Roy B., ed. *Sitting with Job: Selected Studies on the Book of Job.* Grand Rapids: Baker, 1992.

Periodicals

Allison, Dale C., Jr. "What Was the Star That Guided the Magi?" *Bible Review* 9 (1993): 20–24.

Anbar, Moshe. "Changement des Noms des Tribus Nomades dans la Relation d'un Même Evenement." *Biblica* 49 (1968): 221–32.

Bartlett, John R. "From Edomites to Nabataeans: A Study in Continuity." *PEQ* 111 (January–June 1979): 53–66.

Bawden, Garth, and Christopher Edens. "History of Taymāʾ and Hejazi Trade During the First Millennium B.C." *Journal of the Economic and Social History of the Orient* 32 (1989): 48–103.

Ben-Zvi, Izḥak. "Les origines de l'établissement des tribus d'Israël en Arabie." *Muséon* 74 (1961): 143–90.

Bishop, E. F. F. "Arabia in the New Testament." *The Moslem World* 34 (1944): 192–98.

———. "The Bible in 'Arabia Deserta.'" *PEQ* 98 (1966): 103–13.

———. "Some Reflections on Justin Martyr and the Nativity Narratives." *EvQ* 39 (1967): 30–39.

Broome, E. C. "Nabaiati, Nebaioth and the Nabataeans: The Linguistic Problem." *JSS* 18 (spring 1973): 1–16.

Brown, Raymond E. "Meaning of the magi: The Significance of the Star." *Worship* 49 (1975): 574–82.

Cantineau, Jean. "Nabatéen et Arabe." *Annales de l'Institut d'études orientales* 1 (1934–35): 77–97.

Charbel, Antonio. "Mateo 2,1–12: Los Magos en el Abiente del Reino Nabateo." *Revista Biblica* 46 (1984): 147–58.

Crenshaw, James L. "A Mother's Instruction to Her Son (Proverbs 31:1–9)." *Perspectives in Religious Studies* 15 (1988): 9–22.

Cross, F. M., Jr. "Geshem the Arabian, Enemy of Nehemiah." *The Biblical Archaeologist* 18 (1955): 46–47.

Cruveilhier, P. "Le Droit de la Femme dans la Genèse et dans le receuil de Lois Assyriennes." *RB* 36 (1927): 353–76.

Davis, G. I. "Hagar, El-Hegra and the Location of Mount Sinai." *VT* 22 (1972): 152–63.

de Vaux, Roland. "Téman, Ville ou Région d'Edom?" *RB* 76 (1969): 379–85.

Deist, Ferdinand. "Proverbs 31:1. A Case of Constant Mistranslation." *JNWL* 6 (1978): 1–3.

Dhorme, Édouard. "Le Pays de Job." *RB* 20 (1911): 102–7.

Drinkard, Joel F., Jr. "ʿAL PENÊ as 'East of.'" *JBL* 98 (1978): 285–86.

Dumbrell, William J. "The Tell el-Maskḥuta Bowls and the 'Kingdom' of Qedar in the Persian Period." *BASOR* 203 (1971): 33–44.

———. "Midian: A Land or a League?" *VT* 25 (1975): 323–37.

Ephʿal, Israel. "'Arabs' in Babylonia in the 8th Century B.C." *JAOS* 94 (1974): 108–15.

———. "'Ishmael' and 'Arab(s)': A Transformation of Ethnological Terms." *Journal of Near Eastern Studies* 35 (October 1976): 225–35.

Fensham, F. Charles. "The Son of the Handmaid in Northwest Semitic." *VT* 19 (1969): 312–21.

Ferrari-d'Occhieppo, Konradin. "The Star of Bethlehem." *Quarterly Journal of the Royal Astronomical Society* 19 (1978): 517.

Finkelstein, J. J. "The Laws of Ur-Nammu." *Journal of Cuneiform Studies* 22 (1968): 66–82.

Foster, Frank Hugh. "Is the Book of Job a Translation from an Arabic Original?" *American Journal of Semitic Languages* 49 (1932): 21–45.

Fry, C. George. "An Invitation to Ishmael." *Concordia Theological Quarterly* 41 (July 1977): 13–19.

Gadd, C. J. "The Harran Inscriptions of Nabonidus." *Anatolian Studies* 8 (1958): 35–92.

Gibb, Hamilton A. R. "Pre-Islamic Monotheism in Arabia." *Harvard Theological Review* 55 (1962): 269–80.

Graf, David F. "The Origin of the Nabataeans." *Aram* 2 (1990): 45–75.

Grayson, A. K., and J. Van Seters. "The Childless Wife in Assyria and the Stories of Genesis." *Or* 44 (1975): 485–86.

Healey, J. F., and G. Rex Smith. "Jaussen-Savignac 17: The Earliest Dated Arabic Document (A.D. 267)." *Atlal* 12 (1989): 77–84.

Healey, John F. "Were the Nabataeans Arabs?" *Aram* 1 (1989): 38–44.

Horovitz, Josef. "Judaeo-Arabic Relations in Pre-Islamic Times." *Islamic Culture* 3 (1929): 161–99.

Jackson, A. V. W. "The Magi in Marco Polo and the Cities in Persia from Which They Came to Worship the Infant Christ." *JAOS* 26 (1905): 79–83.

Jamme, A. "D. Nielsen et le panthéon sud-arabe préislamique." *RB* 55 (1948): 227–44.

Janzen, J. Gerald. "Hagar in Paul's Eyes and in the Eyes of Yahweh (Genesis 16)." *Horizons in Biblical Theology* 13 (June 1991): 1–22.

Lemaire, André. "Who or What Was Yahweh's Asherah?" *BAR* 6 (December 1984): 42–51.

Lewy, Julius. "On Some Institutions of the Old Assyrian Empire." *Hebrew Union College Annual* 27 (1956): 1–79.

Marsh-Edwards, J. C. "The Magi in Tradition and Art." *The Irish Ecclesiastical Record* 85 (1956): 1–9.

McEvenue, Sean E. "Comparison of Narrative Styles in the Hagar Stories." *Semeia* 3 (1975): 64–80.

Millar, Fergus. "Hagar, Ishmael, Josephus, and the Origin of Islam." *JJS* 44 (1993): 23–45.

Montgomery, James A. "Arabic Names in I. and II. Kings." *The Moslem World* 31 (1941): 266–67.

Mordechai, Cogan. "The Expulsion of Ishmael: No Laughing Matter." *Conservative Judaism* 41 (winter 1988–89): 29–33.

Negev, Avraham. "The Early Beginnings of the Nabataean Realm." *PEQ* 108 (1976): 125–33.

Oded, B. "The Table of Nations (Genesis 10): A Socio-cultural Approach." *ZAW* 98 (1986): 14–31.

Ohana, M. "La Polemique Judéo-Islamique et l'Image d'Ismael dans le Targum Pseudo-Jonathan et dans Pirke de Rabbi Eliezer." *Augustinianum* 15 (1975): 367–87.

Parr, P. J., G. L. Harding, and J. E. Dayton. "Preliminary Survey in N.W. Arabia, 1968." *Bulletin of the Institute of Archaeology* 10 (1971): 193–242.

Patrich, Joseph. "Prohibition of a Graven Image among the Nabataeans: The Evidence and Its Significance." *Aram* 2 (1990): 185–96.

Pfeiffer, Robert H. "Edomitic Wisdom." *ZAW* 12 (1926): 13–25.

Rosmarin, Trude Weiss. "Aribi und Arabien in den Babylonisch-Assyrischen Quellen." *JSOR* 16 (1932): 1–37.

Ryckmans, Gonzague. "De l'encens, de l'or, et de la myrrhe." *RB* 58 (1951): 372–76.

Ryckmans, Jacques. "Aspects nouveaux du problème Thamoudéen." *Studia Islamica* 5 (1956): 5–17.

Savignac, R., and J. Starcky. "Une inscription nabatéenne provenant du Djôf." *RB* 64 (1957): 196–215.

Schmid, H., "Ismael im Alten Testament und im Koran." *Judaica* 32 (1976): 76–81, 119–29.

Starcky, J. "The Nabataeans: A Historical Sketch." *The Biblical Archaeologist* 18 (1955): 84–106.

Thomas, Kenneth J. "Covenant in Relation to Hagar and Ishmael in Galatians." *Bible Translator* 37 (1986): 445–46.

Thompson, John L. "Hagar: Text, Terror, and Tradition." *Perspectives* 10 (April 1995): 16–19.

Van Beek, Gus W. "Frankincense and Myrrh." *The Biblical Archaeologist* 23 (1960): 70–95.

Van Seters, J. "The Problem of Childlessness in Near Eastern Laws and the Patriarchs of Israel." *JBL* 87 (1968): 401–8.

Waltke, Bruce. "The Book of Proverbs and Ancient Wisdom Literature." *Bibilotheca Sacra* (1979): 221–38.

———. "The Book of Proverbs and Old Testament Theology." *Bibilotheca Sacra* (1979): 302–17.

Wenning, Robert. "The Nabataeans in the Decapolis/Coele Syria." *Aram* 4 (1992): 79–99.

Willis, Steve. "Matthew's Birth Stories: Prophecy and the magi." *Expository Times* 105 (1993): 43–45.

Window, William H. "Prophecies Concerning Ishmael." *Methodist Review* 20 (July 1838): 316–20.

Winnett, F. V. "The Daughters of Allah." *The Moslem World* 30 (1940): 113–30.

Zadok, Ran. "On Early Arabians in the Fertile Crescent." *Tel Aviv* 17 (1990): 223–31.

———. "Arabians in Mesopotamia during the Late-Assyrian, Chaldean, Achaemenian and Hellenistic Periods Chiefly According to Cuneiform Sources." *ZDMG* 131 (1981): 42–84.

Zwemer, Samuel M. "Hagar and Ishmael." *EvQ* 22 (1950): 32–39.

UNPUBLISHED MATERIALS

Baldwin, Gary Dean. "Nabataean Cultural Influences upon Israel Until 106 A.D." Th.D. diss., Southwestern Baptist Theological Seminary, 1982.

Dumbrell, William J. "The Midianites and Their Transjordanian Successors." Th.D. diss., Harvard University, 1970.

Heitzer, A. "Hagar. Eine kritische und exegetische Untersuchung zu Gen. 16 und 21:1–21." Th.D. diss., Bonn: Neuendorff, 1934.

Sarna, Nahum. "Studies in the Language of Job." Ph.D. diss., The Dropsie College for Hebrew and Cognate Learning, 1955.

Shehadeh, Imad Nicola. "Ishmael in Relation to the Promises to Abraham." Th.M. thesis, Dallas Theological Seminary, 1986.

———. "A Comparison and a Contrast between the Prologue of John's Gospel and Qur'anic Surah 5." Th.D. diss., Dallas Theological Seminary, 1990.

Staats, Carl G. "A Study of the Basic Interpretive Problems of Galatians 4:21–31." Th.M. thesis, Dallas Theological Seminary, 1967.

Thompson, Glenn L. "Ishmael and Judah: Two Notes on Genesis." Paper presented at the ETS Annual Meeting. Washington, D.C., 1993.

GENERAL INDEX

Citations of material in the endnotes are indicated by the suffix "n." after the page number, followed in turn by the note number. For example, the citation 287 n.23 refers to note 23 on page 287.

A

Abbasid caliphate, 27, 30
Abd-el-Muttalib, 24
ʿAbdullah, 24
Abiateʾ, 163
Abigail, 119
Abimael, 133
Abraham, burial of (Gen. 25:9), 74, 114; call of (Gen. 12:1–3), 49–50; covenant with (Gen. 12:2–3, 7; 15; 22:18; Gal. 3:16), 50; Isaac and, 47; Ishmael and (Gen. 16:15; 17:23, 25; 21:11; 25:9, 12), 92; modern conflict and, 17, 18; Muslim tradition of, 48; Qurʾanic view of, 47
Abrahamic covenant (Gen. 12:2–3, 7; 15; 22:18; Gal. 3:16), 50, 76, 80–84, 106, 220, 255 n.58
Abu Bakr, 27
Abû-l-Hasan bar Bahlûl 195
Abu-Talib, 24
Achaemenid Persian rule, 169–70
Adam and Eve, 49
Adbeʾel, 151, 153, 296 n.40
Adha, 47
ʿAdnan, 46, 48
Aelius Gallus, 22
Agur (Prov. 30), 137–43, 145, 154, 283 n.3, 288 n.1, 291 n.47
Ahab, 111, 159
Aherah, 282
al-Aqsa Mosque, 11
al-Aus tribe, 25
al-Djurhum tribe, 48
al-Jawf area, 126, 152
al-Khazraj tribe, 25
al-Mansur, 27
Allah, 25, 131, 132, 227 n.31
Alexander the Great, 22, 177
Ali, 27
Amalekite, 113, 116
American University of Beirut, 33
Ammon, 167
Ammuladi, 163
Animal metaphors (Gen. 49; Deut. 30), 70
Anti-Arabism, 36
Anti-Semitism, 29, 30, 32, 35, 36
Antigonus the One-Eyed, 22, 177
Antiochus Epiphanes, 178, 189–90
Arab-Babylonian coalition, 163

Arab-Israeli conflict: Arab nationalism and, 33–34; resolving, 37–39, 223–24; Christians and, 36–37; Palestinians in, 230 n.92; causes of, 28–29, 35; Zionism and, 31–32
Arab League of States, 28
Arabia, 12, 110–12, 176, 263 n.21, 292 n.1; Arab, 45–46, 48, 263 n.21, 292 n.1; Islam in, 24–28, 191; Jews in, 187–89; pre-Islamic, 21–24
Arabian Desert, 207
Arabian Peninsula, 112, 129, 171
Arabic language, 20, 46, 129, 141–42, 320 n.46
Arabicized Arabs, 45, 46, 48
Arabs, 20, 110–12, 113, 260 n.4; anti-Semitism of, 29, 30; Arabian, 45–46, 48, 263 n.21, 292 n.1; Arabicized, 45, 46, 48; Ashurbanipal and, 162–64; biblical story of, 20–21, 219–24; British mandate and, 34, 35; Chaldaeans and (Jer. 49:28–33), 165–69; Christianity and, 20, 33, 222, 223–24, 320 n.45; circumcision of, 83–84; Esarhaddon and, 161–62; history of, 20–39, 45–46, 149–79, 220–22; intermarriage of, 176; Ishmaelites as, 103–4, 110–12, 176; Jews and, 191, 217, 189–92, 222–24; literature of, 143, 145; messiah and (Isa. 40–66), 183–84, 192, 202–3, 221, 222; monotheism of, 132–35; Moses and, 135, 216; nationalism of, 32–34; Persian Empire, 169–70; pre-Islamic, 21–23; prophets and, 164, 277 n.69; restoration plan for, 185–86; Sargon II and, 160–61; Sennacherib and, 161; Spain's, 27, 31; Tiglath Pileser III and, 159–60; trade monopoly of, 21, 22, 159; wealth of, 186, 209, 218; Western image of, 19–20, 38
Aramaeans, 112, 122, 172, 175, 262 n.17, 312 n.3
Aramaic-Arabic dialect, 172–73, 175, 277 n.68
Aramaic language, 23, 130, 141, 142–43, 173
Aretas I, 178
Aretas IV, 22, 178, 190, 191
Aristeas, 191
Aristobulus II, 191
Asher, 235 n.29
"Asherah of Yahweh," 134, 281 n.93
Ashurbanipal, 111, 162–64
Assur Naserpal, 112
Assyrians, 207, 208, 233 n.18; Arabs and, 159–60, 163–64; Ishmaelites and, 170, 173, 178–79; Israel and, 157–58; Qedarites and, 152; Samaria resettled by, 111, 160, 262 n.12, 301 n.32
Astrology, 194, 196, 200–201, 217
Astronomy, 200–201, 202, 205
Atarsamain deity, 153, 162
Atheism, 129
Augustine, 195
Augustus Caesar, 23
Aurelian, 23
Ayyubid dynasty, 28

B

Babylonians, 163, 165–69, 195, 206, 207, 208, 217, 220, 233 n.18
Baghdad, 27, 30
Balaam, 196, 287 n.23, 325 n.33
Balfour, Arthur, 33
Balfour Declaration, 33–34
Baptism, 214
Basma, daughter of Ishmael, 122, 130, 247 n.59, 268 n.50, 277 n.66
Basma, daughter of Solomon, 118–19, 144
Bazu, 160, 300 n.23
Bedouins, 46, 71–72, 112, 142, 161, 175, 201, 206
Benê qedem, 112–13, 156, 206, 264 n.22. *See also* Children of the east.
Benjamin, 70
Biblical history, as framework for solving Arab-Israeli conflict, 37–39
Bilhah, 51
Birnbaum, Nathan, 31
Birth annunciation, 66, 68, 105
British mandate, 28, 34
Burckhardt, John L., 23, 171
Byzantium, 23, 27, 164

C

Caanan (Gen. 13:15–18), 50, 116, 133, 134, 216
Caananites, 233 n.18
Caleb, 56
Caliphs, period of, 27
Cambyses, 169
Camels, 111, 159
Cattle trade, 160, 186, 266 n.41
Celsus, 195
Chaldaeans, 165–69, 170, 178, 196, 200
Children of the east, 112–13, 116, 122, 143. *See also Benê qedem.*
Christ: Abraham and (Gen. 12:1–3), 183, 221; as Light to the Gentiles (Exod. 19:6–7; Isa. 42:6; 49:6), 213, 218, 221; birth of, 82; crucifixion of (Acts 2–3), 18; natures of, 227 n.24; second coming of, 218, 222
Christian radio, 17
Christianity, Arabs and, 12, 20, 23, 24, 222, 223–24, 233 n.18, 320 n.45; Ishmael in, 39; Israel and, 36–37; Jews and, 12, 29, 31; missions of, 33
Chrysotom, 195
Circumcision (Gen. 17:10–14), 76, 81, 83–84, 98, 105, 221, 253 n. 40, 258 n.3
Clement of Alexandria, 195
Clement of Rome, 199–200, 206
Code of Hammurabi. *See* Hammurabi, Code of.
Concubines, 56–57
Constantine, 23
Cornelius Palma, 22, 178
Cosmas Indicopleustes, 195
Crusades, 27–28
Cush, descendants of (Gen. 10:7), 21
Cypros, 190
Cyril of Jerusalem, 195
Cyrus, 38, 169, 207

D

Dakhlah, 53
Damascus, 23, 27, 125, 163, 168, 191
Dan, 70, 235 n.29

Daniel, 122, 196
Darkness of Israel period, 37, 38, 150, 167, 179, 183, 221
David, 29, 38, 56, 118, 144, 157, 213
Deborah, 117
Dedan, 297 n.62, 305 n.77, 306 n.78
Der Judenstaat (The Jewish state), 32
Dhimmi category, 26, 29–30
Diaspora, Jewish, 21, 22, 35, 191
Diodorus, 21, 45, 172, 173, 177, 209, 210, 211, 292 n.1, 333 n.25
Dome of the Rock, 11
Dreyfus, Alfred, 31–32
Dumah (Isa. 21:11–12), 151–52, 266 n.41; 305 n.75

E

Edomites, 22, 114, 124–25, 126, 130, 134, 178, 189
Egypt, 22, 27, 28, 136, 140–41, 168, 169, 188, 215, 282 n.1
El, 131, 132, 133, 179, 279 n.76, 280 n.84
Election, Abrahamic Covenant and, 250 n.5
Eliezer, 54
Elijah, 63, 65, 133
Eliphaz, 123, 124
Elisha, 47
Elmodad, 133
Elô(a)h, 131
Elohîm, 131
Elymas of Paphos, 194
Ephah tribe, 186
Epiphanius, 200, 206
Esarhaddon, 162
Esau, 74, 114, 119, 130, 134, 250 n.5, 268 n.50, 277 n.66
Esirtu class, 56
Ethiopians, 21–22
Ethnic partiality, 20
Eusebius, 196–97, 206
Ezekiel, 122, 167

F

Faith, 53–54, 55, 98–100, 104, 259 n.19; Abrahamic covenant and, 76, 106, 220, 255 n.58
False gospel (Gal. 1:6–10), 98
Fatimid dynasty, 27
Ferdinand of Spain, 27, 28, 31
Frankincense, 21, 169, 175, 199–200, 208–9, 216, 232 n.14, 316 n.3, 333 n.21

G

Gabriel, 25, 48
Gad, 70, 117, 235 n.29
Gentiles: Christ and, 215, 217; Paul and (Gal. 1:15–17), 103–4, 186, 191–92, 217, 257 n.2, 317 n.8; restoration of, 184–86. *See also* Arabs; Ishmaelites.
Geshem the Arab, 170, 295 n.29
Ghassānid kingdom, 23
Gideon, 56, 116, 117
Gindibu, 111, 159
Ginsberg, Asher, 32, 35
God: Abraham and (Gen. 12:2–3, 7; 15; 22:18; Gal. 3:16), 50, 76, 80–84, 106, 220, 255 n.58; Arabs and, 167; Hagar and (Gen. 16:13), 65–66, 77–79, 84, 95–96, 105, 170, 219, 249 n.69, 259 n.5; restoration plan of, 184–86; sovereignty of, 18, 51, 53, 55, 104, 216; visions of, 65
Gold, 160, 208–9, 216, 316 n.3
Grace, 98

H

Hadad, 156
Hagar, 17–18; alienation of, 73–77; as symbol of Sinai covenant (Gal. 4:21–25), 100; cultural place of, 56–58, 85, 240 n.64; descendants of, 176, 220; dismissal of (Gen. 21:14–21), 89, 90–92, 93–96, 238 n.53, 255 n.60; flight of (Gen. 16:7–9), 60–65; God and (Gen. 16:13), 65–66, 77–79, 84, 95–96, 105, 170, 219, 249 n.69, 257 n.67, 259 n.5; Muslim tradition of, 48; promise to, 65–67, 84, 95–96, 105, 170, 219, 239 n.56, 250 n.5; Sarah and (Gen. 16:2, 4–6), 50–51, 57–58, 64, 75, 86–87
Halley's Comet, 200
Hammassāʾ, 137, 138–40, 286 n.20, 287 n.21
Hammurabi, Code of, 51–52, 91, 240 n.64, 251 n.12
Hanifs, 132
Hannah, 254 n.43
Hazaʾel, 151, 161–62
Hazor, 166, 307 n.93
Hera, Mount, 24, 25
Herod Antipas, 190, 318 n.26
Herod Antipater, 190
Herod the Great, 190–91, 198, 202, 203, 216, 217, 319 n.29, 334 n.36
Herodias, 190
Herodotus, 118, 150, 153, 161, 169, 174, 177, 194, 208, 232 n.14
Herzl, Theodore, 31–32, 33
Himyarite dynasty, 21
Hira, 23
Hitler, Adolf, 34
Holocaust, 34
Horeb, Mount, 65, 133–34, 214, 281 n.86
Hussein-McMahon correspondence, 34

I

Iataʾ, 162, 163, 303 n.54
Ibn al-Kalbi (Hisham ibn Muhammad al-Kalbi), 44
Ibn Ezra, 127
Idolatry, during Darkness of Israel period, 37, 129, 150, 221; God's reaction to, 117, 166–67, 307 n.92; Ishmael and, 86; Muhammad's response to, 26; among Nabataeans, 179; during the period of the Judges, 144
Idris, 47
Idumaeans, 191
Incense, magi gift of, 208–9, 216; trade, 159, 160, 161, 164, 168, 178, 186, 187, 191, 210, 266 n.41, 301 n.32; uses of, 332 n.12
Inheritance rights, 65, 76, 88, 89, 91–92, 95, 96, 101–2, 103, 221, 255 n.57
Intermarriage, between tribes, 176, 247 n.60, 293 n.10
Iraq, 27, 28, 30, 34
Isaac: birth of (Gen. 17:17, 21:1–7), 55–56; burying Abraham (Gen. 25:9), 74, 114; God and, 250 n.5; inheritance rights of, 76, 95, 96, 221; plan for (Gen. 17:15–22), 81, 83; Qurʾanic view of, 47; Rebecca and, 62; weaning of (Gen. 21:8–13), 85–86, 90

Isabella (queen of Spain), 27, 31
Isaiah, 65; Arabs prophecy (Isa. 21:13–17), 164, 305 n.75; magi and (Isa. 60:6), 212; messiah in (Isa. 60:1–7), 203–4; restoration oracles of (Isa. 40–66), 184
Ishmael, 43, 44; Abraham and (Gen. 16:15, 17:19–20, 23, 25; 21:11; 25:9, 12), 81–82, 74, 92, 114; Abrahamic covenant and (Gen. 17), 80–84; Arabs and, 44–46; biblical image of (Gen. 16), 29, 49–60; character of (Gen. 16:12), 67–77, 80, 219, 243 n.23, 248 n.63; Christian view of, 39; descendants of (Gen. 25:12–18), 20, 45, 301 n.27; Esau and, 250 n.5; exile of (Gen. 21:14–21), 93–96; Isaac and (Gen. 17:18–20; 21:8–13; Gal. 4:29), 18, 76–77, 85–90; life of, 23–25, 48, 81, 83, 105, 221, 253 n.40, 100, 101–4; Mideast conflict and, 17; Muslim view of, 38, 44–45, 46–49, 109, 48; naming of (Gen. 16:11), 66; nomadic lifestyle, 71–73, 105; Paul's view of (Gal. 4:21–31), 97, 100–104; plan for (Gen. 16:12; 17:20), 55, 56, 64, 81, 89, 92, 94–96, 104–5, 109, 170, 219–20, 239 n.56; sons of (Gen. 17:20), 74, 83–84, 111, 114, 151–56, 293 n.6. *See also* Ishmaelites.
Ishmaelites: Arabians as, 110–12, 176; biblical references to, 74–75; children of the east, 112–13, 116; history of, 114, 140; Israel and (Psalm 83), 29, 114–15, 116, 117–18, 144, 157, 179; incense and, 186; Jews and, 114–15, 116, 117–18, 144; Job as, 122–23; Midianites as, 247 n.60–61; monotheism among, 130–31; Nabataeans as, 175–76; in Song of Songs (Songs 1:5, 6), 143–44, 145; tribes of, 151–56; wealth of, 186; wisdom literature of, 138–43, 145. *See also* Arabs; Gentiles; Ishmael.
Ishtar deity, 153
Islam: Ishmael in, 38, 46–49, 109; the migration, 25; Muhammad, 24–27; origins of, 21; as primary Arab religion, 20; rise of, 24–28; tolerance of Christians and Jews, 29–30
Islamic fundamentalism, 11, 36
Israel: Arabia and, 135, 211; Arabs and, 222–24; kingdom of, 118, 129, 149; "Light to the Gentiles", 130; missionary purpose of, 38; nation of, 35, 215; twelve tribes of, 69, 235 n.29
Itureans, 156

J

Jacob, 69, 70, 90, 250 n.5, 271 n.11
Jael, 117
Jaziz the Hagarite (1 Chron. 27:31), 29
Jeremiah, 105, 112, 124, 155, 165–66, 167, 307 n.92
Jerome, 195
Jerusalem: crusaders' capture of, 27; sacking of by Nebuchadnezzar, 177
Jether the Ishmaelite (1 Chron. 2:17), 29, 267 n.43
Jethro, 117, 267 n.43

Jewish Question, 34–35
Jews: Arab converts, 189–92; in Arabia, 187–89; in the Arab world, 28–37; Christian converts, 29; Christian persecution of, 29, 31; commonalities with Arabs, 189–92; conflict with Arabs, 179; destruction of, in Europe, 230 n.92; under a divided monarchy, 149–50, 157; enslavement of (Gen. 15:12–17, Exod. 1–2), 50, 54–55, 60, 68; and Holocaust, 34; immigration of, into Palestine, 32, 34; Ishmael-Hagar line as representatives of, 103–4, 106; and Ishmaelites, positive relations with, 114–15, 116, 117–18, 144; in Medina, 25; messianic, 11–12; and Muslims, early relations with, 29–30; in pre-Islamic Arabia, 22, 24, 187–89; trade with Arabs, 191
Joab, 118
Job: Arabic origins of, 113, 114, 120–23, 124–35, 144–45, 221, 275 n.46, 276 n.64, 277 n.69; dating of, 123–24, 265 n.30; identity of, 121–23, 275 n.46, 276 n.64, 276–77, n. 66; monotheism of, 130–35, 145; literature of, 127–30; 145, 270 n.9, 275 n.46, 276 n.64; lifestyle of, 126, 274 n.40; Qurʾanic view of, 270 n.6
Jobab, 122–23
John Hyracanus I, 191
John the Baptist, 190
Joktan (Gen. 10:25–30), 20, 45, 46, 133
Jordan River, 22, 207
Joseph, 70, 74–75, 84, 114, 214, 215, 216
Josephus, 45, 125, 176, 190, 196, 231 n.7
Jubilees, book of, 45
Judah, son of Jacob, 70
Judah, kingdom of, 149–50, 165, 166
Judaizers (Galatians 3–4), 98, 100, 101, 102, 103, 258 n.3
Judges, period of, 116–18, 144, 260 n.1
Jundub, 111
Justin Martyr, 197–98, 199, 200, 206

K

Ka'ba, 48
Kedemah, 156
Keturah (Gen. 16:3; 25:1–6; 25:6; 1 Chron. 1:32), 20, 45, 57, 89, 114, 116, 175–76, 186, 200, 206, 221, 297 n.62, 301 n.27
Khadijah, 24
Kinda, kingdom of, 295 n.25

L

Lakhmid, kingdom of, 23
Lataʾ, 162
Law, Mosaic, 98
League of Arab States, 20
League of Nations, 34
Leah, 51, 236 n.29
Lebanon, 34
Lemuel (Prov. 31), 137–43, 145, 154, 283 n.3, 288 n.1, 291 n.47
Light of Christ period, 37, 38
Light of Israel period, 37, 110, 143, 150, 183, 221
"Light to the Gentiles" (Exod.

19:6; Isa. 42:6; 49:6), 213, 218, 221
Line of Isaac (Gen. 17:19), 18
Line of Ishmael (Gen. 16:10; 17:20), 18
Lipit-Ishtar, laws of, 91
Literacy, 33
Livestock trade, 160, 186, 266 n.41
Lot (Gen. 13; 19:14), 50, 89, 239 n.56, 266 n.39
Luke, 145

M

Maccabeans, 178, 189
Macedonians, 173, 178
Magi: Arabian origins, evidence for, 196–204, 205, 206–12, 217–18; gifts of, 208–12; identity of, 195; Isaiah expectations and (Isa. 60:1–7), 203–4; Matthew account of (Matt. 2:1–12), 193–94; questions about, 193–94; restoration plan and, 192, 221; revelation to, 202–3; traditions concerning, 194–96; typology, 38, 212–16
Magos, 196–97, 217
Mahalath, 247 n.59
Malichus, 190
Mamluk sultanate, 28
Manassah, 117
Marco Polo, 195
Marriage, 51–53, 236 n.30
Marwan II, 27
Mary Magdalene, 257 n.69
Massāʾ, Ishmael's son, 151, 154; kingdom of, 136–41; Proverbs 30 translation of, 136–43, 285 n.12, 286 n.18; tribe of, 151, 154
Mazdaism, 323 n.8
Mecca, 24, 25, 48, 168
Medina, 25, 168
Medo-Persian Empire, 169, 178
Melchizedek (Gen. 14:18–19), 50
Messianic Jew, 11–12
Mibsam tribe, 29, 115, 156
Midianites, 113, 116–17, 133, 135, 144, 186, 216, 247 n.60–61
Migration, Islamic, 25
Mishma tribe, 29, 115, 156
Missions to Arabs, 33
Moab, 167
Monogamy, 236 n.30
Monophysitism, 23, 227 n.23
Monotheism: Ishmaelites, 130–31, 221; Arabian, 24, 192; Islamic, 25, 26, 29–30; Job's, 129, 130–35, 145; magi and, 201; Nabataean, 175, 179
Moses, 65, 68, 196, 214, 215; Arabs and, 135, 216; as translator of Job, 127, 274 n.43; well symbolism and, 62
Mount of Moses, 133
Mu'awiyah, 27
Muhammad, 24–27, 44–45
Myrrh, 21, 175, 199–200, 208–9, 216, 232 n.14

N

Nabataea, kingdom of, 22, 220
Nabataeans: as children of Ishmael, 45, 116, 231 n.7; history of, 177–78; Ishmael as, 232 n.7; language of, 172–73; lifestyle of, 174–76; as Nebayots, 176–77; origins of, 172–77; religion of, 174; trade routes, control of, 152–53, 155–56; and zodiac, interest in, 201
Nabonidus, 155, 167–68, 187–88, 309 n.106

Nafud desert, 154
Naphish, 156
Naphtali, 235 n.29
Natnu, 163, 164
Nazism, 34
Nebayot tribe, 151, 172, 176–77, 186, 316 n.2
Nebuchadnezzar, 165, 177, 196
Nehemiah, 153, 170, 312 n.127
Neo-Assyrians, 150, 165
Neo-Babylonians, 150, 165, 169
Nestorianism, 23, 227 n.24
New Testament, 37
Noah, commission of (Gen. 9:1), 49; monotheism of, 132; righteousness of, 122; sons of (Gen. 9:25–27), 69
Nomadic lifestyle, 70–71, 111–12, 115, 121, 158, 175, 220, 298 n.71, 299 n.7
Nuhuru, 164

O

Obil (1 Chron. 27:30), 29
Object-deity worship, 132, 179, 201
Omar, 27
Oracles, Arabs and, 219–24; concerning Dumah (Isa. 21:11–12), 305 n.75; concerning Ishmael, 68, 80; Proverbs translation of, 136–40; restoration (Isa. 42:1–10, 60:1–7), 183, 185–86, 187, 221, 222
Origen, 195
Ottomans, 28, 33, 164

P

Paganism, 26
Palestine, British in, 33–34; diaspora, 35; Israeli reprisals against, 230 n.92; Jewish colonization of, 32, 34; location, in relation to journey of the magi, 206–8, 330 n.7; Nebuchadnezzar's threat to, 165; partition of, 35
Palmyra, 23
Papias, 206
Patriarchal period, 113–14, 123–24, 129–30, 135
Paul, faith conception of (Gal. 3–4), 98–100, 259 n.19; Ishmael in (Gal. 4:21–31), 97, 100–4, 105; ministry of (Gal. 1:15–17), 186, 191–92, 217, 257 n.2, 317 n.8
Pentecost, 83, 191, 202, 217
People of the book, 26, 29
Period of ignorance (*Jahiliyyah*), 21
Persia, 23, 27, 195, 206–7, 208, 217, 311 n.120
Persians, 152, 169–70
Petra, 22, 134, 171, 178, 211
Philip the Arab, 23
Phoenix, 199
Pliny, the Elder, 194, 196, 208, 211, 333 n.21
Polo, Marco. *See* Marco Polo.
Polygamy, 236 n.30
Polytheism, 132, 175
Predictions, 67
Promised Land, 50
Promised seed. *See* Seed promise.
Proselytes, 25, 191
Proverbs, 136–44, 283 n.3; Arabic influence on, 141–42, 282 n.1; Aramaic influence on, 142–43; author of, 288 n.27, 289 n.31; ethnic considerations, 140–41; textual considerations, 138–40;

translation of, 137–38, 140
Perôzâdh, 195
Ptolemy, 22, 154, 191

Q

Qahtan, 45. *See also* Joktan.
Qedar, 151, 152–53, 165–67, 170, 172, 177, 178, 186, 306 n.79, 311 n.121, 316 n.2
Qedemites, 112–13
Qumran, 188
Qur'an, 12, 26, 46–47, 84, 132, 270 n.6, 302 n.34
Quraysh tribe, 26

R

Rabbel II, 178
Rachel, 51, 236 n.29
Rebecca, 62, 90
Redemption, God's plan for (Isa. 42:1–10; 60:1–7), 18, 82, 222
Rehoboam, 57, 149
Religious minorities, 20
Religious tradition, early Semitic, 131–32
Reprisal generation, 34, 36
Restoration oracles (Isa. 42:1–10; 60:1–7), 183, 185–86, 187, 221, 222
Reuben, 117
Romans, 22, 152, 178

S

Sabaea, kingdom of, 21, 209, 297 n.62
Saladin, 27–28
Salvation, Christ as, 214, 227 n.24; Plan of (Gen. 17:5–6), 55–56, 186; by grace (Gal. 3:2), 98
Samaria, resettling of nomads in, 111, 160, 262 n.12, 301 n.32
Samaritans, ethnicity of, 111
Samsi (Queen), 160
Samuel, 254 n.43
Saracens, 260 n.5
Sarah, barrenness of (Gen. 11:30, 16:1–2), 50, 51, 53, 104, 219, 234 n.27; Hagar and (Gen. 16:5–6), 50–56, 58–60, 75–76; Muslim tradition of, 48; covenant and (Gal. 4:26–27), 100–2; Isaac and (Gen. 21:8–13), 85–92, 100–4, 238 n.53
Sargon II, 111, 160–61, 164, 262 n.12, 301 n.27
Sassanid Persians, 22
Saul, 37, 56, 117, 144
Saᶜy, rite of, 48
Sect of the Law, 192
Sedentary deities, 132
Seed of the woman, 82
Seed promise (Gen. 12:1–3, 7; 13:15–16; 17:18–22; 22:18; Acts 7:3; Gal. 3:16; Heb. 11:11–12), 50, 51, 54–55, 77, 79, 81, 92, 105, 183, 221, 255 n.58
Seir, 134
Seir, Mount, 22, 177
Semitic religions, 131–32
Sennacherib, 151, 153, 155, 161
Shahba, 23
Shalmaneser III, 111, 125, 159, 261 n.8
Shamash-shum-ukin, 163
Sharon, Ariel, 11
Sheba, kingdom of, 21, 118, 186, 209, 211, 267 n.47, 268 n.48, 301 n.27, 302 n.36
Sinai, Mount, 133, 134
Sheikhs, 126, 274 n.39
Simeon tribe, 29, 115, 156
Simon (Atomos), 196

Simon of Samaria, 194
Sinai Peninsula, 112, 133, 296 n.40
Social classes and divine favor, 66
Solomon, 37, 56–57, 118, 149, 157, 221; Arabs and, 118–19; Ishmaelites under, 144; Queen of Sheba and, 118, 211, 268 n.48; wisdom of (1 Kings 4:30), 119, 120, 136, 143, 183
Song of Songs, 143–44, 145, 291 n.52
Spain, 27, 31
Spice trade, 208
Star of Bethelem, 200–204, 330 n.80, 331 n.9. *See also* Magi.
Stephen, 214
Supernova, 200, 202
Surrogate wife, practice of providing, 53, 54, 240 n.64
Sykes-Picot Agreement, 34
Syria, 27, 28, 34, 165, 178
Syrian Protestant College, 33
Syro-Arabian Desert, 112, 116, 122, 130, 135, 152, 171, 178, 206, 260 n.4, 266 n.41

T

Tacitus, 194
Taymāʾ (caravan city), 128, 154–56, 167–68, 266 n.41, 297 n.54
Taymāʾ (oasis), 158, 278 n.71
Taymāʾ, son of Ishmael, 124, 154
Teʾelhunu, 161
Teiman, 123–24, 271 n.18, 278 n.71
Temple Mount, 11
Terrorist attacks, 12, 19–20, 34, 36
Tertullian, 198–99, 200, 203, 206
Thamud, 302 n.34
Theophany, 63, 76, 79, 96
Tiglath Pileser III, 111, 141, 153, 154–55, 159–60
Trade: Arabian, 21, 22, 159; Babylonian, 168–69; incense, 160, 161, 164, 178, 186, 191, 266 n.41, 301 n.32; Nabataean, 210–12; routes, 152, 168, 266 n.41; Taymāʾ, 154–56
Transjordan, 34, 113, 116, 117, 122, 156, 178, 189, 206, 211, 218
Tribes, Arabian, 115
Tribulation (Dan. 12:1; Matt. 24:21–22; Rom. 11:25–32), 222–23
Tunisia, 27, 30
Turkish Empire, 28, 33
Typology: Arabia's wealth, 215–16; Christ's infancy, 216–17; community threat, 214–15; Egypt's might, 215; magi, 212–17; Paul's use of, 103, 106; Tribulation, 222

U

Uateʾ II, 163
Umayyad caliphate, 27, 31
United Nations, 28
United Nations Palestine Conciliation Commission, 35
Uranius, 46
Uthman, 27
Uz, 124–27, 278 n.71

W

Wādî Sirhān, 126, 152
Weizmann, Chaim, 32, 33
Well, symbol of, 62–63, 74, 94
West, 34
Wisdom literature, 21, 110, 120, 136, 145
World War I, 28, 33

X

Xenophon, 150, 172, 292 n.1

Y

Yahweh, 132, 133, 134–35, 145, 280 n.84
Yahwism, 280 n.84
Yathrib. *See* Medina.
Yemen, 21, 331 n.7
Yetur, 156
Yhwh, 131

Z

Zabibi, 160
Zamzam, well of, 48
Zarathustra, 194, 323 n.8
Zeno, 195
Zenobia, 23
Zilpah, 51
Zionism, 12, 31–32, 34–35
Zionist Congress (1887), 32
Zodiac, 201
Zoroastrianism, 194–95, 196, 323 n.8
Zul-Kifl, 47

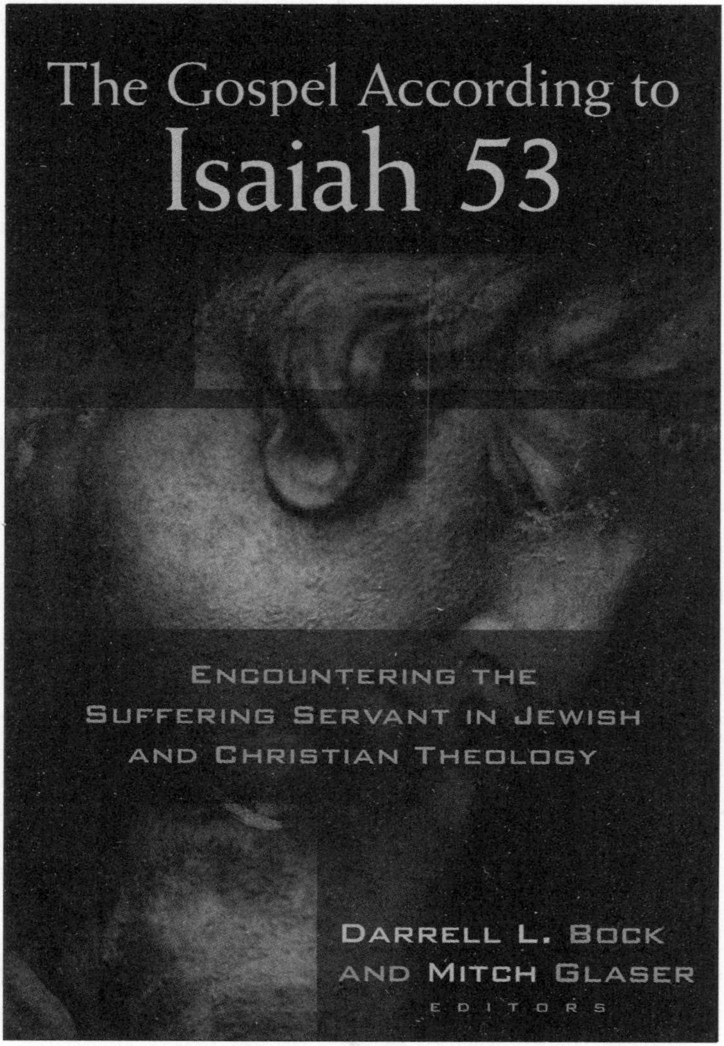

"It is certainly time for a precise and well-researched explanation of Isaiah 53, and this book fills this void for the evangelical world."

—Paul D. Wegner, Professor of Old Testament,
Phoenix Seminary

KREGEL
ACADEMIC